Other books by the author

The Church Hesitant

THE REAL
MRS MINIVER

YSENDA MAXTONE
GRAHAM

St. Martin's Press ⚏ New York

To Michael

Illustrations for *Sycamore Square and Other Verses* (1932) and *The Modern Strewwelpeter* (1936) copyright E. H. Shepard, reproduction by permission of Curtis Brown Ltd., London

www.stmartins.com

ISBN 0-312-30826-4

First published in Great Britain by John Murray (Publishers) Ltd

First U.S. Edition: November 2002

10 9 8 7 6 5 4 3 2 1

Contents

Like rays shed
  By a spent star
The words of a dead
  Poet are,
That through bleak space
  Unchecked fly on,
Though heart, hand, face
  To dust are gone;
And you who read
  Shall only guess
What thorn-sharp need,
  What loneliness,
What love, lust, dream,
  Shudder or sigh
Lit the long beam
  That meets your eye:
Nor guess you never
  So well, so true,
Shall comfort ever
  Reach from you
To me, an old
  Black shrivelled sphere,
Who has been cold
  This million year.

'Dedication: to an Unknown Reader'
  from J.S's collection of poems
The Glass-Blower, *1940*

Prologue

THIS WAS THE programme at Radio City Music Hall in New York on the evening of 4 June 1942:

1. Music Hall Grand Organ
2. The Music Hall Symphony Orchestra
3. 'At Ease!'
   'Bless 'Em All'
   'That's Sabotage'
   'Ladies in the Dark'
   'Two of a Kind'
   'You Can't Say No to a Soldier'
   'Finale' (danced by the entire company)
4. 'Mrs Miniver'
   Directed by William Wyler
   Produced by Sidney Franklin
   Starring Greer Garson and Walter Pidgeon
   Based on the novel by Jan Struther
   A Metro-Goldwyn-Mayer Picture

The high-decibel music and high-kicking dancing were standard splendid fare at the 'Showplace of the Nation'. But the film which held its première after the floor-show caused an unusual sensation. It was normal for audiences to emerge from the theatre blowing their noses: MGM were experts at activating the tear-ducts. But these tears were different. They were shed not just for the Minivers, whose wartime family tragedy the audience had just witnessed. They were shed, also, for the whole of homely civilization – village life, families, whistling milkmen, kindly old station-masters – that was being destroyed, at that very moment, by Hitler's war in Europe.

Mrs Miniver, more than any film which had yet been made

1

during the Second World War, brought the meaning of 'a people's war' into the minds of Americans, millions of whom had been opposed to joining the war until forced to do so by the Japanese and the Germans in December 1941. Greer Garson and Walter Pidgeon, as Mr and Mrs Miniver, helped them to see what they were fighting for. No film had ever run for more than six weeks at Radio City Music Hall: *Mrs Miniver* ran for ten, breaking box-office records. (It had to be taken off to make way for *Bambi*.) Across the United States, across Canada, in Britain, Australia, South Africa, New Zealand and India, the story was the same. People queued round the block.

'Propaganda Bureaus Are Struck Dumb With Envy' ran a headline in the Toronto *Globe*. Propagandists had been striving for years to make the war effort understood by the populations of the United States and Canada: and here, in a little family movie whose central plot was nothing more bellicose than a rose competition at a village flower show, that aim was achieved with little apparent effort. Winston Churchill (an uninhibited weeper during the sad bits of films) is said to have predicted that *Mrs Miniver*'s contribution to defeating the Axis powers would be more powerful than a flotilla of battleships. President Roosevelt was so stirred by the film's closing sermon that he requested it to be dropped across Europe in leaflet form and broadcast to the world on Voice of America. Even the Nazi propaganda minister Josef Goebbels, who loathed the film's hero and heroine, admitted that it was an exemplary piece of propaganda, which the German industry should emulate.

Mrs Miniver became synonymous in the public mind with all that was saintly and self-sacrificing in wartime womanhood. Chicago launched a 'Name Chicago's Mrs Miniver' contest. The winner, smilingly photographed on the centre pages of the Chicago *Times*, was Mrs Leonard Youmans, of 5109 Kimbark, 'who, in her patriotic accomplishments, typifies thousands of other stout-hearted local women in this war year of 1942! She has two sons, Donald and Clifford, in the Navy Air Force. Clifford was wounded on Atlantic duty and is convalescing in hospital. Mrs Youmans has a record of over 1,000 hours of service at the Chicago Servicemen's Center. She is a Travellers'

Aid for troops in transit. She is chairman of the Home Hospitality committee of the Navy Mothers' Club of Chicago. And she does all her own housework besides!'

The original Mrs Miniver was a pre-war creation who first appeared on the Court Page of *The Times* on 6 October 1937. Once a fortnight for two years, a 'Mrs Miniver' piece was published: 'Mrs Miniver and the New Car', 'Mrs Miniver and the New Engagement Book', 'The Minivers on Hampstead Heath'. The articles were anonymous, signed 'From a correspondent'. But there seemed no doubt that they must have been written by a contented, well-balanced, happily-married woman who longed to share her joy in life, and her peace of mind, with *Times* readers. The articles were all about the gentle pleasures of a modern upper-middle-class marriage. Their position at the top of the Court Page was reassuring: if His Majesty The King was holding a luncheon at Holyrood in the left-hand corner, and Mr and Mrs Miniver were attending the Highland Games in the right-hand corner, then surely civilization (in spite of the horrors going on in Spain and the threatening noises from Germany) must be safe.

When the articles were published in book form by Chatto & Windus in October 1939, the author's name was revealed: Jan Struther, the pseudonym of Joyce, née Anstruther, whose married name was Mrs Anthony Maxtone Graham, resident of Chelsea and mother of three. The book – an ideal Christmas present in its pink and grey slip-case – was loved by some readers and detested by others. The rightness, the relentless optimism and the exquisite sensitiveness of the heroine got on many British people's nerves. But when it was published in America in 1940, it became the Number One national bestseller. 'Mrs Miniver will place a gentle hand on your elbow,' said the *New Yorker*, 'and bid you stop to observe something insignificant; and lo! it is not insignificant at all. That touch – the touch of Charles Lamb, even of Shakespeare in a minor mood – is one of the indefinable things that English men and English women are fighting and dying for at the moment.'

Jan Struther was my grandmother. But this is not a book about a dear old grandmama with whom I went to have scones for tea in the 1980s. I sometimes imagine the kind of grand-mother she might have turned into, if she really had been the 'Mrs Miniver' of her own creation. She would have been one of those paper-thin, white-haired Chelsea ladies who live in mansion flats off the King's Road, and who occasionally venture out in their tweeds and pearls to make the journey to Peter Jones on a number 11 or 22 bus. Her drawing room would have been a chintzy, scented haven of pot-pourri and lilies, with pink-and-white striped sofas and silver-framed photographs of her deceased husband in a kilt. She would have managed to keep on a loyal old retainer, who baked the scones and laid her tray for breakfast. We would have sat together by the fire (gas-flame, perhaps), and she would have talked about what the King's Road used to be like in the 1930s.

But Jan Struther never reached old age. She died at fifty-two, nine years before I was born. Even if she had survived till her eighties, she wouldn't have been that kind of grandmother at all. She would have lived on the Upper West Side of Manhattan in an untidy apartment strewn with open reference books and wood-shavings and long-playing records not put back into their sleeves. We would have sat by the air-conditioning unit drinking gin and tonic out of chipped glasses and talking about love and politics. Her venturings-out would have been to the drugstore for malted milk, or to the hardware store for carpentry tools.

During the height of *Mrs Miniver*'s fame and success during the war, Jan toured America as an unofficial ambassadress for Britain, giving hundreds of lectures about Anglo-American relations to enchanted audiences. The public wanted to believe that she was the embodiment of her fictional creation, a sen-sible, calm, devoted wife and mother. She felt it was her wartime duty not to disappoint them. No one guessed – no one could pos-sibly have guessed – that she was in fact living two parallel lives.

She foresaw the unreachableness of her dead self in the poem quoted at the beginning of this book. We can never know her. But she had a remarkable capacity for writing important things down. I hope in these chapters to throw some light on the thorn-sharp need, the loneliness, the love, lust, dreams, shudders and sighs which guided her path through her short life.

Part One

Part One

Chapter One

In my own private Revised version, the commandment would read: 'Honour your father and your mother, your Nannie, your brother, your parents' cook and parlourmaid and housemaid and gardener and groom and chauffeur, and the man who comes to do odd jobs, and all the other people who take care of you and, above all, who teach you things.'

From J.S's unfinished autobiography

'IF I HAD a face like that, I'd pawn it and lose the ticket.'

Joyce Anstruther, aged five in 1906, was having her gloves put on by her nannie inside the front door of 9 Little College Street, Westminster. She was screwing her face up: her two pet hates were whites of egg and woollen gloves. 'Come on, Lamb,' said her nannie, whose name was Lucy Hudson, or 'Lala'. 'Quick's the word and sharp's the action. We're off to the Army and Navy Stores.'

'But can we go for a picnic afterwards?'

'Picnic? I'll give you picnic!'

Joyce was almost an only child. Her brother Douglas was twelve and away at boarding school. Her daytime companion was Lala. Nannie sayings would form the bedrock of her life's vocabulary.

Joyce spotted an advertisement in Victoria Street.

So . . . Ap,' she said.

'Soap, Lamb.'

That was the way she learned to read. Lala never deliberately set out to teach her anything. But nor did she ever stop her from finding anything out.

They bought a length of hat ribbon at the Army and Navy Stores.

'Whom shall I put it down to, Madam?'

'Number one-oh-nine-four-one,' Lala said. 'The Horrible Mrs Anstruther.'

And on they went for their walk, over the bridge in St James's Park, past the cowshed opposite the Horse Guards where you could buy a glass of milk for a penny, Joyce wondering all the while, but not asking, why her mother was described as 'horrible' in the Army and Navy Stores. It was years before she realized that the word was 'Honourable'.

They walked home the long way, through Strutton Ground where Lala picked up a bag of winkles for her tea. Street life held a fascination for Joyce which was to remain with her all her life. She loved seeing the naphtha flares, the shouting men, the scrap metal at A. Smellie, Ironmonger, the occasional drunk being arrested and taken to Rochester Row Police Station. If she saw a traffic accident – a horse which had slipped and got tangled up in the shafts, or a runaway horse with its van swaying behind – it made her afternoon. 'Let me get this straight,' she wrote later. 'I did not *want* disasters to happen, and I would have prevented them if I could, but if they were happening anyway I wanted to be there to see.'

In The Sanctuary, they passed the man who sold hot potatoes off a barrow.

'Well I never! Did you ever see a monkey dressed in leather,' said Lala.

'Oh, please may I have one?' said Joyce.

'I don't see why not,' said Lala. The Honourable Mrs Anstruther had no idea that her daughter's favourite treat was to eat a buttery barrow potato in bed, washed down with two mouthfuls of Lala's nightly pint of stout.

After this treat came the most anxious time of day for Joyce, when Lala went downstairs to have her supper with the servants in the kitchen, leaving Joyce tucked up in bed. Would Lala never come back upstairs? Had she 'run away for a soldier' as she often said she might? No: there, at last, was the sound of her footsteps. Joyce now felt safe to drop off to sleep.

'A world without Lala was as monstrously inconceivable as a world without my parents or brother,' Joyce wrote later. 'I used to read books, sometimes, about children whose mothers or fathers died, and I had bad dreams afterwards and woke up shivering and sweating. But no one ever bothered to write a book about a child whose nannie died or went away for no apparent reason, which was why I was so completely defenceless when it eventually happened to me.'

Joyce's mother, Eva, eldest daughter of the fourth Baron Sudeley, was not horrible, but she was odd. When she died in 1935, she left Joyce all her books. They included sixty-six cookery books and thirty-seven books on black magic. Joyce also found, in a drawer of the desk, a photograph of her mother's lifelong enemy Lady George Campbell, with pins stuck into the body. This confirmed Joyce's belief that her mother was a witch.

The sixty-six cookery books were a mystery, because the only cooking Eva ever did was on a silver chafing-dish brought to the table by a servant with all the ingredients prepared. The single piece of culinary advice she gave to Joyce on her marriage was not that of an active cook: 'Always order a pint of cream a day. It can be used in everything.'

In her speech, Eva combined the two Edwardian fads of 'g'-dropping (she liked pokin' about and pickin' up a bargain at a country auction and sellin' it at a profit to a London dealer) and 'r'-rolling (saying 'garage', 'chauffeur' and 'corridor' as if she were French).

She never once dressed or undressed herself without help from her lady's maid, or did her own hair. She insisted, throughout her life, that her stockings and shoes be put on before her drawers, which were lace-edged. At least three times a week the heel of a shoe tore the knicker lace, and it had to be mended by her maid.

The servants stayed, in spite of Eva's oddness; the young Joyce liked to spend time below stairs, listening to them talking, and learning to twist Bromo paper into a fan-shape with her fist. The impression she got from the servants was that with Mrs A. There Was Never a Dull Moment, while with Mr A. You Always Knew Where You Were. A bell rang.

'That's Her.'

'Oh, well. No peace for the wicked.'

'And precious little for the good.' And upstairs the parlourmaid went.

'There's been some friction up there today,' Joyce heard the parlourmaid say on her return. The servants had only an inkling of what Joyce knew and felt deeply: that Mr and Mrs A. were, in fact, extremely unhappily married. Joyce had plenty of love as a child, but something essential was missing. She wrote about it later, in the beginning of an autobiography which never progressed beyond the age of fourteen.

'To make the complete emotional circuit which is the most important thing about family life,' she wrote, 'a child's love should flow up to one of its parents, across to the other, and down to the child again, strengthened and enriched by their mental understanding. In my family this did not happen. My father adored my mother, but he did not understand her. She understood him pretty well but could not stand hair nor hide of him. Therefore there was a break in the circuit. The electrical force flashed back and forth between me and my mother, and flowed more steadily between me and my father: there were streaks of brilliant lightning, but much driving power was lost, and it was all a considerable strain. If I expressed my affection for him in front of her, I was dimly aware that it made her jealous; if I curled up with her on a sofa in front of him, I was conscious of a vague feeling of sadness emanating from the armchair on the other side of the fireplace. This particular conversation-piece must have occurred early in my life, because since the age of four or five I do not remember them ever sitting together in the same room, unless there was a luncheon or dinner party.'

The family's country house from 1904 till 1911 was Whitchurch House in Buckinghamshire, which had a long, French-pronounced corridor along the ground floor. Mrs A's den was at one end, with its sign on the door: 'No admittance EVEN on business'. She did her writing there: short stories with

Aged two, in Dutch fancy dress

a Boer War backdrop for *Outlook* and the *Saturday Westminster Gazette*, later published in book form.

Mr A's den was at the other end, and if you happened to look in he would probably be sharpening his pencil or a chisel. If there was nothing to sharpen, he would be mending something, and if there was nothing to mend he would be cleaning something, with his shirt-sleeves rolled up to the same level above each elbow. He carried on cleaning his golf clubs with emery paper regularly, long after he had given up the game.

His name was Henry Torrens Anstruther, and his love for his only daughter, and hers for him, was of the unspoken kind which must find outlets for expression in mutual unembarrassing delights such as heraldry, etymology and punctuation.

Things Harry taught me:

Knots and splices
Carpentry
Grammar
Love of reference books, maps, luggage, stationery
Handwriting
Love of Scotland
Not to dog-ear books

A Scot, he was Chief Liberal Whip and Member of Parliament for St Andrews, Fife until 1903 when he resigned on taking up the post of government representative on the Administrative Council of the Suez Canal Company. He was also a Justice of the Peace, an Alderman of the London County Council and a director of the North British Railway Company. But he could have earned his living, Joyce later wrote, and would have led a far happier life, as a jobbing carpenter.

When Eva married him, he was a promising Member of Parliament who seemed destined for the Cabinet. She was the pretty, witty Eva Hanbury-Tracy, aged twenty, brought up amid great wealth in London and at two large and grand country houses, Toddington in Gloucestershire and Gregynog in Wales. She could have made any match she chose.

'My mother had visions of herself,' Joyce wrote, 'as a hostess of some famous London house, standing at the head of a long staircase, welcoming Cabinet Ministers and their wives to epoch-making parties and influencing the destiny of the nation by a diplomatic nod or the quick tap of a fan on a crucial forearm. When this plan went agley, she was terribly disappointed, and she just couldn't take it.'

In 1893, a year before Eva and Harry's first child Douglas was born, Lloyd's Bank filed a bankruptcy petition against Eva's father, and Lord Sudeley was virtually ruined. Though asset-rich, he suffered from what would now be called a cash-flow problem. 'To put it briefly,' Joyce wrote, glossing over the true complications of the affair, 'my grandfather Sudeley, who was incurably optimistic, embarked on a tremendous scheme of fruit-growing but failed to grasp the elementary botanical truth that the trees he had planted would take seven years to mature.'

Queen Victoria wept on hearing of the bankruptcy. Lord Sudeley's great-grandson, the present seventh Baron, has spent most of his life demonstrating, inside and outside Parliament, the unfairness of the treatment of the fourth Baron, and how he was cheated of his estate.

Eva's parents moved to Ormeley Lodge in Ham, which many would now consider one of the most covetable houses in Greater London: Queen Anne red brick with wings, high white gates, and topiary garden at the back. Lady Sudeley considered it 'a villa'. But she carried on living quite grandly. Joyce remembered her grandmother Sudeley at Ormeley Lodge:

'If the unthinkable occurred, and Lizzie Haycock [the head-housemaid] happened to meet my grandmother in a passage, with no nearby doorway in which to take cover, she would flatten herself against the wall, concealing her dustpan and brush behind her back as though they were a jemmy and a blowlamp. My grandmother would nod and smile and Lizzie would murmur something inaudibly apologetic, ending in ". . . m'lady", and stand with lowered eyes until Her Ladyship had passed by. They all did it. It was the way things were.'

Eva found her own finances considerably reduced. She was still comfortably well-off, but no longer a notable heiress. After 1903 her husband wasn't even an MP or Government minister any more. 'My father was a methodical hard-working man,' Joyce wrote, 'with a great eye for detail; he could draft a memorandum with meticulous care and he never composed an ambiguous sentence, but he was sometimes tactless – not out of any lack of consideration for other people's feelings but rather because he hadn't the sense of finesse which makes some people weigh all the subtleties of a situation before they open their lips. Moreover, he hated intrigue, which to my mother was like oxygen.'

Joyce had only one memory of her parents being nice to each other. Her father came home with a bad toothache one evening, and her mother got a bottle of Bunter's Nervine from the medicine cupboard and took it up to him. Joyce was tremendously pleased. 'Perhaps things are going to be better from now on,' she thought. But they were not.

One day she went to tea with her friend Kathleen Gascoigne, and witnessed another episode she never forgot. 'Kathleen's mother was in the schoolroom with us; her father came in, had a mock quarrel with her (how different in undertones and overtones from a real one, and how gentle the ring of tin swords after the clang of genuine steel!) and ended up by picking her up in his arms and carrying her out of the room, talking and laughing. I was almost speechless with wonder, and made a mental note: other people's parents actually talk to each other, and make each other laugh.'

*

In the Housekeeper's Room at Ormeley Lodge, a book called 'Confessions: an Album to Record Thoughts, Feelings, &c' was filled in one afternoon when Joyce was there. Favourite Qualities in a Man: 'A jolly good-tempered old drunkard,' wrote Lizzie Haycock, the head housemaid. Pet Aversion: 'Sunday in on a fine day,' wrote Alice Rivers, another housemaid. Which Characters in History do you Most Dislike? 'Gentry,' wrote a between-maid called Annie McLeod. Here are Joyce's entries, at the age of seven:

> Your favourite qualities in a man: conjuror
> Your favourite occupation: reading
> Idea of happiness: rolling down a muddy bank with your best dress on
> Idea of misery: when Douglas is away
> Pet aversion: meat and eating my dinner
> If not yourself, who would you be? A boy
> Favourite motto: Make hay while the sun shines and no rose without a thorn

That last motto was to prove apposite. The rose and the thorn were inextricably joined in her life.

Joyce played on her own for hours, under and in trees. She had prehensile toes, and she could whistle with two fingers. She invented an imaginary country of which she was king, and drew maps and plans of its coastlines and castles. Every now and then she asked Lala to play the extra pirate, or the Sheriff of Nottingham, or to be a weight on the other end of a see-saw. If Lala didn't feel like it she said 'Oh, no, I've got a bone in my leg.'

One day, when Joyce was seven, she was sitting on the floor in the drawing-room when Lala was brought in to say goodbye. Joyce was absorbed in a jigsaw puzzle and gave her an absent-minded hug. 'Durnie', a former parlour-maid, was put in charge of her for a few weeks, and the weeks extended into months, and it dawned on her very gradually that Lala had retired, and was not coming back. 'I was spared a deep wound,' Joyce wrote, 'but I acquired an infection of uncertainty which took me many years to get over. My mother was spared a heart-rending scene, but she never afterwards had my wholehearted trust.'

Sleeplessness, which afflicted Joyce throughout her life, began now. She also started to develop many of the symptoms of the physically undernourished. 'I was what was known as delicate and nervy, and I had mild St Vitus's Dance. The grown-ups called it, quite kindly, Joyce's "tricks", and it consisted of things like jerking my head, twitching my eyes and making clicking noises in my throat. I also had the habit of developing unexplained blotches and spots all over my body.' Joyce realized, later in life, that all these were nervous complaints, and had the same cause: allergy to parental discord. The nerve tonics, milk, cream, suet puddings, cod-liver oil and malt prescribed by the doctors alleviated but did not cure the problem.

Eva and Harry did not separate until years later, in 1915. A small entry appears in Harry's visitors' book: '8th October. Eva walked out of my house.' Suitable marriages like theirs, Joyce wrote, tended to be bolstered by circumstances. 'When they rot internally the clinging ivy of social routine and feudal responsibility (which often had a hand in strangling them) keeps them standing, though the sap flows no more and the leaves wither. There is always the flower show coming on or the village bazaar which has to be opened; or a General Election is nearly due and One Has to Consider the Party.'

When Joyce's own first marriage was floundering in 1947, she used the same metaphor to describe its sickness; though this time it was a joint love of the children which kept it standing for so long. 'Relationships don't die in one piece. Sometimes the trunk appears dead, and most of the branches, but there is still some hidden flow of sap to one of the boughs which keeps it alive and green. In our case this is just what happened. The whole relationship was dead for most of the time during the last few years; but three times a year, during the school holidays, that one remaining branch – our intense love for our co-parenthood of the children – burst into miraculous blossom, and we could forget the dry twisted deadness of the rest of the tree.'

*

'Educated privately, London,' Jan Struther was to write all her adult life, when filling in forms.

She didn't go to school, quite: she went to 'Classes' in the mornings, for ten years, from the age of six to sixteen. Her first, Miss Richardson's Classes, took place at the house of Mrs Alfred Lyttelton at 16 Great College Street. On her first day there, in 1907, Joyce made a discovery: she found she liked being a new girl. This feeling lasted all her life. 'It didn't matter whether I was being a New Girl at school or a house party or a public dinner or a railway carriage or a ship: I always found it fun to infiltrate, to learn the ropes, to size up the other pupils, guests or passengers and to know that I was being sized up in return.'

Her least favourite subjects were Hist'ry and Jog. Jog was reduced to a network of political boundaries, and Hist'ry to a string of dates. 'It was small wonder that I fell as little in love with history as would a romantic young man with a girl of whom he had seen nothing but an X-ray photograph.' The one item of historical knowledge which inspired Joyce concerned the demise of Henry I: 'He died of a surfeit of lampreys, of which he was inordinately fond.' This sentence, she said, introduced her to the beauties of psalmodic rhythm, and it was still going round and round in her head forty years later when she was queuing for canned tuna fish on the Upper West Side of Manhattan.

In the teaching of Literature, however, Miss Richardson's was superb. Miss Moseley, who taught in a brimmed felt hat, had a taste for Shakespeare, but: 'Children,' she announced on the morning when she handed out the Everyman edition to her girls, 'there are certain words which we are going to leave out whenever we come across them. Now I want you to take your pencils and cross them out carefully so that they can't be read. Ready? Page twelve, line three, word seven. Page nineteen, line eight, word four . . .' The girls spent a delightful morning following her instructions, with the result that 'cuckold', 'whoreson', 'gorebellied' and other Elizabethan rude words were engraved on their memories for ever. Joyce was instinctively keen on swear-words – she used to argue with her brother about the comparative wickedness of Damn and Blast – and there could have been no better way to whet her appetite for Shakespeare.

Whether or not Miss Moseley adopted this ruse deliberately Joyce never knew, but her next was inspired. Rather than start her girls off, as many a felt-hatted teacher might, on *A Midsummer Night's Dream*, she plunged them straight into *Julius Caesar*. She understood children's craving for pageantry, melodrama, rhetoric, unfamiliar words, thundering rhythms, and for the eventual punishment of the guilty, whatever might happen to the innocent.

At once Joyce sensed in Shakespeare a kindred spirit. She experienced for the first time the squeezing of the diaphragm which happens when words or music express the essence of what one feels. She knew just what Brutus meant when he said:

> . . . poor Brutus, with himself at war,
> Forgets the shows of love to other men.

'It might not sink in the very day we read it, but the next time we got in a tangle of temper with ourselves and tried to unravel it by being perfectly foul to our brothers, sisters, mothers and nurses, the meaning of Brutus's words would begin to dawn upon us.' The lines

> When love begins to sicken and decay,
> It useth an enforced ceremony

tallied with her observation of her parents being a little too icily polite to each other; and in Mark Antony's

> For Brutus is an honourable man;
> So are they all, all honourable men

she recognized her mother's confidential tone while talking to a woman friend in the drawing-room: 'My dear, I wouldn't say a word against Angela. She's a thoroughly nice woman. I'm very *fond* of Angela . . .'

Long passages of the plays were learned by heart; in their

smocks and serge skirts, the girls stood up and recited. Joyce used them again for many purposes: to ennoble her daily feelings, to while away the interminableness of church, or to distract attention from brougham-sickness. York's words in *Richard II*, 'Grace me no grace, nor uncle me no uncle' always reminded her of Lala saying 'Picnic? I'll give you picnic.'

From the age of nine until she was twelve, Joyce went to Miss Wolff's in South Audley Street, where her friends were Peggy Lewis, Gena Drummond, Di Darling, Nell Joshua, Vera Jessel, Gladys Hirsch, Rene Lazarus, Elsie Raphael, and Elizabeth Bowes-Lyon, the future Queen, whom Joyce thought beautiful, and whose pigtails she dipped into an ink-pot. Peggy Lewis said 'Oh, Lord!' and 'one' instead of 'I'. Joyce lost no time copying her. When, aged twelve, Joyce went to visit her cousin Ruth Hanbury, the first thing she said to Ruth was, 'Oh, Lord! You're not still playing with that hoop, are you?'

Ruth, sitting with a rug and a Labrador on her lap in her drawing room in Co. Monaghan in May 1999, said: 'Oh, dear, I never played with it again. And I did love that hoop. Joyce was very sophisticated, and she gave me an inferiority complex which I've only really outgrown, perhaps, in my nineties.'

Miss Wolff, who was of German blood, taught her girls to intone 'Der, den, des, dem. Die, die, der, der. Das, das, des, dem,' which appealed to Joyce: grammatical tables, she found, were the only method which worked for getting hold of a language. But strict as she was, Miss Wolff turned to wax when she introduced the girls to German poetry. Joyce felt her diaphragm squeeze again at these words from Heinrich Heine's 'Die Lorelei':

> *Ich weiss nicht, was soll es bedeuten,*
> *Dass ich so traurig bin . . .**

When the First World War began, Joyce was at her third and last educational institution, Mrs Martin Holland's. She had a

---

* 'I know not what it might mean, that I feel so sad.'

pash for Cynthia Lubbock and Cynthia Lubbock had a pash for her. Janet Thomson, on the day war broke out, announced to her classmates that the way to help the war was to be good and not to worry the grown-ups, who were probably worried enough anyway. They all started knitting socks.

In her notes towards her autobiography, Joyce later listed the main points about her sexual awakening.

Facts of life

1 Looking up adultery in dictionary.
2 Thinking babies born fully dressed in red twill frocks.
3 'Nice feelings' when reading about tortures. Still persist. Also when tight-lacing one's stays.
4 Seeing my mother in bath but always discreetly hunched up.
5 Doug given the job of telling me facts of life. Interesting remark (inaudible by my sneeze) about buggery; too proud to ask him to repeat it. Never heard of lesbians till engaged.
6 Masochism – being tied up to trees during Red Indians, etc.
7 Romance: a wall-light seen through an archway; bonfire light on men's faces; a man's torn shirt-sleeve. E. Gosling tearing his thumb, out hunting.

It was about at this time, also, that she first felt 'the lonely melancholy ecstatic feeling when you know you are about to write a poem'.

Eva, meanwhile, was embarking on the work which was to make her Dame Eva, 'the Dame' for short. On microfiche at the Imperial War Museum library, under 'World War I Benevolent Institutions' and among the lists of ladies organizing funds to send Bovril, mouth-organs, chessmen, gramophones, boxing-gloves and walking-sticks to the troops, is to be found The Hon. Eva Anstruther, Honorary Secretary of the Camps Library, which collected books and sent them to the trenches, reinforcement camps and hospitals of northern France and Flanders. People could hand any book over at any post-office counter in Britain and it would make its way, via the distribution office in Horseferry Road, to grateful soldiers whose company commanders wrote back: 'I have often wished that you could see how eager the men are to receive the literature, and how it lessens the monotony of their lives.'

The Camps Library started in 1915, a month before those words in Harry's visitors' book, 'Eva walked out of my house.' The Chairman was Sir Edward Ward, who had been Permanent Under-Secretary of State at the War Office until 1914, and was now Director-General of Voluntary Organisations. He had found in The Hon. Mrs Anstruther, said the *Morning Post*, 'an invaluable executive officer'. It was he who recommended her for an honour, and she was appointed a Dame Commander of the Order of the British Empire in 1918.

But Joyce's best friend Frankie Whitehead was not allowed to visit Joyce at 9 Little College Street because, shockingly, Sir Edward Ward was sometimes to be seen emerging from the house in the afternoons. Joyce knew about the affair. Once, in her late teens, she arrived home as noiselessly as possible late one night, only to encounter her mother also arriving home as noiselessly as possible from the other direction. How long the affair lasted is not recorded. Eva built a house called Pan's Garden in Beaulieu; it had an altar-like chimney-piece in honour of the god Pan, and Sir Edward often visited her there from 1913, until she sold it in 1919.

But as Eva grew older, Joyce wrote, 'her personal unhappiness grew deeper without increasing her spiritual maturity', and she began to depend more and more on her intuitions and psychic powers. She was intensely superstitious about spilled salt, crossed knives, black cats and walking under ladders. She went in for automatic writing and every possible kind of fortune-telling, both as practitioner and as client, and there was always a crystal ball in her room.

Eva encouraged Joyce in her juvenilia: she typed out an adventure story Joyce wrote when she was in bed with chickenpox in 1907 ('You hold the robbers while I go and fetch Father'); she made sure that Joyce joined the Scratch Society, whose members had to write and read out a poem at each monthly meeting; and in August 1918 she saw to it that Joyce's first story was published in the *Saturday Westminster Gazette*. Here the pseudonym Jan Struther first appeared; and from

With her mother

this time on, and throughout the 1920s and 1930s, Jan Struther was a much-published short-story writer, light journalist and poet.

It was her father, though, not her mother, whom Joyce thanked for her understanding of the mechanics of writing. 'He was an excellent critic,' she wrote, 'with a delicate ear for the rhythm and weight of words. As for the finer intricacies of grammar, he was meticulous and, I think, infallible in his judgement. I remember the expression on his face when I showed him a letter from a friend of mine in which the last sentence ran: "I should have loved to have come." "I hope", he said grimly, "that you're not seriously thinking of marrying that young man." I honestly believe he would sooner have seen me married to a jailbird than to a man who used the double perfect. His battle against slipshod language was waged because of his deep sense of the beauty of order. He knew that clarity and simplicity of expression are the outward signs of a writer's inward integrity. By tirelessly pointing out my verbal ambiguities, he made me aware of, and repentant of, the looseness of thought which had caused them.'

Eva and Harry were legally separated but never divorced. Eva moved, with Joyce, first to 51 South Street, and then, in 1920, to 25 Curzon Street. Harry remained in Buckinghamshire, living alone in Whitchurch, in Old Court House (which was smaller than Whitchurch House), and here Joyce spent many beautifully ordered days with him. She always had to be careful to head him away from the subject of genealogical trees, which bored her as much as they fascinated him.

Harry changed for dinner every night of his life. He never owned a motor-car; he went everywhere either on horseback or in his two-wheeled dogcart. One thing he was meticulous about was the opening and closing of gates, which he always did without dismounting. He and Joyce would go out hunting together, and arrive home by starlight, tired and aching. 'We would help each other off with our mud-caked boots, have warm baths with a handful of mustard in the water and then sit down to reminisce about the day over a roast pheasant and a cheese soufflé.'

Then after supper, when the oil lamps had been brought in and the coffee cups cleared away, they sat and sang to the guitar. Most often they sang the old Jacobite songs – 'Charlie is My Darling' and 'Wae's Me for Prince Charlie' – and as the evening wore on they worked themselves into an orgy of sadness over the exiled prince and his long-dead cause.

'I realise now', wrote Joyce in 1948, 'that the main reason why the Jacobite songs appealed to my father was because his own life – particularly his private life – had been something of a lost cause. When he sang "Will ye no come back again?", the image in his mind's eye was not of Charles Edward Stuart but of a witty, pretty woman playing the hostess at the end of a long dinner table, with the sound of Big Ben booming out every quarter hour behind the talk and the laughter.'

Eva lived till 1935, in a house in Swan Walk, Chelsea: 'Dame to tea' and 'Dine Dame' appear in Joyce's engagement books throughout her early married life.

Harry died in 1926, knocked off his horse on 'the narrows' near Whitchurch by a double-decker motor-bus. Joyce was never able to speak of him afterwards without tears filling her

Harry Anstruther

eyes. When she thought of him, she remembered a medley of scents: saddle leather, tweed, warm horseflesh, hawthorn, meadow-sweet and cow parsley.

'The most valuable lesson of all', she wrote, 'was one which he never set out to teach: how comforting and clarifying, in times of loneliness and perplexity, is the companionship of inanimate objects, the touching and handling of wood and stone; and, when larger problems seem insoluble, how steadying to the nerves, how infinitely soothing to the troubled heart, is the painstaking performance of small, familiar manual tasks.'

Chapter Two

Sometimes the bliss within me burning
Leaps to a flame so fiercely bright
That I can feel my body turning
To golden ashes with delight.

Body, beware, whose every sense
Fans in my soul this fire of joy;
Lest, with a heat grown too intense
One day it shall yourself destroy.

'Body, Beware . . .', from J.S's collection of poems *Betsinda Dances*

THIS CHAPTER WAS going to begin 'Joyce did a typing and short-hand course at Kilburn Polytechnic in 1918'. It is the first post-war detail known about her, and it is arresting because 'typing', 'shorthand', 'Kilburn' and 'Polytechnic' are so unexpected after the Shakespeare, Mayfair and nannies which preceded them. Joyce was striking out as a woman, taking buses on her own.

But what kind of person was it who took these buses? She was small (five feet, two inches) with blue eyes and black hair so curly that later, when she lived in New York, she liked to have it cut and dried in Harlem. As a child she used to imitate a King Charles spaniel by pulling curls down over the sides of her face to make ears. She was slim and pretty and her eyes shone with laughter and delight.

The wanting to be a boy which had afflicted her in childhood changed in her teens into the happier state of feeling deliciously feminine as well as wanting to climb trees and shoot with a rifle.

Early married photographs show her bra-less and barefoot on lawns, with boyish knees beneath a sturdy pair of shorts.

She inherited from her father a genuine liking for practical tasks. She preferred unblocking a drain to talking in a drawing-

Aged eighteen

Lined up with her three children at Cultoquhey in 1934

room. She liked sawing and shaping wood. Writing the hymn 'Lord of all hopefulness' in 1930, she put into words one of the things she most admired about Jesus: that his 'strong hands were skilled at the plane and the lathe'. (She was also badly in need of a rhyme for 'faith'. Her rhyming dictionary listed only 'baith' and 'wraith'.)

In her eating and in her household habits, she tended towards the masculine. She drank milk by the glass. She forgot about food for hours, then was suddenly ravenous, but could never eat a whole plateful of anything. 'Why can't you eat it if you were so hungry?' her family asked. 'I have a small but vicious appetite,' she replied.

She didn't notice dust or mess, and her natural inclination was to scribble useful numbers on the wall next to the telephone. She didn't put her clothes away in cupboards but hung them on the back of the chair in her bedroom, day after day, until the weight became too much and the chair fell over. In this she was different from her father, who was described by *Vanity Fair* in 1897 as 'the tidiest man ever invented'.

There was a streak in her which rebelled against what she was supposed to be doing, seeing, saying or wearing. Partly because her mother was so interested in antiques, Jan wasn't at all. Wandering about in a town, she would be drawn not to the shops which sold mahogany chests but to junkier ones where she might pick up an old wooden flute, or a bit of lustre-ware. She liked shininess, and preferred costume jewellery to diamonds. The defiant lyrics of 'The Raggle-Taggle Gypsies' sang in the back of her head. If she met anyone who came of gypsy stock, she was fascinated and jealous. Part of her yearned to swap her goose-feather bed for the cold open fields.

It was perhaps the hanging-around with the household staff throughout her childhood which gave her a lifelong preoccupation with justice and injustice. In her unfinished autobiography she described the moment, at the age of seven, when her social conscience was awakened:

When I think of Lala, one small incident always comes back to me. It had nothing to do with her, really, as an individual, but it has always stuck in my mind because it introduced me to two new feelings. My mother and various grown-up guests were having tea with me for a treat in the downstairs day nursery at Whitchurch House. There was a big fireplace in it and Lala was making drop scones for the whole party. The rest of us were all sitting round the table, but Lala went on standing by the fire, ladling the pale golden batter on to the round iron griddle with the hoop handle. When the scones were done she slathered them over with butter, piled them on to a plate and went back to make a second batch, and then a third. My mother had poured out the tea and we were all eating and talking and laughing. After a while Lala turned her hot red face from the fire and said to my mother, 'Could I please have a cup, Madam?' My mother said:

'I'm so sorry, Lucy, I forgot all about you!' and handed her a cup.

It was the purest oversight, I suppose, but for some reason I was swept by a wave of shame, embarrassment and vicarious remorse. It was the first time I ever had the feeling that I afterwards learned to call a sense of pathos: and it was the first time I was ever consciously aware that the social system was more than a little cock-eyed. This is an opinion I have never had any temptation to revise.

Joyce wasn't one of those voracious readers who work their way through their father's whole library by the age of twelve. A miniaturist in her writing, she was also a miniaturist in her reading, preferring to devour and re-devour old favourites (*Scouting for Boys, Kidnapped, How to Survive on Land and Sea*) than tackle a long book by Dickens. The books she collected were books of poetry, and her favourite poet was Donne. Given a free hour on a train, she liked to look out of the window and gaze into back gardens and allotments, or write a letter. She never travelled without writing-paper, envelopes, stamps, fountain pen and ink.

She loved films: 'I would prefer to be at a bad movie than at no movie at all,' she said. Her favourite films, over her lifetime, were *Casablanca, Brief Encounter, Double Indemnity* and *The Third Man*. She unashamedly liked middlebrow art. She didn't love museums, although (and partly because) she knew she ought to. Their hallowed atmosphere annoyed her. At Miss Richardson's Classes the girls had been taken on gallery outings, and Joyce's eyes glazed over after the first room. She liked Ophelia lying dead in the water. 'Always had a vile taste in pictures,' she wrote in her autobiographical notebook. Her feet hurt. If she stood still for a long time in front of a painting, it tended to be because she was over a hot-air ventilator. There were too many Virgin-and-Childs, and all Joyce wanted to do when confronted with such paintings was to search for the walled town in the distant background and wonder, as she did with back gardens seen from trains, what it would be like to live there.

To sit in rows watching a live spectacle felt like a kind of imprisonment. Of a ballet in the 1930s she wrote in a letter the next day, 'the males wore lime-green tights so tightly fitting that it was only too apparent that their amorous gestures were not, so to speak, heartfelt.' The interminableness of plays reminded her of the interminableness of church as a child. Even at concerts, which she loved the idea of and the beginning of, her mind would take flight in the second half. She wrote poems on concert programmes, round the edge.

'Quartet for two fiddles, viola and cello',
That's what it was called by the Austrian fellow.
Well, some people's *Sitzfleisch* is stronger than mine.
'Quartet for two buttocks, a coccyx and a spine.'

If she turned on the wireless, though, and Schubert's 'Trout' Quintet happened to be playing, or a Bach violin concerto, she was all a-tingle with the beauty of it, and with the sense of luck which happening to switch on at the right moment brought. She liked to come across beauty or good art by chance, rather than be made to sit in front of it.

But she couldn't get enough of the Royal Tournament. This, she never wanted to end. In 1931 she described the Combined Horse and Motor-Cycle Display by the Royal Corps of Signals for *Punch*: 'Side by side the ancient and the modern, the flesh-and-blood and steel-and-rubber go through identical manoeuvres, until one would be hard put to it to know which to fill with petrol and which with oats.' She was enchanted by the two milk-white war horses, Peter and Punch, aged 23 and 25, who had fought all through the war and were due to retire at the end of the year. Horses moved her more than actors did.

Stuck in a train or bus, she would sooner strike up conversation with a man than with a woman. With men she tried harder, and said wittier, cleverer things, and generally shone more. Though she coined the expression 'She's the fondest person that I'm of' to describe her female friendships, she couldn't disguise the fact that she found men more stimulating, a trait which often annoyed the female friends she made in adulthood.

She was attracted to amusing, eloquent men. The man she married in 1923 was, primarily, funny, and amused by the things which amused Joyce. He played practical jokes, and did accents, and redeemed draughty foreign train journeys by writing an apt limerick or starting a competition to spot the passenger with the most gold teeth: brittle humour she enjoyed. But part of her rebelled against the safety of humour – the way being constantly funny removes the need for a real conversation about anything. She was also attracted to sadness, and it was perhaps inevitable that in the late 1930s she was carried away romantically as well as altruistically by the plight of the European Jews.

Beneath her thin skin, sexuality raged. 'Over-sexed' was the word used of her in her lifetime; now she would be described as 'highly sexed'. Men were attracted to the gypsy in her, to the boy in her, beneath the surface of the well-born pupil of Miss Richardson's Classes. She celebrated Armistice Day astride a lion in Trafalgar Square. In sex, too, her taste for the illicit – for what she shouldn't be doing, seeing, saying or wearing – was strong. The price she was to pay for her sensations of rapture was high; in the 1920s, she could have had no idea how high. This, from her book of poems *Betsinda Dances*, published by the Oxford University Press in 1931, is an inkling:

'Evening'

I have looked too long upon the sunset.
  Its spell has stripped me bare
Of all the comfortable thoughts
  That commonly I wear.

Evening's the chink in the soul's armour,
And through it I can feel
The soft cold fingers of desolation
Silently, deftly steal.

Nought's left of joy now but its transience;
Of pride, but its loneliness.
Love's a dim ache, a dying music,
Beautiful, comfortless.

Colour to greyness turns, and slowly
Light fades from the sky:
I sit bowed down by the weight of evening,
Too sorrowful to cry.

Joyce got a part-time job as a secretary at Scotland Yard in 1919. It was one way of satisfying her childhood agony of curiosity about what happened to drunkards when they went inside the doors of Rochester Row Police Station. Her superior, looking over her shoulder one morning, happened to see her typing out a court report riddled with four-letter words: 'I think we'll have one of the *men* finish that one, Miss Anstruther.' For years afterwards she remained friends with the detectives at Scotland Yard, and dropped in sometimes to play poker with them.

She was now a modern maiden, wearing high-heeled shoes and smoking cigarettes. The metaphors she used in her early articles in the *Graphic* and the *Evening Standard* (published in 1920 and 1921) reflect her daily experience: something was 'as bland as a cocktail without ice', and you could as little do something else as 'live on a diet of salted almonds'. The débutante's life involved many iceless cocktails and salted-almond evenings. Polite young men escorted her home to 25 Curzon Street in Mayfair, where she lived with her mother, the Dame.

Joyce's first love was Peter Sanders, whose details are to be found in the leather-bound notebook in which she recorded 'Dances, Dinners, Boys, Girls, Etc.' between 1918 and 1920. Under 'Men, 1920' appears 'Sanders, Arthur (Peter), 3 Eaton Square, VIC 3785. Bayford Lodge, Wincanton, Somerset. 3rd Grenadier Gd., Gds Club.'

The modern maiden

Joyce burned her diaries in 1921 and never wrote about Peter afterwards, so it is only from the spidery handwriting of her best friend Frankie Whitehead that we know Peter to have been 'a wonderful person, good-looking, very clean, very popular and very nice'. The last dance Joyce went to with him was at

Claridge's on 11 November 1920 – the Armistice Dance. Peter went away for a few days' hunting after that, and on 22 November shot himself. Gambling debts were the official reason.

A month after Peter's death Joyce wrote this poem, which she called 'Immortality'. It is not what one might expect from someone soon to be writing hymns.

> They talk to me of the immortal soul:
>   And maybe they speak the truth.
> But O! small comfort, when I want the whole
>   Bright bravery of your youth
> Which grim death stole.
> And yet wise men, forsooth,
>   Try with vague tales of immortality
>   To comfort me.
>
> They talk to me of all eternity:
>   I think it sounds too vast
> And overwhelming just for you and me,
>   Two pagan lovers; we should be aghast
> And shiver at its cold immensity.
> I'd rather be
>   Back in our little past –
> Transient, perhaps, but we
>   Found it sweet, even though it might not last
>   Like this strange solemn immortality
>   They offer me.

The cocktails and salted almonds carried on. The social system may have seemed cock-eyed to Joyce, but she had no qualms about enjoying what it offered to her as a posh (fashionable word) girl in London, or the way it introduced her to suitable young men.

She travelled to Egypt in 1922 with her father in his capacity as a Director of the Suez Canal Company. They took the Bombay Express through France and sailed from Marseilles over Christmas. Joyce got herself up as a gypsy for the Christmas Day fancy-dress dance, and dined in the captain's cabin.

She wrote social notes for *Tatler*'s 'Bystander' pages: 'Among the many visitors to Egypt were Miss Bridget Keir, the artist; Sir Horace and Lady Pinching and their daughter; Lady Somerleyton (who expects to stay in Egypt until the end of April, as does also Lord Mount Edgcumbe), and Sir Henry Webb, the former Liberal MP for the Forest of Dean division.' Her holiday diary is a *Tatler*-ish list of pleasures: tennis-playing at the British Club, French ladies at tea dances, hotel overlooking the Nile towards the Pyramids. 'NB: saw entrance to new tomb – Tut-ankhamen.' On the last day: 'Tea on peak of highest sand dune overlooking sunset. Slid down and came home singing, Gibbs and I barefoot, Tommy Wilson with large tear in seat of bags.' No other girl was present on the sand dune, and Joyce revelled in being the only woman among men.

Another man listed in that 'Dances, Dinners, Boys, Girls, Etc' book was 'Maxtone Graham, Tony, 32 Addison Road, Kensington'. He and Peter Sanders had been friends at Sandhurst, and when Peter died, Joyce talked and cried with Tony about him. Tony told her he was in love with someone who didn't reciprocate, then confessed that the girl was Joyce.

It is often said that 'Tony was the shoulder she cried on' when Peter died, and that 'she fell in love with Tony on the rebound', not phrases which conjure up *Brief Encounter*-type swooning. It was not love at first sight, on Joyce's part at least; it was love at about a hundred and fifty-ninth sight. But it was love. Slowly emerging love could, she discovered, be every bit as strong once it did emerge as the at-first-sight kind. Gradually, and then one day with sudden clarity, Joyce found she was at one in body, mind and spirit with the generous and fascinating man who loved her. Here is her poem called 'Thoughts After Lighting a Fire'.

> When to this fire I held a taper,
> First flared the impressionable paper;
> I watched the paper, as I stood,
> Kindle the more enduring wood;

And from the wood a vanguard stole
To set alight the steadfast coal.

So, when I love, the first afire
Is body with its quick desire;
Then in a little while I find
The flame has crept into my mind –
Till steadily, sweetly burns the whole
Bright conflagration of my soul.

He was the eldest son of a Scottish laird-to-be; Burke's *Landed Gentry*, not the *Peerage*, is the book to look up the family in. His father Jim Maxtone Graham was a chartered accountant, of Maxtone Graham & Sime in Charlotte Square, Edinburgh. Every morning of his working life he said 'Morning, Sime' to Sime and Sime said 'Morning, Maxtone Graham' to him. Tony's mother, Ethel Blair Oliphant, was a writer of history books about the Maxtones, the Grahams and the Oliphants: *The Maxtones of Cultoquhey, The Beautiful Mrs Graham*, and *The Oliphants of Gask*.

The family estate, Cultoqhuey, had been in the Maxtone family since 1429. Surrounded by larger landowners, the Maxtones had with quiet doggedness clung for fifteen generations to their beloved house in the heart of Perthshire. Mungo, the tenth Laird, had dryly summed up his opinion of his powerful and grasping neighbours in the Cultoqhuey Litany which he intoned daily at a well near the house, surrounded by his household.

From the Greed of the Campbells,
From the Ire of the Drummonds,
From the Pride of the Grahams,
From the Wind of the Murrays,
Good Lord deliver us.

His prayer was answered in every line but the third: Maxtones repeatedly married Grahams. The first Maxtone Graham was James, the thirteenth Laird, who combined the names in 1860.

The gabled old house had been knocked down and replaced

by a large new gothick house in 1820. Tony's father did not inherit the estate until his unmarried brother died in 1930, so when Joyce was introduced to the family they were living at Bilston Lodge, near Edinburgh. Spinster aunts came to tea. Tony's mother turned out to be the great-niece of Lady Nairne, author of the Jacobite song 'Will ye no come back again?' The Scottishness in Joyce's own blood came quickly to the surface. She was enchanted.

When she and Tony danced, people stood back from the dance floor and watched. When they talked, their eyes flashed with the pleasure of finding the same things funny. They were so immersed in one another's company that they were often the last to leave a restaurant, forced out at midnight by the sound of chairs being put up on tables.

They started a commonplace book together, writing out their favourite poems, Joyce's hand girlishly loopy, Tony's Etonian and disciplined. Words, and the enjoyment of noticing how other people used them, were a source of constant amusement. They both liked rude words and dirty jokes, a taste neither had ever been able to indulge with anyone else. Being scurrilous together was a new pleasure, and made what Joyce called their 'hanky-panky on the back stairs' all the more uninhibited. Tony encouraged Joyce in her wittiness, and her writing now developed two strands: the brittle, amusing social-observer strand, nurtured by Tony, and the noticing-sadness-in-everyday-life strand, which was her own.

Their parents told them they were too young to marry, which only made them all the more desperate to do so. They were married at the unfashionably early hour of half-past ten in the morning of Wednesday, 4 July 1923, at All Hallows, London Wall, Joyce draped in downward-hanging silvery 1920s clothes. The wedding was quiet, with only fifty-five guests, no bridesmaids and no reception. Officially this was because of 'family mourning', but the fourth Baron Sudeley had died seven months before. The true reason was that Dame Eva and Harry were not on speaking terms. Before settling in her pew the Dame was heard to whisper loudly to Tony's father, 'If that man comes up to speak to me, I want you to knock him down.'

The Evening Standard*'s photograph of the wedding*

Quiet though it was, the wedding was reported in no fewer than ten newspapers and magazines. The heading in the Scottish *Evening Telegraph and Post* of 4 July 1923 was 'Fife Lady Married in London Today. Bridegroom Son of Perthshire Laird.' *The Pall Mall Gazette* noted that Joyce 'carried no gloves, flowers, or prayer-book.' The London *Evening Standard*, searching for copy, reported that Tony wore a red flower instead of the more conventional white in his buttonhole.

One poignant souvenir of the wedding has been preserved, a commemorative paper napkin made by an enterprising printer who hoped to sell it to the guests. It says 'In commemoration of the marriage between Mr Anthony Maxtone Graham and Miss Joyce Anstruther at All Hallows London Wall, 4 July 1923. All Blessings and Happiness to them.' As there was no reception and therefore no cake-encrusted fingers in need of a napkin, it has survived in pristine condition.

'Twenty-three years with the wrong woman', Joyce was later to write about Tony – twenty-three years between that wedding day in the City, with church bells ringing out above the traffic, and the last evening they spent together, washing the dishes in Chelsea in September 1946: 'A long road from the altar in All Hallows, London Wall to the kitchen sink in Wellington Square.'

Chapter Three

Only in two kinds of earth
Can poets bring their songs to birth –
In sorrow's rich and heavy clay,
Or else (and here's the rarer way)
Out of the loamy light caress
Of an abundant happiness.
Therefore, best critic and best friend,
To you these doggerel thanks I send
For each delightful day, each charming year
Your presence has ensured for me, my dear.

Dedication 'To A. M. G.', from *Betsinda Dances*

MRS MINIVER IS a portrait of a woman in a cloudless marriage. When Joyce began to write it, fifteen years into her marriage to Tony, the paradise she depicted was for her a paradise lost. But the very fact that it was out of reach made her perception of it all the sharper, and it is to *Mrs Miniver* we must look for a flavour of the first blissful ten years with Tony. She put her finger on the small but intense daily pleasures of marriage, the eye to catch, the pocketful of pebbles, un-understanding.

'Tell me,' said Mrs Miniver, 'weren't you with an uncle of mine in Singapore – Torquil Piggott?'

'Piggy!' exclaimed the Colonel, beaming gratefully, and plunged into reminiscence. Thank God for colonels, thought Mrs Miniver; sweet creatures, so easily entertained, so biddably diverted from senseless controversy into comfortable monologue: there was nothing in the world so restful as a really good English colonel.

Clem caught her eye across the table. It seemed to her sometimes that the most important thing about marriage was not a home or children or a remedy against sin, but simply there always being an eye to catch.

As she walked past a cab rank in Pont Street Mrs Miniver heard a very fat taxi driver with a bottle nose saying a very old taxi driver with a rheumy eye: 'They say it's all a question of your subconscious mind.'

Enchanted, she put the incident into her pocket for Clem. It jostled, a bright pebble, against several others: she had had a rewarding day. And Clem, who had driven down to the country to lunch with a client, would be pretty certain to come back with some good stuff, too. This was the cream of marriage, this nightly turning out of the day's pocketful of memories, this deft habitual sharing of two pairs of eyes, two pairs of ears. It gave you, in a sense, almost a double life.

Mrs Miniver had long ago discovered that whereas words, for her, clarified feelings, for Clem, on the whole, they obscured them. This was perhaps just as well. For if they had both been equally explicit they might have been in danger of understanding each other completely; and a certain degree of un-understanding (not mis-, but un-) is the only possible sanctuary which one human being can offer to another in the midst of the devastating intimacy of a happy marriage.

Relatives have said that 'When Tony and Joyce were first married they were so in love that when their first son was born they neglected him completely.' This seems unlikely: there are too many photographs of Jamie (born 1924) being hugged. But she certainly handed him back to his nurse the moment he started crying. As Joyce herself wrote of her grandmother's old-fashioned behaviour, 'They all did it. It was the way things were.'

Her babies were born at home: she was modern and brave about childbirth. Twenty-seven years after the first event she described the astonishing pain: ' "Stick to it as long as you can," said my doctor, "but there's no need to get to the stage of biting sheets." "*Me*, bite sheets?" I remember thinking in arrogant

With Jamie in 1929

astonishment; but a few hours later I saw what he meant.' She breastfed her children, but after that she felt she had done her share of hard work, and handed over to Nannie.

Tony and Joyce's first home was a small Georgian house in

Walpole Street, Chelsea. After the hushed grandeur of débutante Mayfair, Joyce loved the vibrancy of Chelsea: the street musicians on the King's Road, and the cheap restaurants with water bottles that had once held Chianti. Their friends tended to be young, artistic Chelsea people with names like Turps (short for Turpentine) Orde. Tony worked for the Lloyds insurance brokers Harris & Dixon; he was also a 'Name' at Lloyds. But he wasn't a businessman by nature. He and Joyce referred to his over-keen colleagues as 'the business bastards'.

Tony came home at six and played with his model trains. In the 1920s and 1930s this was a not uncommon adult male pastime, and Tony's trains were particularly good; he had a real steam locomotive, not just clockwork or electric. But it was perhaps a sign of the schoolboyishness Tony carried with him into adulthood, and never shook off. For him, playing games, telling jokes and doing funny accents – all the things Etonians did between lessons – never lost their appeal. Playing was a way of hiding from the tedium of adulthood, and this, at first, was one of the bonds between Tony and Joyce. Writing to her brother in 1951, Joyce described her own lifelong shunning of adulthood: 'Most people have *some* degree of histrionic sense: certainly nearly all children love dressing up and make-believe and pretending to be Red Indians and so forth. The majority of human beings grow out of this as they get older – some of them, in fact, grow out of it so completely that they become great big fucking bores, as we well know if we've had to sit next to them at dinner parties.' There was a part of her, she wrote, which never stopped being 'the curly-headed girl who would rather have been born a boy anyhow, and who had a strong prejudice against becoming a grown-up *ever* (fostered by many adoring visits to *Peter Pan* – a work of art which is probably responsible for more neuroses among the members of my generation than poor dear James Barrie had ever heard of).'

In the daytime she sat at home writing articles, poems, short stories and fables which were published, at the rate of about one a week, under her pseudonym Jan Struther, first in *G. K's Weekly*, the *Evening Standard*, the *Daily News* and the *Daily Express*, the *Graphic*, and *Eve, the Lady's Pictorial*, and later,

Tony and Joyce in 1928

from 1928 onwards, in *Punch*, the *Spectator* and the *New States-man*. Favourite themes in her earliest pieces were Justice Done to the Underdog, The Dreamer is Revenged on the Prosaic World, and Arrogance Knocked Off its Perch. Editors liked her conciseness, her epigrammatic style, her gift for observing universal daily experience, and her mastery of the irresistible first paragraph.

> Giving a party is very like having a baby: its conception is more fun than its completion, and once you have begun it is almost impossible to stop.

She wrote about party-giving and party-going a great deal, because she was continually doing it in real life and half-liked it, half-loathed it. Tony had a gift for entertaining. Dinner parties at Walpole Street were not sleepy affairs with guests yawning on sofas. After dinner (celery cream soup, roast plover, French beans, rissole potatoes, Hungarian pudding and cheese patties, produced by Ada the cook), jazz records were played in the drawing-room. There was ping-pong (Joyce played until the last day of each pregnancy), or sometimes darts, or Tony would get his model trains working. Late at night, on a whim, everyone would jump into cars and drive twenty miles to Iver in Buckinghamshire, to stand on the railway bridge and watch the Cornish Riviera Express fly past underneath.

They had a small circle of close friends: Guy and Jacynth Warrack, Anne Talbot, Evan and Cynthia Talbot, Klop and Nadya Ustinov, Charles and Oscar Spencer (Oscar was a woman), and Clifford and Peter Norton (Peter was a woman). There was also a wider circle of not-so-close friends to be dined with or stayed with and then invited back. Discussing the characteristics of these friends, and the infuriating conventions which made it impossible to shake them off, was a favourite pastime. 'The Frants? The Palmers? [asked Mrs Miniver.] Really, the unevenness of married couples. Like those gramophone records with a superb tune on one side and a negligible fill-up on the other which you had to take whether you liked it or not.' The necessity of writing the sort of gushing thank-you letter immortalized by Jane Austen's Mr Collins inspired an article for *Punch*, suggested by Tony, entitled 'Snillocs' ('Snilloc' is 'Collins' backwards). It should be the hostess, Jan argued, who wrote the thank-you letter: 'A thousand thanks for coming to stay . . . we enjoyed every moment of your visit . . . it was too sweet of you to go to all that trouble and expense . . .'

For consider what actually happens. The host, or more probably the hostess (since nature has decreed that for what men suffer by having to shave, be killed in battle, and eat the legs of chickens, women make amends by housekeeping, childbirth, and writing all the letters for both of them) – the hostess, I say, is the person who suggests the visit in the first place. She begs, she implores you to come and stay. 'We should so adore to see you again,' she writes. 'So hoping you are not booked up for that weekend – I know how sought after you are!' And again, more briefly and winningly, '*Do* say Yes!!!' Thus far you, the potential guest, are the wooed, the desired, the beautiful maiden whose hand has just been asked in marriage. But as soon as you accept you find yourself de-rated. The beautiful maiden becomes merely another superfluous woman who has been lucky enough to

get off. From now on, you are popularly supposed to be the benefici-
ary, your hostess the benefactor.

The facts, as a brief audit will show, are otherwise. You, it is true,
have saved the price of a few days' food, but that is more than swallowed up by your railway fare and tips. You are richer by a few days
and nights of country air; but against that you must set the discomfort of midge-bites in summer and arctic bedrooms in winter. You
have undertaken, for friendship's sake, two of the most disagreeable
tasks in the world – packing and unpacking. You have had, certainly,
the pleasure of talking to your host and hostess; but you have also
had to talk to their neighbours – or, more likely, to listen to them
talking to each other about people you do not know.

And for all this, if you please, you, and you only, are expected to
write an effusive letter of gratitude: while your hostess, who begged
you to come, whose avowed object in buying a country house was
that it would be such fun to have people to stay; your hostess, into
whose drab herbaceous existence your coming has brought a breath
of refreshing air from a larger and livelier world, is not expected to
scribble so much as a hurried thank-you letter on a postcard.

The ideal relationship was that of guest and fellow-guest.
'Between these two there can spring up the most delightful of
friendships. When they have reached a certain degree of intimacy,
they can slope off together, on the time-honoured pretext of buying
stamps, and have a good gossip about their host and hostess, than
which there is no more satisfying conversation in the world.'

Joyce kept a diary of a week of shooting visits which began
with a flat tyre on the Great North Road, and Tony cursing
while he changed the wheel. They stayed at Burton Hall near
Lincoln, Buckminster Park near Grantham, and Launde Abbey
near Oakham, one after the other, and met the locals at dinner.

Sir Roger Gregory, a wonderful specimen of the genus Old Boy, full
of the richest copy for Tony's study of same: a director of companies, evidently able, but to all appearances quite incredibly stupid
and charming. White wuffly moustache, several chins, shoots in a
stiff collar. Memo: Sir Roger: 'Y'know, in geological times they say
the sea used to come up here.'

I like Lady Monson [the hostess], but find her difficult with that

*Shooting in Scotland, Tony with a 'rook and rabbit' rifle,
and Joyce wih a double-barrelled 20-bore shotgun*

peculiar Edwardian aloofness which is harder to cope with than the
Victorian. *He* is surely the most pompous man that ever lived, and
talks illimitable balls on almost every known subject.

Lady M. has that Edwardian habit of breaking into irrelevant bits
of French, presumably to make things sound less dull than they are.
We passed a herd of cows in the car, who stared vacuously at the
bonnet. 'Ils regardent le motor car,' she said.

'God, I'm glad I didn't marry into a county, hunting family,' she wrote – though she did love 'the barbaric splendour of a pheasant drive – the fusillade, the bright coloured bodies hurtling through the air, the clattering of wings, the breaking of branches as they fell, and the smell of damp earth and gunpowder.' (When asked to give her opinion on blood sports, which she frequently was at dinner parties, her reply was simple: 'Indefensible but irresistible.')

After an interminable rainy afternoon at Launde Abbey, making conversation with their hosts and 'pottering round the bloody garden at a Country House stroll', she and Tony escaped to the Crown at Oakham for a drink.

It was worth being made to potter round other people's gardens and sleep in their icy bedrooms and be introduced to their wuffly-moustached neighbours, because talking about it alone together afterwards was such bliss. Each country house visit or tedious dinner party produced some gem of an incident, and these became woven into Tony and Joyce's marriage. Its paradise was not a walking-hand-in-hand-through-meadows kind of paradise: it was less anaemic than that. It was a paradise of shared laughter, of shared noticing, imitating, discussing and remembering. Time added layer upon layer of such shared memories, so that it became more and more delicious to glimpse one another across the table and know there would be 'an eye to catch'.

'The Accompaniment'

When in chance talk they speak your name
    No common syllables I hear:
Rich with unuttered harmonies
    It falls upon my inward ear.

So a musician, hearing sung
    By idle lips some well-loved words,
Hears, too, beneath the naked tune,
    The richness of remembered chords.

Their inward ears sang with 'remembered chords'. Joyce, on her own, would simply have remembered these shared moments.

But for Tony, all life was potential material for anecdote. He liked to crystallize his experiences into Funny Things that Happened, and give them a beginning, a middle and a punchline. Often, the funny stories were about Scotland.

'Our nearest neighbours at Cultoquhey' (went one of his often-repeated anecdotes) 'were the Drummond-Morays, who, in spite of expensive schooling at Eton, were more a sporting than a literary family. They could hardly be otherwise, when the library at Abercairney seemed to contain almost nothing but bound volumes of the *Household Brigade Magazine*, and *The Grouse in Health and Disease*. This happened in the early 1900s. On a very hot Twelfth of August the guns were toiling up a hill to the next line of butts, and they stopped for a moment to mop their sweating brows. One of the better-read guests said (and I suppose it was meant to be a joke), "A horse, a horse! My kingdom for a horse!" At which the laird of Abercairney looked at the guest in amazement, and then turned to the other guns. "What's that? Did you hear what the feller said? Why, that's a most extraordinary thing – my grandfather said that!"'

'My parents' (went another) 'often stayed with the de la Terriere family in Perthshire. Once, after a Saturday to Monday houseparty there, I asked Mother how they had enjoyed it. "Well," she said, "it was quite extraordinary. The house was absolutely full, and they gave Dad and me a bedroom with no dressing-room. Luckily, there was a screen, so we managed." I may say that by this time they had been married several years and had managed, somehow, to conceive a family of four children.'

They were good stories. But there came a time when Tony was only comfortable in conversation when he was inside the safe walls of an anecdote with its beginning, middle and end.

It was a marriage that needed the constant presence of other people to enhance the pleasure of snatched moments *à deux*.

It was a marriage that needed, particularly, Anne Talbot. Sometimes two very happily married people crave the company of one less happy unmarried person, who is dazzled by their company and envious of their relationship, and reminds them of their luck. Perhaps the fact that they need such a person is a sign that they are not quite as happy as they think.

Big Anne was the sister of Tony's childhood friend Evan. She was man-sized, and she drank beer, played golf and hated going to bed early. She lived with her parents in Chelsea and was at first a secretary to Archbishop Cosmo Gordon Lang at Lambeth Palace but later worked as an interior decorator for John Fowler at Peter Jones. She was romantic and longed for love, but had only short-lived affairs which left her feeling bereft. Tony and Joyce needed her because she was an excellent observer and enjoyer of the present moment, because she loved spontaneity as they did, and liked paper games and scurrilous talk, because she was a good person to play practical jokes on; and because she made them feel better about themselves.

She needed them because she longed to belong, and they made her feel needed. 'I went round to Tony and Joyce . . .' 'Tony and Joyce fetched me at 4 . . .' 'I was woken at 8 by Tony and had morning tea with them . . .' Her diaries, diligently kept through the 1920s and 1930s, are full of Tony and Joyce. She writes of them as a couple dazzling in their togetherness and in their ability to make the world seem all right. Wherever Tony and Joyce were, fun was, and laughter, and new jazz records, and a party in the past or future to discuss, and early-morning tea brought to one's bed, and a new funny story from Tony. ('Joyce and I were in a restaurant the other day sitting near the green-baize door, and we overheard one waiter whisper to another as he carried out a tray of empty plates, "He's eaten it".')

Anne hung around the Maxtone Grahams to such a degree that she earned herself the reputation of a sponger. But it is clear that they requested her presence as much as she was eager to provide it. Tony was conspicuously generous, the kind of man who gets up from the table towards the end of a party in a restaurant and settles the bill with the waiter before anyone can argue. Anne, with a small daytime job and no house of her own, was a gratifying person to practise his generosity on.

Wednesday 30 January 1929. Tony rang up asking me to go round at once – very urgent. I went, rather thrilled, and found him and Joyce saying would I come to Rumania with them for 3 weeks. We discussed the impossibility of me getting £50 for it and finally they said they would pay for it all. *Frightfully* kind of them . . .

And off they went on 8 February 1929, on a night ferry from Harwich and across frozen Europe by train. They were a party of four: Tony, Joyce, a yacht-owning friend called Mike Mason, and Anne. It was supposed to be a duck-shooting holiday, but so long did it take to arrive at the chosen marsh in Rumania that the first day's shooting was not till the 24th. Joyce and Anne both kept diaries. Anne's gives a glimpse of how infuriating Joyce could be, how she liked to be the centre of male attention, and what a hostile reaction she could provoke from other women.

Before they even reach Liverpool Street, Anne is slightly annoyed because Joyce is wearing 'innumerable leather and fur coats etc'. Joyce is happy, enchanted by the exoticism of *wagons-lits* and *café complet*. She gazes first out of the train window and then at the train window, where she goes into a trance with the fascination of comparing 'Do not lean out of the window', 'Nicht hinauslehnen', and 'E pericoloso sporgersi'.

'Joyce and Tony are excellent travellers, Tony always in good spirits as though he was comfortably in London, Joyce efficient and neat,' writes Anne.

'All day in the train we played Nouns and Questions and Telegrams and talked,' writes Joyce. 'Delicious children in head-kerchiefs.' 'We played games a certain amount and we all talked a good deal about sex,' writes Anne. 'There is more vulgar talk in this party than I've ever known.'

'We champed slightly,' writes Joyce, of a nine-hour wait in the train to Nisch, Yugoslavia. 'On the way to Nisch,' writes Anne, 'Joyce, who was tired, was at her very worst – the child-wife business – fussing over her food and changing places because the light was in her eyes, and being kittenish and taking up all the room and then refusing offers of help.'

'We talked about books,' writes Joyce. 'There have been interesting moments with these two,' writes Anne. 'Joyce's snobbery on literature and far less knowledge than she pretends, and

Tony's appalling conceit about his driving and knowledge of cars, for examples.'

There is a jolt, and the train to Nisch is derailed. Anne gives this incident three-quarters of a page. 'In the middle of a flat snowy plain, the train suddenly, with a shaking bump, derailed. Tony and Joyce went green.' Joyce's account covers ten pages, the first entirely taken up by the large inky smudge which it produced. The derailment is by far her favourite event of the whole holiday, providing an excuse for conversations with guards in caps and women with chickens and men with gold teeth. 'The whole thing has been the most terrific fun,' she writes.

In deepest Rumania at last, they go for a day's duck-shooting, and two sheepdogs from the village make friends and spend the day with them. But Joyce decides to spend the next day on her own rather than shooting. 'The others got home at about 8.30, purple in the face from sun and wind.' 'We told Joyce about our day and she said we were all sunburnt,' writes Anne.

On the way back to England, they stay for two nights in Vienna. 'Vienna is lovely and dignified and chic,' writes Joyce. 'We looked at pictures at the Imperial Museum,' writes Anne. 'Titian and Tintoretto, some Dutch and some decayed Italian. I found Giordano well represented. Joyce was bored really but thought she ought to study them. She was very dull about Vienna, and seemed to notice nothing towards the end, such as the beauty of new-fallen snow. They are no good at picking out lovely bits suddenly.'

That last comment seems extraordinary, because as a writer Jan Struther's greatest strength was precisely her ability to 'pick out lovely bits suddenly'. But by now Joyce was longing to go home. She had had enough of making intelligent and poetic remarks about abroad. Though she did not admit it to herself, she had descended into a holiday sulk. If she was not enjoying something, she liked to ruin it for everyone else.

Anne sought revenge in her diary, but Joyce avenged herself in print. In 'A Balkan Journey', published in the *New Statesman* of 1 February 1930, she immortalized Anne – not herself – as the maker of uninspiring remarks.

For an hour or so we travelled at a leisurely pace across a plain of incredible flatness and whiteness. 'It's what a table-cloth must look like,' said T., 'to a caterpillar walking across it.' 'More like Bedfordshire, really,' said A., who, when we are in exciting places, has a perverse habit of making prosaic comparisons.

In the dining-car from Harwich to Liverpool Street they ate bacon and eggs, and read the morning papers. They said goodbye. Anne arrived home 'just as Father was beginning prayers, which he cancelled'. Joyce arrived home and went straight to the nursery.

At the time of their Balkan holiday Tony and Joyce had two children, Jamie, five, and Janet, one. They wouldn't have dreamed of taking the children with them. Children stayed behind, eating potato soup, boiled rabbit and blancmange in the nursery and going for walks with Nannie.

Joyce's early married engagement books contain frequent scribbles about interviewing nannies, or relief nannies to work on the nannie's day off. She described the nannie-agency experience for *Punch* in 1930:

> I felt as a man might feel who had entered heaven in the devout belief that he would get individual attention, and found instead that the place was run on the card-index system by a band of efficient seraphim.
>
> I approached the nearest young woman. She was careful to write a few more lines before raising her head.
>
> 'I am looking for a Nannie,' I said.
>
> 'What kind of nurse were you requiring?' she asked, poising her pen once more.
>
> 'A really *nice* one,' I said. 'You know what I mean – a *really* nice one.'
>
> 'College or nursery?'
>
> 'Oh, for a nursery.'
>
> 'I mean college-trained or nursery-trained?' she explained patiently.

'An hour', for Joyce, had always meant the length of time she had spent after tea in her mother's drawing-room in clean frock and sash. Now, for her own children, 'an hour' was beginning to mean just the same: the length of time they spent each day with their parents in the drawing-room, dressed in clean clothes and playing with the drawing-room toys. Joyce gazed at them, dazzled by the backs of their necks. In her poem 'Betsinda Dances' she described a typical drawing-room scene:

> On a carpet red and blue
> Sits Betsinda, not quite two,
> Tracing with baby starfish hand
> The patterns that a Persian planned.
> Suddenly she sees me go
> Towards the box whence dances flow,
> Where embalmed together lie
> Symphony and lullaby.
> ... Then, as the tide of sound advances,
> With grave delight Betsinda dances:
> One arm flies up, the other down
> To lift her Lilliputian gown,
> And round she turns on clumsy, sweet,
> Unrhythmical, enraptured feet;
> And round and round again she goes
> On hopeful, small, precarious toes.
>
> Dance, Betsinda, dance, while I
> Weave from this a memory;
> Thinking, if I chance to hear
> That record in some future year,
> The needle-point shall conjure yet
> Horn and harp and clarinet:
> But O! it shall not conjure you –
> Betsinda, dancing, not quite two.

This sugary scene took place in Tony and Joyce's new house, 16 Wellington Square, off the King's Road, which they bought in 1930, the house on the left at the bottom of the square as you look down. It is easy to picture the young married Joyce rummaging for her keys.

The key turned sweetly in the lock [she wrote in 'Mrs Miniver']. That was the kind of thing one remembered about a house: not the size of the rooms or the colour of the walls, but the feel of door-handles and light-switches, the shape and texture of the banister-rail under one's palm; minute tactual intimacies, whose resumption was the essence of coming home.

This was a house Joyce grew to love. Robert, her youngest child, was born here in 1931. (Anne Talbot mentions this birth in her diary. Her use of the neuter pronoun gives an idea of the distance between grown-ups and babies: 'Joyce has had a baby. It is going to be called Robert.')

Joyce was now the mother of three, and the nursery floor pattered, as it was designed to, with tiny feet. Distant sounds of crying and coaxing trickled down the stairwell. Inspired by an imagined ideal of a family house, she made a playroom, with a stage and curtains, and put a canvas paddling-pool on the roof-garden, with an outdoor toy-cupboard.

'Modern Home Making. Husband and Wife Each Design a Room.' The *Daily Telegraph*, *The Queen* and the *Evening Standard* devoted a 'Home' page each to Tony and Joyce's modern way of dealing with 'the difference between the sexes'. 'Mr Maxtone Graham, in the dining-room, has chosen a water-lily-green table, cellulosed so that hot plates can be put upon it with impunity, and marks wiped off with a damp cloth.' 'The drawing-room, entirely planned by Mrs Maxtone Graham, might be a room in a pleasant country house. The walls are painted Devonshire cream yellow, and cheerful notes are introduced by the red painted radiators. Built in under one window-sill is the loudspeaker of the radio-gramophone, the control of which is over by the fireplace. Each chair is provided with its own little table, ash tray, and box of cigarettes – a detail which perhaps only a woman would have remembered.' They were being held up as examples of the new-style husband and wife: equals in the home, neither in thrall to the other.

Now the parties could be bigger and better. 'I went to Wellington Sq.,' writes Anne Talbot, 'and found Tony and Joyce preparing for their drinks party. Preparing for festivities is one of the most delightful occupations to find people at, and I realized the heavenliness of that moment.' The dinner was 'excel-

The dining-room at Wellington Square, designed by Tony

lent', the wine 'superb', and later everyone went down to the ping-pong room for a competition organized by Tony. The party ended with scrambled eggs at 2.30 – this on a Wednesday evening.

Joyce retired early to bed at her own parties. Towards the end of a party – just as towards the end of a foreign holiday – she ceased to enjoy what she was supposed to be enjoying, and longed to be unwatched. At these moments, when she mentally withdrew herself from the chatter of her surroundings, she attained the sudden sense of perspective and clarity which gave her the overwhelming urge to write.

Of all emotions, she perhaps felt the emotion of *missing* most acutely. At a party, she missed solitude. Abroad, she missed home. Cut off from her children, she longed to be with them again. When she was, she longed again for solitude. The raggle-taggle gypsy in her head beckoned her to escape.

Chapter Four

Let faith be my shield and let joy be my steed
'Gainst the dragons of anger, the ogres of greed;
And let me set free, with the sword of my youth,
From the castle of darkness the power of the truth.

Verse 3 of J.S's 'When a knight won his spurs', from *Songs of Praise*

IT WAS PERHAPS because Joyce was so unholy that she wrote such good hymns. She could stand back from Christianity and express its essence with childlike simplicity and refreshing vocabulary, from a distance.

Canon Percy Dearmer, though attached to Westminster Abbey, lived with his wife Nan near Joyce, in Embankment Gardens. He and Joyce met in 1929 and had a long talk about hymns, and which were their favourites. He later suggested she write a few hymns for his new enlarged edition of *Songs of Praise*, and she asked if she could write one to the Irish melody 'Slane'. She sat down one morning and wrote 'Lord of all hopefulness, Lord of all joy' – which to this days brings in handsome royalties to the bene-ficiaries of her will. It is included in almost every one of the fifty or so new American hymn books published each year.

Then she wrote 'When a knight won his spurs in the stories of old' and 'Daisies are our silver, buttercups our gold', both of which are apt to bring tears to the eyes of those who remember singing them to the school piano. Not many people know 'When Stephen, full of power and grace, went forth throughout the land', though there are a few who hold it close to their hearts. She also wrote eight other hymns: 'High o'er the lonely hills', 'Round the earth a message runs', 'Sing, all ye Christian people!', 'When Mary brought her treasure', 'Unto Mary, demon-haunted', 'God, whose eternal mind', 'We thank you, Lord of Heaven', and 'O saint of summer what can we sing for you?' These are rarely sung nowadays, but because 'We thank you, Lord of Heaven' contains the line 'For dogs with friendly faces', vicars sometimes choose it for their annual pets' service.

Lovers of these hymns who discover that their author was not herself a churchgoer feel a sense of betrayal. The favourite hymn sung at their own wedding or at their grandfather's funeral turns out to be, so to speak, a fake.

Like most of their generation, Tony and Joyce had been force-fed religion as children, Sunday after Sunday. Tony had suffered the stifling atmosphere of the Scottish Sabbath. As a small child his sister Ysenda was caught by their grandfather playing on a Sunday with a sixpenny tin jar with a handle which, when vigorously worked, caused the jar to emit a few cracked and reedy sounds. 'Nurse, I do not approve of music on Sunday,' said the terrifying grandpapa. 'We must all remember that this child has a soul to be saved.'

Joyce, in itchy gloves, had sat through long services each Sunday, 'and the new puppy was waiting at home to be played with, getting larger and less pick-upable minute by precious minute, and the liturgy dragged and dawdled, always far behind one's eagerness to be gone'.

Avoidance of church was another bond between Tony and Joyce. They even avoided looking at churches. On a rainy day during the shooting visit in Lincolnshire, Joyce wrote in her diary: 'We sat about and sat about. Finally we were reduced to deciding to drive into Lincoln and look at the cathedral (*us!*) but the car wouldn't start.' On a rainy day in Scotland, the younger generation of the family sat in the drawing-room writing clerihews about local ministers of the Church of Scotland. This was Tony's:

> The Minister of Madderty
> Never had a sadder tea
> Than when entertaining at the Manse
> He inadvertently wet his pants.

They were getting their revenge for years of sermons. He and Joyce were always on the look-out for a 'J. in V. B. T.' (joke in very bad taste) or, better still, a 'J. in W. P. T.' (worst possible taste), and many of these were God-related. 'I'm so hungry,' said Tony one Sunday lunchtime, 'I could eat the hind leg off the lamb of God.'

At this stage of her life Joyce had a gift for turning out whatever bits of writing she was asked for. She never lost the schoolgirl's delight in showing work to the teacher and getting high marks. In adulthood, this ability to produce just what the editor required was a kind of flirtation. Editors tended to be attractive and brilliant men: to give them what they wanted in words gave her an intense, even erotic pleasure. If asked, she could turn out cigarette advertisements, such as this 'Capstan Shanty':

When I was Mate of the brig *Carlisle*
(Hulla-balloo-balay!)
We was wrecked one day on a cannibal isle
(Hulla-balloo-balay!)
And there I took up with the chieftain's niece,
A neat little, sweet little coal-black piece.
I was downright grieved when her uncle ate her.
(Better buy Capstan – they're blended better.)

The fact that as an editor Canon Dearmer was not only attractive but also a man of the cloth made the schoolgirl–teacher relationship all the more exciting. A genuine warm friendship sprang up between them. 'I found his faith infectious,' she wrote in the *Manchester Guardian* after his death, 'and his kindliness a warming fire. When one had been with him one felt happier and more alive than before, with widened sympathies, a heightened perception of beauty, and a deepened conviction that – to use a childish phrase – "everything would come out all right in the end".'

Dearmer asked Joyce if she would like to help with the proof-reading and editing of the new *Songs of Praise*. She said yes, and during May and June 1930 she became a daily visitor

at Embankment Gardens, correcting spellings, deleting exclamation-marks ('splaggers'), and choosing between comma, dash and semi-colon. 'My dear Percy,' she said one morning when he was fretting about the theology of Heaven and Hell in one of Isaac Watts's hymns, 'surely you don't believe all this stuff?'

The Dean of Liverpool wrote to Percy Dearmer in May 1930: 'I have completely fallen in love with Jan. Working through these new hymns, I see that she has got us into a new stream that will rive and make glad the city of God. Thank you for this discovery.'

Perhaps Joyce gained an extra *frisson* from her success as writer and editor for *Songs of Praise* by comparing her status, yet again, with that of Anne Talbot, who now had a part-time job as Percy Dearmer's secretary.

It was impossible for Joyce to write a hymn without getting some irreverence off her chest first. 'Serious Admonition by J. S. to Herself on the Occasion of an Almost Overwhelming Temptation' she scribbled one morning, facing the blank sheet of paper. 'Tune: Llanfairpwllgwyngyllgogerychwyrndrobwll-llandysiliogogogoch.'

> When writing a hymn on Bartholemew,
> Remember the subject is solemn. You
> Can't rhyme the apostle
> With 'funny old fossil'
> Or say that his cat had 'a hollow mew'.

Cleansed, she sat down to write the hymn. She flicked throug] her rhyming dictionary, aware that this was dangerous: it enticing possibilities tended to deflect a poet from his origin: purpose. 'I have often wondered', she wrote in an essay (rhymes for the *Spectator*, 'whether mildness (which is by 1 means the same thing as humility) would ever have gained su prestige as a Christian virtue if the hymn-writers had not be at their wits' end for a rhyme to "child".'

But out of all this frivolity and unbelief came some clas hymns with the power to touch people to the heart.

> Lord of all hopefulness, Lord of all joy,
> Whose trust, ever childlike, no cares could destroy,
> Be there at our waking, and give us, we pray,
> Your bliss in our hearts, Lord, at the break of the day.

The break of the day, the noon of the day, the eve of the day, the end of the day: the hymn can be about a day, or about life. The words are simple and understandable, in contrast to Eleanor Henrietta Hull's bewildering line from the hymn 'Be thou my vision', which is sung to the same tune: 'Be all else but nought to me, save that thou art.'

Middle-brow poets arguably write the best hymns, and Joyce was that: a poet who expressed universal thoughts in familiar metaphors. The thought and the image might be simple, but because the words fitted the thought like a glove, and because the scansion was perfect, real beauty was attained.

Writing these hymns, she imagined herself as the child in the pew. 'When a knight won his spurs in the stories of old' was a tomboy's hymn – the sort of hymn she would have liked to sing as a child. She knew that a great hymn speaks not just to children but to the child in us all.

As an adult who never wanted to grow up, she retained a deep compassion for children, and a respect for their way of looking at the world. She couldn't bear adults who were out of touch with magic and enchantment. Possibly she cared more about 'the child inside the man' than she did about actual children. One of her short stories begins:

Nothing out of the ordinary ever happened to Mrs Murple. If she went to stay in a haunted house, the most authentic family ghost would go on strike and refuse to show off; if she entered a room where children were playing at pirates, the nursery table would instantly cease to be a Spanish galleon, and the desert island would automatically change back into a hearthrug. She would have harnessed Pegasus to a four-wheeled cab, and made the golden apples of the Hesperides into dumplings. But she had delicate features and an ethereal expression, and it was almost impossible to guess, when you saw her with that far-away look in her eyes, apparently lost in an exquisite reverie, that she was really making mental calculations

about housekeeping accounts or wondering how to improve her game of golf.

Prosaic grown-ups need to be taught a lesson, and Miss Murple got her come-uppance. Plainly Joyce was not out of touch with nursery life. But she was never in it for long enough to be anything other than enchanted by the child's view of the world.

Joyce claimed not to be a believer-in-God, but her sense of enchantment was so strong that it was akin to spirituality. She had moments of sudden religious vision.

'Intimations of Immortality in Early Middle Age'

On the first of spring, walking along the Embankment,
Light-footed, light-headed, eager in mind and heart,
I found my spirit keyed to a new pitch,
I felt a strange serenity and a strange excitement.

I saw a boy running, and felt the wind
Stream past his cheeks, his heart in ribs pounding;
I saw a nurse knitting, and my own fingers
Knew the coldness of needles, warmth of the wool.

I saw, over the barges, gulls flying:
It was my own wings that tilted and soared,
With bone-deep skill gauging to a line's breadth
The unmapped hills of air, its unplumbed hollows.

I saw a woman with child: a second heart
Beat below mine. I saw two lovers kissing,
And felt her body dissolve, his harden
Under the irrational chemistry of desire.

And I, who had always said, in idle, friendly,
Fireside thrashings-out of enormous themes,
That anybody who liked could have my share
Of impersonal after-life, fusion with the infinite,

Suddenly thought – Here, perhaps, is a glimpse
Of the sages' vision, delight by me unimagined:
To feel without doing, to enjoy without possessing;

To bear no longer the burden of a separate self;
To live through others' senses; to be air, to be ether,
Soundlessly quivering with the music of a million lives.

Pantheistic tosh, one might say. But Joyce said, 'There you have my religious belief.'

Ernest Shepard. the illustrator of Winnie-the-Pooh, became Joyce's illustrator in *Punch* in 1931. Three things about her light verse of this time made it ideal material for Shepard's talents.

The first was her tendency to write simple verses about the daily delights of childhood, which could be enjoyed by children but were really aimed at nostalgic grown-ups.

The second was her depiction of London, whose unsung charms she longed to express. She cherished the sight of tri-cycling children, muffin men, milk ponies, chimney-pots, pigeons, and Belisha beacons.

The third was her light but firm delineation of social class. The children she described (based on her own) were Christopher Robin-like in their well-brought-upness: they were children with nannies, and with smart Mummies in furs; children who peeped out of nursery windows and were allowed out in best coats and hats to tricycle up and down the square before tea. Her street characters – policemen, flower ladies, pavement artists, street musicians and so on –were comically Cockney.

E. H. Shepard was on Joyce's wavelength in each of these three aspects. He, too, drew pictures of children and of childish pleas-ures which, though loved by children, were positively drooled over by grown-ups. He, too, spoke as much to the child inside the adult as to children themselves. He, too, adored London and sought to express its charms on paper. And he, too, was sensitive to social class and uninhibited about delineating it. When you look at one of his well-brought-up children with long dangly legs on a tricycle, you can hear her posh vowels, and when you look at one of his street artists, you can hear him saying, 'Why, bless your heart. It ain't no trouble – I'm *used* to Art.'

Joyce's collaboration with Shepard began in *Punch* on 25 February 1931 with the first of a set of verses about London telephone exchanges called 'Dialling Tones':

DIALLING TONES

AVENUE

When I dial A-V-E,
Back at Limes I seem to be.

Old Mulwinkle's still alive,
Pottering down the western drive,
Pausing now and then to sweep
Fallen leaves into a heap.
Six years old, I follow near
Listening with respectful ear:
(Gardeners' words are always wise—
Age-old truth within them lies).
"Catch," says he, "a falling leaf,
Catch a day without a grief;
Catch three-hunderd-sixty-five,
You'm the happiest man alive!"
Old Mulwinkle sighs, and then
Stoops to pick up leaves again.

Back at Limes I seem to be
When I dial A-V-E.

The idea for a set of verses on this subject was an example of Joyce's ability (when not in a holiday bad mood) to 'pick out the lovely bits suddenly'. In the daily act of dialling 'A–V–E', 'H–I–L', 'P–R–I' or 'R–I–V', her imagination was transported to remembered avenues, hillsides, primrose meadows and riversides. This was an experience shared by many Londoners in the days before all-digital telephone numbers and Joyce, together with Shepard, gave expression to a commonly-felt urge to find poetry in the mundane.

Joyce wrote to the editor of *Punch* at about this time, begging to be allowed to sign herself 'J.S.' or 'Jan' instead of being anonymous. This was an honour permitted only to the most established *Punch* writers; and the editor at first refused. But when her second set of Shepard-illustrated verses began in February 1932, the shortened signature at last appeared: 'Jan'.

'Sycamore Square' was the name of this set of verses. It was about street life in Wellington Square, and at the end of 1932 Methuen published it in book form together with the telephone-exchange verses. Doggerel-like in its simplicity and shortness-of-lines, the verse was an unobtrusive backdrop for Shepard's illustrations, such as the one of the policeman:

THE POLICEMAN

Every few hours
Throughout the night
He comes to see
That the Square's all right.
Slowly and solemnly
Round he goes
On his great flat feet
With their great blunt toes,
Shifting his very
Portentous weight
From side to side
With a rolling gait.
He flashes his lantern
Up and down ;
His brows are bent
In an ominous frown ;

To see him you'd think
No thief would dare
To crack a crib
In Sycamore Square.
Yet when he's at home
You'll probably find
He's a jovial man
And extremely kind,
Who likes his pint
And a kipper for tea
The same as you—
Or, at any rate, me.

There he is at the bottom of the page, jovial, with a baby on his knee, truncheon and helmet hanging on a peg behind him, cup of tea in his hand, kipper on a plate, buxom smiling wife in an apron, two more babies, and three riotous children waving their knives and forks in the air, as the Sycamore Square children *never* would.

Joyce's next collaboration with E. H. Shepard was *The Modern Struwwelpeter*, also published first in *Punch*, and then by Methuen in 1936. It was a set of cautionary verses inspired by the bad habits of Joyce's children and nephews: James, who liked too much ice-cream (and turned to ice); Philip, who didn't cross the road carefully (and got run over by a bus); Peter, who wouldn't take his halibut oil (and was visited by a monstrous fish); Anthony, who said 'You've got it up your sleeve' to conjur-

Says Ruthless Mike to Reckless John :
" These gentle hints must not go on."
Says Reckless John to Ruthless Mike :
" We must bump off Miss Marlinespike."
(This horrid phrase, I fear, had been
Picked up from gangsters on the screen.)
" But how ? " says Mike. " We have no gat,"
(No *gun* was what he meant by that),
" And stainless nursery table-knives
Are not much use for taking lives."
" I know ! " cries John. " We'll have to give her
A good hard push into the river."
But Michael quickly crushes him :
" You fool—Miss Marlinespike can swim."

ors (and was turned into a white rabbit); Charles, who said 'O.K.'
(and was turned into a parrot in the zoo); Janet, who said
'Mamma, I *must* have that' in toyshops (and was turned into a
doll in a shop window); Robert, who dialled 'COW' and 'HOG' on
'his mother's toy, the telephone' (and was terrified when the telephone let out a blood-curdling screech); and Reckless Mike and
Ruthless John, the twins who tried to make their governess Miss

" *Oh, no, you can't,*" a whisper said,
From somewhere just above his head ;
And then he shed unmanly tears,
For unseen hands had boxed his ears ;
While Mike, across a ghostly knee,
Was soon as sore as sore could be.

A wretched life from that time on
Led Hapless Mike and Luckless John :
For unexpected prods and slaps
And cuffs and clouts and tweaks and raps
Were showered all day from empty air
Upon the miserable pair,
While always the reproachful sound
Of whispering followed them around.

Children, pray be warned by them—
Make the best of *your* Miss M. :
Better one you do not love
Than a disembodied gov.

Marlinespike vanish with vanishing cream (but she remained in the air, slapping them invisibly). Though the time Joyce spent with these nephews was limited, she did capture their essence, and many acknowledge that they carried the attributes she spotted into their later lives.

'But why are you allowed to do things, Mummy, if we're not?' Joyce's daughter Janet asked her one morning in 1933.

'If I can't be a shining example to you,' was her reply, 'let me at least be a horrible warning.'

Her children were becoming old enough to ask taxing questions and to remember the answers, and Joyce adored them more and more – though she still avoided the daily drudgery of looking after them. One day in 1933 when a cluster of nannies from different families were all off-duty, Joyce had to drive three or four children to school herself in her Baby Morris, as well as taking Jamie (aged nine) to the school train. The day was so abnormal and so hectic that in the evening she wrote it all down. From Victoria Station she went to Peter Jones to buy nursery chairs, then to Michelin House to buy a guide to France (for a forthcoming grown-ups-only holiday). 'Went to lunch with Dame at 1.30, and as we sat down suddenly remembered we'd got four people coming to dinner tonight, and I hadn't told Ada. So I had to order dinner over the telephone.'

The love she felt for her children was all the more intense because she saw so little of them. An article she wrote for the *Spectator* called 'Half-Term', about visiting Jamie at boarding-school, depicts the cut-offness of parents from children, and the briefness of a 1930s half-term. Children got only the tiniest whiff of non-school life. Parents stayed in a hotel near the school, watched the school cricket match on Saturday, then went to school chapel on Sunday and took the child out afterwards for a picnic on the beach. That was the end of half-term.

On Saturday:

Throughout the afternoon he sits wedged between you on a garden seat, watching the match with unflagging seriousness. You yourself are more occupied with watching him; he is close beside you, yet a thousand miles away; he is still living in an alien world. 'Played!' he says at intervals; and 'Oh, bad *luck*' dutifully, when somebody misses a catch. Only twice during the afternoon does he make any remark unconnected with the game. The first time is when an immensely fat boy of about twelve walks past.

'I bet you don't know what *his* nickname is.'

'Fatty?'

'No.'

'Piggy?'

'No.'

'Er – Suet?'

'My gosh!' he exclaims respectfully. 'However did you guess?'
The second time is when he nudges you in the ribs and jerks his
head towards a round-faced solemn little boy in spectacles. 'That's
Rupert Smith-Twissington. He collects skulls.'

On Sunday:

You spend a hot, happy day on the beach, punctuated only by a colossal lunch of sausage-rolls, bananas and ginger-beer and a hardly-
smaller tea of jam-puffs, buns and raspberry cider. He is still a little
remote to begin with, a little inclined to answer every inquiry with
an automatic 'Yes, thank you, Mummy'; but he soon becomes perfectly at his ease. Leaning back against a sand-dune, you try to look
at him dispassionately. He is certainly much plumper and browner
than he was six weeks ago; his manners have improved and he is
more independent; he is, in fact, a very nice little boy of nine: and if
his chief interest in life seems to be food and his small-talk consists
entirely of age-old riddles and verbal catches – well, little boys of
nine are like that, and you may as well accept the fact. And if you
once thought that he was something a little out of the ordinary, that
he had imagination, that you could talk to him as though he was a
contemporary, then you were deceived; and a good thing too, you
reflect, or he would be having a bad time of it at school.

At this point you notice that he has stopped chewing and is gazing
curiously at the half-eaten jam-puff in his hand.

'What's wrong?' you ask. 'Isn't it a good one?'

'Mm,' he replies. 'But I was just wondering. Do you ever think
things aren't really there at all – only inside your mind?'

'Good Lord! Have they been teaching you about Bishop Berkeley
already?'

'No. But I asked Rupert Smith-Twissington that once, and he said
he'd often thought of it too.'

Joyce liked merriment in a child, but she had a particularly
soft spot for inscrutableness and solemnity. She knew from experience just how frail a child's happiness and sense of security

could be. A child could express all the sadness in the world just by not laughing, or by saying something simple and grave and true. This is a moment on Guy Fawkes night, from *Mrs Miniver*: 'Toby, his feet sticking out over the edge of the seat, was completely immobile, but whether from profound emotion or too many coats, it was difficult to tell.' She understood the complicated feelings of a boy about going back to school:

> Not that Vin disliked school; but it had to be regarded, he found, as another life, to be approached only by way of the Styx. You died on the station platform, were reborn, not without pangs, in the train, and emerged at the other end a different person, with a different language, a different outlook, and a different scale of values. That was what stray grown-ups you met in the holidays did not seem to understand when they asked you the fatuous and invariable question, 'How do you like school?' It was impossible to answer this properly, because the person of whom they asked it never, strictly speaking, arrived at school at all.

And she understood a solemn child's eccentric way of opening Christmas stockings:

> Toby pulled all his presents out, but he arranged them in a neat pattern on the eiderdown and looked at them for a long time in complete silence. Then he picked up one of them – a big glass marble with coloured squirls inside – and put it by itself a little way off. After that he played with the other toys, appreciatively enough; but from time to time his eyes would stray towards the glass marble, as though to make sure it was still waiting for him.
>
> Mrs Miniver watched him with a mixture of delight and misgiving. It was her favourite approach to life: but the trouble was that sometimes the marble rolled away.

The enchantment of Tony and Joyce's family life at its best was captured in that 'Christmas Stockings' piece. 'Words', wrote Joyce, 'are a net to catch a mood: the only sure weapon against oblivion.' Here she caught the mood of Christmas dawn on an eiderdown, and the intricate tracery of the 'family pattern' for which she would one day grieve.

There were cross-currents of pleasure: smiling faces exchanged by her and Vin about the two younger children; and by her and Clem, because they were both grown-ups; and by her and Judy, because they were both women; and by her and Toby, because they were both the kind that leaves the glass marble till the end. The room was laced with affectionate understanding.

This was one of the moments, thought Mrs Miniver, which paid off at one stroke all the accumulations on the debit side of parenthood: the morning sickness and the quite astonishing pain; the pram in the passage, the cold mulish glint in the cook's eye; the holiday nurse who had been in the best families; the pungent white mice, the shrivelled caterpillars; the plasticine on the door-handles, the face-flannels in the bathroom, the nameless horrors down the crevices of armchairs; the alarms and emergencies, the swallowed button, the inexplicable earache, the ominous rash appearing on the eve of a journey; the school bills and the dentists' bills; the shortened step, the tempered pace, the emotional compromises, the divided loyalties, the adventures continually forsworn.

It was a formidable list of parental woes. She couldn't avoid the filth altogether. But down the margin, in her annotated copy, Joyce's daughter Janet scribbled: 'I don't remember my parents forswearing many adventures.'

Chapter Five

This knowledge at least is spared us: we cannot tell
When any given tide on the heart's shore
Comes to the full.
The crown-wave makes no signal, does not cry
'This is the highest. Mark it with a bright shell.
It will be reached no more.'

From 'High Tide' in *The Glass-Blower*

'I WALKED ROUND to dine at the M. Gs,' wrote Anne Talbot in her diary of 27 April 1930. 'We played poker. In the middle there was a lot of telephoning to Edinburgh as one of Tony's uncles died. Joyce, although slightly upset, was a *little* bit proud of it all. We had a lot of journalist rot from her today, and car business from Tony. Their own experiences loom so very large . . .'

The death of the unmarried uncle meant that Tony's father Jim Maxtone Graham was now Laird of Cultoquhey, and that Tony was next in line. Now the Cultoquhey summers could begin. The whole family – two sons, two daughters, eleven grandchildren, four nannies – travelled to Scotland each summer for a house party which lasted from July to September.

The holidays always began in the same way: the children were sent up to Perthshire from Euston by train, with the luggage and Nannie, and were met at Gleneagles station by Welsh, the chauffeur.

Tony and Joyce drove up together, taking turns at the wheel and stopping for a night on the way, at the Haycock at Wansford or the George at Stamford. The sign at the top of the Finchley Road marked to 'The North' gave them a stab of excitement every time, though there were no children in the back to share it with.

Joyce liked the way an annually repeated journey combined the thrills of travel with the comforts of tradition and familiarity. Memory flags, as she called them, accumulated along the Great North Road. The place where the car had once dropped a push-rod, which after a long search they had recovered from the gutter a quarter of a mile back; the tin garage where they had once been stranded for eight hours and played endless games of picquet on a packing-case; the field where they had passed gypsies with a skewbald horse: each of these places became like a friend, which she and Tony looked forward to passing and repassing and thinking the irresistible thought, 'This time last year . . .' At the summit of the road between Bowes and Brough, they stopped to stretch their legs and smoke, and Tony ground his cigarette end into the tinder-dry earth as they took a last look at the southward view.

They bumped along the drive towards Cultoquhey at dusk, as the gong was ringing to dress for dinner. They went upstairs to say goodnight to the children and Tony, wearing starched cuffs, flicked sixpences to make them vanish up his sleeve by the bedsides.

Cultoquhey, from a coloured print of 1861

The family Joyce married into. Tony is bottom left, with Janet. Jamie is second left, top row. Robert is the baby, bottom right

Tony's father Jim could not disguise his penchant for pretty young visiting girls, bitterly remarked upon by Anne Talbot in her diary. He flirted at dinner, and not with her. (This weakness was crystallized into anecdote by Tony: 'When my father was a young man, he was at a dinner party in Perthshire, a grand affair, all the men in their kilts and doublets. He sat next to one particularly attractive girl, and he reckoned he was doing rather well with her when he felt her hand on his knee. He thought he was in for an exciting evening. That was during the soup. During the fish she gave his knee a comforting pat from time to time. But I'm afraid that when the joint was served all that happened was that his hairy knee was offered a morsel from the fair lady's plate.')

After nursery breakfast the children were allowed into the grown-ups' dining-room to watch their grandpapa's daily breakfast ceremony. First he ate his porridge standing up with his back to the wall – a tradition dating from the days when lairds used to stab one another in the back. Then he sliced the top off his soft-boiled egg and drank its liquid contents in one gulp, making a loud noise. Last, he threw his apple up into the air and caught it on the blade of his *sgian-dubh*.

Grown-ups did tricks and organized occasional family concerts and fancy-dress parades, but were otherwise rarely concerned with child care. Nannies, as always, looked after the children. But at Cultoquhey there was the complication of conflicts between the nannies belonging to the different batches of cousins. Joyce, after many fruitless interviews at agencies, had found a Canadian nannie-from-heaven. Even her name was heavenly: Mabel Good. The Smythe cousins also had a nice normal nannie, Scottish Nannie Blythe, under whose benign rule the American Townsend cousins longed to live. *Their* nannie, known as Irish Nannie, was not like other nannies. Instead of eating at the nursery table with everybody else, she took her plate and chair, opened the toy-cupboard door, and ate her meal facing into the cupboard where nobody could see her. Every day she would walk up the long drive to the post office at Gilmerton with a parcel addressed to somewhere in Ireland. What, the other nannies wondered, was she sending? Was it a food parcel which she had secretly been filling behind the cupboard door? Once they spotted her trying to post a letter in a petrol pump.

Irish Nannie was eventually replaced by a French nannie, who was worse. She wore a whistle round her neck which she blew to summon the boys, as if they were dogs. She did not allow them to eat a sweet or toffee unless she had tasted it first and pronounced it fit for consumption, so all sweets and toffees tasted of French saliva.

The weather was unpredictable. Cold garden parties were held in the grounds of Cultoquhey, the guests shivering in their tweeds as they made conversation on the wet lawn, some of them huddling under rugs. In the drawing-room on rainy days the grown-ups played paper games and card games, and such was the addiction to the *Times* crossword that two copies of the paper had to be ordered each day. 'It was extravagance of this kind', remarked one of the aunts, 'that led to the downfall of the Roman Empire.'

Joyce entered into the spirit of all this. She liked the ache in the legs after a stiff walk through deep heather on a grouse moor. Stories of old Scotland, recounted at length by aged in-laws, fascinated rather than bored her. The Crieff Games were an annual delight, and she saw the sword dance at the end

At the Crieff Games

through a mist of tears. 'For I defy anyone', she wrote in 'Mrs Miniver', 'to watch a sword-dance through to the end without developing a great-grandmother called Gillespie.'

The nannies and servants were a constant source of amusement, and at Cultoquhey there was the added spice of the Scottish accent to make the stories better. 'I said to Campbell [the old gamekeeper] at the Games this morning,' recounted Tony, '"I'm sorry to see that Mrs Campbell isn't with you today as usual. I do hope she is not unwell." "Och, the woman's done! She's finished!" Campbell answered. Of course I rushed to make enquiries, and found that poor Mrs Campbell simply had a heavy cold, and thought she shouldn't go out.'

Cultoquhey had an indoor staff of eleven. These servants were treated kindly but also, sometimes, as though they were invisible. Joyce bristled, remembering her happy days in the servants' room at Whitchurch House. She began to take note of precisely how little attention Tony and his family paid the butler and parlourmaid as they served dinner. One evening, to prove her theory, she made an excuse to be late for dinner, then dressed up in parlourmaid's uniform and served at table herself. She helped Tony to potatoes, and he didn't notice her; then he almost fainted with surprise when the parlourmaid sat down on his knee and kissed him.

At their tin wedding party on 4 July 1933, their tenth anniversary, Tony and Joyce were given new rolling-stock for the model railway, three buckets, five trumpets, tins of pineapples, peaches, lychees, pretzels and salted almonds, and fourteen tins of sardines. Alone together after the party, they re-read the love letters they had written before their marriage, and congratulated themselves on still feeling the same. But it was at about this time that in small ways they began to turn away from each other.

Tony had taken to golf. He wasn't good at it, and he never became good at it; but he found in it a deep source of relaxation and pleasure. As he lay awake at night, mentally urging balls into holes, he found that he was becoming addicted – and he did not resist. Golf was a new thing to *play* – and knowing that Joyce liked playing too, he hoped she might share his new addiction. She had a go, but she hated it. Where he saw excitement, camaraderie and rolling verdure, she saw futility, dull businessmen in plus-fours and a soul-destroying fake landscape. To her, golf was the opposite of interesting and the opposite of poetic. In describing the prosaic Mrs Murple at the beginning of her story about an unromantic woman she precisely named housekeeping accounts and golf as the two deadly-dull subjects which preoccupied her anti-heroine. How could Tony, who was so *anti*-bore, suddenly be so keen on the world of the clubhouse?

So Tony played golf with Anne Talbot and her brother, and they had lovely windblown days out at the West Surrey Golf Club, away from sulky Joyce who would have ruined the whole thing. In 1933 Tony took a long lease on a house in the middle of Rye Golf Course. The Chief Officer's House was one of a row of former coastguard cottages between Rye and Camber, and its flower beds were white with stray golf balls. Protective netting had to be put on the windows. The front garden was just like the spot described by P. G. Wodehouse in *The Clicking of Cuthbert*: 'At various points within your line of vision are the third tee, the sixth tee, and the sinister bunkers about the eighth green – none of them lacking in food for the reflective mind.'

Joyce, whose reflective mind was not nourished by that kind of food, retaliated with beachcombing and botany. While Tony played golf with his friends, she wandered alone among the sand dunes, picking up bits of driftwood and sea-holly, and occasionally (if it was the morning after a southerly gale) a bottle with a French name on it – 'a detail', she wrote, 'which has somehow put France on the map for me as no amount of geography lessons ever did.' Every now and again she bent down to examine a tiny patch of dune, to see how many species of flora – speedwell, forget-me-not, pearlwort, white flax, stork's-bill, crane's-bill, white saxifrage, moss – could fit inside the 'O' made by her finger and thumb.

These were the perfect antisocial pastimes for an anti-golfer. When the others came home feeling virtuous with exercise and achievement, Joyce could trump them with new insights into geography and nature in which they felt obliged to feign interest. She wrote enthusiastically about beachcombing and botany in the *Spectator*, with no hint that she was in any way snubbing golf. Yet in writing about even such innocent subjects as these she managed to introduce a new acerbic tone, a briskness, a sort of horticultural leftiness which seemed subtly designed to get her own back on the social world of the golfers. Here she is on gardens:

> As things to sit in, well and good; as things to be taken round, definitely bad: though the possibility of finding an unknown wild flower skulking in somebody's herbaceous border has often enabled me to wear an expression of eager interest which has entirely deceived my hostess. (I scored caper spurge in that way, I remember, hailed it with perhaps rather tactless triumph in the middle of a tedious homily on antirrhinums, and was never asked again.)

And here she is on gardening (which she had never tried until she lived at Rye):

> I had not the faintest idea what I ought to do. Weed? Perhaps. The idea did not attract me. To anyone accustomed to the vigorous and jostling democracy in which wild flowers contrive to flourish and look beautiful, weeding smacks both of mollycoddling and of snobbism. I felt, in fact, about these civilised plants much as a worker in a slum parish, used to the spry and merry hardihood of the Cockney child, might feel if suddenly put in charge of a party of Mayfair brats who could not so much as blow their own noses.

She was expected to entertain Tony's golfing friends for dinner at the Chief Officer's House; and the very sound of their voices, let alone their conversation, brought out a new left-wingness in Joyce.

The 'car business' mentioned by Anne Talbot was another small area of annoyance. Tony, Joyce noticed, was becoming a car bore as well as a golf bore. After the Motor Show each year she had to listen to exchanges like this:

'Well, I must say, I liked the new Scott Hermes.'

'What, the fourteen?'

'No, the twenty-six. Guaranteed to do eighty-five.'

'M'm. Don't like that overhead camshaft. Now, the Skipper Straight Eight . . .'

Her own attitude to cars was sentimental rather than acquisitive. The day when the beloved old car was taken away, never to be seen again, and the new one purred up to the front door in its place was the subject of one of her Mrs Miniver vignettes. 'A car, nowadays,' she wrote, 'was such an integral part of one's life, provided the aural and visual accompaniment to so many of one's thoughts, feelings, conversations and decisions, that it had acquired at least the status of a room in one's house . . . Old horses one pensioned off in a paddock, where one could go and see them occasionally. Or one even allowed them to pull the mowing-machine in round leather boots. But this part exchange business . . .'

Tony bought an expensive Armstrong Siddeley which had belonged to the racing driver Malcolm Campbell. It had the inevitable nickname 'Bluebird', and a flashy registration number, 'ALO 1'. In September 1933 Tony drove it when he and Joyce took the other Talbots on holiday to Majorca: Anne's brother Evan and his wife Cynthia. Evan had such a plum in his voice that when he said 'I beg your pardon' it came out as 'Bom pom'.

They got lost on the way to Dover. They stayed at the Grand Hotel, opposite the municipal bandstand, and the next morning the car was hoisted onto the *S. R. Autocarrier*. Tony handled the car capably on the way out of Calais, driving on the right as if born to it. In French hilltop towns he seemed to know instinctively where to find the prettiest street and the best restaurant. They took another boat from Barcelona to an unspoiled Majorca, where they had three weeks of scorching days in coves, with lots of wine for lunch every day, and grapes which Tony and Evan ate 'à la Bacchus', cramming whole bunches into their mouths and spitting out showers of skin and seeds into the bushes. Each of them had an improving book to read, Milton (Evan), Dante (Cynthia), Dickens (Tony), and Conrad (Joyce), but no one got much beyond page 21. They were woken at dawn on cloudless mornings by what Joyce described as 'the flat golden tonking of a thousand sheep-bells'.

They noticed *New Yorker*-ish sights, such as other couples at the hotel doing vigorous exercises after bathing. Like many other literary Londoners, Tony and Joyce had subscribed to the *New Yorker* since its first issue in 1925. 'Getting' the Peter Arno and Helen Hokinson cartoons enhanced their sense of being cosmopolitan. Captions such as 'Isn't Chile thin?' became part of family folklore. Little did Joyce know that one day she would (on her own admission) turn into a *New Yorker* cartoon figure herself, stealing into her garden in slippers each sweltering Manhattan dusk to measure her gladioli.

In northern France on the last morning of the holiday the car got stuck in the mud, visibility was bad, a cross Frenchman shouted at them, they got stuck behind some pigs, there was a fallen tree across the road, and they had a puncture. 'Our delay', Joyce noted, 'was due to BOG, FOG, FROG, HOG and LOG, and if only I could make out that the puncture was due to a loose COG, my happiness would be complete.' Driving to London from Dover, Tony pretended to be a foreigner and asked directions in Catalan. Then it was back to the nursery again. 'Found everything as right as rain at Wellington Square, and no po-faces among the staff, which does them all great credit, as two separate nurseries in one house has been known to lead to complications.'

Just after this holiday Joyce reviewed for the *Spectator* a book called *The Technique of Marriage*, by Mary Borden. The fault she found with it was that Miss Borden underestimated 'the importance of what one's grandmother calls That Side of Marriage. As a wise man once said, sex doesn't matter all that much when it goes right, but it is very important indeed when it goes wrong.'

It was beginning to go wrong for Tony and Joyce, and it did matter. Embarrassment and awkwardness were seeping in, where seamless union had been. Their daytime irritations with each other led to night-time non-attraction. Joyce saw beside her in bed a golfer knocking back a pink gin in a club-house. Tony saw beside him a sulky, scarf-wearing collector of sea-holly. Joyce suggested that they should visit a doctor to discuss their sexual block, which they did, but to no avail. At about this time they agreed that each could look elsewhere for sexual satisfaction, provided it was done discreetly. There are signs that Joyce had entertained the possibility of infidelity as early as 1927. Her friend Philip Hewitt-Myring, the Leader Page editor of the *Daily News*, became 'P.' in her engagement book, and they met at 12.30 on many Tuesdays and Wednesdays. When he went to America as a holder of the Walter Hines Page Fellowship in Journalism in 1927 and 1928 she kept a note of each letter sent and received: 'To P.', 'From P.' But the affair, if it was one, was short-lived, and P. soon became Philip again and was chosen as godfather to Robert.

Tony, sometime after the 1933 holiday in Majorca, began an affair with Cynthia Talbot. Nannie Good discovered that on her Chelsea walks with the children she had to be careful to avoid taking them along Walpole Street where Cynthia lived, because the Bluebird, with its all-too-recognisable number plate, was often parked there in the late afternoons.

Cracks were appearing in the Wellington Square life which had been immortalized as such a paradise by Joyce and E. H. Shepard. A few doors down, at number 28, the Warrack marriage was breaking up; Jacynth was having an affair, and Joyce let her telephone her lover from the safety of number 16. The sentence 'We talked about Tony and Joyce' – sometimes it was 'We railed against Tony and Joyce' – became common in Anne Talbot's diary. It was a gossipy circle, which seemed to derive more pleasure from talking *about* Tony and Joyce than to them. Their friends, behind their backs, tried to get to the bottom of why Tony and Joyce could be so likeable, and yet so annoying.

Joyce was often a little ill, if there were callers. Not badly ill – just a cough, and a dressing-gown on, and the bedroom door closed behind her. In Rye, to get away from the golf conversation, she made a small upstairs sitting-room for herself, with a sofa-bed, to which she retreated with the excuse of a cold and an article to finish. Being 'under the weather' was the easiest way of bowing out of the jollities. She wrote poems in bed, such as this one, 'At a Dull Party':

In fifty years at most I shall be dead.
  These jaws, which now grind hard to scotch a yawn,
Will gape unchecked; and in a clay-cold bed
  Clamped fast, I'll wait a problematical dawn.
I have less than twenty thousand days to live –
  Six hundred months, a bare half-million hours;
And each new breath, heedless and fugitive,
  Another mouthful of my life devours.
Then, Christ! what spendthrift folly brought me here,
  To breathe stale smoke, and drink, talk, think, small beer?

A sense of mortality was creeping into her consciousness.
This marriage was beginning to make her feel old. In her mid
thirties she began to write about what it was like to grow older.
It was

>   . . . to feel on the first rose
>   The breath malign and fell
>   Of the first icicle,
>   And in the earliest kiss,
>   The handshake of farewell.

It was to see 'Night's poles flash by us, day's wires dip between
them', as one stared from the train window. It was to notice, at
the annual Eton and Harrow cricket match at Lord's, how much
one's acquaintances had aged. Joyce never enjoyed this day out.
'Like the hands of an electric clock which pounce forward once
a minute, the faces you meet at Lord's seem to grow older in
horrid jerks, bringing home the passage of time more cogently
than the smooth, almost imperceptible changing of faces of
intimate friends.' As for the ordeal of having to watch the
cricket match and chat to these acquaintances, this was Joyce's
opinion: 'It may or may not be true that playing games has made
Englishmen what they are. But there is no doubt whatever that
it is having to watch Englishmen play games that has made
English women what they are.'
  Her taste in men changed, in the mid 1930s, from the British
to the central European, and preferably Jewish. Hungarians
didn't rely on anecdotes; they played violins and allowed the

sadness of the world to seep into them. As Tony became less and less communicative, Joyce craved the company of men who were not afraid to talk about the blackness in one's heart. In a letter to her son Jamie after the Second World War, referring to Tony, she wrote: 'This bottling-up habit is the only *bad* fault I've ever had to find with him, but it certainly is a bad one, and is enough to wreck any marriage.' As she put it in 'Variation on an Old Proverb', 1937,

> Hard words will break no bones,
> But more than bones are broken
> By the inescapable stones
> Of fond words left unspoken.

The cheekbones of a Hungarian doctor she met in Chelsea, Tibor Csato, made her knees melt. We have only Anne Talbot's description of this exotic man: 'Good looking and beautifully made, and seems charming. He is a poor dog doing cancer research here.' (The 'poor dog' went on to become a successful London surgeon, with fashionable consulting rooms in Great Cumberland Place.) Joyce wrote nothing down about Tibor, but it is clear that he was a Friend rather than a mere friend (she used that capital 'F' to distinguish sexual from non-sexual friendships). Tibor came to stay at the coastguard's cottage in Rye, when Tony was there: the capital 'F' aspect was kept deeply secret, and Tony was lavish, as always, with hospitality and good wine. Tony and Joyce never ceased to be 'a good team' on social occasions. For the sake of the children, and for the sake of not having to face anything unpleasant, they maintained the façade of a happy marriage.

'The lover, the party-giver and the freelance journalist are the only people who feel a genuine interest in the postman's knock,' Joyce wrote; and, for a time, she was all three. But in public she was still the safe wife, tending to display wit rather than emotion. The brittle social-observer strand in her journalism was being over-used, the noticing-sadness-in-everyday-life strand under-used. At the end of some of her *Spectator* pieces of the mid 1930s, an invisible 'Will this do? is all but legible.

Perhaps the weakest article of her whole career was 'A Brief Guide to Cornwall' written for the *Spectator* in 1935. She and Tony had been on a cheap Cornish holiday, and Joyce frivolously summed up the county using that crutch for the lazy or uninspired journalist, the 'A to Z' method. 'Place-names: Unbelievable. Still, there they are on the map. But don't go to St Anthony-in-Roseland, because no place could possibly live up to a name like that. We avoided it, for fear of disillusion.' (Informationless though it was, this article made its way into the pages of *The Statesman*, Calcutta.)

Why were Tony and Joyce driving around Cornwall being facetious about the place-names, dialect, customs and inhabitants? They were economizing.

They had never been good at hanging on to their money. In 1925, two years into their marriage, they had decided against 'taking care of the pence' in their life – saving money on matches, stamps and bits of string. It was more important, they felt, to take care of the pounds and 'let the pence go hang' – to live in a cottage but have a never-failing supply of first-class cigarettes. At that time, they were indeed living in a kind of cottage – a small house in Chelsea.

But now, in the 1930s, they were trying to maintain a fourteen-roomed house with a triple garage in the mews, and a seaside cottage, and the staff of both – as well as keeping up the supply of first-class cigarettes. Then Tony suffered a blow at work. He had been earning a handsome commission from Lord Beaverbrook's newspapers with an insurance brokerage scheme by which readers could cut out coupons entitling them to free accident insurance. Then Tony's father, the chartered accountant, auditing in Canada, declined to approve the accounts of one of Lord Beaverbrook's companies there. Beaverbrook was furious, and refused to do any more business with anyone called Maxtone Graham. Tony's income suddenly dropped.

It was no longer enough to let Wellington Square for the summer season, as they had been doing. In 1936 they had to let it permanently, and move out. Later, Joyce named the moment of shutting up Wellington Square as the first time she experienced what she believed was depression – 'I fondly thought', she wrote to her brother, 'that I was in the lowest depths, little dreaming that there was a Grand Canyon beyond. Actually, it was eight years before I had anything one could call a real depression.' Here she is, in 1936, on bankruptcy, both literal and metaphorical:

'Audit'

Bankrupt of joy, who once was rich in it,
Must drop pretence at last, no longer hide
Behind drawn blinds rooms ravished by distraint;
Swallow his pride,
And openly admit
His fortune spent.

That over, what remains? Only to sit
By a cold hearth, staring at a stripped wall,
And with humility make
His statement of account;
Recall
The past's transactions; rack the brain, and wonder
What accident, extravagance or blunder
Frittered his pounds to pence
And brought so rich a heart to indigence.

Wonder in vain. It is too late to take
Remorseful vows.
This was a gracious and a lovely house:
But now its floors are bare,
And there are heavy footsteps on the stair.

The family moved, with Nannie Good, to a tiny house in Caroline Place (now Donne Place) near the Brompton Road, where they were woken at three o'clock each morning by the milk ponies of the United Dairies. They couldn't stand it for long, and moved again, to 17 Halsey Street, Chelsea.

On 2 September 1936, during this black time, Joyce received a letter from Peter Fleming, whom she had got to know when he was Literary Editor of the *Spectator*. Now he was a leader-writer at *The Times*, and a favourite of the Editor, Geoffrey Dawson.

Dear Jan,

If you ever read the articles on the Court Page of *The Times*, you will have noticed that they are mostly about stoats. This seems to me a bad thing, and we should welcome a light and feminine touch occasionally. The demand is not for essays but rather for anecdotes: you probably know the form. I am not in a position to commission anything but if you should ever feel inspired to turn out the simple and rather dim kind of stuff that is necessary, it would get very sympathetic consideration.

Come and have a drink tomorrow.

Yours ever,

Peter.

This laconic note set Joyce thinking what she might write. (At the age of eight she had written 'thinking what I might write' in one of the servants' confessional albums, under the heading 'Present state of mind'. It was her state of mind for ever.)

She decided to write about a woman who was as happy as she had once been.

Chapter Six

Stepping lightly down the square, Mrs Miniver suddenly understood why she was enjoying her forties so much better than she had enjoyed her thirties: it was the difference between August and October, between the heaviness of late summer and the sparkle of early autumn, between the ending of an old phase and the beginning of a new one.

From 'Mrs Miniver Comes Home'

THERE HADN'T, ACTUALLY, been any mention of stoats on the Court Page of *The Times* for more than a month when Peter Fleming wrote that letter to Joyce. It was nonsense to claim that the Court Page was 'mostly about stoats': it was mostly about Buckingham Palace, and grand marriages, and the funerals of deans and bishops. But in a deep way, Peter Fleming was accurate. Constitutionally unable to resist comic effect, he had used a monosyllable to express a wide general subject – minority-interest flora and fauna. Almost every day, in the top right-hand corner of the Court Page, there was indeed an article about some kind of wild animal or plant.

In the fortnight leading up to his letter these had included 'Hop-picking – A Midland Memory', 'Pheasants in 1936', 'Woody Plants for Limy Soil', 'Family Cares of the Little Owl', 'Stork Colonies in Germany', and 'Pot-hunting on a Sussex Marsh'. Occasionally the subjects strayed from Nature, but they still tended towards the masculine: 'A 64-Gun Ship at Trafalgar', by Admiral Sir Herbert Richmond, or 'Cars of Today: the Morris Fourteen-Six'.

The only whiff of femininity on the page came from the fashion edicts, but their tone was headmistressy rather than light. 'The simple afternoon dresses are short, straight, and may have front and back panels indicated by ribbed seams.' 'Cloth coats with plain material collars and tailor-mades with which furs can be worn are now the fashion.' It is no wonder that Peter Fleming, with his ear for the arresting detail and his loathing of humourlessness, yearned for 'a light and feminine touch'.

Joyce went, as bidden, to have a drink with him at Printing House Square the next afternoon. 'We want somebody to invent a woman and write an article about her every few weeks,' he said. 'Will you take it on?'

'What sort of woman?' asked Joyce.

'Oh, I don't know – just an ordinary sort of woman, who leads an ordinary sort of life. Rather like yourself.'

Joyce took this as a compliment, and agreed to have a go. 'Right,' said Peter. 'Now, the first thing you've got to do is think of a name for her. You want something that's long enough to sound nice, and short enough not to be a nuisance in narrow column headings; and if possible it ought to begin with an "M", for the sake of alliteration. And it would be better not to have a real surname, otherwise we might go letting ourselves in for libel actions.'

Joyce went out of Printing House Square and walked along Upper Thames Street, thinking of all the 'M'-words she could. Every one she thought of was either too long or too short, or a real name, or didn't sound like a name at all. Then she noticed a man carrying a bundle of skins out of one of the furriers' warehouses, and this set her thinking about the heraldic names for fur which her father had taught her. Vair and counter-vair, potent and counter-potent, ermine and erminois . . . and what was the other one? It was on the tip of her tongue for several minutes. Then she remembered it. She went straight back to Printing House Square.

'What about calling her "Mrs Miniver"?'

'That's not half bad,' said Peter Fleming.

The *Oxford English Dictionary* gives several meanings for 'miniver': '1. A kind of fur used as a lining and trimming in cere-monial costumes. 2a. The animal from which the fur was supposed to be obtained (*obs.*). 2b. (*dial.*) The stoat . . .' So, even after the arrival of Mrs Miniver, the Court Page of *The Times* still featured stoats.

It was easy for Joyce not quite to get around to putting pen to paper. There were many excuses. She was moving house – twice, first to 1 Caroline Place and then to 17 Halsey Street, and feeling all the tension and lowering of self-esteem which moving to a smaller house brings. The family listened to the Abdication broadcast in the cramped drawing-room at Caroline Place. By the time of the Coronation they had moved to Halsey Street, and they watched the procession from the window of Scotland Yard, invited in by Joyce's old detective colleagues.

On hymn-writing mornings, Joyce had written a limerick after breakfast in an effort to clean her mental slate. Now, commissioned to create the perfect housewife, she had first to unburden herself in Ogden Nashese:

Fidelity isn't just a question of who you go to bed with:
It'd be simple enough, if that was all you had to bother your
    head with.
Because, after all, unless you happen to be introduced to a
    ravishing Russian when the weather's particularly sultry,
It's only too easy not to commit adultery.

But anyway, as I said,
Fidelity isn't just a matter of Respecting the Marriage-bed.
It's a matter of not letting other people be able,
At the dinner-table,
To tell whether you are hearing one of his stories for the first,
    second, tenth or twentieth time;
And of understanding, and responding to, his pantomime,
When he is bored at a party and wants you to get up and say
    Goodbye;
And of remembering always to say 'we' instead of 'I'
And 'our' instead of 'my';
And of never accepting a telephone invitation without leaving
    him a loophole for escape;
And of never letting him in for amateur theatricals in any
    form or shape . . .

and so on, ending:

> But pray don't think that I am trying to disparage
> Marriage.

In the spring of 1937 she sat down in the garden at Rye and tried to write about Mrs Miniver, but found she could only write about the impossibility of writing in a garden. The sunshine kept moving onto one's piece of paper 'like an importunate cat', and sun-glasses were no good: 'expensive ones give a depressing effect, as of a November twilight in a slate quarry; while cheaper brands transport the wearer to such a lurid, threatening and phantasmogorical world that he might well imagine himself to be looking at a colour film of the Day of Judgment designed by El Greco and produced by MGM.' The *Spectator* published this. Joyce spent weeks of 1937 building a punt called 'Puffin', badly. It required six strong men to carry it to the water, and it leaked. She and Jamie also started making a cardboard model of Bodiam Castle, which afterwards became a symbol of life's unfinished projects.

Peter Fleming's idea took a year to come to fruition. In September 1937 he wrote again, asking Joyce to discuss the 'embryonic project' – and suddenly, inspired by the beginning-of-school-year bracing air, she got to work. On Wednesday, 6 October 1937, the first article appeared, in the exact spot on the Court Page which 'Rock Gardens in Autumn' had filled earlier the same week: 'Mrs Miniver Comes Home', signed 'From a correspondent'. This is how it began:

> It was lovely, thought Mrs Miniver, nodding good-bye to the flower-woman and carrying her big sheaf of chrysanthemums down the street with a kind of ceremonious joy, as though it were a cornucopia; it was lovely, this settling down again, this tidying away of the summer into its box, this taking up of the thread of one's life where the holidays (irrelevant interlude) had made one drop it. Not that she didn't enjoy the holidays: but she always felt – and it was, perhaps, a measure of her peculiar happiness – a little relieved when they were over. Her normal life pleased her so well that she was half-afraid to step out of the frame in case one day she should find herself

unable to get back. The spell might break, the atmosphere be impossible to recapture.

And this is how it ended, five paragraphs later:

She rearranged the fire a little, mostly for the pleasure of handling the fluted steel poker, and then sat down by it. Tea was already laid: there were honey sandwiches, brandy-snaps, and small ratafia biscuits; and there would, she knew, be crumpets. Three new library books lay virginally on the fender-stool, their bright new wrappers unsullied by subscriber's hand. The clock on the mantelpiece chimed, very softly and precisely, five times. A tug hooted from the river. A sudden breeze brought the sharp tang of a bonfire in at the window. The jigsaw was almost complete, but there was still one piece missing. And then, from the other end of the square, came the familiar sound of the Wednesday barrel-organ, playing, with a hundred apocryphal trills and arpeggios, the 'Blue Danube' waltz. And Mrs Miniver, with a little sigh of contentment, rang for tea.

It was a prose poem on the afternoon happiness of a very lucky Chelsea wife. Nothing was written in any leader to explain Mrs Miniver's sudden appearance. The aura of self-satisfaction exuded by this initial essay was enough to exasperate several readers.

A fortnight later, after 'An Enigma of the Turf' and 'White Sparrows – Experiments of a Bird-Breeder', there she was again: 'Mrs Miniver and the New Car'. Her husband, Clem, was now introduced, a charming and successful architect who had just landed two lucrative commissions and could therefore afford to swap the old Leadbetter for a smart (unspecified) new brand from the Motor Show catalogue. Readers were given a glimpse of the Minivers at home:

Clem put his head in, dishevelled from a bath. Not for the first time, she felt thankful that she had married a man whose face in the ensuing sixteen years had tended to become sardonic rather than sleek. It was difficult to tell, when people were young and their cheek lines were still pencilled and delible. Those beautiful long lean young men so often filled out into stage churchwardens at forty-five.

But she had been lucky, or had a flair; Clem's looks were wearing well. The great thing, perhaps, was not to be too successful too young.

And Mrs Miniver revealed herself as sentimental about inanimate objects. This time she was introduced, in an unsigned Leader by Peter Fleming, as 'an imaginary lady who makes her second appearance in these pages'. Fleming liked to be funnier than anybody else. As well as introducing Mrs Miniver, he outdid her on the subject of the uselessness of one's old car:

Over and again it has delayed us, marooned us, embarrassed us, and covered us with oil. It has subjected us to hardships, humiliations and expense. It has never been our friend. At best it was a reluctant and treacherous ally, and of late it has become, more or less openly, our enemy. Though it may be said to 'stand meekly by', it requires considerable effort on our part to make it do anything else.

Readers began to piece together data about this mysterious woman. Her Christian name was not revealed. She had three children, Vin (Etonian, liked fishing), Judy (took her doll out in new red dress, chain-sucked barley sugar on journeys), and Toby (small, unfathomable, made guitar out of photograph frame and eight elastic bands). Clem was a perfect piano-playing husband and father. The Minivers lived in a stucco-fronted London square, where they gave dinner parties. At weekends, when they were not invited to a country house party, they went to their cottage in Kent called Starlings, where they spent happy afternoons fitting up one of the outhouses like the cabin of a ship. They went to Perthshire each summer.

It was all idyllic enough to make for deadly dull reading – were it not for the fact that this anonymous 'correspondent' had a remarkable gift for expressing small universal truths. Each piece contained a few gems: a spot-on metaphor or two, and some razor-sharp insights into the sensations of daily life. Here was Mrs Miniver on rear-view mirrors: 'She wondered why it had never occurred to her before that you cannot successfully navigate the future unless you keep always framed beside it a small, clear image of the past.'

On friends whom one half-dreads seeing: 'There was nothing really the matter with the Lane-Pontifexes. They were quite nice, intelligent, decent people: yet for some reason one's heart sank. Their company, as Clem said, was a continual shutting of windows .'

On choosing an engagement book: 'She rejected the leather-ette at once. In a spasm of post-Christmas economy she had once bought a very cheap engagement book, and it had annoyed her for twelve months; everything she put down in it looked squalid.'

On the first 'Wedgwood day' – blue sky and scudding white clouds – at the beginning of spring: 'On certain days, the bar-riers were down. Mrs Miniver felt as though she and the outside world could mingle and interpenetrate; as though she was not entirely contained in her own body but was part also of every person in the street. This was the real meaning of peace – not mere absence of division, but an active consciousness of unity, of being one of the mountain-peak islands on a submerged con-tinent.'

On a hot summer which goes on for too long: 'As day after day broke close and windless, and night after night failed to bring any refreshing chill, she began to feel oddly uneasy. The year, now, seemed like an ageing woman whose smooth cheeks were the result, not of a heart perennially young, but of an assured income, a sound digestion, and a protective callousness of spirit.'

On a child's inability to grade its misfortunes: 'One never knew, when setting out to comfort Toby, whether to prepare first aid for a pinprick or a broken heart.'

On the sound of a father and child walking together: 'Toby trotted off to the pond with Clem, his feet beating crotchets against his father's minims.'

On the sound a pneumatic windscreen-wiper makes: ' "Suc-cessful?" asked Clem, seeing her festooned with parcels. "Look here," she said, "that screen-wiper – I *think* what it says is 'Beef Tea.' " "My goodness," said Clem. "I believe you're right." '

It became an oasis of gentle wit and wifely common sense, this fortnightly patch of the Court Page; it was a safe, framed world to retreat to after facing the news on the previous pages, which was steadily getting worse. This analysis of happiness, written by a modern independent wife, was something quite new. Fundamentally contented readers who also bought new cars, had family firework displays, bought engagement books, did Christmas shopping, sent their children back to school and so on, saw their own thoughts expressed for the first time.

There was, perhaps, something a little suspicious about the utter happiness of the Minivers. An author genuinely blissfully happy with her husband can dare to criticize him. Today's columnist will complain cheerfully about 'the dreadful Simon' who forgets to turn taps off – and it is plain that really she is flaunting the success of her marriage. There was not a single criticism of Clem, or of married life, in the 'Mrs Miniver' columns. To cynical modern eyes it seems obvious that the author may have had something to hide.

By inventing a happily married woman and describing her thoughts, Joyce was turning out what Peter Fleming had asked for, and Mrs Miniver was an ideal vehicle for her minute observations of daily life. But with hindsight it seems that Joyce was describing the marriage she once had, which perhaps she wished she could have had for ever, and which she might regain if she wrote about it with enough enthusiasm. She and Tony were equally loath to face up to failure: the Miniver essays, which Tony read and approved of, were an exercise in mutual convincing, an effort to cover over the cracks and pretend they were not there.

The question which occupied readers' minds in 1938 was not why the pieces were written, but who had written them. A friend of Tony's overheard two colonels in a golf club on the south-east coast. 'I say,' said one, 'do you know who writes those "Miniver" articles in *The Times*?' The other replied, 'I've never been able to find out; but of one thing I'm quite certain, and that is that they couldn't possibly be written by anyone but a man.'

At first, Joyce received letters saying either 'Dear Madam: I simply love your Miniver articles – do go on with them', or 'Dear Sir: I simply loathe your Miniver articles – do stop.' Some of Mrs Miniver's most bloodthirsty critics, as well as several of her most enthusiastic fans, were clergymen; Joyce could not decide whether this was proof of inconsistency in 'Mrs Miniver', or of schism in the Church.

After a time, she noticed that people were no longer writing 'Dear Sir' or 'Dear Madam': it was 'Dear Mrs Miniver', as though she were a real person. In one article Mrs Miniver found a new charwoman at number 23, Block H, The Buildings, a fictitious hunting-ground for people in search of daily help. The next day there was a letter for Joyce enclosing a stamped addressed postcard: 'Dear Mrs Miniver: Do be an angel and let me know exactly *which* block of dwellings it was. I have been looking for a charwoman for weeks and am quite distracted. Forgive my bothering you, but I know what a good housekeeper you are.' The last sentence made Joyce feel guilty, since she knew only too well that she herself was *not* a good housekeeper.

Even friends and relations who knew she was the author of the 'Miniver' pieces began to confuse Joyce's real life with Mrs Miniver's. For Easter 1938 Mrs Miniver and Clem went off to Cornwall. The following week a friend rang Joyce and said, 'Oh, you're back, are you? Cornwall must have been heavenly. I wish I'd been there.' 'So do I,' said Joyce. In August, wanting to inflict some pain on her character, she sent Mrs Miniver to London to the dentist, for a filling. 'Darling,' one of Joyce's aunts wrote to her, 'I'm so sorry you've been having such a nasty time with your teeth.'

These reactions were all quite gratifying in a way, but they were also alarming. Joyce began to feel that she wasn't in charge of her own life any more. 'In fact,' she wrote later, 'I felt rather like a ventriloquist whose doll has suddenly struck up an independent conversation with the audience.'

Deductions about the precise social status of Mrs Miniver and sightings of flaws in her perfection became a running game on *The Times* Letters and Leader pages. The name of the Minivers' country cottage, Starlings, was a clue. 'These homely old rural names', said a Leader on 19 April, 'always suggest not a family house but a purchase.' Mrs Miniver, it seemed, was not 'top drawer': she was 'top drawer but one.' And her teeth seemed to have something wrong with them. 'It was a shock to learn that she had to go to the dentist, and to come up from Starlings for the purpose. That could not have been for one of the regular half-yearly assurances that her teeth, like her taste, were flawless: it must have been a special visit, denoting a defect. How Mrs Miniver must loathe to have anything about her that is not perfect – Mrs Miniver, so delicately sensuous that she can take delight in the feel of her own fluted steel poker!'

Joyce later insisted, in lectures and interviews, that though her husband and children were remarkably similar in age, habits and temperament, she was not Mrs Miniver. Many of the incidents, it was true, were drawn straight from life, but heightened by Joyce's own, real, poetic way of looking at things. Yet, unlike Mrs Miniver, she was no longer living in a large house in a Chelsea square; she had moved to a small house in a Chelsea street. The 'little sigh of contentment' as the tug hooted from the river and Mrs Miniver rang for tea were echoes from Joyce's past. The utterly good-natured Clem, in perfect mental union with his wife, handsome, sardonic rather than sleek, turning out his 'pocketful of pebbles' for her each evening, was not quite the golfing, clubbable, gin-drinking man Tony was becoming; tellingly, there was no mention of golf in 'Mrs Miniver'. And there was no hint of the dark side of Joyce's mind, the side which could blot out beauty and see nothing but barrenness; the side which, at the height of her success at *The Times*, wrote this poem:

> This is the measure of my soul's dis-ease:
> I, who for love of life,
> Once grudged each moment of the night's oblivion,
> Now seek out sleep, unearned;
> Cling to its depths, and wake reluctantly
> As though to bodily pain.

Mrs Miniver's outlook on the world was the polar opposite of the depressive's, who sees futility in everything. Nothing was futile for Mrs Miniver: even a rear-view mirror, even a swing-door, even a dentist's ceiling, could inspire a thought about the human condition.

It is too simple to say that in 'Mrs Miniver' Joyce was re-creating a lost paradise. Officially she and Tony were still a stead-ily married couple: the laughter, the funny accents, the brilliant thoughts, the impetuous adventures continued, and there was no feeling, even in private, that the marriage itself was threatened. It has been suggested that Tony did not like having a wife who was successful and clever, but this was not the case. What he did mind, more and more, was having a rebellious wife, a depressed wife, a left-wing wife, a sulky wife, a wife who felt fenced in. Tony and Joyce visited the *Times* offices, and became friends of Geoffrey Dawson and R. M. Barrington-Ward, the successive editors. It was another world to discover together and laugh about. Tony was heartened by the 'Mrs Miniver' articles: if Joyce could capture the sparkling days of their marriage and co-par-enthood so vividly and lovingly in print, maybe this was how she still saw their marriage: and maybe everything was all right.

For Joyce, writing 'Mrs Miniver' actually had the effect not of helping her to regain her lost state of serene Chelsea wife but of making her realise that she didn't want to be that type of person ever again. It was almost as if the creation of 'Mrs Miniver' was a way of writing the exquisiteness out of herself. Readers saw Mrs Miniver's life as an enviable paradise; Joyce, privately, was beginning to see it as a cage to which she was ready to say good riddance.

The first inkling that Joyce might not be able to get away from her creation came the day after the appearance of the second 'Mrs Miniver' article. The publishers Lovat Dickson, having discovered her identity, wrote to her care of *The Times* to ask whether they could publish the pieces in book form when there were enough of them. Between October 1937 and November 1938 Joyce received letters from Constable, Black, Methuen, Arnold, Chatto & Windus, Cassell's, Harrap, Jonathan Cape, Hodder & Stoughton, Macmillan, Longmans Green, Dent and Hamish Hamilton, each of them courting her favour. Each found a different way of sounding attractive: 'All of us in the firm are very hopeful that you may be interested . . .'; 'If you can be persuaded – and I do so hope you can – I know there will be no difficulty about terms'; 'Do you want any more of these obviously boring requests from publishers?' Peter Fleming wrote to ask. 'Or shall we turn them down ourselves and pass on their letters to you already answered?' Wooed, desired, popular, choosing and rejecting suitors, Joyce was in the foothills of fame, and loving it.

She already felt a sense of loyalty to Chatto & Windus because they were publishing her book of collected journalism, *Try Anything Twice*, due to come out in October 1938. Harold Raymond's courting letter ('May I tell you how delighted I have been to make the acquaintance of the Minivers? My wife drew my attention to "Three Stockings" on Christmas Eve . . .') was the proposal which won her hand. She accepted Chatto in March and gracefully refused the other thirteen.

Perhaps, suggested Peter Fleming, Mrs Miniver should dare to mention the political situation: 'Now that you have your readers purring, a little astringency might do them good.' Joyce did not want to raise the decibel level of her prose by inserting ill-informed comments about Hitler and Mussolini. But she did continue, now, to puncture Mrs Miniver's serenity with occasional pricks of gloom. 'Mrs Miniver was conscious [seeing a placard with the word JEWS on it] of an instantaneous mental wincing, and an almost instantaneous remorse for it. However long the horror continued, one must not get to the stage of refusing to think about it. To shrink from direct pain was bad enough, but to shrink from vicarious pain was the ultimate cowardice. And whereas to conceal direct pain was a virtue, to conceal vicarious pain was a sin.' Again she struck a chord with readers, putting her finger on the small ways in which one's heart sank in 1938.

But the reader who searches the book *Mrs Miniver* for scenes of Dunkirk, air-raid shelters, bombs, ranting German pilots, death of heroine's daughter-in-law, death of station master, destruction of parish church roof, and so on, all of which later found their way into the Hollywood film, will find hints only of the looming war. Mrs Miniver was a pre-war character, requisitioned by MGM.

'I scratch for light leaders like a hen in the barren dust,' wrote R. M. Barrington Ward to Joyce. As well as her fortnightly 'Miniver' pieces, Joyce wrote more than sixty unsigned Fourth Leaders for *The Times* between January 1938 and June 1940. Writer's block afflicted her at home, so she was given a room of her own at the *Times* offices. She was so small that her legs dangled off the office chair. But she turned out just what was required. Subject: arachnophobia in the English psyche. 'There is mental horror, because the character of spiders is so unattractive. They have all the most revolting copybook virtues – prudence, patience, perseverance, foresight, and so on. As for their vices – well, every living creature must catch its food as best it may, but there is something about the spider's methods which is very far from cricket.' Subject: the terrifyingness of fairy tales (inspired by news that an 'Adults only' certificate might be given to the Walt Disney film *Snow White*). 'No more hair-raising piece of dialogue has been written than the world-famous conversation between Red Riding Hood and the wolf in grandmother's clothing.'

Subject: advice to the young. Here, Joyce mentioned a 'superb example' of advice which had come from Nazi Germany that week (in June 1938). Julius Streicher, in a speech to 25,000 young Germans on the summer solstice, had exhorted them to 'Be beautiful, godlike and natural'. 'It is a commandment audacious in its simplicity,' Joyce wrote. She was impressed: the word 'Nazi' was by no means synonymous with evil – yet. Most British people, apart from a few hardened pessimists and far-sighted politicians, were still trying to see the best in the Nazis. The following merry observation, from Joyce's leader on the 1938 summer sales in Berlin, seems unbelievably naïve now: 'Berlin housewives are putting Aryan pride in their pocket and going to banned Jewish shops for bargains in the sales. It is a thought which cannot fail to bring a pang of sheer delight to all who are interested in psychology, ethnology, drapery, dictatorship or women.'

Then, in September 1938, came the Munich Crisis, when war suddenly seemed imminent. Anonymously, in her 'Mrs Miniver' articles and in her *Times* leaders, Joyce summed up the emotions of the nation's optimists: first, the tension and anxiety; and then, after Neville Chamberlain returned from Germany waving his piece of paper, the relief.

One of the things that gave Joyce her misguided confidence in Neville Chamberlain was the fact that he was a botanist. She tried to cheer *Times* readers with this wishful thought: 'Both statesman and botanist', she wrote in a leader, 'must be able to handle other human beings, to inspire their confidence and to justify it: let anybody who thinks otherwise watch a clumsy novice trying to worm out of a suspicious innkeeper in Teesdale the exact habitat of the Alpine Bartsia. The botanist (like the statesman) must be neither afraid to reach up for what he is seeking, nor ashamed to kneel down for it.'

The word 'escapism' was being bandied about: and Joyce, in a leader entitled 'Poets and the Crisis', wrote a defence of escapism. 'If to draw comfort from poetry or music or painting is "escapism", then the word has lost the meaning which the sceptics gave it: it has changed in mid-air from a missile to a crown. For to "escape" by any of these means is not to hide in an underground cavern, or even to retreat across some neutral frontier. It is to climb a mountain-top, to rest the eyes on a wider horizon, to breathe for a time a rarer, clearer air, and to come down strengthened and refreshed.'

The Minivers, meanwhile, queued up outside the Town Hall to collect their gas-masks, taking the cook and housekeeper with them.

(In real life, when Janet and Robert were told that their day-school in Tite Street was to be evacuated to North Wales, the first thing they said was not 'Is Mummy coming with us?', but 'Is Nannie coming with us?' This exchange did not find its way into 'Mrs Miniver'.)

'It's so nice to be back to normal again,' remarked Mrs Adie, the cook, in the 'Mrs Miniver' article of 6 October, subtitled 'The Afterthoughts of Mrs Miniver'. The crisis was over; but they weren't quite back to normal, thought Mrs Miniver, and they never would be. They were poorer by a few layers of secur-ity, though richer in other ways:

THE MINIVERS AND GAS MASKS

THOUGHTS IN A QUEUE

FROM A CORRESPONDENT

Clem had to go and get his gas mask early, on his way to the office, but the rest of them went at half-past one, hoping that the lunch hour would be less crowded. It may have been; but even so there was a longish queue. They were quite a large party—Mrs. Miniver and Nannie; Judy and Toby; Mrs. Adie, the Scots cook, lean as a winter aspen, and Gladys, the new house-parlourmaid: a pretty girl, with complicated hair. Six of them—or seven if you counted Toby's Teddy bear, which seldom left his side, and certainly not if there were any treats about. For to children, even more than to grown-ups (and this is at once a consolation and a danger), any excitement really counts as a treat, even if it is a painful excitement like breaking your arm, or a horrible excitement like seeing a car smash, or a terrifying excitement like playing hide-and-seek in the shrubbery at dusk. Mrs. Miniver herself had been nearly grown-up in August, 1914, but she remembered vividly how her younger sister had exclaimed with shining eyes, "I say ! I'm in a war !"

But she clung to the belief that this time, at any rate, children of Vin's and Judy's age had been told beforehand what it was all about, had heard both sides, and had discussed it themselves with a touching and astonishing maturity. If the worst came to the worst (funny how one still shied away from saying, "If there's a war," and fell back on euphemisms), if the worst came to the worst, these children would at least know

that we were fighting against an idea, and not against a nation. Whereas the last generation had been told to run and play in the garden, had been shut out from the grown-ups' worried conclaves: and then quite suddenly they had all been plunged into an orgy of licensed lunacy, of boycotting Grimm and Struwwelpeter, of looking askance at their cousins' old Fräulein, and of feeling towards Dachshund puppies the uneasy tenderness of a devout Churchwoman dandling her daughter's love-child. But this time those lunacies—or rather the state of mind which bred them—should not, must not, come into being. To guard against that was the most important of all the forms of war work which she and other women would have to do. There are no tangible gas masks to defend us in war-time against its slow, yellow, drifting corruption of the mind.

glory. She carried away with her, as well as a litter of black rubber pigs, a series of detached impressions, like shots in a quick-cut film. Her own right hand with a pen in it, filling up six yellow cards in pleasurable block capitals ; Mrs. Adie sitting up as straight as a ramrod under the fitter's hands, betraying no signs of the apprehension which Mrs. Miniver knew she must be feeling about her false fringe ; Gladys's rueful giggle as her elaborate coiffure came out partially wrecked from the ordeal ; the look of sudden realization in Judy's eyes just before her face was covered up ; the back of Toby's neck, the valley deeper than usual because his muscles were taut with distaste (he had a horror of rubber in any form) ; a very small child bursting into a wail of dismay on catching sight of its mother disguised in a black snout ; the mother's muffled reassurances—"It's on'y Mum, duck. Look—it's just a mask, like at Guy Fawkes, see ? " (Mea mater mala sus est.

A typical 'Mrs Miniver' article, as published anonymously on the Court page of The Times, *28 September 1938*

They had found themselves looking at each other, and at their cherished possessions, with new eyes. Small objects one could send to the country – a picture or two, the second edition of Donne, and the little antelope made of burnt jade; others, like the furniture, one could more or less replace: but one couldn't send away, or replace, the old panelling on the stairs, or the one crooked pane in the dining-room window which made the area railings look bent, or the notches on the nursery door-post where they had measured the children each year. And these, among their material belongings, were the ones that had suddenly mattered the most.

And they had learned to appreciate the value of dullness. As a rule, one longed for more drama in one's life. But now, thought Mrs Miniver, who was 'tired to the marrow of her mind and heart', 'nothing in the world seemed more desirable than a long wet afternoon at a country vicarage with a boring aunt'.

The Munich Crisis had been exhausting and terrifying; but it had woken people up, and Joyce was grateful for this mental awakening in herself. 'The most prosaic of us', she wrote in a *Times* leader, 'has begun to live at that pitch of tireless intensity and awareness which in normal times is known only to children, poets, lovers and other fanatics.' If, as she hoped, war was finally averted, they had been granted the privilege of skimming the cream of war without having to live through a real one.

Chapter Seven

Those whose love's no more
Than a blind alley –
A cul-de-sac
Which can have no other end
Than turning back
Or beating with bare hands
At a wall without a door –
These must go slowly.
These at a measured pace
Must walk,
And linger in one place
Often, to gaze and talk;
Even retrace
A yard or two, perhaps,
Their careful steps,
And take them over again.
By such fond strategy,
They may a long while cheat
Themselves into content,
And not too deeply care
That Fate across the threshold of their street
Has scrawled 'No Thoroughfare'.

From 'The Cul-de-Sac' in *The Glass-Blower*

'IT OCCURS TO ME,' suggested Peter Fleming in a letter to Joyce in November 1938, 'that Mrs Miniver's Xtian name is Mabel, and that you should reveal this shameful fact at some festival, as it might be Christmas.'

Surely not Mabel, thought Joyce. It was her children's

nannie's name. It would be one 'M' too many. And how could she reveal the woman's name without introducing some contrived snatch of conversation which would wreck the poetry of the interior monologue?

So she did it on the Letters page instead, on 17 December: 'I am, Sir, yours faithfully, Caroline Miniver.' Mrs Miniver's letter to *The Times* was a motherly appeal to her readers to search their 'put-away cupboards' for clothes to send to Lord Baldwin's Appeal Fund for Refugees, and it was effective. Five days after its publication, the one room previously in use at the clothing depot in Westbourne Terrace had multiplied to seven, and parcels were arriving steadily throughout the day by post, rail, car and hand. They often came with a covering letter, such as this one, from 'Highgrove', Sunbury Hill, Torquay: 'Mr Nicholls is sending the enclosed dress suit. Some years ago he took up conjuring as a hobby in winter evenings, hence the unusual pockets. He hopes it will be found in some form to be of use to a refugee.'

Joyce helped out at the clothing depot as often as she could: her Scottish spinster friend Ruth Berry was the organizing secretary and told her what to do. A refugee, Mr A. Miesels, described the scene at the depot for the *Jewish Times* (it was translated from his original Yiddish):

> The clothing department occupies three stories. Smart ladies of highest social standing in the English Aristocracy, and young girls are engaged in sorting and picking out the most useful articles. Miss Ruth (who by the way is very proud of her Biblical name) explains to me that one has to be careful not to hurt the feelings of the Refugees by sending them unworthy cloths. She also introduced me to a young lady, to whose recent appeal in the 'Times' the English population responded most generously from the farthest corners of England.
>
> At tea-time a wooden box was brought into the office and the ladies around that improvised table talked, not about weather, kittens, but about Lord Balfour, Dr Herzl, Palestine . . . One's heart is growing with joy when one realises the marvellous attitude of the noble Gentry towards the unfortunate refugees . . .

(This was a year before thousands of such refugees, so dazzled by British kindness, were interned as enemy aliens.)

'Mrs Miniver' was beginning to bring Joyce the power to do good in big, public ways. She was fascinated by the Jewish refugees, with their heart-rending combination of intellectual wealth and material destitution. She was meant to be sorting clothes, but she was easily distracted into conversation (in English or schoolgirl German) with the violinists, poets and scientists who wandered in. Romantic and lacking in political perspective, she would take up the cause of a single musician and fire off imploring letters to men in high places. 'As you will appreciate,' came a reply from the headquarters of the Lord Baldwin Fund, 'musicians are even more difficult than writers, when it comes to a question of placing them in work. People can be induced to take a domestic servant, or even a doctor, but musicians are even normally regarded as a luxury.'

'T. out.' 'T. to Manchester.' 'T. to Sandwich.' 'T. stayed at Rye.' Joyce's engagement book for 1939 (not leatherette: a Walker's 'Flexor' in red morocco) suggests much time spent apart. But at least now there was an excuse for escaping. She was truly busy. *The Times* was commissioning a leader once a week and still expected its fortnightly 'Mrs Miniver'; Chatto & Windus were collecting the 'Mrs Miniver' pieces for publication; and Joyce was lying awake at night, worrying whether the sensitive-fingered Mr Hans Mahler would find a domestic position.

'Three times a year, during the school holidays, that one remaining branch – our intense love for our co-parenthood of the children, and our joy in their company – burst into miraculous blossom . . .' So Joyce wrote years later, looking back at this time. In the holidays there were still days of marital happiness. That Easter of 1939, Tony, Joyce and the children were united in a next-door-garden-tidying project at Rye. A day of apple-tree-pruning and bonfire-tending did not need to be improved on when Joyce used it for 'Mrs Miniver': it really was as idyllic as a typical Miniver day. 'Constructive destruction is one of the most delightful employments in the world, and in civilised life the opportunities for it are all too rare.' Sitting up in the branches, Joyce/Mrs Miniver watched as the two eldest children raced snails up the gate-posts and the youngest made an elaborate entanglement with twigs and cotton over some newly

The Maxtone Grahams in the school holidays, 1939

sown grass, and regretted only that 'circumstances had never led her to discover that the way to spend the spring was up an apple tree, in daily intimacy with its bark, leaves and buds'. Tony/Clem handed her up a glass of beer.

'We've made a lot of difference today,' he said. 'You can almost see the shape of the trees.'

'I suppose', said Mrs Miniver between gulps, 'the brambles would try to make out that the apple-trees had been practising encircle-ment.'

'That reminds me,' said Clem. 'We ought to be getting home pretty soon if we don't want to be late for the news.'

The stabs of Hitler-induced anxiety were becoming more fre-quent, for the Maxtone Grahams as for the Minivers. But Joyce's naïve optimism carried on. In a *Times* leader of 18 July, she was still saying, 'During the War – we must on no account allow ourselves to get into the habit of referring to it as "the previous war" . . .'

'Worked at Bloomsbury House, 2.30–8': Joyce was the kind of

person who put some of her nobler achievements into her engagement book after they had happened, so that she could flick back with pride. Bloomsbury House, in Great Russell Street, was one of the headquarters of the Jewish Refugee Committee: in a slow queue, German, Austrian and central European refugees made their way to the desk for a small weekly hand-out of money, a square meal, help with financial paperwork, and advice about employment. Joyce was drawn to Bloomsbury House, haunted almost to the point of obsession by the arriving Jews and longing to help them in some way. The man behind the desk in the Financial Guarantees office was her friend Sheridan Russell, cellist, Jew, and do-gooder, with whom she had made friends at the clothing depot. Sheridan-Christ, she soon came to call him, for not only did he work tirelessly and unpaid at Bloomsbury House; he also introduced her to the man she was to love.

Tony and Joyce drove up the Great North Road to Cultoquhey in time for the Twelfth of August. The cousins gathered, the nannies argued, boiled rabbit was served in the nursery, the children rode their bicycles on the gravel: all was as normal, and London seemed far away. But suddenly the black clouds were overhead. Neville Chamberlain made his broadcast to the grown-ups on Sunday morning, 3 September, and the grown-ups rephrased it to the children, telling them that war with Germany had broken out.

'To children,' wrote Joyce in 'Mrs Miniver', 'even more than to grown-ups (and this is at once a consolation and a danger), any excitement really counts as a treat, even if it is a painful excitement like breaking your arm, or a horrible excitement like seeing a car smash, or a terrifying excitement like playing hide-and-seek in the shrubbery at dusk. Mrs Miniver herself had been nearly grown-up in August 1914, but she remembered vividly how her youngest sister had exclaimed with shining eyes, "I say, I'm in a war!"'

With bombing expected, there was no going back to school in London. Jamie was at Gordonstoun, the school founded in 1934 by Kurt Hahn in a huge mansion in the far north of Scotland.

Joyce had sentimental feelings about Gordonstoun, partly because she had spent summers there with her cousin Ruth as a child, when they had smoked the butler's cigarettes and written poems sitting on gravestones; and partly because of Kurt Hahn, whom she hero-worshipped for being both Jewish and a scout: she imagined school life there would be one long knot-tying, camp-fire-lighting adventure. But Jamie, a highly intelligent, lazy and non-games-playing child, loathed the school. It was remote, it lacked kindred spirits, and the days consisted of a succession of physical discomforts, many involving cold water.

Janet and Robert were sent daily to Morrison's Academy in Crieff, with new uniforms and gas-masks. Joyce stayed in Perthshire for a fortnight to settle them in and returned to London on 23 September. It was turning into a childless city. Separated from her own children, she wrote with feeling in a *Times* leader:

> In many of the more well-to-do houses there may have been other valuables which had to be removed to the country or lodged in the bank. But in the poorest homes the children were the only treasure: and now that they are gone the parents must be feeling destitute indeed. Some of them, looking at an empty cot, a stray slipper, a doll lying face-downwards on the floor, may be tempted to think that the burden of anxiety which has been lifted from their minds by the evacuation was almost easier to bear than the burden of silence and loneliness which succeeded it. It is astonishing how loud a noise children can make simply by not being there; and how large a table for six can seem when there are only two to sit at it.

Her instinct, as a wartime writer and later lecturer, was to console: to focus on small inspiring sights, and renew her readers' or audiences' faith in the fundamental benignness of the world. But she no longer felt able to write her 'Mrs Miniver' pieces in the serene essay style. In peacetime, the thoughts of Mrs Miniver about windscreen-wipers or tree pruning or doorknobs were all very well; but now, with the black-outs, the evacuations and the genuine fear of death in the air, exquisite prose poems no longer seemed apposite. She changed to the epistolary style, and wrote to an imaginary sister-in-law: 'Dear Susan . . . With love, yours ever, Caroline.' These letters are less good, as writing, than the earlier essays. It is as if Elizabeth Bennett had stepped out of *Pride and Prejudice* and started chatting on the telephone: the gossipiness jars. The essence of the pleasure of the earlier essays lay in the way one was distanced from Mrs Miniver by the third-person narrative, while gaining intimate access to her thoughts. In letter form, some of her mystery is lost and she becomes just an unusually observant, talkative female.

But as bits of bracing journalism which in November and December 1939 made *Times* readers sit up straight, the Miniver letters were good. 'It oughtn't to *need* a war to make a nation paint its kerbstones white, carry rear-lamps on its bicycles, and give all its slum children a holiday in the country. And it oughtn't to need a war to make us talk to each other in buses, and invent our own amusements in the evenings, and live simply, and eat sparingly, and recover the use of our legs, and get up early enough to see the sun rise. However, it *has* needed one: which is about the severest criticism our civilization could have.'

She found endless things to be uplifting about: the nice 'damp jutey smell' of sandbags, and the sight of people sitting on them eating sandwiches; the way London was beginning to look and sound like a country town, with its tinkle of bicycle bells and clopping of hoofs; the cheerful brightness of white clothes; the way people's figures were improving through exercise; the beauty of buildings' silhouettes in the moonlight of the black-out, and the enhancement of the sense of touch, when you clutched hold of railings which you couldn't see; the singing of the barrage balloon cables which made you feel you were 'going to sleep on a ship at anchor, with the sound of wind in the rigging'; the way Londoners were learning to carry gas masks with panache, as if they were going off to a picnic with a box of special food.

But there were two things Caroline Miniver missed:

The first is golden windows. It used to be so lovely, that hour after the lamps were lit and before the curtains were drawn, when you could catch glimpses into other people's lives as you walked along the street: a kitchen table with a red cloth and a fat cook writing a letter, laboriously; or a ground-floor sitting-room, very spick and span, full of obvious wedding presents, with a brand-new wife, rather touching and self-important, sitting sewing, her ears visibly tuned for the sound of a latch-key; or an old man by the fire, doing a crossword, with an empty afternoon behind him and an empty evening in front. And occasionally, by great luck, a dining-room with a child's birthday party going on; a ring of lighted candles round the cake and a ring of lighted faces round the table; one face brighter than all the others, like a jewel on the ring. But now all this is gone. Houses slip straight from day to night, with tropical suddenness.

The other thing I miss, terribly, is children. Not only my own – I do at least see them (and plenty of others) at weekends: but children in general, as an ingredient of the town's population, a sort of leaven. It may be different in some parts of London, but certainly round here they have acquired rarity interest. They used to be daisies and are now bee-orchises. One looks round with a lift of pleasure on hearing a child's voice in a bus . . .

The reason why Mrs Miniver saw 'plenty of other' children at weekends was that the Minivers had taken in seven 'tough, charming' evacuees at Starlings. 'To tell you the truth [gushes Mrs Miniver], I think Mrs Downce [the housekeeper] is delighted to have some Cockney voices in the house. It makes her feel at home in Darkest Kent. She had quite a Dr-Livingstone-I-presume expression on her face when she welcomed them in.'

Mrs Miniver is scathing about a grand lady she meets who insists on having only 'really nice children' as evacuees. Snobbishness about evacuees is one of Mrs Miniver's bugbears.

But Tony and Joyce were not asked to take in any evacuees at *their* country cottage. It was too near the coast to be officially regarded as safe. The closest they came to evacuees was seeing those from the Glasgow slums who were housed in a stable-block at Cultoquhey. Joyce was preaching, in 'Mrs Miniver', what she was not able to practise in real life. In the matter of evacuees, the saintly Mrs Miniver was an idealized Joyce.

On 26 October 1939, the book *Mrs Miniver* was published.

Covered in what looked like spare-room wallpaper ('a gay binding', said the Chatto advertisement), it came in its own slip-case, the perfect present, for 7s. 6d. It contained only one of the wartime Miniver letters: apart from the last five pages, all was pre-war.

The book was widely and favourably reviewed, but two famous authors were scathing. E. M. Forster wrote at length in the *New Statesman*:

> What answer can the villagers make to a lady who is so amusing, clever, observant, broadminded, shrewd, demure, Bohemian, happily-married, triply-childrened, public-spirited and at all times such a lady? No answer, no answer at all. They listen to her saying the right things, and are dumb. They watch her doing the right things in the right way, and are paralysed. Even if they disgrace themselves by spluttering smut in her hearing, she is not put out, for the class to which she belongs has grown an extra layer of thickness of skin in the last thirty years. 'Touchée!' she would exclaim, with her little ringing laugh, and pass on untouched.

(No one, in the book, ever splutters smut in the direction of Mrs Miniver. Where did Forster get this from, and why? 'He is a cock-eyed intellectual,' wrote Barrington Ward in a consoling letter to Joyce, 'full of internal distortions and disorders.') Forster continued:

> There is something the little lady has not got – some grace or grandeur, some fierce eccentricity, some sense of ancient lineage or broad acres lost through dissipation. She may be able to give chapter and verse for a distinguished ancestry, but distinction does not course in her blood. She has her own style, but she has not Style . . . Her shabby old car, her unsnobbishness in living only in Kent, are deftly exploited, and serve to snub another lady who has smarter cars and lives in Gloucestershire. But dinginess is a dangerous weapon. It may break in the hand if used carelessly.

Then he discussed the class to which Mrs Miniver did, he thought, belong:

It is a class of tradesmen and professional men and little Government officials . . . and we who belong to it still copy the past. The castles and the great mansions are gone, we have to live in semi-detached villas instead, they are all we can afford, but let us at all events retain a Tradesman's Entrance. The Servants' Hall has gone; let the area basement take its place. The servants are unobtainable, yet we still say 'How like a servant!' when we want to feel superior and safe.

(To which Joyce replied, in her first lecture about *Mrs Miniver*, given at the Mayfair bookshop Heywood Hill: 'Now I don't deny that I have heard that sort of remark made – though just as often by the "top drawer" as by the "top-drawer-but-one". But I myself would never dream of making it, nor would "Mrs Miniver". And if Mr Forster himself has ever made it, then all I can say is that he is not the man I took him for, and all his books must have been written by Francis Bacon.') Forster ended his review:

Just as Gloucestershire and Kent have become alike, so will England, Germany, Russia, and Japan become alike. Internationalism, unavowed or avowed, is a cert. Bloodstained or peaceful, it is coming. As it looms on the eastern horizon, the little differences of the past lose their colour, and the carefully explored English temperament seems in particular scarcely worth the bother that has been taken over interpreting it.

(Down the margin of which, in her collected edition of Forster's essays, Joyce scribbled 'Balls'.) If Mr Forster's prophecies were correct (and Joyce didn't believe they were), it was the best justification one could have for writing a book like *Mrs Miniver*. If things were going to disappear, whether they were wild flowers or duck-billed platypuses, it was doubly important to write about them. Forster (said Joyce in her lecture) seemed to be confusing class-consciousness with class hostility.

Class-consciousness is not in itself a bad thing, any more than any other kind of consciousness. On the whole, there is far too little consciousness in the world. No; what matters is what use people make afterwards of the impressions which their senses have collected. There is no harm whatever in noticing that one class pours out the tea first and puts the milk in second, while another class makes a point of doing the exact opposite. The harm only begins when one member of the former class says to another, 'What sort of girl is it that Maud's boy's goin' to marry?' and the second one replies, 'My dear, quite impossible – she puts the milk in first.'

Rosamond Lehmann wrote a vitriolic review in the *Spectator*:

Mrs Miniver is, we know, secure in the hearts of the majority of her public; and I must be taken as speaking only for a minority, upon whom she exercises an oppression of spirits which, since it is caused by such a charming person, appears at first sight due to mere jealousy and spite. Yet surely it is odd that anyone so tactful, kind, tolerant, popular, humorous and contented, should arouse such low feelings, even in the ever-dissatisfied minority? And then, if one happens to dislike the spectacle of so much success, why not simply ignore it, and turn away? Why read, as one must, with exasperation, the column she has with such modest triumph made her own? Why does one look out for her next appearance with such feelings as the deserving poor must entertain for the local Lady Bountiful, or the inmates of a Borstal Institute for a certain kind of official visitor?

As a fortnightly column in *The Times*, Mrs Miniver had lived quietly in the minds and hearts of her readers. Now, dressed up in her gay binding in a book-in-a-box, she seemed fair game for mockery. 'She is always so smug, so right, such a marvellous manager,' wrote M. F. Savory of Worthing in a letter to *The Times*.

It would be so much more helpful if Mrs Miniver would tell us how she would behave if her husband had an affair with a pretty ARP worker, if her son refused to join up, and if some of the workers at the hospital supply depot rose up in revolt and told the lady exactly where she got off. No, I think the only thing for Mrs Miniver is a direct hit from a bomb, and I am certain that within a month Clem would marry again a young and pretty, untidy woman, who never said or did the correct thing, and they would be enormously happy, and so should I.

Joyce sought revenge in small ways. Competition No. 512 in the *New Statesman* of 16 December was to write a parody of one of a choice of authors, including 'Jan (Mrs Miniver) Struther'. Joyce sent in an entry, under a pseudonym. It began, 'Curious, thought Mrs Miniver, pensively nibbling a *langue-de-chat* . . .', and it won.

Sir [wrote Joyce to the editor of the *New Statesman*], I am afraid I must plead guilty to a slight deception. When I saw the announcement of your competition, I felt pretty sure that I could write a far crueller satire on 'Mrs Miniver' than could any of my detractors. I therefore tried my hand at it, and sent in the result over the name of my friend, Miss K. Watkins. As I seem to have succeeded beyond my wildest hopes, and as my close connection with Mrs Miniver precludes me from accepting the prize, I have no choice but to reveal myself.

Would you be so good as to send the prize to the competitor who was next in order of merit – or, if you would prefer, to the Association for the Relief of Distressed Gentlewomen?

Jan Struther

The vitriol helped the sales: 6,500 copies of *Mrs Miniver* were sold in the first eight weeks. Though she was hurt by the sarcasm and loathing, Joyce distanced herself by nursing the thought that she herself was not Mrs Miniver, and was indeed becoming less like Mrs Miniver every day.

Jewish refugees in their hundreds shuffled towards the Financial Guarantees desk at Bloomsbury House, their gait suggesting hearts broken, their brows suggesting university degrees. So why Sheridan Russell picked out one of these refugees and beckoned him to the front of the queue no one – not even Russell himself – quite knew. There was something about his face.

Adolf Placzek, the man in the queue, trembled with fright at the moment of this beckoning. Having spent the last twelve months in Nazi Vienna trying not to be noticed, he had learned to dread, more than anything, being singled out by a man behind a desk. But he went, as bidden. He was asked questions.

'Are you a poet?'

'Yes .'

'Also interested in the arts, and music?'

'Yes .'

'It's all in your face. There's not much I can do now, but I might be able to get you occasional work as a tutor.'

Then he took Dolf back to his place in the queue.

A few days later, Joyce asked Sheridan if he knew of anyone who could help her to improve her German.

Dolf had arrived in London in March 1939, virtually penniless and with a single suitcase. He had been born in Vienna in 1913. His grandfather had been Grand Rabbi of Moravia, a scientist, poet and ornithologist who corresponded with Darwin. Dolf's father died in the Spanish influenza epidemic of 1918, and his mother, Pauly, married Fritz Eisler, a distinguished X-ray physician who had severely damaged his hands through using an X-ray machine without wearing lead gloves. Dolf's childhood in the highly respectable Neunte Bezirk of Vienna consisted of piano lessons, violin lessons, Latin and Greek lessons, lessons in German poetry, and hours spent at his desk in the evenings after school. When he was fifteen, in 1929, Joyce was within a mile of him during her sulky visit to Vienna.

If Dolf, at the piano, stopped practising his examination piece and began to experiment with chords, his stepfather would tell him to get on with his practice. 'Mucking about at the piano' had its own word, *klimpern* ('jingle, jangle, clink, chink, tinkle'). Dolf longed to *klimpern*.

When he was eighteen he was summoned to his stepfather's study.

'You have been accepted at medical school, and you are to start in September.'

'But I don't want to be a medical student. I want to be an art historian.'

'That's enough for tonight.'

That was the end of the argument. For three years, Dolf went to medical school. Each evening for three years, he sat at the same supper-table as his stepfather, in silence. Dolf had never failed an exam at his *Gymnasium*; but at medical school he

Dolf in Vienna, at his studies

failed every one. He had no aptitude for medicine; and he was squeamish about surgery. One of his early 'practicals', on a cadaver, was a simple appendectomy. Dolf was told that he had 'killed' his 'patient' in fourteen different ways, and still hadn't managed to get the appendix out.

After nine terms of exam-failure, Dolf was allowed to give up medicine and begin a History of Art course at Vienna University. He flourished. The history of art, and particularly of architecture, fascinated him He read widely and studied deeply. He fell in love with a poet, Maria Santifaller. But the atmosphere of anti-Semitism was beginning to cast a shadow over his hopes. Three days after the Nazis marched into Vienna in March 1938, Jews were declared to be no longer members of the University. Dolf was summoned into the Director's office. 'There will be a way for you, but not here. I wish you well.'

Maria, a non-Jew, could have betrayed Dolf but did not. She said they should run away together, to Michigan. But how to get out? Dolf's passport had been renewed: 'Deutsches Reich', it now said; there was large inky 'J' on the front page, and a photograph of a persecuted-looking man in glasses. For the next few months Dolf queued at one consulate after another, trying to get a visa. A rich old lady friend in New York, Anne de Tapla, who was half-mad, turned out to be the key to freedom. She sent an affidavit to Vienna which got Dolf and his mother and sister Susan a place on the waiting-list for the United States. With this, Dolf could now get a transit visa for England: 'Good for one journey only.' Before leaving Vienna he went round his old apartment in the Wasagasse taking photographs of the corner of the drawing-room, his desk, the cook in the kitchen, the favourite tea service – all his familiar surroundings – in case he should never see them again.

His sister Susan arrived in London in the autumn of 1938 and found a job as a nurse at a Quaker hospital. Dolf arrived in March 1939, a year after the *Anschluss*, with his cousins Ernst and Franz Philipp, who had also managed to get out. They found lodgings in a seedy attic room at 100 Denbigh Street, Pimlico, and they queued at Bloomsbury House. Thanks to Sheridan Russell, Dolf soon got a part-time job there as an

Farewell photographs of Dolf's Viennese home

interpreting clerk. In the evenings the three cousins walked the streets, for mile after mile. During the lonely London weekends, uprooted and under-occupied, they sat in their room tearing one another's poetry apart.

Their landlady, Mme Luhn, was a kind-hearted former Madam who insulted her lodgers while ladling them bowlfuls from great vats of *pot-au-feu*. One evening after supper, when the cousins were sitting upstairs as usual, scorning one another's use of cloud-imagery, Mme Luhn called up the stairwell: 'Monsieur Placzek. Le téléphone.' Dolf trembled again. He ran down four flights.

'Hello, you won't know me. I'm Joyce Maxtone Graham, a friend of Sheridan Russell's, and he gave me your number because he said you might be interested in giving German lessons.'

They arranged to meet outside Lyon's Corner House in the Strand, at 4.30 on Tuesday, 21 November. 'I'm very small,' said Joyce, 'and I'll be carrying a white gas-mask.' 'Placek, 4.30' she wrote in her engagement book, spelling his name wrong. (Later, in the United States, Dolf was careful to emphasize the 'cee-zee', as he learned to call it, in the middle. The name is pronounced 'Plah-chek'.)

They met; and so strong was the instant attraction that neither of them could eat their rock cake. 'I don't feel too

good in my stomach,' Dolf said. 'We don't call it "stomach"',
said Joyce. 'We might possibly call it "tummy".' 'Pardon?' Dolf
needed to learn the social subtleties of English, she noticed,
as much as she needed to improve her German. He told her
he had learned his colloquial English on an exchange visit
to Ramsgate in 1935. Joyce advised him at once to 'forget
Ramsgate'.

Dolf was a foot taller and thirteen years younger than Joyce.
She was in love with the idea of him before their initial encounter: being Jewish, Viennese, twenty-six and recommended by
Sheridan Russell, he could hardly fail to fascinate her. As soon
as they met, they both felt an overwhelming sense that they
were (as they later called it) 'one river'. It was not a case of irresistible cheekbones: Dolf did not have film-star good looks.
Joyce described his face as 'tragic-humorous': the nose was
large, the forehead wide, the smile neither sardonic nor sleek
but boyishly uncontrolled, the eyes hidden behind round spectacles, the gestures gawky. If Dolf needed to scratch his right
temple, he brought his left arm over the top of his head and
reached down to the itch. But he had immense sex appeal, and
Jan's string of scurrying thoughts at the moment of their
meeting might have run like this: tall, thick black hair, couldn't
be less like Tony, lean, young, hands of a pianist, Viennese
accent exuding high intellect and high passion, only pleased by
the finest things in life, but intensely and sensually pleased by
them.

Feeling light-headed, unhungry, and already at home in one
another's company, they read the notice-board outside the
National Gallery. 'Concert, 5.30 today.' 'Let's go in,' said Joyce.
She had already been to one of the new Myra Hess National
Gallery concerts: Mrs Miniver, in her letter of 16 October, had
described it:

All sorts of people, young and old, smart and shabby, in uniform and
out of it, soldiers, nurses, Salvation Army girls, typists, office-boys,
old ladies with ear-trumpets, and a few of the regular 'musicals'
with coiled plaits. A few were there, perhaps, out of curiosity, but
most of them because they were suffering from a raging thirst for

music, and for some assurance of pattern in a jangled world. She played magnificently and thoughtfully, almost as if she were discovering – no, *un*covering – the music for the first time. Bach, Beethoven, Brahms – ironical, isn't it, how the world has to turn to the great Germans to find healing for the spiritual wounds inflicted by the ignoble ones? There were so many people in tears that it might have been a revivalist meeting. So it was in a way. And the curious thing was that everything she played seemed to have a kind of double loveliness, as though she had managed to distil into it all the beauty of the pictures that were missing from the walls.

This time, all Joyce said, as she and Dolf came down the steps after the concert, was 'Bach is so all-right-making, isn't he?' The compound adjective struck Dolf as perfect. 'Who is this magical creature,' he wondered, 'who can express what I have always thought about Bach but have never found the right words?'

The German lessons started at once, three times a week, at Halsey Street. The subjects discussed tended to be metre and botany. The daily letter-writing also began. Each wrote in the other's language: 'Lieber Herr Placzek!,' 'Dear Mrs Graham'. Joyce wrote on 'Mrs A. Maxtone Graham' postcards, and Dolf, in italic handwriting which spoke of years steeped in Goethe, on torn-out sheets from a Pimlico stationer's pad.

Joyce, on Christmas Eve, from Rye: 'Anne Talbot ist gestern abend angekommen. Jetzt spielen sie alle Golf (Anne, mein Mann, Jamie und Janet). Um vier Uhr werden wir den "Messiah" auf dem Rundfunk zuhören. Heute nacht die drei Kindern werden die Strümpfe aufhängen. Leider kann ich nach London diese Woche nicht fahren. Meine nächste deutsche Stunde muss deshalb im Jahre 1940 sein!'*

Dolf: 'The refugees – I can recognise them in the street at the first glance. I shun them whenever I can. I never suffered more

---

* 'Anne Talbot came yesterday evening. Now they are all playing golf (Anne, my husband, Jamie and Janet). At four o'clock we are going to listen to the "Messiah" on the wireless. Tonight the three children are going to hang up their stockings. Sadly I can't come to London this week. My next German lesson will therefore have to be in 1940.'

than when I was a clerk at the Bloomsbury House, not even in Germany. There one could show courage, dignity, heroism. Now, in safety, free (while the less agile and lucky who have not been able to get out slowly die at home) – what remains? Outside the petty financial misery, and inside aimless emptiness. Dante was right who said that the worst what can happen to a human mind is exile.'

The tone could not have been more different from one of Tony's letters. Here was raw emotion, sadness examined head-on.

On Christmas Eve, the three Viennese cousins were sitting in the attic as usual when the doorbell rang. It was the postman, and he handed over a large parcel addressed to Herrn Placzek and Philipp: 'With all best wishes for Christmas, from Joyce.' It was a basket of peaches. Peaches in winter! The symbolism was not lost on the three poets. The attic room seemed suddenly full of the warmth of a Mediterranean country, of abundance, indulgence, and hope. They ate some of the peaches, and got to work incorporating the event into their verses.

The first days of 1940 were dark and cold. Joyce was with her family at Rye, writing postcards to Dolf by the fire. She said how dangerous it was to make new friendships in a world where separation and death were becoming commonplace: you laid yourself open to the risk of severe pain. Dolf sent her some of his poems. They discovered they had used the same images, almost word for word, in poems they had written before they met. 'Dear, dear Dolf,' wrote Joyce on 13 January, breaking into English, 'This becomes more and more extraordinary, and almost uncanny. All poets, perhaps, come from the same springs in the same mountain, but occasionally two of them seem to come from the identical spring, and that is what has happened here. It is not as though we can have been influenced by reading the same lyrics in our childhood. I give it up – it is a riddle.'

Janet and Robert, still being kept away from London, started at Rye Grammar School. Joyce returned to London, through snowdrifts, to take Jamie to the overnight train for Gordonstoun. London was white with snow. The school train left at 7.30

on Thursday 18 January; and in the hours afterwards Dolf and Joyce became lovers.

'Ich bin sehr schläftig,' wrote Joyce to Dolf the next day, 'und voll von einer Süsse, friedliche, traümende Glück. Ich habe dich lieb, und ich freue mich dass wir bald wieder zusammen sein werden.'*

Writing in German made Joyce feel it wasn't quite Joyce Maxtone Graham who was writing. It was akin to the pleasantly guiltless feeling of spending foreign currency: you could convince yourself that it wasn't quite real, and that you would not have to suffer the consequences.

But within days, the implications began to weigh on their hearts. If you fell in love with a man on a waiting-list for a visa for the United States, the 'severe pain' of parting wasn't a risk, it was an inevitability. 'Ours is "eine Schiffskameradschaft",' Joyce wrote to Dolf, a friendship between two people thrown together on board ship, who would have to part when it docked. They must remember this; they must not depend on each other's presence. As soon as Dolf got his visa for the United States, he would have to leave the country. After months of losing sleep over not getting a visa, Dolf was now losing sleep over getting one.

For someone as susceptible to mood swings as Joyce, the situation was precarious. Elated, dancing on air, she would make her way from Halsey Street to 113 Cheyne Walk, where she and Dolf met on their 'Zusammentage' – their days together while Tony was in his office or playing golf at Rye. Her friend Charles Spencer had lent them a room, overlooking the river. It became 'their' room, and all the sounds outside – the tugs hooting (as they had in Mrs Miniver's hearing), the houseboats lapping, the evening newspaper-seller chanting the war headlines – were for ever after associated in their minds with these days of intense secret happiness. Their hours together, Joyce wrote later, were 'full of the sweet flowing interchange of thoughts and feelings, which is the mainspring of our rare relationship:

---

* 'I am very sleepy, and full of a sweet, peaceful, dreamy happiness. You are close to my heart, and I'm glad that we will be together soon.'

physical love-making, though the most ecstatic and satisfying that I have ever had, is between us only the overflow from a deep lake.' They walked together in the early evenings, over the bridge to Battersea Park, or along the river to a National Gallery concert, trying to live in the present moment.

Joyce would return to Rye by train, writing to Dolf on the journey. The children would be waiting for her; she hugged them; they had supper together, chatting about school. She and Tony sat by the fire afterwards, late into the evening. Joyce switched the wireless on and tuned it to the Home Service. Beethoven's 'Archduke' trio sent her into a reverie. She was with Dolf as she listened. She was divided into two, and she was full of a sense of foreboding. She had already known the guilt of an adulterous love affair. But she had never known the 'guillotine feeling' – the knowledge that at some moment in the near future the loved one would sail away and she would not see him again.

The guillotine began to hover over their meetings: Joyce found it impossible to banish it from her imagination. 'I wish I could live in the present like you,' she wrote to Dolf on 14 February. 'But I can't. When I love, especially, I need the future as a kind of sounding-box in which the sound of the present can ring clear. A present with no future, to me, has a muffled sound, as though one struck a bell in a box. Anyway, I will try, on Saturday, to forget that there is not an unlimited vista of Saturdays stretching before us . . .'

On that next Saturday Joyce made excuses to be away from Rye – an article to finish at *The Times* – and she and Dolf went to Brighton together, where they were snapped by a street photographer as they squinted in the south-coast glare: spring lovers enjoying a stroll. As Europe began to fall apart around them, they stole what private happiness they could. When she found herself with an unexpected free day, Joyce sent Dolf a telegram saying when and where to meet. There were wartime regulations against using foreign words in telegrams, so instead of writing 'Deine J.' at the end, she wrote 'Dinah J'. From that day on, she signed her letters to him 'Immer deine kleine Dinah'.

Taken by a street photographer in Brighton

Dolf's visa for the United States arrived on 28 April. (His mother had managed to escape from Vienna, and had sailed to New York the month before.) He secured a passage on a ship to New York which would leave from Liverpool on 29 May. On hearing the dreaded date, Joyce lay awake for most of the night. 'Ich bin um 6 Uhr aufgewacht, so voll Verlangen und Begierde fur dich, dass ich fast in Flammen war. Ach, Gott, wie verliebt bin ich in Dir . . .'*

On their last day together, they took photographs of each other on a bench in Battersea Park. 'My sweetest beloved darling,' wrote Dolf, after the final goodbye, 'Now this first day is over, which was so sad, so hopeless, that I didn't write even. I don't know how I spent it, only that I sat at the piano and played again and again "Auld Lang Syne", and "Comin' through the rye" and "Ach, wie ist's möglich denn" . . .'

Joyce did not go to Liverpool with Franz Philipp and Dolf's sister to see him off. She wrote a letter to him instead, addressed to the hostel in New York where he would be staying. Franz was glad she had not gone to Liverpool: 'It was an awful crowd of refugees there,' he wrote to her in his broken English, 'much crying and oriental gesturing, as we called it. Suzy was very, very brave. Only a little sobbing when we stepped the platform back. Really, it was very good you weren't there. It makes everyone miserable.'

Dolf was gone. Again, Joyce was divided in two. Half of her, crushed and exhausted by the loss, wanted to die.

There's no way of knowing
What like the day will be,
The day he must be going,
My true love, from me.

There's no way of knowing
(And it's little I shall care)
If the wind will be blowing
Or the sun shining fair.

But oh, I'm praying only
That the tide may be low
When I stand there lonely
To watch my true love go.

* 'I woke up at 6 o'clock, so full of longing and desire for you that I was almost on fire. Oh, God, how I love you . . .'

For then, as I wander
Back across the strand,
I'll see a while longer
His footprints in the sand.

The tide, inward creeping,
Will steal them one by one,
And I'll not start weeping
Till the last of them is gone.

But there, where it vanished,
I'll lay my body down,
And cry, 'My true love's banished:
Christ, let me drown.'

But the other half – the optimistic Mrs Miniver half – wanted to live, and do good, and see justice done. 'It does seem a little hard, I must say,' says Mrs Miniver's friend Agnes Lingfield over coffee in Sloane Street, in one of the last 'Miniver' letters, 'that one should have been unlucky enough to live in a time like this.'

'Good old Agnes, how she clarifies one's feelings,' writes Mrs Miniver – and this is Joyce speaking. 'Till that moment I had not realized how passionately I felt that I would not live in any other time if you paid me. I didn't say so; after all, the coffee was on her. But when I left her I found myself crossing the street with particular care, because it would be so awful to get run over just now and not be there to see what was going to happen.'

Part Two

Chapter Eight

You need not envy lovers who are never apart:
For not in the pin-point starry conflagration
Of touch or kiss
Deepest contentment is,
But in the memory of delight, and its anticipation –
The interstellar spaces of the heart.

'You Need Not Envy', from *The Glass-Blower*

CONNOISSEURS OF THE film *Mrs Miniver* will remember that on the night Dunkirk fell to the Germans, 7 June 1940, Clem Miniver (played by Walter Pidgeon) was woken by a telephone call in the middle of the night. 'What? Uh? Oh, emergency, I see . . . I'll be right over.' It is River Patrol, summoning him for duty. Yawning in his white monogrammed pyjamas, he gets out of his single twin bed and Mrs Miniver (played by Greer Garson) gets out of hers. 'Sandwiches. Thermos. If you're going out on night duty you'll need them.'

Clem goes down to the village pub, which has been opened especially, and finds it full of mystified men in mackintoshes. 'I say, Miniver,' says one. 'What d'you make of it? I'm willing to do anything for my country, but this digging us out of bed at two in the morning – it's taking the war a bit far, don't you think?'

They are instructed to go to Ramsgate and await further announcements. We see fifty little ships chugging along in the darkness and arriving at what looks like a medieval town, with smoking chimneys, a church on a hillside, and a twin-turreted tower on the bridge. The scene was shot early in 1942, six thousand miles away from Ramsgate. The 'little ships' were models.

'Attention, please! Attention, please!' An amplified voice speaks to the waiting men from a naval vessel. 'Switch off engines. As you know, the British Expeditionary Force is trapped between the enemy and the sea. Four hundred thousand men are crowded on the beaches, under bombardment from artillery and planes. Their only chance to escape annihilation rests with you. Your destination is Dunkirk . . .'

Kay Miniver – for that is her MGM name – cannot sleep. She comes downstairs at half-past five in the morning, nudging the hands of the grandfather clock forward ten minutes as she passes them on the stairs. (This is one of the motifs of the film which mark it as the work of the great and perfectionist director William Wyler. Wyler had a fixation about clock hands. He grew up in Alsace during the First World War, in a village which was captured and recaptured many times. When the Germans marched in they moved the clock hands to Berlin time; when the French recaptured, they moved them back to Paris time. After a while, Alsatian children believed that battles were only about time.)

In the undergrowth of her blooming Kentish garden, Mrs Miniver sees a uniformed Nazi lying asleep, wounded. There is a pistol beside him on the grass. He must be the escaped German flyer Clem was talking about yesterday. He stirs as she is trying to remove his pistol, and forces her at gunpoint towards her house. 'Move, or make noise, I shoot.'

In the kitchen he demands food and milk, which he wolfs, and spills down his front. On Greer Garson's face terror is blended to perfection with motherly concern for the German's wounded arm. (William Wyler used to insist on as many takes as it needed to get this kind of thing right.) The milkman goes by, whistling 'With the tow-row-row-row-row-row-row of the British Grenadiers.' The flyer points his gun at Mrs Miniver.

Then he collapses. Mrs Miniver calls the police. He regains consciousness, and Mrs Miniver gives him a cool flannel for his neck. 'You'll be much better off in hospital,' she says. 'Really. You'll be well looked after.'

'I may be finished. But others vill come,' says the flyer, in a spitting German accent. 'Ve vill bomb your cities, like

Barcelona, Warsaw, Narvik, Rotterdam. Rotterdam ve destroy in two hours.'

'Thousands were killed,' says Mrs Miniver. 'Innocent—'

'Not innocent! Zey were against us! Tirty tousand in two hours! And ve vill do ze same here.'

The police car arrives, and the flyer is led away. 'Mummy! Who was that, Mummy?' Toby comes downstairs in his dressing-gown, the picture of innocence and sweetness.

It is the most unsubtly anti-German scene of the film. In the early stages, when shooting was being scheduled, Louis B. Mayer wanted to cut it. 'We don't make hate movies,' he said. He was horrified by the idea of offending any country which might buy the film. Wyler, an unashamedly anti-Nazi, war-mongering director, wanted to keep the scene in. He got his way: within a fortnight of the start of principal photography, war had been declared between Germany and the United States, and Mayer relaxed his rules. Mrs Miniver, the perfect wife and mother, would after all come face to face with malignant Nazism in her own kitchen.

If Louis B. Mayer had known what the supposed original 'Mrs Miniver' – Jan Struther – was doing the night Dunkirk fell, he would have been surprised. Joyce was in a drawing-room in Edinburgh, singing madrigals. Tony was in London after a day at the office, Jamie was at Gordonstoun, and Janet and Robert were lodging with friends in Berkshire.

The drawing-room was that of Tony's sister and brother-in-law Ysenda and Pat Smythe, whose company was balm for the bereft Joyce. She could not tell them her secret, but she needed to escape to Edinburgh to stay with them, in their plain, draughty spare bedroom on the top floor of 38 Heriot Row. They were frugal, and good. Ysenda had been a nurse in France in the First World War and later became a policewoman in this one. Pat was a Bach-loving lawyer with a good tenor voice who knitted his own knickerbocker stockings. 'It was a beautiful warm light midsummer evening,' Joyce wrote later; 'the windows were wide open and the scent of red hawthorn came floating in from the gardens on the other side of the granite-setted street. We sat round, happy and absorbed, completely at one, weaving anew in the air patterns of sound which were three or four hundred years old. I remember thinking, suddenly, "This is what we are fighting for." And when we finally stopped, my brother-in-law said, "I've just realised – I haven't thought about the news for three hours." Nor had any of us.'

As she sang 'Adieu, sweet Amaryllis' and 'Draw on, sweet night', Joyce was singing for civilization. She was also, in her deepest heart, singing for Dolf, who was at that moment crossing the Atlantic, moving further and further away from her by the minute. Beautiful music always had the effect of making her feel he was in the room with her. She was not a good sight-reader, and relied heavily on her co-soprano sister-in-law for her entries; but for civilization, and for Dolf, she persevered. Later in the evening she sat up writing to him, shoring up pillows between her spine and the iron bedstead. She wrote in English: the time had come, she decided, to drop the German veil. The letter was addressed to a refugee hostel at 611 West 114th Street, Manhattan, and marked 'personal'.

The imminent invasion of Britain was on everyone's lips, as the Germans drew closer and closer to Paris. Every precaution was being taken, and one of these was the systematic wiping-out of place-names on signposts across Britain. Joyce – always apt to focus on the minute consequences of national events – felt a pang of compassion for the imagined German parachutist (disguised as a commercial traveller) asking an English yokel for directions. She expressed this in a letter to *The Times* on 10 June, entitled 'Our Secret Weapon'. With tongue in cheek, she envisaged the following monologue from the mild-eyed farmer leaning on his hayfork, speaking to the bewildered invader:

'Clodborough Junction? Ah! Not Market Clodborough, or Nether Clodborough, or Clodborough Canonicorum? No? Oh, well, if the gent is quite certain it's Clodborough *Junction* he wants . . . Ah. Well, you go along this road for half a mile, or maybe three-quarters, and then there's a by-road on the right – but you don't take no notice of that. And then about a furlong further on there's a big tithe-barn on the left – but you don't take no notice of that neither: except that if so be as there's a chap with a wooden leg alongside of it, loading dung, you might just let him know as young Fred's home on leave and O.K. And then you take the second turn on the right (that is, the second if you don't count the little lane as goes down to Starvecrow, but the third, of course, if you do), and keep straight on past the Jolly Soldiers. (What? Lord bless you, no, it's just the name of a pub. And let me tell you, the draught bitter there is summat like; but they won't be open for another two hours.) Of course, if you want to save time, you can cross the stile just beyond the duckpond and go across the fields alongside Ribstone Wood. Only mind out for old Perigoe's bull in the Ten-Acre; he's a terror, especially when the flies 've been at him . . .'

But what is this? A rifle-shot rings out! The Local Defence Volunteers, having discovered the parachute, have had time to creep up silently behind the hedge. The *ersatz* commercial traveller lies prone upon the tarmac. The mild-eyed yokel goes on with his haymaking. Our secret weapon has triumphed once again.

It was all couched in hilarity and parody; but Joyce, again, was expressing what Britain was fighting for: the lovely ancient unliteralness of the Englishman in his fields and by-roads, threatened by an invasion of Nazi militarism and precision.

Also in the clarity of the Edinburgh spare bedroom, she wrote for *The Times* a leader in defence of the heart, which was published on 17 June, the day France capitulated. Readers could have had no inkling of how close to the writer's heart this anonymous leader was.

A girl in love was recently heard to say, 'I feel I ought to be ashamed of myself for being so happy'; and a woman whose child had just died wrote to a friend: 'I don't feel that I've even got the right to cry: one's own individual sorrows seem so unimportant nowadays compared with the vastness of the world tragedy.'

Both these opinions are understandable; yet both are based on the same profound mistake. World tragedy, or world triumph, is only an abstraction, a mosaic pattern made up of the individual joys and sorrows of countless human beings. These joys and sorrows are no less important in time of war than in time of peace; and indeed, in this particular war, they have acquired a heightened significance. For in this war, above all, we are fighting for the rights of the individual against the tyranny of the state machine. Whatever happens, we must not restrict our capacity for delight and grief. For this is the only thing that keeps us human among all the inhumanities of war; this is our life-line, which will one day haul us back again from these monster-haunted depths to the world of light and sanity which we used to know.

The Bishop of St Albans wrote a rapturous letter to *The Times*, thanking them for this leader: 'It is so sound, so healthy, so invigorating, so timely, and so Christian.'

It was the last article Joyce wrote for *The Times*, ever.

Dolf tried to keep a diary on board ship, as Joyce had said he should, but after the first day it didn't work. What was there to describe, apart from Nelson's shadow, glimpsed in the starless night as he had driven towards Euston, and the grey damp dawn in Liverpool, and his co-passengers on the ship, whom he didn't much feel like talking to? Joyce could always be jolly about things, and engage in fascinating conversation with strangers, but he didn't seem to have that gift. He found it more natural to sit in apathy in his cabin, not even writing poetry. He had left his homeland, he had left his new love; and his reputation in Vienna as a brilliant young art historian had been eradicated. In America, he would have to start all over again.

But at least he would see his mother. She had been lent a room in New York by Anne de Tapla, the benefactress who had sent the affidavit which made the journey possible.

Dolf arrived in Manhattan at dawn on Saturday, 15 June, with twenty dollars in his pocket. 'Welcome to the land of the free!' said a taxi-driver, lowering his window. 'Would you like a ride? I'll take you wherever you want for ten dollars!' Dazzled by the man's enthusiasm and his shining yellow car, Dolf accepted. 'Well, here you are! And a good day to you, sir,' said the driver, drawing up outside the apartment building where Dolf's mother was lodging. Dolf gave him ten dollars – a colossal sum, ten times what the ride should have cost – and walked into his mother's room. She was asleep.

'Mutti?'

'Ach, mein Gott!' said Pauly, waking up. She seemed more surprised than pleased to see him. She was not at all pleased when
he told her how much he had given the taxi-driver.

Pauly Eisler ('Pauly' was pronounced the Austrian way,
rhyming with 'Cowley') was an exquisitely-mannered Viennese
mother who had brought Dolf up strictly according to the rules
of Viennese etiquette: she had stood by while he struggled at
medical school for three years, because submitting to one's
husband's will was the done thing; and she had seen to it that
at twenty-three Dolf lost his virginity to a prostitute attuned to
the needs of the bourgeoisie, because it was the done thing. She
adored Dolf, and worried about him, fussing about him being
driven too fast in cars. In Vienna the family had had a maid and
a cook, and Pauly had rarely needed to enter her own kitchen.
Now, in New York, having lost all her possessions, she had
taken on a weekday job as a charwoman. She never revealed any
kind of self-pity.

Later, taking a bus this time, Dolf found his way to the
refuge hostel at West 114th Street. There, pinned to the notice
board in the hall, waiting for him, were three airmail letters
addressed to A. K. Placzek, all from Joyce. He opened them as
he stood there with his suitcase. Her loving voice, ringing
clearly out of her prose, gave him the courage to announce
himself to the porter. He was shown to his bed, which was in a
dormitory for six.

'Thank you for the letters – I was unspeakably glad to find
them when I arrived here,' he wrote to Joyce that evening. (It
was her first censored letter from him, 'opened by Examiner
5513'.) 'One can't be alone here for a minute or concentrate, the
house is full of noise, Jews and the smell of wet paint (because
Mrs Roosevelt will pay a visit next week, everybody cleans and
polishes the whole day). I think of you all the time, sweet
darling, and don't want to see anybody. But I will not lament
about individual things in a time when immortal nations break
down like putrefied trees and the hopes and lives of millions die
overnight . . .'

Joyce had given him one important telephone number, and

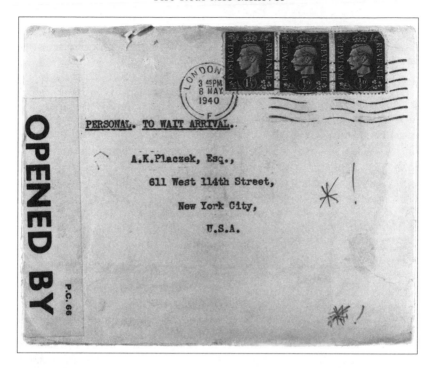

implored him to dial it as soon as he arrived in New York. It was that of Tony Maxtone Graham's other sister, Rachel Townsend, who was as extravagant as Ysenda was frugal, and who would, Joyce was sure, give him a warm welcome and pull strings to find him a job worthy of him. Dolf fumbled with the unfamiliar coins and rang her up, explaining that he was a friend of Joyce's.

'Do come to dinner, and do bring your mother,' said Rachel.

So Dolf and Pauly put on their best clothes and went to dinner with Tony's sister, at 1 Beekman Place, a grand apartment block near the East River. It was a strained evening. Rachel had no idea that her forlorn-looking guest was her brother's wife's adulterous lover: it struck Dolf that he was there under false pretences. A fellow guest sat playing the piano throughout the evening, and he was not, by any means, practising his Mozart: this was *klimpern* on the grand American scale, a medley of songs from the shows and jazzy chords, and it made Pauly feel jumpy. Rachel chatted away on the sofa, but she did not see Dolf through Joyce's eyes, as an attractive, brilliant art historian and musician. She saw him as a pitiful refugee whom Joyce must have picked up in the course of her good works. 'Mrs Townsend was very nice and very intelligent,' Dolf wrote to Joyce afterwards, 'but rather cool and not very interested in my fate as a whole (I can't blame her).'

Dolf found a job on his own, in Union Square, wrapping and sending parcels, some of which had to be insured and some of which had to be registered. His boss was an old east European Jew with a long beard and a wet cigar in his mouth. He didn't quite trust Dolf not to make a terrible mistake.

Joyce, cycling, on the day France fell, along hawthorn-scented lanes in Berkshire from Twyford Station to the house where Janet and Robert were staying, had no premonition that her life was about to change dramatically. She was living from hour to hour, as everyone was during that terrifying day. 'The Battle of France is over,' Winston Churchill was telling the House of Commons. 'I expect that the Battle of Britain is about to begin.'

She was fortified by a strong feeling – the belief, perhaps, of all separated lovers – that a star was watching over her and Dolf, bringing them the promise of reunion. And surely what happened in the next ten days was such a miracle that it could only have been achieved by the power of a benign star.

She was effectively being *sent* to New York.

It began with the New York publishers Harcourt Brace, who sent a telegram in early June to Chatto & Windus: 'Mrs Miniver Book of the Month Club Choice for September. Publication date 29 July.' The author's presence was requested, to help to promote the book.

Then Rachel Townsend, who like thousands of people in America wanted to do something to help the British in 1940, rang Tony and implored him to send the children over to America to stay with her for the duration of the war, with or without Joyce.

Then Tony himself left a telephone message for Joyce in Berkshire on 17 June: 'I think you should take Janet and Robert to New York as soon as possible.'

Finally Sir Frederick Whyte, head of the American Division of the Ministry of Information, summoned Joyce to a meeting on 19 June – a meeting now untraceable in the Public Record Office, so one can only guess what was said. The gist was that Joyce, if she were to undertake a lecture tour in the United States, representing Mrs Miniver, could play an effective role as a propagandist for Britain. Americans still isolationist after the horrors of the First World War needed to hear the viewpoint of an archetypal British wife and mother, now faced with total war.

Love plays havoc with priorities, and at this pivotal moment in Joyce's life the line between what she ought to do and what she wanted to do were blurred. Sail to America! Of course she jumped at the chance. Not only would she be reunited with Dolf – she would also be able to stretch her wings, constricted by years of country house visits and golfing weekends. She would be able to travel thousands of miles by train, through 'Ole Virginny' and Dixieland and the Wild West. The British Information Services *wanted* her to do this. Her duty and her heart's desire seemed, miraculously, to be one and the same.

Once the idea had taken hold of her imagination, there was no looking back: the magnetic force pulling her across the Atlantic was too strong. She was determined to go. Why should she stay? Tony would shortly be away on active service in the Army. In Britain, she would be just one more hungry mouth. She felt single-minded and confident as she queued, with Janet and Robert, at the American Embassy, the passport office, and the US Consulate. She was going because she had been sent. It was not her idea. No one could say it was. (But oh! Where would she first meet Dolf? By a lake in Central Park? On Broadway? Outside the Waldorf Astoria? Only a month before, they had said goodbye for ever.)

On Sunday, 23 June, Rachel Townsend invited Dolf for a drink at Beekman Place.

'You know, I had a cable from Tony today, saying that Joyce is bringing the children over here for a while. She's leaving England on Wednesday, and she'll be here in ten days' time.'

Dolf could hardly speak.

'Jan, darlingest,' he wrote that night. 'I just heard from Rachel Townsend that you might come over here with the children. I can hardly believe it – it's too wonderful for any words . . .'

Things were happening quickly now for Joyce. Jamie was allowed out from Gordonstoun to say goodbye, and arrived in London at midnight on 24 June, just before an air-raid warning. He was too old to be evacuated: he had another year to go at Gordonstoun, then he would be called up into the Army. The next day – her last day before sailing – Joyce took Jamie to a National Gallery concert (Mozart's violin sonata in C Major K296 became 'their' piece, ever afterwards), and Tony took Janet and Robert to Regent's Park Zoo. Janet and Robert, aged twelve and nine, could not know how long the impending separation would be: months, they supposed. No one guessed that it would be five years.

Tony and Jamie took them to the station to catch an early-morning train from Euston to Liverpool the next day. Now it was Joyce's turn to drive past Nelson's Column, Joyce's turn to experience the dampness of maritime Liverpool. Nannie came with them on the train, to see them safely onto the *Duchess of Atholl*. Two years before, during the evacuations of the Munich Crisis, when the children had asked 'Is Nannie coming with us?' the answer had been 'Yes': Nannie had been allowed to go with them to Wales. But this time the answer was 'No': Nannie was staying in Britain. Joyce knew only too well how devastating this separation from Nannie would be for Janet, and especially for Robert. And on board ship, for the first time in her life, she would be in sole charge of her children, for eight whole days.

Joyce had not had time to read her morning's mail before she left London: but now, on the train, she opened her letters. There was one from her friend Sheridan Russell which gave her a brutal shock. She expected – she needed – words of loving encouragement and farewell, but Sheridan had written: 'I am disappointed in you, that you should be running to your lover at this terrible moment for your country.'

Joyce felt sick. In the last nine days, since that message from Tony suggesting she should take the children to America, she had been so busy (or she had made herself so busy), shopping and queuing for visas and packing, that she had not given herself a chance to examine her conscience fully. She had been all a-flutter with the intoxicating mixture of public responsibility and private excitement, and with the pre-travel urgency of everything. She had repressed any inclination to stop what she was doing, stand back from her busyness, and ask herself, unemotionally, whether she should go or stay.

Now, as she looked out of the train window at the Midlands disappearing behind her, she felt the first icy shafts of guilt. Running to her lover? Was that what she was doing? Sheridan had said so, the saintly Sheridan-Christ, who had worked so hard for Jewish refugees: he had seen straight through her.

But no, she thought, watching drops of rain running into each other down the 'No smoking' sign: the facts did not fit Sheridan's accusation. He knew – she had hinted to him – that she and Dolf had fallen in love; but he could not know that she had been *sent* to America. She would never be running in Dolf's direction if it were not for the young children, Harcourt Brace, the Ministry of Information, Rachel Townsend, Tony, and the Book of the Month Club. A burning sense of the injustice of Sheridan's letter began to smother her feelings of guilt. She hated Sheridan for writing such hard words to her. She never wrote back.

There was worse to come, an hour later. Whom should she meet in the next compartment, also travelling to Liverpool with her two young children, but Vera Brittain?

'Are you going to America with your children?' Joyce asked her: the two were acquainted, having met at literary parties.

'No,' Vera Brittain answered. 'I'm only seeing them off.'

Joyce's heart sank, again, with feelings of pity and guilt. Vera Brittain described the episode in *Testament of Experience*:

'I feel as if I were running away,' Jan Struther said brokenly. 'But I thought that if I didn't go I might never see the children again.'

I looked at John and Shirley, and felt sick at heart. In that inexorably speeding compartment, familiar words seemed to hang in the air between Jan Struther and myself.

'Lord, let this cup pass from me!'

How many times, all over the world, had our women contemporaries uttered that prayer during their numerous Gethsemanes?

Who was right, she or I? We had made different decisions, but so great was our mutual anguish of irresolution that neither could blame the other for her choice . . .

The small gallant figures which disappeared behind the flapping tarpaulin of the *Duchess of Atholl* have never grown up in my mind, for the children who returned and eventually took their places were not the same; the break in continuity made them rather appear as an elder brother and sister of the vanished pair.

Joyce went through the flapping tarpaulin with her children. She reminded herself, as she did so, that her conscience was clear: she was being sent. But one small corner of it was not clear, and never would be. She would never be able to erase those words of Sheridan's from her memory, or to forget the encounter with Vera Brittain, who had chosen to say goodbye to her children rather than desert her country. There was a new small self-accusing voice inside Joyce's head which would not go away; and its nagging presence went some way towards explaining the course of her life during the next five years.

Chapter Nine

Through space and time I range
Seeking these two alone:
The savour of the strange,
The solace of the known.

From 'Sleeveless Errand', in *The Glass-Blower*

SHE BOARDED THE ship on 26 June 1940 as Joyce; she disembarked a week later as Jan. From the moment she left the shores of Great Britain, she never introduced herself as Joyce, always as Jan; Dolf called her Jan, and Jan she will be from now on. The almost unisex name suited her: 'Joyce' had overtones of the pampered hostess she had once been, who rang a bell in the drawing-room for tea. Released from that world, she wanted to be a tomboy again: someone who wore jodhpurs and lit camp fires and knew how to splice rope.

The first day at sea was fine and warm, and she was on deck all day with the children. They had never seen their mother so funny and relaxed. She was being an impudent New Girl, pointing out stock characters among the passengers and whispering nicknames for them. The sea-breeze made them all feel hungry and full of laughter.

After tea it began to blow harder, and it got worse, and by the next morning whole dining-roomfuls of passengers were groaning in unison as lights swung and bowls clattered. Jan was supposed to be keeping an eye on six children during the voyage: her own, Vera Brittain's, and two little Jewish refugees who (unlike Jan) were travelling First Class. Nausea dented both her aptitude for the task and her willingness, and by the third day the cabin steward was complaining that the children were running wild. The ship was teeming with children and teenagers too excited to worry about the danger from U-boats: the voyage took place at the height of the British government's programme of evacuating children to the United States and Canada, before the torpedoing of the *City of Benares* in November put a stop to it. Twelve-year-old Janet, unwatched for the first time in her life, experienced her first kiss, with Jeremy Harris, aged thirteen, in a distant corridor.

On the fifth day the ship passed an iceberg. On the seventh it arrived in Canada, and the rush of impressions began, familiar to so many evacuees to North America: first the bright lights of Montreal (dazzling after the blackout), the Royal Canadian Mounted Police and the glorious banks of the St Lawrence River; then, arriving in New York, the Statue of Liberty, the shimmering heat, the skyscrapers, the noise, the yellow taxis.

The plan was not for Jan to live with her children: she would have had no idea how to deal with the cooking or washing. They would lodge at 1 Beekman Place with Aunt Rachel Townsend, who had two sons of her own, Anthony and David, as well as another evacuated nephew, Charles Smythe, son of the Edinburgh madrigal singers, and whose apartment was geared towards nursery life. Jan took a cab straight to Beekman Place so she could shed the children. The door was opened by the cook, the children vanished with their cousins to the train-set room, and Jan breathed freely. She was off-duty at last. Dolf must have sat in this very drawing-room when he came to dinner here. He must be less than two miles away from her.

Of course she could use the telephone, Rachel said: and Jan dialled the number Dolf had given her – his mother's number.

'Mrs Eisler? This is Jan Struther speaking . . . Yes, I'd love to meet you, too. Tomorrow evening? I'll come round after dinner. And Dolf will be there too? Oh, I'm so glad . . .' The Viennese accent made Jan's diaphragm contract.

On their first evening, Rachel Townsend's husband Greenough drove the new arrivals out to the New York World's Fair at Flushing Meadows. They saw sensational sights (man-made lightning, and swimmers in the Aquacade forming themselves into flower and star shapes), and rode a toy train which instead of blowing its horn played the first line of 'When Irish Eyes are Smiling' again and again. They had supper at the Swiss Pavilion. The contrast to blacked-out and terrified England was macabre, and made pure enjoyment impossible.

From her first day, Jan seemed to fit seamlessly into the social world of New York: there was no emptiness in her diary, no touristy wandering round museums to fill in time. In anticipation of Jan's arrival, Rachel had entered her name in the *New York Social Register*, at which Jan was furious. She insisted on having her name removed from the list at once. The whole point of America, she hoped, was that one could escape from the social snobbery which would include her in a 'set' but exclude someone like Dolf.

Listed or unlisted, she was sought-after. Editors, dramatists and broadcasters wanted to meet her. Far from making her wilt, the heat and noise of New York gave a new spring to her step. Everything seemed possible. She strode down Third Avenue on that first Saturday afternoon, feeling more free than ever before, squinting up at the Elevated Railroad and making detours into numbered streets which looked too interesting to resist.

Then, after dinner at the Townsends', she let herself out quietly and walked to Mrs Eisler's apartment. Dolf came to the door.

The certainty of separation-for-ever had hovered so low over Dolf and Jan during their last week in London only forty days earlier that they had felt like ghosts. Their way of making the imminent ending bearable had been to behave, in the last hours, as if the end had already passed. On that last day in Battersea Park they had been, as Dolf put it in a poem, 'blessed shadows of souls which died long ago'.

They had become used to living at this pitch of tragic intensity. And now, for the time at least, that could change. As they sat in Pauly's room, listening as she chatted on about the horrible speed of New York cars and her trunk of beloved possessions which had never arrived from Trieste (and never did), they looked across at one another with amazement and trepidation. Now they were no longer ghosts. They must readjust to being flesh-and-blood secret lovers living in the same city.

Pauly guessed, in an unspoken way, that the two were in love. She was more pleased than shocked, because she wanted Dolf to be happy and could see that Jan made him so. Her motherly Viennese goodness touched Jan deeply, and she fell willingly into the role of second 'daughter' to Pauly, and co-adorer of Dolf. (Pauly's real daughter, Susan, remained in London all through the war.)

Within a few days of her arrival Jan rented a tiny apartment which she had spotted on one of her walks – tiny, because wartime regulations had prevented her from taking money out of Britain. It was on East 49th Street between Second and Third Avenue, within sight of the 'El' track which so fascinated her. She set up a desk by the window and watched the trains taking commuters downtown in the morning and uptown in the evening, and the Italian newsagent's wife hanging out three little blue striped frocks in the morning and taking them down in the evening. She was enchanted and distracted. From a Third Avenue junk shop she bought an old bed, which had bedbugs. She wrote to Tony, describing all this in detail.

Everything seemed possible – even living two parallel lives. Three thousand miles to the east of her, Tony was at Pirbright Camp in Surrey, as a Second Lieutenant, learning to be a Weapons Training Officer with the Scots Guards. He had rejoined the army, with an immediate commission, just after Joyce and the children sailed from Liverpool. He and Joyce, as he of course always called her, were still very much a married couple, separated only by the necessities of war, and wrote to each other every few weeks. The letters have not survived.

There was no question of setting up house with Dolf. He found an apartment with his mother at 215 West 101st Street, and Jan took a lodger at East 49th Street, her friend Bea Horton (the writer Beatrice Curtis Brown), who helped pay the rent. Dolf and Jan's meetings still had to be conducted in secret, and their craving for each other was intensified, as ever, by a sense of forbiddenness.

From the very beginning the secrecy of their love affair was of paramount importance from the family point of view. Tony must never find out, the children must never find out, Rachel must never find out. But later, in the extraordinary weeks after *Mrs Miniver* was published in America on 29 July, the secrecy started to become important from a patriotic point of view. As the author of a book about a supremely happy marriage, Jan was representing her country. Try as she might to dissuade them, her American readers would equate her with Mrs Miniver. And she could not have guessed how many hundreds of thousands of Americans would read the book, or how wide its influence would be.

It was far from Jan's intention to rise to fame in the United States *as* Mrs Miniver, the perfect, 'cute', saintly housewife from plucky little England, torn apart from her husband by war alone, who never thought a wicked thought. But that was just what happened. Americans, it seemed, were in search of a wifely role model from across the Atlantic, and the publication of the book was perfectly timed by Harcourt Brace. England was standing alone in Europe under the Nazi threat; gradually, consciences across the United States were awakening; and here, touring American bookshops and lecture halls in the person of Jan Struther/Mrs Miniver, was the embodiment of what the Nazis were trying to destroy.

The Davenport, Iowa *Times*, in its bestseller lists, classed *Mrs Miniver* as fiction, the Springfield, Ohio *News* as non-fiction. The truth, as we know, was somewhere in between. 'So *you're* Mrs Miniver!' someone said to Jan at one of her first book-signings. 'No, I *write* Mrs Miniver,' Jan corrected her. 'But I have begun to wonder whether it wouldn't be more true to say, "Mrs Miniver writes me".'

By 3 August, four days after its publication, the book was on its third printing. By the third week of August (the week, incidentally, when Alice Duer-Miller's *The White Cliffs* was published, also to instant acclaim) *Mrs Miniver* was selling in America at the rate of 1,500 hardback copies a day, and it jumped in that week from twenty-first to seventh on the national bestseller list.

'What Albany Is Reading' . . . 'What Chicago Is Reading' . . . 'Philadelphia Likes . . .' – *Mrs Miniver* was everywhere. Wives sitting on their porches in the prairies revelled in it – though what they made of the men in kilts tossing cabers and doing the sword dance, Jan could only guess. The Highlands, and Eton, and Piccadilly, must have been as exotic and fascinating to them as the Grand Canyon and the Badlands were to her. What seemed to appeal to readers was the mixture of foreignness and universality: on every page there were uplifting words of wisdom about marriage, or children, or Christmas, or growing older, which cut across all nationalities.

There was none of the vitriol the book had engendered in Great Britain. There were no E. M. Forsters or Rosamond Lehmanns to point out the infuriating rightness of the heroine. Critics were enchanted: their only problem was how to review the book without merely quoting it. 'The book defies review,' said the Flemington, New Jersey *Republican*. 'There are no fireworks, no dramatic climaxes, nothing, as a matter of fact, but the delicious experience of meeting in print a woman whose philosophical musings are always interesting, sometimes amusing, and never dull. I urge you just to read it, and then you will understand why persons have pounced on it with a fervor that is astonishing.'

'If there are thousands of English women like Mrs Miniver,' said the Battleborough, Vermont *Reformer*, 'for whom the whole of England is covered with memory flags, who listen absorbed to the windshield wiper to find what it is saying – if England is full of Mrs Minivers, then it is going to be mighty hard to soften Britain. And we are inclined to think that Mrs Miniver is the most winning and remarkable ambassador that embattled people could have sent to this country just now.' 'Men fortified by the spirit of the millions of Mrs Minivers in England', said the Lincoln, Illinois *Courier*, 'form a fighting army which neither accepts nor knows defeat.' 'The book is perhaps unintentionally tragic,' said the Grand Island, Nebraska *Independent*, 'for what is happening to the England

Latest portrait of forty-one years old Jan Struther, left, creator of Mrs. Miniver who to millions has become the personification of Mrs. Britain. Above, Jan Struther at a celebration of Mrs. Miniver's record-breaking run at New York's Radio City

Just after the last war Joyce Anstruther "came out." Left (below) is a picture taken at her début with the man she married when she was twenty-two. Right (below), Jan Struther's husband, Anthony Maxtone Graham, now a prisoner of war

Mrs. Jan Struther, author of Mrs. Miniver, acts in America as our

UNOFFICIAL AMBASSADRESS

EVERYONE knows that Lord Halifax is our official ambassador in America. Few people know that Jan Struther is our unofficial ambassadress in the U.S.A.

American journalists disagree as to what is so taking about her," but they agree that "she has what is best about the Britishers." Kindness, tolerance, courage, endurance—you can finish the list. All these virtues are in Mrs. Miniver, creation of Jan Struther.

In the American mind both Jan and Mrs. M. have come to typify Britain.

One evening in New York, Jan Struther and I were fellow guests in an enormous drawing-room, cross between a studio and a medieval hall. Jan stood in front of its vast fireplace, looking very small and fragile. She is five foot two inches tall, and weighs just under eight stone. Her profile was lit up by the flames, and as she looked into them

Mrs. Miniver of film fame has become a personality. But she knows the real Mrs. Miniver—the author of the book from which the film was taken. In this article the Countess of Listowel tells the story of Jan Struther and her family who were the inspiration of "Mrs. Miniver."

I noticed that she had blue-grey eyes, sensitive hands and nice legs.

In that smart, rich New York drawing-room, Jan Struther was dressed in an inexpensive—frankly—inelegant frock, and my guess was that she had hurriedly set her own hair. She had no varnish on her nails, and hardly any rouge on her lips. She looked an English "open air girl," in pointed contrast to the super-dressy New York women.

When I next met Miss Struther having

They have all been good sportsmen, and pride themselves on their love of horses. Jan, too, is a first-class horsewoman, though she cannot play games! Like every busy person she has hobbies. She collects wild flowers in remote mountain districts, and "hot jazz records" in London and New York.

Jan's grandfather, Sir Robert Anstruther, was M.P. for St. Andrew's burgh. Her father followed in his political footsteps, and was for many years Government Whip, and later became Government Director of the Suez Canal.

Jan's mother, Dame Eva Anstruther—descendant of Count de Tracy, one of the "murderers" of Thomas à Becket—was a very forceful personality. Before the last war, when women definitely did not write for the papers, Dame Eva was a regular contributor to the Westminster Gazette, and also published some moving short stories. She founded the camp libraries of the last war. They have been revived in this war and are very popular with the troops.

luncheon in a drug store she melted into the crowd. She belongs to the ordinary people—on both sides of the Atlantic—whom she so admirably portrays.

Yes her background is almost " feudal." Her real name is Joyce Anstruther, from which J. Anstruther, then Jan Struther. Originally the Anstruthers were Danish pirates. They landed in Scotland 800 years ago. They have been in every scrap since, from the Crusades to the present world war.

of Mrs Miniver? There is no place in war for truly civilized people, and when this war is over, there may be no place in England for them.' 'Of Mrs Miniver's philosophy,' said the St Petersburg, Florida *Times*, 'one can truly say that she has found the true art of living, the art of loving, the art of marriage, the art of family life, the art of happiness. There are no triangular love affairs, not an indecent suggestion. It is a book any granddaughter can safely put in the hands of her grandmother.' (In the margin of that last clipping, Jan pencilled a small exclamation mark.)

The newspaper and magazine interviews began: Jan found herself scrutinized by journalists, some of whom had not read the book. They wanted 'heart-rending human incidents', details of what it felt like to part from one's home and half one's family. They wanted revealing nuggets about her life – and here was a good, safe one to fob them off with: Jan Struther didn't like tea. But surely all English ladies drank tea? Especially Mrs Miniver, to go with those crumpets and small ratafia biscuits? No, Jan said: 'You see, in reality in England I was at a typewriter in a newspaper office at four o'clock with a thick mug of coffee beside me.' She really *didn't* like tea. She had expressed her loathing for it in one of her early articles for *Punch*: 'It is difficult to make perfectly but nauseating when anything less than perfect. Neat, it is pleasing to the eye but acrid to the palate; diluted with milk, it is passable in taste but revolting in colour.' The drink became one of the banes of her life in America. She was constantly given imperfect cups of it by kind hostesses who wanted to make her feel at home.

'Dear Nannie,' Jan wrote on 5 August, 'We have arrived safely, and we are now at Cape Cod staying with Mrs Patrick's mother [Tony's brother Patrick's American mother-in-law, who had a large house on the Cape]. The children are being very good, and if ever they get quarrelsome, I mutter 'H. and P. of the B. E.' (Honour and Prestige of the British Empire) and they pull themselves together. *Mrs Miniver* is selling well, and all the chaps who really matter here seem to agree that it's exactly the right book to put Great Britain across over here, and that it will do a great deal of good, especially among American housewives . . . ! It really is an extraordinary development, considering how little I was thinking about the US when I wrote the bloody things.'

While the children were canoeing and eating banana splits with their cousins on Cape Cod, Jan kept dashing back on trains to New York for meetings in grills, hotel lounges and 28th-floor offices. On 7 August she met Clark Getts: 'Clark H. Getts, Inc., Waldorf Astoria Hotel, New York City' – she was to become all too familiar with that showy sans serif letter-heading over the next four years. Clark Getts were prestigious lecture-circuit agents, and among their fifty-three lecturers for the coming season, many of them advertised in the papers as 'eye-witnesses of the war', were Carl J. Hambro, President of the Norwegian Parliament and of the League of Nations Assembly ('I Saw it Happen'), Sir Evelyn Wrench, Editor of the London *Spectator* ('What is Happening in Europe'), and Norman Alley, 'Ace of the Newsreels' ('War on Review'). Now Jan Struther was to join their list. She was particularly pleased to be with the same agents as the children's author Munro Leaf: she loved *Ferdinand*.

'It is understood that I will assume my rail and Pullman lower berth fares, that I will assume all other travel expenses incident to engagements . . . It is also understood that if it becomes necessary for me to cancel any engagements, I will reimburse you and the local management for all expenses incurred . . . For and in consideration of your services, you are to receive 40% of all earnings before remitting the balance to me . . .' She signed up with Getts on 24 August, with no qualms that they were sinking their claws into her. Lecture tours sounded thrilling. You travelled from state to state and there was somebody waiting on the platform to greet you. What better way to meet the real America? She wouldn't mind a bit about the tiringness of long-distance travel, if it was all in the cause of putting Great Britain across to isolationists. She had always been at her happiest and most creative on trains, anyway.

On another of her dashes from Cape Cod she met Clifton Fadiman, who was 'master of ceremonies' (that is, the man who asked the questions) on the famous radio quiz programme *Information, Please!* He was in search of a female guest for the programme, and Jan said she would be happy to have a go. Her first *Information, Please!* broadcast was scheduled for 10 September, and she would leave for her first lecture tour on 2 October.

Pictured right is the first of 276 Details of Engagement which Jan was to receive from Clark Getts over the next four years. What would the West High School in Minneapolis look like?

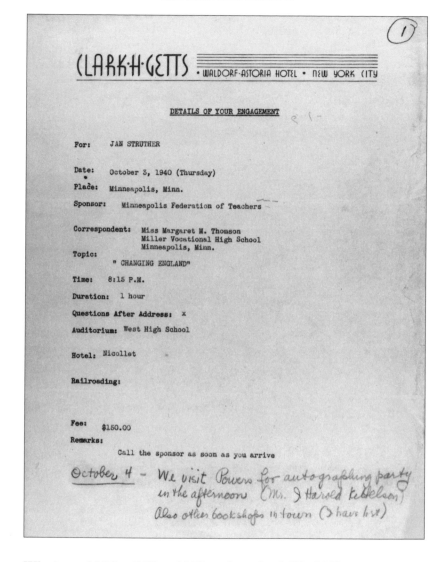

CLARK·H·GETTS · WALDORF-ASTORIA HOTEL · NEW YORK CITY

DETAILS OF YOUR ENGAGEMENT

For: JAN STRUTHER

Date: October 3, 1940 (Thursday)
Place: Minneapolis, Minn.
Sponsor: Minneapolis Federation of Teachers

Correspondent: Miss Margaret M. Thomson
Miller Vocational High School
Minneapolis, Minn.
Topic:
" CHANGING ENGLAND"

Time: 8:15 P.M.

Duration: 1 hour

Questions After Address: x

Auditorium: West High School

Hotel: Nicollet

Railroading:

Fee: $150.00
Remarks:
Call the sponsor as soon as you arrive

October 4 – We visit Powers for autographing party in the afternoon (Mr. & Harold Kettelson) Also other bookshops in town (I have list)

What would Mrs J. Harold Kettelson look like? Who would turn up to listen to the lecture? Jan was intrigued.

Fizzing with excitement after meeting influential people all day, Jan collected Dolf from his work in the evening – he was still wrapping parcels in Union Square. The unworthiness of the job filled her with rage. 'How *can* you work there? The smell of that man's cigar! I *know* you'll find something better soon . . .

I did a lovely book-signing today at the British War Relief, and I had a hilarious lunch with the Morleys at Harcourt Brace . . .' Jan talked away as they walked together up to East 50th Street. 'D'you like the top of that building?' Dolf gave an architectural appraisal shining with art-historical wisdom, and Jan was dazzled by the fineness of his mind.

He did, eventually, make the terrible mistake which got him sacked from the parcel-wrapping job: he registered a large consignment of parcels which were supposed to be insured, and insured a pile which were supposed to be registered, and sent them all off to South America before the mistake had been spotted. 'You will be happier somewhere else, Herr Doktor,' said his boss. 'Get out!'

Dolf was grateful for that final 'Herr Doktor': it implied recognition that he had been too bright, rather than too dim, for the job. Jan was delighted, but not for long. Dolf did indeed soon get another job, but it was addressing envelopes: he was paid by the hundred. Now at least he could work at home.

'It's 8.30 p.m. Welcome to *Information, Please!*' This was Clifton Fadiman speaking into his microphone at Radio City. 'And with us tonight on our panel we have Jan Struther, the author of *Mrs Miniver*, and John Gunther, author of *Inside Europe* and *Inside Asia*. They are joining our usual friends Franklin P. Adams and John Kieran. As you know, the aim is to send in a question the panel can't answer. If you succeed, we will send you ten dollars and all twenty-four volumes of the *Encyclopedia Britannica*. But first, a word from our sponsor.'

'Canada Dry is the aristocrat of the table . . .'

Help, thought Jan. The sponsor was bringing momentary respite, but any second now the ordeal would begin. She was sitting uncomfortably on a copy of the Manhattan telephone directory, which she had been given to raise her to the level of the microphone.

'Now, Miss Struther and gentlemen, Lois B. Walker of Mill Valley, California has sent in the following question: What practical use is made of these scientific facts: (a) helium is lighter than air and non-inflammable; (b) silver chloride is sensitive to light; (c) liquid ammonia absorbs heat when it vaporizes; (d) wood alcohol has a low freezing point?'

This was awful. They hadn't done much science at Miss Richardson's Classes. The first one must be something to do with balloons . . . But Mr Adams had put his hand up. 'The first is airships. Silver chloride and light: that's photography. Liquid ammonia: that must be refrigeration. Wood alcohol: isn't that the anti-freeze they put into automobile radiators?'

'Attaboy, Mr Adams! Now, Mr Frank J. Mason of Laurel, Mississippi asks us the following: What pitcher (a) holds the Major League record for strikeouts in one game; (b) holds the Major League lifetime record for strikeouts? (c) holds the record of the greatest number of consecutive hitless innings?'

Surely she couldn't be expected to know that. Even the others on the panel had to confer. Wasn't it Bob Feller, or someone, of Cleveland, who struck out eighteen Detroit Tigers back in 1938? And surely Walter Johnson must be the record-holder for strikeouts? Correct; but they couldn't answer the consecutive hitless innings question. They were stumped, Jan noticed. And they wouldn't even know what 'stumped' meant.

'Congratulations, Mr Mason. The *Encyclopedia Britannica* is on its way to you. And now another word from our sponsor.'

These men knew their stuff. They knew their chemical elements, their Bible, their Greek myths, their Swinburne, their Longfellow. Their hands went up before Jan had time to think. But her moment of glory came. 'Mrs Donald G. Dempsey of Sharon, Ohio asks the following: Name a work of fiction in which: (a) five sisters are among the principal characters; (b) four sisters are among the principal characters; (c) three sisters are among the principal characters; (d) two sisters are among the principal characters; (e) one sister is the principal character.'

'Well, *Pride and Prejudice* is five,' said John Kieran, 'and *Little Women* is four, and *King Lear* is three . . .'

'And what are the names of the Little Women?'

'Let me see. There's Amy . . .'

But the men didn't know the others. Joyce put her hand up.

'They are called Meg, Jo, Beth and Amy March,' she said in a quiet and startlingly English-sounding voice.

'Good on you, Miss Struther.'

She would be invited again.

Term began for the children, at Trinity School, a private day school on the West Side of Manhattan, where all the cousins went. Rachel Townsend, a great 'fixer', managed to persuade the maintenance man of 1 Beekman Place, Al Cominucci, to agree to be the family chauffeur for the school run. Off the children went each morning; and Rachel sat in bed for another two hours. Her breakfast tray had slots on the sides for the post and the papers.

The news pages were full of the forthcoming presidential elections. Rachel supported Roosevelt, because she sensed (in spite of his cautious words) that he would not stand by and let Nazism triumph in Europe. Greenough (being right-wing Eastern Seaboard) was anti-Roosevelt. Jan felt the same way as Rachel, but she went further: she loved Roosevelt for his quiet rhetoric and his vibrant face which belied his physical frailty. She admired him for daring to be unpopular with the rich to help the poor, and she could read on his face the anguish of a man torn in two directions, between Winston Churchill and Congress. She even started dreaming about him from about this time. 'I've been dreaming fantastically, mostly FDR-politically,' she told Dolf.

And still *Mrs Miniver* crept up the national bestseller list. On 22 September 1940 it was second, and on 29 September it was Number One. 'TOP!' wrote Jan, next to the *Herald Tribune* headline 'What America is Reading'. The next four, in descending order, were *How Green Was My Valley* by Richard Llewellyn, *The Beloved Returns* by Thomas Mann, *Stars on the Sea* by F. van Wyck Mason, and *To the Indies* by C. S. Forrester. On the non-fiction list, *Mein Kampf* was seventeenth.

Jan boarded a train in the direction of Minneapolis on 2 October, as bidden by Clark Getts. The paint was olive-green, the upholstery was brownish plush, and Jan was full of curiosity. 'I love seeing the approaches to small towns from the train,' she wrote, '– the children's toys in the yard, the bright-coloured washing hanging on the line: there was a beautiful old patchwork quilt just now hanging outside a very poor little frame house – probably their only heirloom and treasure. Glimpses like that, to me, are the real essence of America – not the skyscrapers or the Statue of Liberty.'

Then, as night fell, there was the new experience of sleeping in a curtained berth above or below the berth of an American stranger. 'I'm sharing with a pleasant moon-faced middle-aged man with rimless glasses,' Jan wrote, 'who has slept most of the way, awakening only at intervals to enquire from new passengers about the progress of the Ball Game at St Louis. He has the Lower Berth, I have the Upper. I know nothing about him and he knows nothing about me. We will never see each other again. Yet just for this night I shall sleep suspended 3 feet above him in that curiously impersonal proximity which seems such a fascinating part of American Pullman life.'

The man turned out to be a public-health official from Oklahoma who specialized in venereal disease, 'which he discussed with the same cool, dispassionate interest as if his subject had been insurance or tractors. When the porter asked him what time he wanted to be called he said "6.30". I said, "An hour out of Chicago – 6.40." "Then make it 6.40 for both of us," said Lower Four coyly. I felt we were almost married.'

She awoke to a sparkling morning and found herself in a land of white grain elevators, which looked to her like medieval castles. At Chicago she changed trains, and at Minneapolis she took a taxi to the Nicollet Hotel: creamy-brown walls, creamy-brown bed-cover, telephone screwed to the wall too high up to reach unless she stood on the Bible 'placed by the Gideons'.

The teachers at Minneapolis were delightful. They were unashamedly dowdy, and told her that in their language, 'PhD' stood for 'petticoats hanging down'. And the lecture, Jan wrote to Dolf (she was beginning to use American expressions) 'went over swell'.

Dolf was beginning to use American expressions, too. 'Gee, it was nice to hear your voice on the telephone,' he wrote back to her.

There were two main messages that Jan wanted to get across in this first season of lectures. The first was that she was *not* Mrs Miniver:

> You see before you, Ladies and Gentlemen, a haunted woman. And if my husband and children were here today as well, you would see before you a haunted family.
>
> Now most families, if they are haunted at all, are haunted by the people who used to live in their house in the past. But we, as a family, are haunted by five people who have never lived in our house at all. I should like to take this opportunity of stating in public what I have so often explained in private, that is, that I am NOT 'Mrs Miniver'; my husband is NOT 'Clem'; our three children are NOT 'Toby', 'Judy' and 'Vin'. It is quite extraordinary how difficult it is to make people understand this. I suppose it's the penalty one has to pay for writing in a paper with such a reputation for truthfulness as the London *Times*.

The second thing she wanted to impress on her audience was the similarities, as opposed to the differences, between Americans and British people. 'If John Doe from Ohio meets John Doe from Yorkshire, they discover how fundamentally alike they are.' Anglo-American relations, she believed, were a matter not just for politicians but for ordinary people: they began at home. 'I seem to be talking a lot about "ordinary people". Well, everybody talks about them nowadays, thank goodness! They've come into their own at last, in the centre of the picture.'

What ordinary people felt and said and did was important: 'The private opinion of today is the public opinion of tomorrow, and the public opinion of tomorrow is the legislation of the day after.'

> So, to anybody who is trying to get to know the people of another country, I would offer this advice: scrap your old filing system. Put new labels on your mental pigeonholes. When you meet somebody of a different nationality, see if you can't match him up with somebody in your own country. For instance, you or I cross the Atlantic for the first time, and it so happens that one of the first people we meet is a very crotchety, difficult, overbearing old man. Our instinct is to say

to ourselves immediately, 'Oh, so this is what Americans are like, is it?' or 'So this is a typical Englishman?' What we ought to do is to nip that thought in the bud right away, and cast our minds back in all honesty and fairness to our own side of the Atlantic. If we do, it won't be more than a matter of minutes before we find ourselves saying, 'Why, of course; he's the spitting image of my Great-uncle Benjamin.' You try it, and see. The more you play this game, the more convinced you become that the ordinary people of the United States and the ordinary people of Great Britain are amazingly alike. They are alike in the 'mental climate' which they breathe – in the things which they think worth living for and, most of all, in the things they think worth dying for.

At Milwaukee on 5 October she spoke to the American Assembly of University Women: two hundred of them, crammed into the College Club for a luncheon with table decorations to match the book cover of *Mrs Miniver*, and a quotation from the book folded up inside each napkin. The university women lapped up her lecture. Among the questions they asked at the end were these: 'Where do you go when your house is bombed?', 'Where are the little princesses?' and 'Will you please tell me how to make an English trifle?' To that, Jan (who had no idea how to cook anything) replied that the English were currently more preoccupied with making rifles than trifles.

'Oh boy, how I do like *people*,' she wrote to Dolf. 'There are so many nice ones around that one hardly dares to stop still and not meet any for fear of missing something good. (I am not drunk, only heady with relief and success.)'

Places which had just been names on maps – York, Pennsylvania; Flint, Michigan; Oak Park, Illinois; St Paul, Minnesota; Cleveland, Ohio – came to life for her: she used the *Sleeping Beauty* analogy of kissing places awake by touching them. At each town she was fêted, interviewed by the local press and radio, and listened to by enthralled audiences. The American enjoyment of lecture-attendance amazed her. Who were these smiling people who gave up their lunchtimes and evenings to sit in rows and listen to someone else talking for an hour? *She* wouldn't go to a lecture if she were paid. It would be far too much like choosing to sit through a sermon.

On the last day of October 1940 she sent a cable to Nannie in England: 'JAMES HILTON WRITING STORY & DIALOGUE MINIVER FILM GREER GARSON PROBABLY STARRING SHALL GO HOLLYWOOD LATER CHECK ENGLISH AUTHENTICITY BOY OH BOY WISH YOU WERE HERE.'

MGM had summoned her. The character she had invented for Peter Fleming of *The Times* was to appear on the big screen. She set off on 10 November, pausing to give lectures at Worcester, Mass. on the 11th, Rochester, N.Y. on the 12th, Toledo, O. on the 13th and Chicago, Ill. on the 14th and 15th (she liked using the correct abbreviations for states). Then she boarded the *Los Angeles Limited*, bound for the West Coast.

Chapter Ten

I was a citizen, once, of a great city.
  Its buildings were of mellowed brick and of weathered stone.
I woke up every morning to its sparrows' chatter
  And lay down every evening to its traffic's drone.

It had its faults. It was shabby in parts, and sooty;
  Its water-front could have done with tidying up.
It was shapeless and vast: but I loved it like a village.
  It was my home. It held my life like a cup.

Its sky-signs were my earliest constellations.
  My nursery-rhymes were the legends of the town.
I sang, 'London's burning, London's burning.'
  I sang, 'London Bridge is falling down.'

I learned to walk and talk there. By its times, its spaces,
  Are measured for ever my thoughts of space and time.
A hundred yards is the length of the Square garden:
  An hour is Big Ben's chime to Big Ben's chime.

Its seasons are my seasons. For me, winter
  Is the sound of a muffin-bell through the gathering dark;
And spring, for me, is neither a lamb nor a primrose,
  But a crocus down by the lake in St James's Park.

Summer's the smell and the feel of hot asphalt,
  With costers selling geraniums down the street;
Autumn, for me, is a bonfire in Kensington Gardens,
  And the rustle of plane-leaves over the children's feet.

It is peaceful here. Yet here, where maple and sumach
  Cut unfamiliar patterns on a moonlit sky,
I am a citizen still of the same city:
  I feel its houses crumble and its people die.

Heavy at heart, I lie awake at midnight
And hear a voice, five hours nearer the sun,
Speaking across the ether from a grim daybreak,
Calmly reciting what the night has done.

I think, 'London's burning, London's burning.'
I think, 'London Bridge is falling down.'
Then something wiser than thought says, 'Heart, take comfort:
Buildings and bridges do not make a town.

'A city is greater than its bricks and mortar;
It is greater than tower or palace, church or hall:
A city's as great as the people that live there.
You know those people. How can London fall?'

'A Londoner in New England, 1941', from J.S's *A Pocketful of Pebbles*

THE POWERLESSNESS OF the original author to control the plot and script of a Hollywood movie 'based on the book by . . .' became clear to Jan within minutes of shaking hands with her first 'man behind a desk' at Culver City. The matter, she realized, was out of her hands. MGM were going to make a movie of *Mrs Miniver*, it was going to be a war film, there was to be bombing and death – and all she could usefully do was stand back with her fingers crossed. If these Hollywood moguls really thought they could use the character she had created to show Americans the plight of a typical British family, and if this would really help to turn the tide of public opinion in favour of joining the Allies, then they should be left to get on with it.

Within a fortnight she had signed on the dotted line, selling the rights for a lump sum of $32,000, renouncing all editorial control. 'I got the worst contract of any author ever, second only to Margaret Mitchell for *Gone With the Wind*,' she stated later, when the film had grossed $8,878,000. In fact, it is thought to have been, at the time, the largest lump sum ever paid by a film studio for a first novel.

'Hollywood is an awful, phoney place,' she wrote to Nannie, 'and I'm sure you wouldn't like it any more than I do.' She met James Hilton (the author of *Lost Horizon* and *Goodbye Mr Chips*), who had been commissioned to write the screenplay: they had cocktails one night and dinner the next, and she tried to explain to him the difference (though she was not quite sure of it herself) between the British middle class and upper-middle class. She wished him luck, and fled back to New York.

'Now, Miss Struther and gentlemen, Mrs Henry J. Shipment of Baltimore asks you this: Here are four famous American names translated into various foreign languages. Can you identify them? (a) Heinrich Langerkerl; (b) Alfredo Ferrero; (c) Benito Buonomo; (d) Giuseppe Sarto.' 'Benny Goodman!' cried Joyce, shooting her hand up before the others had a chance. She felt much more at home among these New York brain-boxes than she had among the Los Angeles millionaires. At the *Information, Please!* anniversary party she talked and danced until four in the morning, and Wendell Willkie, the man who had recently failed to be elected President of the United States, made an unsuccessful pass at her.

Jan on Information, Please!

Christmas was coming, and Harcourt Brace were spending $5,000 on their Christmas advertising campaign for *Mrs Miniver*. Jan and the children sent parcels and loving messages to Tony, Jamie and Nannie. On 24 December Jan had Christmas dinner and present-giving with her secret 'family', Dolf and Pauly, and on Christmas Day with her official family at 1 Beekman Place.

'Liebes, Liebes, I have had *such* fun at Kalamazoo,' Jan wrote to Dolf on 7 March 1941: she was in Michigan, and had just given her forty-first lecture. 'A perfectly charming college, charming Faculty, charming boys and girls, and an ENORMOUS audience: about 800 people, including rows and rows standing up or sitting on the floor, and hundreds were turned away too. The sponsors took me on a fascinating 150-mile journey through apple orchards and vineyards . . . I think I am in love with the world; and the best of it is that it seems to *last*. The love, I mean. Just as – thank God – yours and mine does.' But on the back of her Details of Engagement for 13 March (Place: Buffalo, N.Y. Sponsor: The Garret Club. Correspondent: Mrs J. M. Mitchell, 70 Oakland Place), she scribbled 'Mrs J. McC. Mitchell. Yellow-faced old bitch.'

Sponsors sent gushing letters to Clark Getts to thank the agency for sending them Jan Struther, who was 'as cute as a bug', and whose humour, light-heartedness, infectious laugh, charm, grace, radiance and joy had warmed hundreds of hearts. The income from the lectures, and from the MGM contract, made it possible for Jan to make donations of thousands of dollars to the British War Relief Fund.

She helped to raise yet more money by editing and writing the Introduction to a book called *Letters from Women of Britain*, which Harcourt Brace published in 1941 on the understanding that all its profits would go to the Air Raid Victims Relief Fund. It was a collection of letters (some to Jan but mostly to her friends and acquaintances) from women living through the Blitz. It demonstrated how British women were beginning to get used to the absurdity of going down to the cellar or into an air-raid shelter each night: it was becoming as routine as brushing one's teeth. 'How gloriously adaptable we shall all be after the war!' wrote one correspondent. 'S. and I used to make an awful fuss at a hotel if we could only get a double-bedded room – and now we share a single mattress on the floor in the greatest luxury.' 'Last night I slept a whole night in my bed, which was a most delightful experience,' wrote another. 'Today,' wrote a third, 'as I was vacuuming the sitting-room carpet, it suddenly came over me how silly it was to be doing it, with a house blown to smithereens nearby – and yet one must and does. One even renews one's kitchen utensils at Woolworth's, and worries about the moth in the curtains. One must and one does.'

Real names were changed to initials, so there were tedious sentences like 'We have Z. living here now – she moved from the O— Street flat – but we don't see a great deal of S.' The book was put together quickly, and it showed. But it was a vivid document, full of such domestic detail as the way people planted rockeries with gnomes and rabbits on top of their garden air-raid shelters. Perhaps Jan felt a rush of reassurance when she chose to include the following, in which the anonymous writer advises her friend 'C.' to stay in America and *not* come back to Britain: 'It is of the greatest importance to us all that some people should remain in full possession of a kind of pre-war sanity, not muddled and dérangé like us. Not, I mean, in order to regulate the world, but just so we can restore ourselves by getting back our old balance from them, serenity and so on.' Yes, there was another good reason for staying in America.

Between lecture engagements, as she looked out of her train window at 'moonlit and flat grain fields with their drifts of snow lying about the edges, and lonely farmhouses sunk in isolationist slumber', she wondered whether anything could wake America up to the danger of the world's situation. Roosevelt, thank goodness, had been re-elected, and had managed to get the Lend Lease bill through Congress: America had now agreed to be, at least, 'the arsenal of democracy', giving 'all aid to Great Britain short of war'. FDR's analogy of a man lending a hose to a neighbour whose house was on fire had helped to get the idea across to millions of Americans clinging fearfully to their isolationism. But in the air there was still an almost tangible hatred of Roosevelt and everything he stood for. Jan bore the brunt of this loathing more and more in 1941. In her lectures she was beginning to introduce rallying words which did not go down well with isolationists. She quoted Sydney Smith, the nineteenth-century canon of St Paul's Cathedral, whose essay on the subject of possible Napoleonic invasion seemed amazingly apposite to the United States in 1941:

Be not deceived, there is no wall of adamant, no triple flaming sword, to drive off those lawless assassins who have murdered and pillaged in every other land. Heaven has made with us no covenant that there should be joy and peace here, and wailing and lamentation in the world besides. I would counsel you to put on a mind of patient suffering and noble acting; whatever energies there are in the human mind you will want them all; every man will be tested to the very spring of his heart, and those times are at hand which will show us as we really are, with the genuine stamp and value, be it much or little, which nature has impressed upon every living soul.

The children had noticed a growing anti-British element among the teachers at Trinity School: Jan decided to take them away. Robert would board at the Harvey School in Westchester County, New York and Janet would go to the George School in Pennsylvania, an enlightened Quaker boarding-school.

'What a different 1st of June this is from last year's one,' Jan wrote to Dolf. She was spending the weekend with Lord and Lady Halifax, the British ambassador and his wife, at their residence in Washington. 'You had just sailed away and I was wandering about feeling disembowelled . . . I'm having a lovely time here – just a small dinner party last night, and I sat next to the Greek Minister.' Lord Halifax had taken a liking to Jan from the moment she told him, in a direct-but-kind way, that he mustn't go about fox-hunting with the smart set in Virginia because it would give Americans a damaging impression of what the British were like. She described the Halifaxes' drawing-room to Dolf: 'On the table where visitors can't fail to see it, there is a solemn thick book about India, inscribed "Their Excellencies" by someone there, and sticking out of it, instead of a bookmarker, a piece of unmistakable BUMF! (loo paper). In no other country's embassy could this occur. Don't worry, we'll win the war, because we know how to improvise.'

As her lectures began to merge into one another in her memory, she took more care to 'catch' each one by writing notes on the back of her Details of Engagement.

Mrs Harriet Collins [she scribbled, after 'The Truth About Mrs Miniver' at the Matrix Club of Columbus, Ohio]: husband died a year ago – very fat, fair, jolly – insomnia. I recommended rum milk punch at night. Knows Thurber.

Mrs Harriet Allen – husband in jewellery store.

Mrs Florence Horchow: née Smith. Married a Jew – Austrian insurance broker. Delicate girl, 9, Hester, brain tumours. I did orange-peel teeth. Mrs H. *very* nice, ugly, efficient, became Jewish by religion on marriage.

Mrs Bricker: wife of State Governor. V. nice, distinguished-uglyish.

Mrs Bevis: wife of Univ. Pres. Oldish. ?Jewish.

'Jewish' was one of the most frequent words in these scribbles. She was still more interested in Jews than in anyone else, and gushed to Dolf in her letters about the delightful ones she had met. Dolf wished she wouldn't, sometimes: anti-Semitism was despicable, but indiscriminate pro-Semitism was not healthy either.

Where should they spend the summer? Summer *loomed* in America, more than it ever had in England. There, a gentle breeze blew, and she could rely on Nannie, Kensington Gardens and the cottage at Rye to get her through July, before the ready-made holiday at Cultoquhey which soaked up August. But here it was sweltering from mid June onwards, there was no Nannie, and the summer school vacation was three months long. She yearned to go on a real holiday with Dolf, away from everyone: she envisaged them riding horses together through the Wild West. What she didn't want was to go with him on a local villagey holiday: 'I feel I'd rather have a hellish hot six days' drive than potter around New England all summer.'

July and August would present no problem, because Robert

would be staying with the Townsends in Rhode Island, and Janet would be at summer camp. But there was still June. Jan decided to be brave and motherly and take Janet and Robert camping on her own.

'I am going to have fun with the children but you know I hate leaving you,' she wrote to Dolf, giving him some addresses in upstate New York and Vermont. 'Please *type* envelope, mark Personal, *and* enclose your letter in an inner envelope. With these provisos, you can write freely.'

It was lovely, on the surface. They stopped by the sides of lakes and cooked 'Wieners' on Jan's Sterno stove. They went to movies in obscure New England towns in the afternoon and ate strawberry cheesecake afterwards. They slept in a log cabin in a wood on the edge of Lake Placid, with a bathing beach, a canoe and no electric light. 'Don't be a "Mutti" about traffic accidents, my sweet!' Jan wrote to Dolf. 'Really and truly I drive very carefully when I'm with the children. I never go more than 60 mph, mostly about 40, and we are wandering along doing about 150 miles a day.'

But she was beginning to notice a new pattern of aliveness and deadness in herself. When she was with Dolf, she felt phys- ically and mentally alive – able to respond fully to the sensa- tions around her: the beauty of trees, the deliciousness of food, the soothingness of water, the sparkle of conversation. When she was away from him for any length of time, there seemed to be a smothering of these feelings: life lost its savour. She expressed this later in a poem, using the Cinderella analogy.

> While you are here, Beloved, while you are here,
>   Happiness clothes me round like a golden gown.
> The young men smile, and turn their heads, and stare,
>   As I step light-footed through the enchanted town.
>
> But when you are gone, Beloved, when you are gone,
>   The slippers of glass will vanish, and the golden gown;
> And no one will look at the rags that I have on
>   As I walk with feet of lead through the desolate town.

'I am as sterile as hell,' she wrote to Dolf from Hillsborough in upstate New York. 'I eat, and swim, and write letters, and sleep, and dream, and then wake suddenly. I am getting very sunburnt.'

Their star was still watching over them. At a literary luncheon at the New York Public Library a few weeks before, Jan had sat next to the eminent librarian Jenny Flexner (of Jewish descent), and had mentioned that she knew a young Viennese immigrant who would make a brilliant library student. Strings were pulled; and in the log cabin by Lake Placid Jan filled in a reference form about Dolf: 'Ability of candidate: more than average, considerably. A real scholar and book lover.' Dolf got a scholarship to library school at Columbia, and the course was to begin in September. He could give up the envelope-addressing job – and the dream of a secret holiday in the West could come true.

It was, Dolf later said, 'among the most magic things we ever did. It was our last chance.' They set off in Jan's second-hand Plymouth and drove across the United States. For the whole month of July they could ignore the screeching of time's wingèd chariot, and could live together day and night, away from the world's gaze. At hotels, they registered as Don and Judy Eisler (Don – joke-typical American name; Judy – Mrs Miniver's daughter; Eisler – Dolf's stepfather's surname). They stopped for the night at Cleveland, Ohio, at La Porte, Indiana and at State Center, Iowa, where they bought local papers to catch up on the world's news. (The German Fourth Panzer Division was encircling Smolensk.) They pulled off the road for snacks at 'Joe's', or 'Nick's Eats', or 'Ma Schmitt's Place'. In the washroom at O'Neill, Nebraska, Jan had a narrow escape. She was chatting to the woman at the next-door basin when the woman stopped in mid-hand-wash and said, 'Wait a minute – I recognize your voice. Now, where have I heard that voice before?'

'I've no idea,' said Jan. 'My name's Judy Eisler. I'm a housewife.'

'No – come on, it's so familiar. Let me guess. Haven't I heard you on the radio?'

Jan shook her head, smiled, dried her hands as calmly as possible, left the washroom, and left O'Neill, Nebraska ten minutes later.

Dolf and Jan headed for the Black Hills of South Dakota. There, at last, they were out of earshot of the *Information, Please!* audience. They stayed at a dude ranch and rode horses side by side all day, getting lost on purpose. Jan's ability to appreciate beauty had come flooding back: every sunset, every picnic, every view, every siesta, every conversation was memorable. They felt they were literally discovering the New World together.

They crossed the Rocky Mountains at Kremmling, Colorado, where Jan spotted gentian, wild columbine, larkspur, monkshood and Alpine rue. They swept down into scorching Arizona and rode horses with Western saddles in the Canyon de Chelly. They bought tough Western shoes at a J. C. Penney store. Their car got stuck in the mud between Ganado and Chambers, Arizona, and was pulled out by the sheriff of the Apache country. Every adversity merely enhanced the sense of adventure.

Very reluctantly, after three weeks of this existence, they turned eastwards again and were drawn back towards New York. The routes across America – just like the Great North Road in Britain – were now lined with 'memory flags' for Jan, to be noticed and hugged to herself in private reverie each time she passed nearby, on future, solitary journeys.

'Greer Garson *probably* starring,' Jan had cabled Nannie at the end of 1940: and it took many months of Hollywood meetings for that probability to become a certainty.

First, the whole *Mrs Miniver* project had to be passed by the sceptical Louis B. Mayer. The producer Sidney Franklin had taken on the project with zeal, and had set up a team of five scriptwriters (James Hilton, Arthur Wimperis, George Froeschel, R. C. Sherriff and Claudine West) who had worked for six months to adapt (which is to say, completely rewrite) the book for the screen. They handed the screenplay to Mayer at the end of August 1941, and he didn't like it. Too many anti-German films seemed to be filtering out of the Writers' Building, he said, and MGM could do without them while it was clinging to a declining, war-torn international market. Mayer became even more worried in September, when Senator Burton Wheeler, a prominent member of the America First Committee, accused Hollywood of 'conspiring with the Roosevelt administration to conduct a violent propaganda campaign intending to incite the American people to the point where they will become involved in this war.'

Greer Garson was not happy about accepting the role of Mrs Miniver. How could she – a beautiful, thirty-three-year-old actress with what journalists called 'a nimbus of red-gold hair' – possibly play the mother of a man aged twenty-one? It was absurd. Surely, if she accepted the part, she should be 'aged', with wrinkles, greying hair, horn-rimmed spectacles and padded hips? William Wyler, the director, disagreed. He said she looked just the right age as she was. 'That hit a nerve,' wrote Michael Troyan in his biography of Greer Garson, *A Rose for Mrs Miniver*. (Actually, Garson was not thirty-three but thirty-seven: she always subtracted four years from her true age, and it was only after her death that her year of birth was found to be 1904, not 1908.)

William Wyler had the reputation of being an impossibly demanding director to work with. Both Greer Garson and Walter Pidgeon had to be begged by Sidney Franklin to say 'yes', but at least there was no need for begging when it came to casting the twenty-three-year-old (and already-divorced) Richard Ney as Mrs Miniver's son Vin: 'I picked him out of a bunch of silly kids,' said William Wyler, 'because he seemed the silliest.' Ney, who had merely stopped by at MGM to visit a friend and decided on a whim to do a quick screen test, could not believe his luck when he was offered the part. Culver City seemed to him like the Garden of Eden: 'I was in paradise, eating apples everywhere.'

Was it love at first sight? The scene, in Sidney Franklin's office, was imaginatively described in an article by Beth Emerson entitled 'Secret Romance': 'Greer looked up, prepared to see the usual young actor. Instead, she observed a tall, slender fellow with a sensitive, studious face. Richard Ney looked down . . . His startled blue eyes flashed to her slender ankles, even as Greer's startled green eyes took heed of the width of his shoulders; and then their delighted glances met again, met and locked and held.'

The burgeoning clandestine love-affair between screen-mother and screen-son was a new sub-plot in the *Mrs Miniver* story. Jan was unaware of it as she set off from Pennsylvania Station on 4 October for her longest lecture tour so far.

She perused her time-table.

Schedule for Miss Struthers [the Clerk Getts secretaries often spelt her surname wrong]:

Saturday, Oct. 4th: Lv Pennsylvania Station, train 31, 6.05 EST. Lower Berth 12 in Car 318.

Sunday Oct. 5th. Arrive Terre Haute, 11.13 am CST. Change trains. Lv Terre Haute, Chicago & Eastern Illinois R.R. 1.45 pm CST. Ar. Evansville 5.05 pm CST. Reservation at McCurdy Hotel . . .

This went on for three pages. She would be travelling on *The American, The Spirit of St Louis, The Blue Bonnet, The 20th Century, The Morning Zephyr, The Black Hawk* and *The Rocket*. (What would Tony give to ride on these famous trains! She must write to him during the journey.) She was to give twenty-three lectures in six weeks, and local newspapers from Michigan to Texas were growing excited. 'In a full week of activities ahead,' said the Evansville, Indiana paper, 'probably the one most talked about is the appearance of Jan Struther, the English woman whose much-read *Mrs Miniver* has made her to the public "Mrs Miniver" herself.' She mustn't disappoint her public.

In Evansville, she certainly didn't. The lecture went across 'swell' again. She wrote to Dolf on 'Hotel McCurdy' paper embossed with a picture of a dreary building with too many windows. 'Loew's Theatre was completely crammed – about 2,500 in the audience. They laughed at all the jokes and (to judge by the comments from the mob at the bookstore later) took the serious bits to heart with *gratitude*. And this is Indiana! I'm not exactly tired, but I have done (today) one lecture, four interviews, a "sidewalk" broadcast, & a two-hour autographing party at a bookstore (where we sold out completely).'

The most tiring bit, Jan found, was the morning after lectures, when she was collected from her hotel by the sponsors and taken on sightseeing tours of the Old Governor's Palace, or the Angel Mounds Historical Site. Sightseeing was never a pastime she enjoyed – she preferred street-wandering. At Fort Wayne, Indiana she got her own back by taking two of the sponsors (Mrs Mary Ann Doody and Mrs Myron R. Bone) to the cinema in the evening. 'I think they were pretty exhausted,' she wrote to Dolf, 'and they never go to Westerns, but of course they couldn't get out of it, so I led them off to a very low common mean little movie house where everybody was eating buttered popcorn, & they unbent considerably from their ladylikeness and became quite girlish . . . I thought it would be a piquant change for the lecturer to outlast the sponsors' vitality for once.'

Jan could see the isolationists' point of view. She understood why the northern Midwest states were the most isolationist of all: for not only did they contain a great many people of German descent, and not only were they midway between the two oceans, but they were almost literally isolated by the vast north–south expanses of the Great Lakes. But she was not prepared for the level of anger her presence could induce. At Grand Rapids, Michigan on 11 October she was woken in her hotel bedroom at seven by the first of a stream of abusive anonymous telephone calls. 'I don't particularly mind the abuse,' she wrote to Dolf, 'but I get as mad as hell when they refuse to give their names. Finally I left a message that I considered anonymity un-American & that I would only talk to people who had the courage to give their names. That stopped *that*. I did manage to lure one America Firster (a man, a doctor, by the way. I LIKE men better than women, I do) into (a) giving his name & (b) having coffee with me at my hotel. We talked civilly for an hour, & neither of us convinced the other.'

Over coffee and rolls in the palm court, the America Firster raged against the 'war-mongering' Roosevelt administration;

Jan replied (quoting William Howard Taft), 'Too many people don't care what happens so long as it doesn't happen to them'. When they were about to part, Jan said, 'I just want to say one more thing. Did you notice that waiter who has been standing behind the palm-tree listening to us?'

'Yes, I was aware of him,' said the doctor. 'Why?'

'Well, do you realize how lucky you are to be living in the kind of set-up where he won't go off and report you to the SS men for the things you've been saying about your own government?'

'You do not understand,' he explained. 'This is America.'

'Neither do you,' Jan said. 'This is the world.'

'We parted as courteous adversaries,' Jan wrote to Dolf, '& really he was very nice and polite, but oh God! so hopelessly out of touch about Europe. I was left with a feeling of impotence. Those folks HATE Roosevelt. They hate him more than they love the ultimate good of their own country. I almost believe he could do us more good if he pretended to be against us: they might then rush to our help. And there are 15 million of them . . .'

As she crossed the border from Wisconsin into Iowa, she wrote, 'I miss you more and more, the further west I go towards "our" country . . .'

'They Think She Is Like Mrs Miniver And Offer Her Tea' ran a sub-headline in the El Paso, Texas *Herald* three weeks later, in early November. All eyes were on this exotic woman's habits. 'She Drank Coffee.' Jan's distaste for tea was intensifying. She had discovered that at women's afternoon meetings it was an honour to be asked 'to pour'. Jan hated pouring tea, but as the guest of honour she could not avoid it without giving offence. Tea at these gatherings was made with teabags immersed in less-than-boiling water, with their cardboard labels attached and also immersed, gradually dissolving. The sight made Jan turn away in revulsion.

The El Paso *Herald*, after commenting on the non-tea-drinking, went on to quote from the lecture: 'Miss Struther believes that the feeling that Hitler must be beaten has been solidifying in the Midwest of the US in the last six months. "This country is like a body of water," she said. "When you tip it one way it rushes in that direction. It's rather terrifying."'

On the morning after *that* lecture she was taken to Radford College for Girls, 'where [she wrote to Dolf] to my horrified surprise I was expected to get up in front of 1,300 schoolchildren and give them an Uplift Message.' Two days later, in the Town Hall at San Antonio, Texas, she found herself addressing 'the entire troupe of this year's débutantes'. Her favourite question from the floor was, 'Will you please tell me whether you prefer Bach or Boogie-Woogie?' The next day's report in the San Antonio *Express* was devoted entirely to describing what members of the audience were wearing. 'Mrs Walter Grotehouse wore a black pinstripe tailored suit with a striking pin of turquoise, amber and gold', and so on.

In Texas, Jan noticed that she had ceased to be hounded by abusive telephone callers. Maybe she was right: perhaps the great American 'body of water' really was starting to tip in the Allied direction. Nobody will ever know what the outcome of the isolationist-versus-interventionist argument might have been if the Japanese had not attacked Pearl Harbor on the morning of Sunday, 7 December. Four days later, America was at war with both Japan and Germany.

Chapter Eleven

No, Mrs Poppadum, I didn't write the film. I always think it's better for authors who know nothing about script-writing to keep their fingers out of the pie. Yes, Mrs Marchpane, I simply loved the film. Since I had nothing to do with making it, I can speak quite freely. Why, yes, Mr Syllabub, I thought the casting was excellent. The station-master? Oh, yes, exactly the way I always imagined him to be. (And then I would know that Mr Syllabub hadn't read the book, because the station-master didn't come into it.)

From J.S's unfinished book on America, 'Cactus and Columbine'

THE ABBREVIATIONS FOR American radio and television stations, CBS, WNEW, WSB, KTMS and WEVD, pepper the pages of Jan's engagement book for 1942. 'B'cast, 5.30.' Her voice, speaking to a country at war, was becoming a national morale-boosting presence on the airwaves. Often, the 'b'cast' was preceded by 'H.D.' – hairdresser's – in the morning.

For these hairdressing appointments, Harlem beckoned. When no one was looking, she took a bus northwards up Third Avenue, on and on, as the buildings grew seedier and the hair curlier, like her own. Sitting in the salon of her choice, which throbbed with Afro-American life, she flicked through the hair-styling magazines and discovered that the advertisements here were not for permanent waves, but permanent straightening. She returned to Upper East Side, refreshed by this glimpse of the other New York which carried on its gritty existence fifty streets to the north.

'Morale is something like vitamins,' she said, speaking to five continents through the microphone at NBC on 1 March. 'You can't see it, you can't touch it, you can't taste it, yet if you haven't got it you're sunk.' 'If we begin to make plans now for a better world structure,' she said during a broadcast in favour of Federal Union, 'we shall have no moments of despair. We shall only have moments of acute impatience, because we cannot start to build it straight away. Nothing on earth is more fun than planning a new house in which we shall live. The thoughts that we are thinking now will be its bricks and mortar.' It was quotable oratory, and America lapped it up.

Almost as frequent as the word 'b'cast' in the engagement books is the word 'dentist'. Between January and March 1942, it appears ten times. The London *Times* had pointed out the 'flaw' in Mrs Miniver's perfection, betrayed by her mid August dentist's appointment. Four years later, her creator was still dashing from glamorous luncheon to dentist's chair with alarming frequency. Sometimes her mouth was numb for broadcasts. 'I had a fever, an ice-bag and a left cheek the size of a football,' she wrote to her lawyer Melville Cane after her Easter broadcast, 'and I talked out of the side of my mouth like a Brooklyn gangster. I hope it came through on the air all right – personally I remember nothing about it except that somebody dragged me out of bed and got me to the studio five minutes before airtime, and somebody else shoved a mike in front of me and said Okay, Miss Struther, you're on right after the Ave Maria and the Lord's Prayer. The rest was delirium.'

Jan made two new male friends at about this time. The first was this lawyer, Melville Cane, of Ernst, Cane & Young, whom she had employed to negotiate her contracts, but whom she quickly saw to be a kindred spirit, a poet at heart, unfulfilled in his legal job. The second she met at a fund-raising Republican dinner-party given by the heiress of the Wells, Fargo and Company mail-carrying service. Sitting on her right was a man who spoke like an Englishman, called John Beverley Robinson, whom Jan instantly warmed to and instinctively trusted. Such wisdom and understanding shone out of his eyes that she was disarmed. She felt an overwhelming urge to divulge to him the secret she had been holding inside her breast since her arrival in America. She could not stop herself. 'He's called Dolf. I know you'd like him,

Tony in Egypt, 1942

and he you ... I don't know why I'm telling you. I've only known you for an hour ...'

Her instinct was right: 'Bev' Robinson was a truly compassionate man, who kept Jan's secret and did not condemn her for her double life. He was sixteen years her senior, and married. His family lived in Toronto and he spent his weeks working in New York, living at the Westover, a residential hotel. He and Jan became great friends. A week later she invited Mel, Bev and Dolf to supper at East 49th Street, and they sang folk songs to a recorder she had picked up at a junk shop in Mission, Nebraska. The room was alight with candles, music, poetry, wine and laughter, and for a fleeting evening Jan and Dolf basked in the illusion that they were an accepted 'couple'.

Tony, 'five hours nearer the sun', was preparing to go to North Africa on active service with the 2nd (Motor) Battalion of the Scots Guards.

At Culver City in Hollywood, meanwhile, a new Mrs Miniver was coming into being. 'You allowed your tear to spill over just a second too soon,' William Wyler said to Greer Garson. 'Now, if you can get the tears again, I want you to hold them there. And *then* I want you to let that tear run down your cheek.'

At her wits' end over the impossibility of pleasing this director, Greer Garson thought herself back, for the hundredth time that day, into Mrs Miniver's skin. The camera moved in, and, amazingly, she felt tears stinging her eyes. She held them in, counting the seconds, until one ran down her cheek. Wyler nodded and smiled. It was awful working for him, but it could not be denied that he was a master craftsman.

Greer Garson had been scooped up by Louis B. Mayer on his talent-spotting tour of London theatres in 1937. She came to live in Hollywood with her mother, and had a miserable first year, offered demeaning parts (such as the woman who gets papered to the wall by the Marx Brothers in *A Day at the Races*), which she refused. Reluctantly, in 1938, she accepted the small part of Katherine Chipping in James Hilton's *Goodbye Mr Chips*, and was nominated for the Oscar for Best Actress. Vivien Leigh won, for *Gone With the Wind*, but Greer Garson was now a star, and her luminous beauty was recognized. Mrs Miniver was an ideal role for her. When she threatened to walk off the set after William Wyler had made her light Walter Pidgeon's cigarette so many times that she became ill from the smoke, her friend Bette Davis encouraged her to carry on. 'You will give the great performance of your career under Wyler's direction,' she said. It was true.

The film's sets were full of Hollywood fakery. The Minivers' house was unlike any ordinary English country house of the 1940s: to suit the camera lens, it was open-plan. The village, Belham (a name invented by the script-writers), crawled with roses on trellises at every corner. As for the plot, it bore only these resemblances to the original book: Mrs Miniver is a loving, loyal, wise wife and mother, married to a charming, witty man named Clem; their children are Vin, Judy and Toby; Mrs Miniver gets off a bus in a hurry to rush back to a shop, deciding to buy something after all (originally an engagement-book, a hat in the film); Clem buys a new car.

Out of the fertile imaginations of the producer and his five script-writers came astonishing additions to pad out these four vestiges of the book. Jan blinked with surprise when she went for her early viewing. A village flower-show was the running sub-plot of the film: Lady Beldon (played by Dame May Whitty) expected to win, as usual, but was horrified to hear that Mr Ballard the station-master (played by Henry Travers) was entering 'The Mrs Miniver Rose'. Jan could only admire the film's creators, who had brazenly invented the flower-show, Lady Beldon, Mr Ballard, and 'The Mrs Miniver Rose'. On and on it went, for an hour and a half: an unfolding love-story and war-

The air-raid-shelter scene from the film of Mrs Miniver

story, full of new material, totally gripping, and impossible to watch without soaking a handkerchief.

The aura of excellence about the film derived from various sources. William Wyler's directing was one, with his instinct to pare down rather than fill out. In the original screenplay, when Vin was called up to join the Royal Air Force, Mrs Miniver's lines were: 'I'm all mixed up, thinking about Vin. Oh, you men! What a mess you've made of the world! Why can't we leave other people alone?' But during filming, that was all cut. In the finished version Mrs Miniver simply says, 'Isn't he young? Even for the Air Force?' and Clem answers, 'Yes, he's young.' In the Dunkirk sequence, too, Wyler leaves the horrors to the imagination. Clem sails off in the middle of the night, and returns with five days' growth of beard. 'You've heard it on the news,' he says to his wife. 'I'm glad. That means I don't have to tell you about it.'

Then there was the acting, which despite Wyler's insistence on endless takes gave an impression of naturalness. Mr and Mrs

Mrs Miniver with her daughter-in-law Carol Beldon (played by Teresa Wright), also from the film

Miniver teased more than they praised one another: the strength of family love was not stated outright, but hinted at through casual snatches of conversation. Judy and Toby (played by Clare Sandars and Christopher Severn) spoke their cringe-making sugary lines, but the sight of them peacefully asleep in the air-raid shelter, only waking and crying with terror and bewilderment when their own house was hit, was deeply touching. No scene went on for too long.

Then there was the shocking twist in the plot at the end of the film. It was the producer Sidney Franklin's idea that Vin's young wife Carol Beldon (played by Teresa Wright) should die, rather than Vin, the RAF pilot: a civilian death would bring home to American audiences what this war was really like for the British population. William Wyler sat up late into the night with Henry Wilcoxon (who played the vicar), rewriting the film's final sermon. It began quietly – 'We, in this quiet corner

of England, have suffered the loss of friends very dear to us' –
and worked its way to a climax: 'This is the people's war! It is
our war! We are the fighters. Fight it, then! Fight it, with all
that is in us! And may God defend the right!' The film, they
decided, would end with the closing hymn, 'Onward, Christian
soldiers', sung by a dazed congregation with gaps in the pews,
and bomber planes visible over the roofless church.

'THIS was their finest hour and THIS is your finest attraction',
ran MGM's advertisement in *Kinematograph Weekly*. 'Not only
the best of the year . . . Not only the best of the War . . . but the
best EVER produced by Metro-Goldwyn-Mayer!' Mayer had told
Greer Garson that she must on no account let her romantic
attachment to Richard Ney become public knowledge at this
delicate time. The hint of incest would be disastrous for publicity.

Jan was a guest of honour in the audience at the film's première at Radio City Music Hall on Thursday, 4 June 1942. The
MGM lion roared. Two paragraphs of scene-setting gothicky
words rolled down the screen, to the stringed strains of a familiar tune:

> Oh God, our help in ages past,
> Our hope for years to come,
> Our shelter from the stormy blast
> And our eternal –

The final cadence was an unresolved minor chord. It was the
signal to sit back and prepare for tears.

Jan decided, wincing every now and then during the performance, that she would never be rude about the film in public.
Whatever she might think privately about the liberties MGM
had taken with her book, whatever she might feel about the
idealized representation of English village life or the irritating
ladylikeness of Greer Garson's Mrs Miniver, she knew that it
was her duty, as an unofficial ambassadress for Britain, to
uphold the film without reservations. 'I was apprehensive' – this
was the message she put across in interviews – 'but as a matter
of fact I got a lovely surprise when I saw how closely the film

had followed the characterisations in the book. The whole Miniver family behaved in the film exactly as I had always believed and hoped they would behave when the bad times came. I feel convinced that there are Mrs Minivers in every freedom-loving country in the world, and that they and their families, like the characters in my book, will be able to meet any trial that may come with the same courage, fortitude and faith.' She instructed Janet and Robert, also, never to say a bad word about the film to anyone outside the family.

She dashed from Radio City to Grand Central Station, to go to Janet's school play. While she was contemplating the small-ness of the school auditorium compared with the one she had just left, film critics across New York were at their typewriters.

Some of them, it turned out the next morning, were almost lit-erally lost for words. 'I have wasted all the superlatives in the dictionary on lesser films,' wrote Lee Mortimer of the New York *Mirror*. 'Mere words are inadequate to express the emotional impact of this superb picture,' said the Albany, New York *Times*. 'Out of the rather casual jottings that were made into a best-seller called *Mrs Miniver*,' said the *New Yorker*, 'a movie has evolved that might almost be called stupendous.' 'Perhaps it is too soon to call this one of the greatest motion pictures of all time,' said the *New York Times*, 'but certainly it is the finest yet made about the present war, and a most exalting tribute to the British who have taken it gallantly. One cannot speak too highly of the superb understatement and restraint exercised throughout this picture.'

Audiences emerged from the film shocked and red-eyed. Word spread fast. In its first four days at Radio City, the film was seen by 98,207 people, and people carried on seeing it at the rate of 20,000 a day. Its value as propaganda quickly became apparent. The head of the US Office of War Information, Elmer Davis, called for the film to be released nationally 'to convey its mes-sage to as many Americans as possible, as soon as possible'. As it opened in Loew's theatres across the the United States, Jan travelled from city to city, a useful component of MGM's pub-licity machine, giving first-night talks immediately after the screenings. She walked on to the stage, into the spotlight, holding one of MGM's 'Mrs Miniver' roses, produced for publicity purposes by the American botanist Dr Eugene Boerner, and stood peering out at her audience. 'I feel certain that if your cities here have to undergo the bombing ordeal that England's cities have, your ordinary people are going to behave in the same way we have, in the same way as the Minivers you have just seen.' She walked out through the foyer, where war stamps and war bonds were being sold, and went back to her hotel alone.

At Atlanta, Georgia on 13 July there was a message for her in the hotel pigeon-hole. She had sent a cable to Tony in North Africa six weeks before: he had let her know that he was in charge of No. 19 Anti-Tank Platoon. 'Pommel Rommel good and hard' she had cabled – she knew he would enjoy the rhyme. Now she opened the envelope: Tony was 'missing on active service, presumed captured'.

It had happened at the Battle of Gazala, the costly struggle which ended with the Allied surrender of Tobruk after a week of siege. Jan sank down onto a chair in the hotel lobby to absorb the news. A member of staff brought her water: Atlanta was proud to help Mrs Miniver at this terrible moment. And what forbearance she showed! said the papers in the following days, when word spread that 'Mr Miniver' had been captured. 'She telephoned her children, attended a luncheon given for her, and visited wounded soldiers at Lawson Hospital, showing none of the fear and sorrow which must be in her mind.' The journalists could not know that fear and sorrow were only two of the multitude of emotions which swarmed in Jan's mind, heart and conscience.

She decided not to break the news to Janet and Robert until she had heard for certain whether Tony was alive.

Mrs Miniver went into its sixth week at Radio City Music Hall, equalling the record held by *Rebecca* and *The Philadelphia Story*. It opened in Britain at the Empire, Leicester Square, on 11 July. Critics once again sat at their typewriters; predictably, they were crueller than their American counterparts, just as they had been about the book. *The Times*: 'The picture of England at war suffers from that distortion which seems inevitable whenever Hollywood cameras are trained on it.' *The Manchester Guardian*: 'The eldest son comes down from Oxford sporting a bowler hat and a Canadian accent, a naïve and inarticulate college boy who could not possibly be the product of Eton and Oxford.' The *Observer*: 'No gents' outfitters of our acquaintance supplied Mr Miniver with his pyjamas.' *Time and Tide*: 'The village church has a medieval circular tower which seems to have strayed from Conwy Castle.' The *Spectator*: 'The film ponderously reveals us on Sunday September 3rd 1939 as a collection of simple-minded innocents basking in a smile from the squire's pew and without any inkling whatsoever that we may be at war before the service is over.'

'But...' Nearly all these reviewers, having vented their spleen, succumbed to a final 'but' clause: 'But it is years since I remember being so touched by any film' ... 'But it would be the grossest ingratitude to do anything but thank our American friends for this warm-hearted picture' ... 'In spite of the foregoing, it is my duty to certify that in my vicinity two medical students, three naval officers and a sergeant in the RAF sobbed loudly and continuously throughout.' (This last from the *Tatler*, which carried a photograph of Jan's brother Douglas Anstruther at the British première. He was now Major Anstruther, and he was becoming quite an eccentric. He wore a judge's wig when dining, to keep the draught off his neck. Jan had sent him funds for an ambulance: he bought the body and fitted it to the chassis of his Rolls-Royce, named the ambulance 'Mrs Miniver' and proudly showed it off. 'It can carry ten men into action, or carry two stretchers and two sitters, or be a canteen. It carries fourteen gallons of drinking-water and eight for washing up.')

There was no 'but' clause in Harry Ashbrook's quiveringly angry article in the *Sunday Pictorial* of 26 July. Jan read it and felt once again the mixture of guilt and a sense of unfairness that Sheridan Russell's letter had engendered. 'She's a Disgrace to the Women of Britain!' ran the headline.

This is England – the England of the miners. Settling into their comfortable beds, exhausted by a day's shopping, Mr and Mrs Miniver congratulate each other for being born into the British upper middle class. 'We are very lucky people,' they chorus. Talking of lucky people, in the North of England is a town called Jarrow. Nine out of ten men of Jarrow were out of work before the war. While Mrs Miniver drifted around village flower shows, the men of Jarrow looked for work. I'll say you were lucky, Mrs Miniver. Mrs Miniver's creator Jan Struther said recently, '*I plan to stay in America for the rest of the war because my children are happily settled here and I don't want to disturb them.*' The ordinary working people of Jarrow, Clydeside and Coventry are fighting this war and all the old nonsense of tea-parties and flower-shows has gone. Their life would make a grand film, Mrs Graham. But you've got to come back to see them before you can write it.

Vera Brittain saw the film twice in the weeks after its British release. 'I love it,' she wrote in her diary, 'but I think Jan Struther is a charlatan posing as a patriot in the safety of the USA.'

Tony was safe, a prisoner-of-war. Jan received airmail letters from both Tony and Jamie, and she smiled with relief when she found that Tony's experiences had already become the stuff of anecdote.

He had been captured on 13 June at a place in the desert called Maabus-el-Rigel, known as 'Wriggly Ridge'. He was forty-two, twenty years older than his fellow subalterns; helmetless, and almost completely bald, he was taken by the Germans for a high-ranking officer. The finer points of British badges of rank were a bit of a mystery to them. 'Daddy was put into an enormous staff car,' Jamie wrote, 'and whisked off amid a flurry of Teutonic salutes.' 'What are you doing in that car?' asked a fellow prisoner. 'They think I'm a general,' answered the departing Tony. That night, two or three of the Scots Guards officers taken at the same time managed to slip past the sentries, back to the British lines, but Tony was by then far to the rear of the German position. Eventually, he was discovered to be just an elderly lieutenant.

*

Mrs Miniver-mania continued to grip the United States. The millionth ticket was purchased on 19 July by a Mrs Harry M. Simon, blushing as she was photographed. The film went into its ninth week at Radio City Music Hall, and its tenth. Jan was a guest of honour at Radio City, with Walter Pidgeon and William Wyler, to celebrate the film's record run. Now, at the height of her celebrity, she moved house, from East 49th Street to an address worthy of it: 214 Central Park South. This time, she didn't take a lodger. Dolf and she could at last spend days and nights 'at home' together, when no one was looking.

Mrs Miniver opened in Canada, and a journalist named Roly, in his weekly column 'Rambling with Roly', took the art of rambling to new heights: 'A couple of days ago, I came back to the office after seeing *Mrs Miniver* and tried to write a review of the film. I think I made a hash of the attempt. It was the toughest review I ever tried to write because my mind was in an emotional turmoil and I couldn't seem to find the words to say what I wanted to say . . .' Like so many others, he was lost for words. The film was shown to the British Army in Cairo, and generals and colonels wept: many had not seen their families in England since the Blitz. Major Eric Sandars, the father of Clare Sandars, who played Judy, was one of those who saw it in Cairo. His daughter had been evacuated to the United States at the outbreak of war, and spotted by Hollywood scouts as a 'typical English child'.

When it was shown in Buenos Aires, the German Embassy there protested strongly to the Argentine government against the showing of such an anti-Axis film. It was the last Hollywood film to be shown in Budapest before the Nazis put a stop to all US film imports.

In neutral Sweden, as in Switzerland, Axis and Allied films vied for popularity. The Germans took half-page spaces in the Stockholm newspapers to boost the new Jannings film about Frederick the Great which had won first prize at the Venice Film Festival; it ran for seven days in a half-empty cinema. *Mrs Miniver* ran for twenty weeks, showing at four cinemas in the centre of Stockholm.

*

'I'm sitting in a Pullman pouring with sweat,' Jan wrote to Dolf on the way from Louisville to New Orleans in mid July. 'At every big-town stop (even for five minutes) there is an MGM man, a Loew's man, a photographer, a reporter, and a local Lady Beldon on the platform to give me a bo-kay, usually so-called 'Miniver' roses, but if unobtainable, orchids. It's all very, very comic.'

Janet and Robert were at summer camps in Maine, and Jan was travelling incessantly, signing rolls of honour, selling war stamps, autographing stamp books, recording scripts to be used in broadcasts such as the 'Cleveland at War' programme, and running along station platforms and jumping onto trains just as the man was calling ''Board!' It was impossible to get away from America's *Mrs Miniver*-itis. Leafing through a Boston magazine she came across this:

> Mrs Miniver's Haircut – it's soft and pretty and easy to manage. It's very wearable with the new hats and a joy to take care of, especially if you assure it with a new Slattery permanent wave. Phone HANCOCK 6600 for appointments.

Sitting down to lunch a week later at a restaurant in Toledo, Ohio, she found 'Mrs Miniver's Fruit Salad Plate' on the menu.

America launched contests to name its 'Mrs Minivers' – women who 'served on the home front'. 'Vote for YOUR favourite Mrs Miniver and vote today!' cried the Lewistown, Pennsylvania *Sentinel*. The Los Angeles *Herald* printed the names of Los Angeles's Mrs Minivers, 'who run their houses smoothly and still find time for the war effort; the women who have sacrificed sons and husbands, and carry on with indomitable courage.' Los Angeles even awarded a bouquet of Dr Eugene Boerner's roses to its 'Mrs Miniver of the Day'.

Surely, Jan hoped, with the film so successful, and with Mrs Minivers popping up in major cities all over America, she could escape from the burden of being mistaken for her saintly fictional creation. And gradually during 1942, the longed-for release did begin to take place. Greer Garson willingly took over as the embodiment of Mrs Miniver in the public imagination.

Greer Garson and Jan in Hollywood

And the public were relieved to discover that Greer Garson's favourite drink was afternoon tea: two bags, cream in first.

Up until this time, during her journeys across America, Jan had known that sooner or later she would be going 'home' to Dolf in New York. Wherever she travelled, she could rest assured that he was within a three-mile radius of Columbia University, and waiting for her. (He had crossed the campus at

Columbia in June 1942 for a job as an assistant bibliographer at the Avery Architectural Library.) But suddenly at the beginning of 1943, this changed. Dolf, who had been granted American citizenship in 1942, volunteered to join the United States Army. He knew he would eventually be drafted, and hoped that as a volunteer he would be allowed to choose his 'combat theater': he wanted to go to Germany to kill Hitler with his own hands. In a thick Viennese accent he swore his oath of allegiance, and became Private A.K. Placzek. For his basic training, he was to be stationed in California. Once again *force majeure* was sending him three thousand miles to the west, away from Jan.

Chapter Twelve

The westbound train is running four hours late.
A dozen times at least it's pulled into a siding,
And the passengers listen, and wonder,
And listen, and wait
For the growing thunder and then the dying thunder
Of troop train or freight
Taking the right of way.
The conductor's an old man, patient and grey:
He's ridden this road for thirty years or more,
And he *knows the score.*
'Yes, Sir,
Wartime riding's not peacetime riding.'

Six hours late. The slim quicksilver bar
On the wall of the coach has climbed to ninety-four.
It isn't a real coach, but a baggage car
Hauled from retirement, fixed to meet the rush:
The seats are upright, covered in dirty plush;
The sides, windowless iron, vibrate with the heat.
In back, two businessmen unfasten their collars
And loosen their shoes to ease their swollen feet.
They missed the Limited — scrambled on at a run.
'This is a hell of a train,' says the paunchy one.
'I wouldn't take it again for a thousand dollars.'
But the thin one has a son
In Africa or the Arctic (he doesn't know which –
This is a crazy war),
And to him it doesn't matter any more
Whether he travels the poor man's way or the rich.
He *knows the score.*
Yes, *Sir.*
Folks know things now they never knew before.

From 'Wartime Journey', published in *Atlantic Monthly*

'GELIEBSTER SOLDAT' – 'Beloved soldier' – Jan wrote to Dolf from Durham, North Carolina on 13 February 1943. She was determined to be a tower of strength for him as he left for the Army. 'I am *really* glad they accepted you after all. It is hell to be separated, but I know you'd have felt disappointed if you hadn't got in. The great thing is that it's only "limited service" so that somehow or other we'll be able to meet sometimes. I feel I'm actually in the Army myself, or possibly the Navy, as I've spent so much time travelling with them all. I made friends yesterday with a bunch of four Naval Reserve men & we pooled all our meagre provisions during an interminable journey from Greenboro' to Durham. They had some candy and I had some bananas.'

Dolf was worried: would there be any kindred spirits in the Army? Jan reassured him.

I spent a gorgeous evening yesterday with the Army at Fort Bragg, watching a show being put on for the benefit of their Soldiers' Lounge Fund. One of my poems was set to music by Otto Guth, a sergeant, Viennese Jew, late of the Prague Symph. Orch. Then a beautiful youth came on & played music, & the Master of Ceremonies said, 'You see? In the daytime he learns to fire the big guns – and in the evening he practises his violin. Let's give him an extra-big hand.' Which we did. I only hope to God that you get into as nice a camp, and that they discover about your piano-playing. Sweetheart, I know you must be dreading it in a way – I mean things like woollen underwear & bean farts & the lack of privacy – but DO remember that it isn't an army of hicks & bloggs & toughs – I've met dozens of mild spectacled cultivated-looking soldiers during this journey, who all must have dreaded it.

Jan was on another lecture tour. Topic: 'A Pocketful of Pebbles', said her Details of Engagement from Clark Getts. Englewood, Glen Ridge and Summit, New Jersey; Greenboro, Durham and Charlotte, North Carolina; Greenville, South Carolina; Cincinnati and Delaware, Ohio; Detroit, Michigan; Indianapolis, Indiana . . . she travelled for two months, giving three or four lectures a week.

'There is one great – and, so far as I can see, insuperable – problem in a lecturer's life,' she said to her audiences.

Speaking engagements are usually planned many months ahead, and it's only natural that the programme's chairmen, who have to deal with publicity, should want to know well in advance what one is going to talk about. Now, this wouldn't present any difficulty if one was a learned professor with some highly specialized subject like 'Ancient Chinese Music' or 'The History of English Painting in the 18th century'. But if, like me, you are not an expert or a specialist in anything at all, but only a quite un-highbrow human being whose main interest is in the day-to-day feelings of other un-highbrow human beings – well, then it's practically impossible to decide on a topic months ahead, because it all depends upon what's going to happen to the world in the meantime. So when this date was first arranged, and my lecture manager called me up and asked what the title of my talk was going to be, I replied that I hadn't the faintest notion. He said, very patiently, 'Well, but you see, the sponsors want to know.' I said that this was just as bad as being asked to decide on a Monday morning what you were going to talk to your family about at supper a week from Saturday. And then I had an idea. I remembered having once described how 'Mrs Miniver' used to save up all the thoughts and incidents of the day so that she could discuss them in the evening, and how 'Clem' did the same thing, and how it was as if each was turning out a pocketful of pebbles that they'd collected for each other during the day. So I said to my lecture manager, 'Look! You just tell them that the title of my talk will be 'A Pocketful of Pebbles', and that'll leave me entirely free to speak about anything which occurs to me between this and then.

Audiences enjoyed this friendly babble: it was the antithesis of lecturely pomposity. The loose title enabled Jan to break the lecture up into sections rather than droning on about a single subject for sixty minutes. She liked to give an impression of off-the-cuffness in her lectures, though in fact she honed them for hours in the silence of her hotel rooms. 'I know a lot of folks who say they always make their talks extemporaneously,' she said in an interview for the Charlotte *Observer* in February 1943 before one of her lectures. 'Yes, and they sound like it, too.'

'Please tell us something about your husband,' said the

Charlotte journalist. 'If you want my husband's name,' replied Jan, smiling, 'you'd better get out your pencil, because it's pretty long. He's called Anthony Maxtone Graham. He's a prisoner-of-war in Italy. And he's doing nicely. I had a letter from him only four days ago. It was written last October.'

That letter had taken fourteen weeks to arrive. Some took longer. Most did not arrive at all, whether to or from Tony. The weekly allowance for a POW to send was one airmail letter form, and one postcard. Out of a total of fifty Tony sent to his family from Chieti Camp in Italy, only three were delivered. To judge from these three that have survived (none to or from Jan), it is clear that captivity (or rather, the consequent freedom from the responsibility of being grown-up) had an inspiring effect on Tony. He blossomed. Jan, in her scathing Ogden-Nashese poem about fidelity, had advised against 'letting him [one's husband] in for amateur dramatics in any shape or form'. But now she wasn't watching. Tony's latent talents as an impresario were reflected by his election as 'Chairman of Chieti Entertainment'. To Jamie and Ysenda he wrote:

I have written a longish 1-act play & am going to embark on the most ambitious play-writing project shortly . . . Music is going strong; we have a theatre variety orchestra, a dance band & a chamber-music orch., all of which come under my aegis. We had a Mozart concert on Sunday which was hugely successful. We are lucky in having Tommy Sampson, a dance band leader in private life, & above all Tony Baines, the Philharmonic player, who is superb. They work from dawn till lights out, scoring & rehearsing . . . We have not had any scores supplied to us yet, tho' we got the instruments without too much difficulty. The theatre is great fun, & we have produced an enormous variety of entertainments. Again we have no play scripts but James Oliphant [Tony's middle names – his POW *nom-de-plume*] has been kept busy! I have done three 1-act plays, one full-length thriller, and one full-length trial so far – very successful, though I say it. Every show runs for 4 performances – about 300 of an audience at each . . . I have had good letters from USA but no acknowledgement of any of mine . . . Tobacco is my principal want; and books on playwriting, and books of plays.

An illuminated testimonial given to Tony by his fellow prisoners mentions the forty-five plays he produced, including *The Admirable Crichton*, *The Man Who Came to Dinner*, and *HMS Pinafore* (there was much ironic cheering at the line 'Or an Ital-i-an').

A prisoner-of-war-camp theatrical production. The 'bead' curtains are made of thousands of rolled-up cigarette papers

While Tony had respected Rommel's soldiers, he held his Italian guards in contempt and up to ridicule. Notices were put up warning the prisoners not to walk or loiter too close to the barbed-wire fences, drafted by the commandant, too proud to ask for a translation from the Senior British Officer, with the help of his pocket commercial dictionary: 'PASSAGE AND DEMUR-RAGE NO ALLOW'. As a marine insurance broker, Tony knew that 'demurrage' was the charge paid by ships which loiter too long in port. The pompousness of the notice inspired Tony and his fellow prisoners to all the more fun, in spite of the guards.

While Jan was keeping up the morale of the lecture-going public in America, Tony was doing the same for the Chieti prisoners, many of whom might have sunk into despair but for his contagious good spirits.

Dolf, in uniform, boarded his Army train, and set off westwards across America with 'the buddies'. Far from being the violin-playing types Jan had hoped for, they were sweet-natured, thick-necked men who talked about girls and tried to prise from Dolf the truth about his love life. Catching his first sight of the Mississippi, one whistled and said, 'There she is, the big mother fucker.'

Mother – *what*? Dolf had never heard the expression before, and his Viennese sensibilities were ruffled. Saying that about a *river*? He tried not to think of Pauly.

His address, in the coming months, was 'Company B, 77th Infantry Training Battalion, Camp Roberts, California'. As soon as it was discovered that he could type, he was marked out for desk work, rather than combat duty. His wartime service, as he later described it, was 'on the typewriter front'. Three thousand miles away from anyone he knew, six thousand miles away from his homeland, he relied on Jan's letters for sustenance. And they came.

'When are you going to write your next book?' journalists often asked Jan. 'A sequel to *Mrs Miniver*, or a book about America?' 'Next week, positively next week, I *will* begin writing that book,' she sometimes replied. But, in truth, no such book was germinating inside her. Apart from her lectures and occasional poems, all her creative energy was channelled into communicating with Dolf. It was the only writing which seemed worthwhile to her.

The war was causing a great slowing-down of transport across America. Trains ran six, seven, eight hours late, and Jan spent these hours at a standstill with pad and pen. Gasoline rationing meant that people had to share rides and forgo non-essential journeys, but despite the shortage three thousand people attended her lecture in Greenville, South Carolina, a fact which astonished her. Would nothing stop them from going to lectures? One thing the gasoline shortage did put a stop to, however, much to her relief, was the compulsory sightseeing drive the morning after.

Darling [she wrote on 16 February 1943], I managed to catch the Cincinnati Express – the station authorities at Richmond were persuaded to hold it for me! (The station-master was a Miniver fan, & had heard me speak at Loew's Theatre last July.) So I rushed across the tracks, & clambered on to the train to find there was no food on it. However, the conductor gave me his only apple, and the Pullman porter came up to my bunk & shyly said, 'Ah hev an orange yew could hev ef yew lakke . . .' I ate them and then slept for eight hours & feel fine.

Don't worry about me: I'm tired but at the very TOP of my form, making gorgeous speeches & writing gorgeous poetry. I can't be unhappy when I'm in my present state of acute, starry, clear-headed but burning-hearted inner fertility. I've gone down to 108 lbs & am size 10 again. I feel all the time as though I'm walking – no, dancing – on air & my head is bursting with poems and ideas. Forgive my arrogance but who wouldn't be arrogant if they had my luck? – The greatest part of which is to have been your lover for three such perfect years & to know that I am still loved by a great poet who I know is also going to be a great soldier . . .

Dan [Jan's friend Dan Golenpaul, the businessman behind *Information, Please!*] is going to put me on *Inf. Pl.* at least once a month, if not oftener, as the 'anchor' guest on the opposite week from Oscar Levant: and as I now get $400 a time instead of $200, you can see what a difference this will make to my finances. But you know nothing changes me inside, whether it's success or revenues, just as long as I have enough vitamins and red corpuscles. (And love. Not sex, but LOVE.) Sweet love, I adore you, & I carry round with me two of the photographs I took of you in Battersea Park just before our last agonizing farewell!

Dolf didn't feel that he was being a great soldier. What he was experiencing for the first time in his life – like so many people new to the Army – was boredom. Jan longed for his news: for hilarious details about barrack rooms, or about any violinists he had unearthed. But Dolf could think of little to report, except which film he had seen in downtown Los Angeles during his twenty-four-hour pass. 'Just came back from my pass, which was on the lonely side, as usual.'

From Jamie in England, too, Jan received letters hinting at the loneliness and newslessness of the soldier. Jamie was at Pirbright Camp, having joined the Scots Guards in October 1942. Army life was too repetitive and dull to write about. The only news Jamie – like Dolf – felt inspired to give was what he had done on his leaves. There was no home to go to in London (the lease on Halsey Street had been given up, and Wellington Square was shut up, its rooms draped with dust-sheets), so he stayed in friends' flats, and went out for solitary dinners at the Martinez in Swallow Street. For spiritual sustenance, he went to National Gallery concerts: in one letter he enclosed a programme of Schubert songs accompanied by Gerald Moore, to which he went alone on 19 April 1943. These concerts always reminded him of the one he had been to with his mother on the day before she sailed.

Both Dolf and Jamie, cut off though they were from Jan, could see her name on the screen and hear her voice on the airwaves. '*Mrs Miniver* was shown at Pirbright cinema at the weekend,' Jamie wrote. 'I thought Vin was awful, but it is getting a terrific reception here.' He also heard Jan on a transAtlantic Brains Trust programme, broadcast from New York. Dolf sometimes tuned in to *Information, Please!*, just to hear Jan's voice. And, knowing he might be listening, she secretly spoke to him, or sang to him: 'Oh, *if* you listened last night I hope you got my message! There was a question – "Sing a line of a song containing the word 'Johnnie'." So I upped and sang, "I would give them all for my handsome winsome Johnnie", and thought so *so* longingly of you while I sang.'

She was still being strong for them both. 'The Placzek–Struther Axis is strong and we'll lick the world yet, whether we're in each other's arms or not. When I'm up on a platform trying to sway an audience, you're standing invisibly beside me saying, "Stand up *straight*, & let's have a nice Joycerl smile." And when you're on kitchen duty peeling potatoes with hands that should be playing Mozart, then *I'm* beside *you*, saying "Hold the knife the other way, you sweet left-handed son of a bitch."'

At about this time, though, she began to betray small hints of the exhaustion which was beginning to seep into her body and mind. Adrenalin enabled her to sail, glowing, through evenings like this one at the Weir Cove Community Women's Club of West Virginia:

PROGRAM

Theme Song: "Moonlight and Roses"

"Hail West Virginia"_____Miller-McWherter

"Your Land and My Land"_____Romberg

"The Song of the Jolly Roger"_____Candish

"A Lullaby"_____Ford

"Song of the Marching Men"_____Protheroe

"The Mulligan Musketeers"_____Atkinson

"The Creation"_____Richter

Theme Song: "Moonlight and Roses"

WEIRTON STEEL MALE CHORUS

T. Herbert Davies, Director
Harry Elliott, Accompanist

"THE TRUTH ABOUT MRS. MINIVER"

JAN STRUTHER

But she was finding it harder and harder to wind down after these lectures, and she was beginning to resort to sleeping-pills. Here she describes to Dolf, in one unbroken paragraph, a typical forty-eight hours of her spring 1943 lecture tour.

I was talking to people almost without a break from 10 a.m. till midnight . . . An autographing 'Do' from 2–3.15 & another from 3.15 to 4.30. Back to my hotel, where an Irish-Minnesotan guy called Kennan interviewed me (and gave me a drink). Then a rapid dressing, then dinner [with the sponsors] . . . Then the lecture, at which I talked to a packed theatre (2,000, I shd think) for an hour and answered questions for another half-hour . . . [Then she had agreed to be driven to Toledo by a stranger, Mr Hardgrove, a necessity of the gasoline shortage.] I was relieved to see that Mr Hardgrove was a kindly respectable humorous blondish 'family man'. By the time we set off from Akron it was 12.30 a.m. & the roads were a sheet of ice, & we were running through thick white fog, with trucks suddenly looming up. But I was so utterly exhausted that I slept more than half the time. I had to ask him to stop once, so I could get out and p— in the snow, but we were neither of us in the least embarrassed. Exhaustion reduces people to complete simplicity. We finally got into Toledo at 3.45 a.m. The car doors were frozen & my eyes were gummed up with sleep. I opened them just long enough to check in & get to my room & then collapsed into bed, hoping to sleep till 9. But my blasted mental alarm-clock woke me at 7.15. Then at 9.30 a visit to Edna Rowe's school – and the heartrending experience of being presented with a flower-posy by a boy called Chuck (four years old), who was born blind & is terribly cross-eyed & very ugly & very sweet, while the press photographer struggled to get a picture of the ceremony without showing Chuck's eyes. Chuck kept stroking me and snuggling up to me but turning his face to the camera, & I had to keep trying to get him to turn the right way without saying anything obvious. And the photographer kept saying 'You just keep right on smiling and talking, Miss Struther.' 'Keep smiling' – my God, I wanted to cry all the time . . . I managed *not* to cry during that, but when the singing class of the school began singing 'London Bridge is falling down, my fair lady' which is for me the quintessence of *Heimweh*, I'm afraid I pretty well broke

down. Not in their sight, but in Miss Rowe's office . . . [That same
evening, she gave another lecture, to 1,000 people.] I spoke for one
and a half hours to an absolutely *tops* audience . . . I think I had
more applause here than I've ever had before – maybe my technique
is improving; I know I stand more still & speak more flowingly than
I used to. Then half an hour of questions (good ones, too, giving lots
of opportunities for stories & wisecracks & sly digs at *U.S.* class dis-
tinctions, etc.) Then a biggish party at a 'By*ood*iful Home', where I
drank punch and was forced by Edna Rowe to read some of my
poems . . . I went back to my hotel at 12.45 and thought, Now the
Day is Over . . . But the telephone rang . . . It was Harold [Harley,
Editor of the Toledo *Times*], asking if I'd like to come over to his
room and have a nightcap. So I said I'd come for 10 minutes. I went,
& stayed till 3 a.m., lying on a sofa & discussing poetry, philosophy,
medicine, psychology, love – with particular reference to *his* love
life, not mine . . . To bed at 3.15, took a sleeping-pill (which I hadn't
for several nights) and planned to sleep till noon. I need hardly tell
you that I woke up at 8.30. I am a *little* tired. (Department of British
Understatement.)

One of the poems she read out at the 'byoodiful home' was a
ballad she had just written, 'The American Way of Life':

> I met an old man
>   The other day:
> His eyes were small
>   And sharp and grey;
> His paunch was fat
>   And his lips were thin,
> And his cheeks were as dry
>   As a rattler's skin.
> And all the time
>   As he talked and ate,
> In went victuals
>   And out came hate.
> Like a burst of hail,
>   Like a creek in spate –
> His own particular
>   Hymn of Hate.

'I don't know whether
  You share my views,
But it makes me mad
  When I read the news.
Helping the Russians
  And helping the Jews . . .
Rationing sugar
  And rationing shoes . . .
All these orders
  And all these bans,
Cutting out coupons,
  And counting cans.
Oh, I know – the war . . .
  And I know – Lease-Lend . . .
But where is the whole thing
  Going to end?
I view with fear
  And deep misgiving
This change for the worse
  In our manner of living:
In fact, as I frequently say to my wife,
We're in danger of losing our own way of life –
      Our own,
      Known,
      Sure,
      Secure,
Great American way of life.'

Said I to him,
  'Well, that may be.
I'm only a guest
  From across the sea,
And I've only been here
  Two years or three;
But this is the way
  It seems to me.

'The men who founded
  And built this land –

They didn't do it
  On food that was canned,
But on home-made broth,
  And home-cooked hash
And hominy grits
  And succotash.
The men who trudged
  Through Cumberland Gap
Wore buckskin boots
  And a coonskin cap;
And the men who crossed
  The Great Divide,
They slept rolled up
  In buffalo hide.
The things they owned
  Were simple and few;
They used them well
  And they made them do.
They made their own songs,
  And they loved to sing 'em;
They thought their wives
  Looked fine in gingham;
And though they ached
  From their own day's labours,
They were never too tired
  To help their neighbours.
They'd strength in their arms
  And breadth in their backs;
They won this land
  With rifle and axe,
They followed their stars
  And they earned their stripes,
And they didn't have time
  For groans and gripes.

'Now I've travelled this land
  Two years or three;
I love it next
  To my own countree;

And from what I hear,
　And from what I see,
This is the way
　It seems to me:

'Something was lost –
　Not lost but hidden,
Like a sleeping hound
　That wakes when it's bidden;
But out of this danger and out of this strife
Is springing afresh your own way of life –
　The plain,
　Sane,
　Old,
　Bold,
True American Way of Life.'

She sent a copy of the poem to Eleanor Roosevelt, on the off-chance that she might like it.

'LATE STAR FINAL! BLUE STREAK EDITION!' she wrote to Dolf, at the end of her letter of 19 March. She enclosed the following:

> The White House
> Washington D.C.
>
> Dear Miss Struther,
> 　Many thanks for your letter & for the ballad. I love it! It is a grand answer. Would you be willing to have the President read it on his next broadcast?
> 　　　　Sincerely yours,
> 　　　　Eleanor Roosevelt

'Oh boy, oh, boy, oh Jesus *F. Christ* . . . my cup is full (very nearly – if you were here it would be quite!). Oh, oh, *oh* I'm so excited. I called her up at once (as soon as I'd got my breath back) & talked to the sec. as she was out of town. You ought to have seen Anne's [Jan's secretary Anne Curtis Brown's] face of utter deliberate gloating nonchalance as she put through the person-to-person call and heard the operator gulp.'

*

At the Academy Awards ceremony, *Mrs Miniver* won five Oscars: best actress (Greer Garson), best supporting actress (Teresa Wright), best directorial achievement (William Wyler), best written screenplay, and best achievement in black-and-white photography. Greer Garson made a long speech through her tears, thanking everyone, including the doctor who had brought her into the world.

She bought a new home in Los Angeles, 680 Stone Canyon, and her Miniver-esque life there was described by visiting journalists. 'You feel as if you were walking into the Miniver home when you visit Greer Garson,' wrote Mary C. McCall. 'It's a homely, mildly Tudor white brick manse secreted in its own little canyon through which a brook flows, with some artificial goading, under ancient sycamores.' The rooms were panelled in bleached oak, with Scottish crests on the doors. Tea, by the poolside, included cucumber sandwiches, Banbury tarts and marmalade rolls, and Greer Garson loved to chat about her favourite poet, John Donne.

'If you come to Washington,' wrote Eleanor Roosevelt to Jan on 28 March 1943, 'do let me know. Both my husband and I will be happy to see you.'

Jan replied: 'Thank you for your lovely letter. It was sweet of you to write again, and as for the invitation, I am at a loss how to answer it except with the all-expressive phrase, "You bet".'

To Dolf she wrote, ' *Will* I go to Washington? *Will* I drop in on her and her old man? I have waited almost three years for this, and it has come exactly the way I hoped it would, without official wangling but through human recognition of a co-guerrilla fighting for the same cause.'

She stayed the night at the White House, as a guest of the Roosevelts, on 16 June 1943, and her hours there were perhaps the pinnacle of her ascent to fame and success. 'Darling,' she wrote to Dolf, on White House writing paper, 'I am writing this IN LINCOLN'S BED (stark naked, incidentally, because it is a terribly hot night) . . . The President is a perfectly GORGEOUS man, more than up to my wildest hopes & much *funnier* than I ever imagined. Mixes an excellent cocktail (his own special, with his own hands), & you can say absolutely anything to him. We were just six of us, & I sat on his right, & we ate dinner on the terrace with softshell crab & strawberries & fireflies & lots of amusing talk (with serious undertones). There's a bell by my bed with 3 buttons saying "Maid", "Butler" & "Usher". I can't imagine what I could need an usher for, unless Lincoln *walks*. More when we meet. All my love.'

She sealed the letter to Dolf and began one straight away to Tony. To conceal her whereabouts from the Italian censors, she used her own blank paper and headed it 'Casablanca'. Naked in Lincoln's bed, dashing off letters to her lover and her husband, she felt in control of her parallel lives.

So desperate and determined was she to see Dolf that she was ready to jump at any opportunity to go to California. And one came. Louis B. Mayer wanted another box-office phenomenon like *Mrs Miniver*. He wanted Jan to write the original material for MGM to spin, once again, into Hollywood gold. It could be a sequel to *Mrs Miniver*, it could be something new – anything she liked, Mayer implored her, but please could she produce it soon?

Jan liked the idea: it was a good one in theory. She sat on trains with her pen poised over a blank sheet of paper, hoping a new character would walk onto it. She couldn't write any more Mrs Miniver. She was becoming sick to death of Mrs Miniver, and she had lost the desire to describe married life. What she could write about was love – sudden, magical, illicit love, and wartime separation from the beloved, and living three thousand miles to the west of one's husband and three thousand miles to the east of one's lover; about exiled Jews, and the dreadful, paradoxical feeling that you half-wanted the war to end, and half-wanted it to carry on for as long as possible because it postponed the moment of having to make a heart-breaking decision.

But she couldn't possibly write about that. It was deeply secret. Such a storyline from 'happily married' Jan Struther would cause a catastrophe in the family and a scandal across

America. It was unthinkable. So she wrote to Dolf instead: 'Darling, I adore Oklahoma. The train service was impossible y'day but I had the luck to be driven from Tulsa to Okla City – about 120 miles – along Route 66, & I got such secret delight out of passing places where we'd stopped to eat together.' Or she wrote to Eleanor Roosevelt, describing inspiring sights she had seen. One of her favourite things about America were mail-boxes, which had come into being through 'R.F.D.' – rural free delivery, which ensured that mail was delivered to every home across the country. The mail-boxes stood in coveys on the sides of roads, perched on top of crooked posts at all angles, each reminding you that there was a home and hearth to which it belonged, hidden along a drive or down a wooded path. With their rounded tops, mail-boxes seemed to Jan to be the ghosts of covered wagons, and she wrote to Mrs Roosevelt, 'Much as I love almost the whole of this country, the two things I like best about it are FDR and RFD.'

But none of this got her any nearer to writing profit-making script material. Perhaps, Louis B. Mayer suggested, if Jan were actually to live in Hollywood for a few months, the muse might come to her. Surely, if she spent enough time fraternizing with script-writers, producers and film-stars in such magic surround-ings, she could not fail to be inspired?

'You bet' was once again the gist of her reply. *Paid* to spend the summer in Los Angeles! She would bring the children with her, and Gracie, the daily, to do the housekeeping. She would be only a short drive away from Dolf, who was now stationed at his regiment's headquarters at Culver City, in the personnel section. It was perfect. Their star seemed to be watching over them with amazing attentiveness.

The working holiday was doomed to fail, as Jan, had she thought it through properly, could have foreseen; but she was swept along by the power of the Culver City coincidence.

She was there, with Janet and Robert and black Gracie, from mid June to early September. It was sweltering in Los Angeles that summer: much hotter than California was supposed to be. The only way to cool down their soulless rented house (paid for by MGM) was to spray water over the roof. Janet and Robert

Mail-boxes like those Jan loved

were now fifteen and twelve – old enough to crave freedom and
the company of friends. At number 1061 of an interminable
road off the interminable Westwood Boulevard, they were isolated, and there was nothing much to do.

Jan, in the mornings, sat looking out at other similarly soulless houses, trying to write the story for a book or film, but no story came. Rather than inspiring her, Hollywood had the opposite effect: it seemed to paralyse her creative spirit entirely. Partly, she was both physically and mentally tired: her months of travelling from city to city, and the endless succession of lectures and hotel rooms, were beginning to take their toll on her energies. And partly she was 'blocked' by the fact that the only storyline which preoccupied her at the moment was the one she must keep secret. But there was also a sort of cussedness in her, almost a wilful refusal at the last fence, which made her stall when success was so easily in her reach. All around her were movie moguls, producers and script-writers, hungry for her words. The conditions were too perfect: and the pressure was too great.

She took the children to a grand dinner at Louis B. Mayer's mansion – Robert's first-ever grown-up dinner party – and all the men went off and played pinochle in a darkened room fuggy with cigar smoke, and everyone drank too much, and Robert and Janet yearned to go home. Jan arranged for Janet to spend a tedious day on the beach with Shirley Temple. Jan and the children had breakfast with Groucho Marx, who wasn't funny, and lunch with the screen 'monster' Boris Karloff, who was sweet. She went on her own one afternoon to see Greer Garson at 680 Stone Canyon, and was treated to tea with cream in first. Greer Garson was now a navy wife: she married Richard Ney in July 1943 (much to the disapproval of the press – Ney was fifteen years younger), and after the honeymoon he went to sea as Ensign Ney. Jan had much in common with Greer which she could not discuss.

Longing to proclaim her love for Dolf from the rooftops, Jan found a brazen (but oblique) way of doing so at a lecture in Los Angeles in aid of the United Jewish Appeal. She stood on a platform and spoke passionately about the plight of the Jews, with particular reference to a few individuals she knew well, giving them made-up names. Elizabeth, Max, Liesl and Willi, the characters whose plight she described, were disguised members of Dolf's family held in Nazi concentration camps – cousins,

The 'goldfish-bowl prison-visit'

aunts, uncles and grandparents – and Jan loaded her lecture with heartbreaking detail. The lecture raised thousands of dollars from the wealthy Jewish audience: one member came up to Jan afterwards and said, 'My dear, I feel PURRRGED.'

Janet and Robert had no idea that nice Viennese Dolf, who came to visit them fairly often during the summer in Los Angeles, was anything more than a great friend of their mother's. The pretence was faultlessly maintained, but it was a strain. This was admitted at the end of the holiday: 'I'm glad you didn't come to the house to say goodbye,' Jan wrote to Dolf on 10 September. 'I knew that if I had another harrowing farewell with you I should *really* vomit. I couldn't bear to have another travesty of a meeting with you, with no time alone & no chance for even our eyes to kiss each other. Our relationship has stood up to so much, but I honestly think this sort of goldfish-bowl prison-visit period is the hardest of all. We shall be nearer together, I think, when geographically apart, than in this farcical set-up. But we have had *some* beautiful hours this summer, and we will have lots more, darling, somehow, somewhere. I know it.'

In this letter of 10 September 1943, there was the first hint that the balance of the relationship was changing: 'It is *you* who keep up *my* morale, rather than the other way round.' For nearly four years, Jan had been the dazzling one – the acclaimed author, the English beauty, sought-after wherever she went. Dolf had been the dazzled one: the penniless refugee, the addresser of envelopes, the lowly private in the Army, hardly able to believe that the illustrious Jan Struther could love him. But now, returning from the strained summer in California, Jan felt herself ageing and her powers of writing dwindling, and she knew that Dolf was becoming the stronger of the two.

Chapter Thirteen

In small countries the landscape is a roomful of pictures
Framed in the window of the train.
There is composition – an old mill in the centre
With a cow on one side of it and a horse on the other,
Or a manor-house, perhaps, set among elm-trees,
Or old men on a bridge, and a boy fishing.

In large countries the landscape is a wallpaper
Lining an enormous room.
It slides past the window of the train
With variation, repeated variation,
Yet no real change.
A wooded hill, a lake, a long white town,
A hill, a lake, a town, a wooded hill,
A lake, a long white town.
There is length, but never any centre
For things to cluster round.

From 'Small Countries', 1944 (unpublished)

IT SEEMED TO come quite suddenly, this new phase of Jan's life, when blackness of heart rather than resolute cheerfulness was her dominant emotion. Over that summer of 1943 she changed from the powerful and frivolously confident guest in Lincoln's bed to a much frailer woman, at the mercy of short-lived 'highs' and long-drawn-out 'lows'.

She had experienced mild depression before: hints of it had appeared in her early poems, and she had even managed to project it, twelve years before, onto Mary Magdalene in her hymn 'Unto Mary, demon-haunted' for *Songs of Praise*. The refrain went:

Banish, Lord, our minds' confusion,
Fear and fever drive away;
Down the valleys of illusion
Spread the kindly light of day.

There was a streak of depression in the family: a surviving teenage diary of Jan's mother Eva suggests that she too experienced it, and later, in 1951, Jan's brother Douglas suffered a depressive nervous breakdown. In Jan's case, confusion seemed to be its overriding symptom. This poem, written in 1944, echoes her earlier hymn's refrain:

It took me forty years on earth
To reach this sure conclusion:
There is no heaven but clarity,
No hell except confusion.

It felt, during these periods of 'confusion', as if her way was lost in what she called 'the mind's jungle': the tangled, chaotic mass of entwining worries and fears which existed in her head where once was 'starry, clear-headed inner fertility'. In an effort to befriend and make light of this new, recurring affliction, she gave it a nickname, 'the Jungles'.

As the tide of the war turned in the Allies' favour and talk of the invasion of mainland Europe began to be heard on people's lips, Jan knew that the time was coming when she would have to make a decision about the situation which she had allowed to develop in her life. During a war, the rules were slackened: you could live in a state of suspended reality, basking in the present moment, not questioning the consequences. But at the end of a war you had to emerge again, wake up from the dream, and pick up real life where you had left it.

The subject had to be broached with Dolf. Out of their preliminary talks came an awareness, devastating for Jan's confidence, that the relationship was not set in stone. Nothing had ever been promised: the love-affair had survived, so far, on trust alone.

Jan told Dolf that when the war ended, she would have to go back to Tony. She couldn't simply abandon him, so that he would return from his POW camp to wifelessness. He and the children needed her: the 'family pattern' was the foundation of their sense of security.

But having broken this news to Dolf, she could not then expect him to be loyal to her; he had every right to look elsewhere for love if she intended to go back to her husband when the war ended. Dolf falling in love with somebody else did not bear thinking about: but she did think about it, and her love for him, her need for him and her fear of losing him became more rather than less intense.

This was a major cause of her 'Jungles'. There was also physical exhaustion, panic at the loss of her magic touch as a writer, a sense of anti-climax after stepping down from the pinnacle of fame, and an increasingly acute feeling of missing Jamie.

As soon as she returned to New York from the Los Angeles summer she became physically ill, with gastritis. Her physical and mental states were from now on closely linked. When she was depressed she couldn't keep food down, or sleep, and this made her feel worse. 'Maybe it's not good for two human beings to get so happy in one another's company,' she wrote to Dolf from her bed, 'when they are doomed to live in separate cages of skin and flesh which may be separated by circumstances at any moment and for oh! so long. In one way, though, I feel closer to you here than I did in that farcical pseudo-proximity without privacy in California. At least I am living in the home we shared together, among furniture & books on which our eyes have rested.'

Her doctor, Max Schurr (who had been Sigmund Freud's personal physician), advised her to cancel her October 1943 lecture tour. 'I'm horribly disappointed,' she wrote to Dolf, 'but I can't go trailing about the country in this state, never knowing whether I'm going to throw up into the next microphone or otherwise disgrace myself in front of The Ladies.' The cancellation was a relief and brought about a gradual physical recovery, so she did not have to cancel her sixteenth appearance on *Information, Please!*

I am getting stronger physically [she wrote a month later], but it appears that with every increase of strength comes an increase of

awareness & therefore of sadness. I seem to have no heart for anything except you. Everything else is empty and senseless. This is all
WRONG, & it's sort of undignified for any human being to become so
dependent on another human being for mental & spiritual sustenance. But I don't even care about that. The hell with dignity. I only
want to be in your arms – No, that's not true. If it were, I should say
the hell with my duty to Tony & my compunction about the children's peace of mind & my value as Allied propaganda, & just leap
on a train & come to you. But that would be going AWOL – and you
know that we can't do that, whether we are official or unofficial soldiers. There are some things that one could not DO, if one wanted to
retain one's self-respect & peace of mind for ever afterwards. But I
just want you to know how I wish I could see the slightest chance of
our spending our future lives together.

Dolf had been promoted to the rank of corporal, and was now
Classification Clerk at Inglewood, California. 'I am still having
fun,' he wrote to Jan, 'or at least some part of me is having fun,
while the rest is numb and dead. I was so disappointed that I
couldn't get my call through to you, but the lines were jammed,
i.e. the waiting time was 8–10 hours, so I had placed the call too
late. Furthermore, hearing your voice on *Inf. Please* stirred so
many things up in me that I felt a little weak anyway, and when
it didn't come off I felt something like "a cowardly relief".'

He had found, among 'the buddies', a confidant whom he
told about his love affair with an English married woman. Jan's
reaction to this information revealed how sensitive she still was
about her reasons for coming to the United States in 1940: 'I
know it sounds more romantic and simple, the way you put it to
him, but don't you see that it isn't fair on *me* to imply that I left
GB just at that crucial moment simply and solely to be with
you? I didn't, as you know: if the children hadn't been coming
I'd just have had to stick it out and mend my heart with Scotch
tape or something. So please revise that version before I come
– otherwise, I promise you, I shall get hold of him and do it
myself.'

For Mrs Miniver, and for Jan in her early marriage, privacy
and free time had been two of the most cherished privileges. In
'Mrs Miniver and the New Car' she had quoted the Chinese

proverb, 'To be entirely at leisure for one day is to be for one day an immortal.' But now, in late 1943, she dreaded solitude, and feared the emptiness of being 'at leisure'. The woman who had once made sure there was a permanent nannie between herself and her younger children now dreaded them going back to boarding school. This was another symptom of her depression. If there was nobody in the apartment with her, she was paralysed with loneliness. Pauly came and spent the night with her often, to keep her company: they were brought together by both missing Dolf. 'Ich weiss wie tief dankbar ich sein muss,' Pauly wrote to Dolf in 1943, 'und ich darf bestimmt nicht klagen, aber ich bin oft so schrecklich allein.' (She ended the letter, 'Wirst Du nie fotografiert von den Buddies?')* But Pauly now had a job as a paid 'lady companion' to a wealthy American lesbian, Miss Frank, and had to travel with her wherever she went. Jan's secretary Anne Curtis Brown had left, to get married.

'I miss Anne dreadfully,' Jan wrote to Dolf on 22 October 1943.

It was lovely to feel that she would be turning up every morning – moody as the devil, but human. The early mornings are the worst. Gracie comes at 10.30. Pauly (when she sleeps here) leaves at 8.30. Those two hours, especially after a bad night, are purgatory. I don't know what we can do, darling, except wish on our star and wait. The Russian (& other) news is marvellous, & that's what we ought to fix our minds on. Hell, when people are being killed all over the world, & nine lovers & sweethearts out of ten are being separated, the fate of two scraps of humanity like us ought to seem insignificant. But oh God! how it hurts. If everybody – I mean all lovers – who are torn apart like this are feeling as we do, the world seems too small to carry such a load of exquisite misery. I know we have no right to think of ourselves as exceptions – it's only that most of them can at least look forward to some focal point in the future when they can take up their lives together again, whereas *we* – but what's the use of going into all that again every time I write . . .

---

* 'I know how deeply thankful I should be, and I really shouldn't complain, but often I'm so terribly alone . . . Have you ever been photographed by the buddies?'

This was an eighteen-page letter, and it ended: 'Darling, I've just made myself a dry Martini, & I'm lying on the bed drinking it. As it penetrates down to my fingertips & up to my braincells, I find I can almost imagine us happy again one day, & falling asleep in each other's arms with nothing more formidable than an alarm-clock for the next morning. Sweet, foolish, heavenly dream . . . I'll cling to it while I can.'

Pauly, when she stayed with Jan, went downstairs each morning to collect the mail. If there was a letter from Dolf, she woke Jan; if there wasn't, she let her sleep on. Jan read the letters aloud, leaving out the private bits and the bits which might worry Pauly. On 23 October she had to leave nearly everything out. 'There is a chance that I might be sent overseas,' Dolf had written.

'Please don't even *mention* the overseas idea to me at present,' she wrote back. 'I am not strong enough to stand it.' Her thoughts were 'going round and round like chipmunks in a cage' – and the only way to regain any peace of mind, she realized, was to countermand the cancellation of the second half of the autumn lecture tour. At Jan's request, Clark Getts had arranged for her to be in Los Angeles over Thanksgiving, after giving four lectures in Illinois, two in Texas, two in Oklahoma, two in Washington state, and three in northern California. 'Darling, I am on my way to you,' she wrote on 7 November, 'travelling in a slow and rather cold train through an illimitable waste of snowy prairie. I am sitting with a nice Pittsburgh housewife who is on her way to Seattle to see her husband (an Army doctor) for a little while before he goes overseas. She has 3 small children at home & can't therefore do war-work to take her mind off things. She is obviously miserable. Just one more of the millions of torn-apart and disembowelled . . .'

In her engagement book, the inch-deep space for Thanksgiving Day has a diagonal mark across the top left-hand corner: her secret sign. The Clark Getts Details of Engagement say: 'We presume you have your own plans for accommodation in Los Angeles.' She and Dolf stayed at the Biltmore, for three nights. By 2 December she was lecturing at Houston, Texas, and she would not be able to see Dolf again until his furlough, which could be months away.

Her lectures, she felt, could do with rejuvenating. She needed new material, first-hand, up-to-date information about wartime civilian life in Britain. She made an application for a two-way passage. Surely she would have priority, with the excuse of 'collecting material for British publicity in the US.' She dared to dream about it: and, having started to dream, she let herself go. She would see Jamie again, and small fields, and beloved London! Homesickness overwhelmed her, and she was now as set on returning to Britain as she had been on leaving four years before.

But her plan was constantly foiled. Later in December, a fibroid was found in her womb ('apparently innocent,' she wrote to Tony's sister Ysenda, 'but obstructive, so that I am absolutely crippled with pains for the four or five days when I have the curse, and have to stay in bed with my knees doubled up, feeling as though I'm giving birth to twins'). Then the British Information Service told her there was a long list of essential people trying to get to Britain, and she would have to wait some months. 'I expected to have left by now,' she wrote to Dolf on 2 March 1944, 'but it seems it may be another couple of weeks at least. I feel discouraged and on edge.' She could not get to sleep without a sleeping-pill or a drink. 'DON'T call me "a brave girl", sweetheart. I am not brave, & you know it. My only strength is that I do not fear death any more – only injury, and sea-sickness, and lecture audiences, and going home to a Heimat which will be stranger than any strange land.'

Then news came from England that Jamie, having injured his leg on a training exercise, was in an Army hospital with haemorrhoids. And she still had no definite date for leaving. 'You can imagine my present state of mind,' she wrote to Dolf on 20 March. 'The suspense of this journey business is awful. In addition, everything else has been going wrong at once – financial worries about income tax, Getts chivvying me about lectures, and, underlying everything, my ever-present sadness at being separated from you with oh! so little hope of seeing you again till God knows when . . . I saw two letters from Tony in the mailbox yesterday at long last – but when I looked at them I saw that one was 7 months old, from Italy, & the other (a postcard) 5 months old from the German transit camp. Oh dear, it's so hard to keep in touch with people when the news one gets is so stale. The postcard sounded very depressed (for him).'

In the course of the Allied liberation of Italy, some prisoners-of-war had been released to make their own hazardous way to the Allied lines. But Tony had been among the less fortunate ones who were sent on in closed cattle trucks to Germany, by way of transit camps in Central Europe. 'You may imagine my disappointment at finding myself here,' he had written to Jamie from Stalag VIIA in southern Germany on 8 October 1943. His postcard could not say more.

By 16 April 1944, Jan's journey to England was definitely off. 'Nothing can make the Home Office give any guarantee of my being able to get back here again,' she wrote to Dolf, 'especially with things being about to pop (invasion etc.) & I simply cannot risk getting myself stranded *there* & the children stranded here . . . I feel desperately disappointed on Jamie's behalf. For myself, I feel ghastlily disappointed at not seeing him. I feel like a snapped string, and I have now *no* focal point to look forward to.'

> I have forgotten even the smell of happiness –
> As one who has been many months at sea
> Forgets the scent of grass on summer evenings.
> I remember only that it was sweet, and lifted the heart.
>
> One of these days, perhaps, there will be landfall,
> And I shall smell it again, and my heart be lifted.
> But for now there is nothing except the bitter salt,
> Day after day after day.

While she was working on this poem, called 'At Sea', in the black fortnight after the final cancellation of her plans to return to England, Dolf sent her one in German he had just written, about being in a strange sun-land where there was no rain, and *no sweet smell of grass* in the evening. It was another of their poetic coincidences. 'Oh, darling,' Jan wrote back, 'I try so hard to orientate myself away from the life which you have

been the centre of for so long: I think I am making headway –
and then suddenly a poem of yours strikes me right to the heart
and makes me realise how absolutely "one river" we are.'

A period of 'Schneeschmeltzen' – the thawing of Jan's iced-up
spirit – followed in April, with the help of Dr Pardee, a neurol-
ogist with whom she sat for many hours, talking things out. He
told her she was going through a kind of battle fatigue as a
result of trying to deal with insoluble problems until her brain
was exhausted and congested. He could not solve the problems,
but he at least clarified what was happening, and this shaft of
light tipped Jan in the other direction, from depression to a new
kind of high – elation spiced with dottiness. She dashed off
poems every day – 'A poem a day keeps the doctor away':

> I'll never see, where'er I roam,
> A tree as lovely as a pome.
> A tree is just a thing that growed –
> But only man can make an ode.

She and Dolf were frank, in their letters, about their 'randi-
ness'. 'When I'm in camp I don't miss sex so much,' Dolf wrote,
'but as soon as I get out and especially after catching up on my
sleep, it bothers me – not enough, though, to get into the gutter.
What I really miss is LOVE – the whole thing, the physical and
mental.' Jan was having calcium injections and had discovered
that they 'reduced local desire in other parts of the body'. 'This
is a major discovery,' she wrote to Dolf, 'though rather comic in
a way. I never knew about it before, because it is so many years
since I have been sex-starved (awful word).'

They were both aware of the possibility of the other 'getting
involved with' somebody else. 'Are you?' Dolf wrote. 'No, sweetheart, I am NOT,' Jan replied. 'Temptations are many & strong
because I'm meeting so many fascinating people – but (a) I'm
too physically tired to be very randy very often & (b) I love you
too much. This is not a promise – we *neither* of us made a
promise – but only a statement of fact.'

Dolf had every reason to fret: Jan was meeting lots of attractive, eminent men, the very fact of her affair with him proved her capable of infidelity, and she did have crushes. 'Don't worry, I haven't the least letch on Morris Ernst [President Roosevelt's personal representative on missions to England],' she wrote to Dolf. 'I had for about 2 days, but got over it when I'd lunched with him for the 3rd time & seen his handwriting in a notebook.' (Amateur graphology was one of the dozens of subjects which fascinated her.) She was great friends with the singer Paul Robeson, crush material even though he was married (and it was Janet, not Jan, on whom Paul Robeson turned his seductive charms). Dolf hardly met any women from one year's end to the next, but Jan still felt jealous. She used the expression 'a blonde' to describe the kind of woman Dolf might be tempted go to bed with: someone of great superficial physical attraction, but not much brain. It was a cunningly derogatory term, designed to make Dolf feel ashamed if he did succumb to such a person's charms. It became one of their private comic words; but underneath the comedy there was genuine fear on Jan's part. When she saw 'a blonde' in her imagination, it was always somebody *young*, with bouncy hair and a bronzed West Coast complexion. Dolf was thirty, she was forty-three. Her own hair was becoming silver-flecked, and she occasionally caught sight of a double chin in a right-angled mirror. (She had recently sent Dolf a funny photograph of herself looking donnish and double-chinned in a mortarboard while being awarded an honorary degree by the University of Pennsylvania.) It was a sign of the shifting balance of power in their relationship that she felt the more insecure.

She telephoned Dolf one morning and he was short with her. He didn't say, 'Is that you, darling?' but 'Is that New York?' Feeling sick with foreboding, she wrote to him.

The possibilities, as near as I can figure them out, are these:
1 You were desperately sleepy and early-morning-new-born-kitten-ish, and couldn't rouse yourself to talk much. OR
2 You were feeling really sick, either in the stomach or in the head. OR

3 You were feeling depressed about the boringness and smallness of your job, and longing to get overseas or at any rate into something more interesting. OR

4 You weren't alone, and therefore couldn't speak freely. This again splits up into various possibilities, viz:

5 You were sharing a room with another GI, owing to space shortage. OR

6 You were sharing the room with a GI blonde. OR

7 You were sharing the room with Janie [a married acquaintance, in whose house Dolf sometimes spent the night on his leaves]. OR

8 You were sharing the room with somebody else, not a GI blonde, but some other, new, 'real' person.

She made herself face and analyse each of these possibilities in turn. It was an utterly un-'blonde' letter, drawing on their deeper-than-physical bond of words and candour. It was an exercise in preparing for an end with Dolf, whenever it might come. This was how she dealt with the final three possibilities:

6 I want you to know, darling, that I don't mind in the very least. I know what you must have been going through about sex, partly because I've been going through it myself. I don't want to risk getting emotionally involved with anybody, so I stick to Miss Bates. But, as you know, if it were possible for a woman to go to a convenient and hygienic brothel, or to pick up the equivalent of a GI blonde, I would do so at the drop of a hat (or should I say at the rise of a clitoris?) So that's that. I wish circumstances were not such as to make it necessary, but seeing that they are, and seeing that you are so heavenlily, heavenlily highly sexed (thank God) – well, as I said, don't worry.

7 I also don't mind, sweetheart. I expected something of the kind to happen in that quarter, and I have had a feeling for some time that something has. Partly because you don't seem to go there as often as you used to, and partly because you don't mention her in your letters any more . . . Maybe you fell in love (or started to) with her and felt you oughtn't to go there any more because of [Janie's husband] Ted: or maybe you just both felt that electric something growing up in the air between you, and agreed that you'd better not meet. Or perhaps you both fell in love, or in lust,

and you *are* meeting. Well, you needn't feel badly about it, if this is so.

8 Well, that's the worst of the possibilities, I admit, and when I thought that one out I did have a quarter of an hour of fairly acute pangs: but even that I managed to digest after a while, and get the sting out of it, by reflecting that you and I are no longer just 'you' and 'I'. We have been mixed up with each other so long and so sweetly and so intimately that from now to the end of our lives we shall be part of each other: therefore I shall always share in any loveliness you have, and you will share in mine. It is only by thinking oneself into this frame of mind that one can overcome or transmute jealousy. It is not easy, but it can be done, and genuinely, if one's love is deep enough.

Well, there, as they say, the case rests, until I hear from you. All I implore, darling heart, is that you tell me the truth. For the sake of everything we've been to each other in mind and body; and for the sake of Mozart and Donne and Shakespeare and Goethe and Placzek and Struther and all the other poets and musicians alive or dead; and for the sake of all the beauty that our love for each other has helped us to discern and enjoy – PLEASE write soon and truthfully.

It turned out that Dolf had simply been sharing his room with a GI from Alabama, 'a lazy son-of-a-bitch who wouldn't get up and go to the bathroom while I was talking (*any* Viennese would have).' 'Oh, blessed, blessed possibility five!' wrote Jan. 'How I love him, the fat slob. I could kiss him on his solid southern arse.'

In her new state of elation-after-depression, Jan turned her apartment at 214 Central Park South into a busy haven of helpers, friends, children and eccentric pets. 'If you *knew* what life has been like for the last 3 weeks,' she wrote to Dolf on 2 August. 'I've only been able to get scrappy help so I've been cooking and cleaning and looking after Robert's livestock (1 snake, 1 baby alligator, 2 turtles & 3 salamanders), & training Margie (the new secretary), and giving the baby its bottle & changing its diapers & I don't know WHAT all. Oh, I forgot, you don't know about the baby. She is called Barbara & is COAL black

& very sweet. She belongs to the temporary maid (Rose) whom I captured in Harlem 2 weeks ago when I went up & raided the Slave Coast in despair. It's simply *heavenly* having a baby around again . . .'

Jan could say deliberately provocative things like 'raided the Slave Coast' because she had a genuine love of black people. She craved their company. She and her black maids had coffee round the table each morning (not at all the done thing in 1940s New York), and this was not a mere patronizing gesture. There was real unselfconscious friendship. She would have despised the 'politically correct' people of half a century later who refused to ask for 'black' coffee but never had black friends in the same way as they had white friends.

Carl Sandberg, Jan and Paul Robeson at a gala dinner

Jan made two new 'bosom friends' in the spring of 1944: one was the black actor Canada Lee, whom she had met while selling war bonds. 'He is 37, very dark skin, and a swivel eye (from having been badly hit when he had to give up prize-fighting). He has a son called Carl, even blacker, a brother called "Lovey", who is a postman; a divine old uncle called Mr Gaddesden (Gaddy) who is from South C'lina & fries chicken like a dream; & a host of friends, some Negro, some white.' The other was Bennes Mardenn, aged twenty-eight, a friend of a friend of Janet's, who was a struggling actor working as an elevator attendant. 'Through him we've got to know a whole raft of struggling actors, musicians & dancers, mostly Jewish of Russian background but not in the least ghetto-ish, so don't start snorting, you old Viennese snob . . . These two new worlds converge in our apartment, and we sit up playing the mandolin, guitar, concertina, etc. & talking & drinking beer, wine & Coca-Cola till anything between 2 & 5 every morning. It is the kind of "student" life which I never had, and it's *heaven* compared with the depression & gloom I was in all last winter & spring. The only thing lacking is you, playing the piano in the jam session & being host with the wine & so on.'

Staying with Bev Robinson and his wife Marian in Canada in late August, she listed to Dolf the skills she had acquired in the last few weeks, many of them picked up at Robert's summer camp, Camp Kieve in Maine, which she visited on the way: 1 using a long-hafted woodman's axe, 2 using a scythe, 3 playing the guitar, 4 using a soldering iron, 5 making knotted string belts in different patterns, 6 whittling, 7 graphology, 8 cooking, 9 Yiddish, 10 Russian, 11 rifle-shooting.

I did (11) brilliantly at Rob's camp: he practically embraced me in front of the councillors. I was able to put over a WHALE of a talk against racial intolerance at supper, & they LISTENED, which I knew damn well they wouldn't have on the strength of any mere literary achievements. And later, sitting on the stoop of the council hall, I took a live snake out of the Nature Room & sat with it coiled round my wrist & fingers while I pursued the same line of talk. God, how they need it – at least half of the boys are from Baltimore & points south, & they stink on the Negro problem, & even on anti-Semitism. I had quite a run-in with one brat in the workshop on the same subject. Luckily I was, at that time, helping *him* to use a soldering iron, which was the best possible position to be in. I had a primeval longing to shove the white-hot soldering iron up his fat little Arsch . . .

Dolf's heart sank slightly when he read letters like these. When he first heard that she was feeling happier, he wrote: 'This was really the greatest Sunday gift you could send me, Kleines.' But he now feared that she could only escape from 'the Jungles' by throwing herself into this almost manic over-activity. He would have been more convinced of her recovery if she had taken up one new skill, rather than eleven. And as for all the shooting, snake-wielding and shoving things up arses – he detected suppressed rage which might turn dangerous if her mood changed.

She crawled under the foundation posts of the house in Canada, shot a porcupine, then skinned and dissected it. 'I got out its heart, lungs, stomachs, 9 feet of intestines – I measured them – liver, kidneys, spleen & vagina; then I made the meat into a stew with onions & we all ate it for dinner; then I boiled down the head & four paws to get their skeletons to keep for Robert. I'm going to make the teeth & claws into a bracelet. A perfectly glorious day.'

This behaviour was Jan's final two fingers to ladylikeness. She was flaunting her tomboyishness and her taste for the shocking and disgusting, and had it not come after a period of depression it would have been purely hilarious. But again Dolf sensed that she was over-compensating.

Janet now had a boyfriend, whom she had met at the George School: Thomi Schmidt, a German-Jewish immigrant whose father had been murdered by the Nazis. 'Mummy, I wonder how one ends a love-letter in German?' she asked, sitting at the desk at 214 Central Park South. 'I bite my tongue out at the root,' Jan wrote to Dolf, 'swallow three times, & then say casually, "Why not look it up in the dictionary?" I get a lot of gorgeous private pleasure out of the irony of the situation . . .' Trying to be a liberated modern mother, Jan took Janet to a doctor to get her fitted with a contraceptive diaphragm; her unshockability shocked Janet. Jan was adamant that Tony must not be told, in any letter, of Janet's love for a German, even this anti-Nazi one.

Dolf's furlough came up in September, and he went to New York for a fortnight. Reunited with him, Jan felt almost calm again, and whole. And for once, she left before he did. On 6 October she boarded *The Mohawk*, Train 5, Car 30, Upper 4, for what she rightly guessed would be her last lecture tour of the war years. 'The farewell wasn't so bad this time, was it?' she wrote to him on the train. 'Definitely it is *far* easier to be the one who goes away first. Next time let's arrange to go simultaneously in different directions – nearly as difficult as arranging to come simultaneously! (A propos of that, I am as randy as hell. But don't worry. I am so full of the sweetness of love that lust has no attractions.)'

She kept an un-private diary of this six-week trip, as well as writing private letters to Dolf. Reading both, the contrast between her outward stiff upper lip and her increasing inner exhaustion and loneliness stands out. Exactly the same ingredients which she had found so exhilarating on previous tours – staying in strangers' houses, looking out of hotel-room windows, being taken out for dinner, shaking hands with hundreds of people, being the centre of attention at the coffee-party after the lecture – now wore her down. She saw their dark rather than their light side. Remarks on her Details of Engagement – 'You will be required to attend a private luncheon and make a 10-minute speech. This is a special privilege they require from all our speakers' – were merely tiring to contemplate. 'Privilege', indeed!

She was not sure which was worse: staying with people (in which case you had to be on best behaviour), or staying in a hotel (in which case you were lonely in a room 'which contained everything you needed but nothing you ever wanted to see again'). At St Louis she was a guest, staying with Mrs T. N. Sayman of 5399 Lindel Boulevard. There was a butler, and an over-sophisticated daughter, Do-Jean, who discussed the steak and kidney pie with her mother over the luncheon-table. 'Do-Jean, they've made this much better this time.' 'I don't know, mother. I think the kidneys ought to have been soaked still longer in red wine.' The atmosphere reminded Jan of 'pre-pre-war big country houses in England', and she had a nightmare afterwards of going back to Britain and being forced to live in a Big House with a butler. 'I woke up almost in tears. God, how awful it would be.' After the St Louis lecture she slipped away to Walgreen's delicatessen for a peanut-butter-and-jelly sandwich, to avoid dinner at the Saymans' table. At Wichita, Kansas, where she lectured at the University, she made friends with five college girls (Betty, Beverley, Joanie, Francie and Darline) and spent three relaxed evenings in their house drinking Cokes and 7-Ups and reading old copies of *The New Yorker* in front of the fire. She was becoming allergic to best behaviour.

At this very time Tony, a prisoner at Oflag 79 near Brunswick in Germany, was dreaming about precisely how wonderful it would be to live in a Big House with a butler. He was imagining the blissful reunion with his family. He wrote to Jan (she quoted the letter to Dolf), saying that he hoped 'having a grown-up family would not make him feel too ancient', and that he was 'longing to take up the threads of family life'. Waiting for the war to end, he was planning the future. He and his co-prisoners would establish the Brunswick Boys' Clubs, an idea they had dreamed up together, and for which many of them had promised generous sums of money. He might stand for Parliament, as a Conservative candidate in Perthshire. There would be long, happy summers at Cultoquhey (which he had by now inherited, his father having died in 1940). He would make the most of the house, as his parents never quite had . . . the food needed improving, and the wine cellar . . . he would install new bathrooms, and make sure there was endless hot water . . . he would invite his friends up for golfing house-parties, and for shooting, fishing and stalking . . . the gong would ring to dress for dinner, the last course would be a savoury (devils on horseback? cheese soufflé?), and there would be jazz records and billiards till late into the night.

Lecturing in city after city, staying at the Abraham Lincoln, the Leland, the Statler, the Commodore Perry, Jan put across the gist of her message: that 'it's no manner of use the politicians working out a democratic world set-up if the individual members of each group are going to go on behaving like bastards in their personal lives.' 'I know for certain,' Dolf wrote to her, 'that you are going on fighting your lovely private war against stupidity and indolence . . . I wish I could be with you

or sit somewhere at the back of the room during that terrible
moment when you begin to talk. And you would touch your hair
with your left hand, as a sign that you had seen me . . .'

At Memphis, in the segregated South, she began to feel 'the
Jungles' coming on, and her lecture, far from 'going over swell',
seemed 'to come out as a god-damned boring mess.' The Peabody
Hotel was the gloomiest yet; luncheon with the ladies of the
School of Art Committee was 'pure hell'; and a concert given
'by a [white] man with a cold who had the effrontery to sing
Negro songs in Negro dialect to a mixed but segregated audi-
ence' was excruciating. In her diary, it was the injustice of seg-
regation which was blamed for her misery; but in her letters to
Dolf, it is clear that the misery was mainly inside herself. 'I wish
I was a riveter in a factory, or a carpenter, or a cowboy, or anything except what I'm being at the moment. I'm beginning to
think lecture touring is the most loathsome thing in the world
. . . I'm so TIRED . . .'

She could not telephone Dolf, because he was deep in the
Mojave Desert on manoeuvres. This was a refreshing adventure
for him, and he was feeling like a true buddy of 'the Buddies'.
'We've been sleeping in foxholes for the last 7 days', he wrote to
Jan in Buddy-speak, '(and does my back ache!), eating miserable
cold grub (and did I throw up!), and shaving out of steel helmets
(and did I cut myself!). But my health has never been better.'

Dolf's morale was also lifted by the fact that there were
German prisoners nearby, and he could watch them playing in
the way he had played as a boy. 'What a complete change of
circumstances,' he wrote to Jan. '*They* are the prisoners and *I*
am the non-com with the rifle!'

One day, though it was strictly forbidden, he and some fellow
GIs went and talked to the prisoners.

We took our truck down to the salvage dumps where the Krauts
work. The guards – especially curious to have an interpreter –
joined us and soon I and my buddies stood on the truck surrounded
by 30 German prisoners and shooting questions back and forth. It is
hard to realise (and yet it is an undeniable fact) that these hard-
working, well-disciplined and quite humorous boys are the same

who goose-stepped arrogantly through European capitals, murdering and bullying . . . They are all recently captured (in the South of France), partly by the French whose guts they hate. They are scared stiff of the Russians . . . their greatest fear is what the Russians are going to do with Germany, and that is their single reason for fighting on. Some of them, even married men with children, have been in the Army for seven years, unable to lead a normal life, and they are pretty tired of it. The wheel has come full circle . . .

If Dolf was out of reach, whom could Jan turn to? Feeling 'utterly sunk' in Kansas, she telephoned Bev Robinson at midnight to cry. At Columbus, Ohio, sobbing with loneliness at the Deshler-Wallick Hotel, she picked up the telephone and rang Janet, who was at boarding school. She had never heard her mother in this state: it came as a shock. She got permission to take some time off school, and went to Cleveland to be with Jan for the last days of her tour. It was a rescue: Jan got through the final lectures, with Janet by her side. But she did not tell her daughter the true reason for her misery.

On Thanksgiving Day Jan was back in New York, on Dr Pardee's couch, talking about the insoluble problems which had once again congested her mind on the lecture tour. And on that same day, at the Albert Hall in London, the United Thanksgiving Service was taking place in the presence of Winston Churchill. Jan's poem 'A Londoner in New England, 1941' (quoted at the beginning of Chapter Ten) was read aloud by the actress Celia Johnson. When she finished the last line, 'How can London fall?', the orchestra swept into the final bars of Elgar's 'Cockaigne' Overture. Churchill spoke: 'We are moving forward, surely, steadily, irresistibly and perhaps, with God's aid, swiftly, towards victorious peace.'

Janet took her mother and brother to spend Christmas with Thomi Schmidt's family at Binghampton, New York. It was a time of rest and stability, before unknown upheavals to come. '1944 wasn't quite as much "our" year as the preceding ones,' Dolf wrote to Jan on New Year's Eve, 'but our love hasn't changed. It walks into 1945 without too much hope but with the old feeling of perfection and never-ending meaning. Darling, I couldn't say "Happy New Year" to you, but my thoughts are with you very much.'

An inspecting officer inspected Dolf's office in January 1945, and said that his were the best records he had seen in all his years of inspecting. Dolf would not be sent overseas after all; and he was even invited to supper by the inspecting officer. 'His wife was beautiful,' Dolf wrote to Jan, 'and when I heard her call him "Honey" I felt suddenly nostalgic for you and for our home, a feeling I always have when I see a happily married couple at home. "Nirgendwo fühlt der Fremdling sich fremder, als wo die Liebenden wohnen." '*

The spring of 1945 struck both Dolf and Jan as beautiful, coming – as it must be – before an end. 'Spring is in the air,' Dolf wrote, 'an irregular, unsystematic kind of spring, with bitter winter and full hot summer in it, an American kind of spring, but it makes me restless again. I wish at moments like this that it was all over, but the future is such an empty canvas, and we have nothing to print on it.' Sitting by a lake in Central Park, Jan wrote, 'I am just melting inside with the exquisiteness of the spring & the greening trees & the prospect of your coming.'

He did come to New York, on 10 April, and they had once again what Dolf called their 'ghost-days' together – the days of 'bitter bliss' just before parting, when it was almost as if the parting had already happened. Jan had not resolved her dilemma by travelling to America in 1940: she had merely postponed its resolution. The scene of farewell had moved from Battersea Park in May 1940 to Central Park in April 1945.

On 27 April, the morning after Dolf left to go back to California, Jan received a cable from Frankie Whitehead to tell her that Tony had been liberated ten days previously, and expected to be home shortly. Later that day there was a cable from Tony himself to say that he had reached England safely.

'I cabled back suitably and lovingly,' Jan wrote to Dolf, 'and said we'd get a passage back as soon as possible. I feel sort of

---

* 'Nowhere does the stranger feel more strange, than where lovers live.'

numb and stunned and I can't keep any food down – the usual thing. Oh God, I'm so *genuinely* thankful that he's safe and well. I am not a ghoul, darling, and I am *really* fond of him and anxious to see him again. It's only that my heart is all yours, and I cannot take it back with me.'

The Ministry of War Transport telephoned Jan on 4 May: there was a passage for them on the 8th. Frantic busyness was a merciful anodyne. Janet and Robert came home from school. The 'raft of struggling actors, musicians and dancers' helped with the packing, breaking off occasionally to make last-minute records on Jan's recording machine. Trunks were sent off, loaded with gramophone records, teddy bears, soldering irons and musical instruments. The Golenpauls, Jan's friends whom she had met through *Information, Please!*, gave a farewell party on the last day, during which Jan slipped into her hostess's bedroom to sign a contract with Harcourt Brace for a collected edition of her poems, lectures and stories, to be called *A Pocketful of Pebbles*. Jan described the final hour to Dolf: '. . . And then I opened my last bottle of wine & we all drank our healths. And in the middle of all this, VE Day was announced on the radio & paper began falling through the sky like snow-flakes, & we drove to the station, nearly unable to get there because of the Times Square celebrations, & finally we LEFT, with all of them expressing their emotions in their characteristic ways. The whole thing was so ridiculously fantastic that I didn't cry at all, but took a swig of rum & slept all through Connecticut.'

They were caught up in the Halifax Riots, when soldiers and sailors celebrated victory in Europe by smashing glass and looting beer, and their ship (the SS *Bayano*, a converted banana boat) could not leave for three days. On the voyage, they had little time to think: a gale blew for twelve days and nights, the ship rolled at forty degrees, and they had to lash themselves to the deckhouse in order not to be swept overboard, and to sling their elbows through ropes at night to stay in bed. The ship was travelling in convoy, and had to heave-to in mid Atlantic for sixteen hours because the deck cargo carried by the rest of the convoy was being broken up. Jan gave splicing lessons to

FYFFES LINE

MENU

"Bayano"   26th Mawn 1945

BREAKFAdT.

Rolled Ov
Corn Flake. Graps Ny.
chrwdded Wheat.

cmoked Fill3t. od Codlig

caute of Px Lver.

Egg.:)-Frntee, Boiked & Turn3dd.
Griklee Bsakga..t Bavon.
Bre.kf.b Roll. Roll. Currnat cxone. To.

Breakfaa.t Roll. qu;tan coo ene. Totaao.t.

Ja J   Mr.;a,te;f½

     Tr.½   Coffr.

          COvoa.

sprawling groups of children, to distract them from seasickness. The crew had a drunken all-night party on the last night, after which an only-just-legible breakfast menu was typed.

Aching and bruised, Jan, Janet and Robert emerged onto the bomb-scarred *terra firma* of Liverpool. A row of old ladies of the WVS gave them bread and margarine on the quay. They noticed how old the dockers and porters looked: all men of normal working age, they supposed, must still be in the Forces. They took a slow train southwards, and eventually drew into Euston Station. Tony was waiting for them on the platform. Jan ran to him and hugged his thin frame.

Part Three

Chapter Fourteen

Wandering, I have discovered
Much treasure on my way, and none more precious
Than the meaning of Going Home, the real meaning.
One traveller said: 'Home's where I hang my hat.'
Well, there's some truth, but not all truth, in that.
Add two more letters – then, instead of part,
You'll get the whole: 'Home's where I hang my heart.'

Part of 'Going Home', from *A Pocketful of Pebbles*

OUTSIDE EUSTON STATION, Tony hailed a taxi. 'To the King's Road, please.' As it swept southwards through bombed streets and past Nelson's still-standing Column, Jan basked in the sound of Robert and Janet laughing with their father over the drunken breakfast menu. It was like music. In Tony's smile to her from across the seat, she felt once again the warm, shared pleasure of co-parenthood which she had not known for five years. Tony was gazing with delighted amazement at his fourteen-year-old son and elegant seventeen-year-old daughter.

Only Jamie's presence was needed was to make his happiness complete, but Jamie was in Yugoslavia with the Scots Guards, having been refused compassionate leave. During rough games in the Officers' Mess a few days earlier, Tony explained, Jamie had squirted a brigadier with a soda siphon, and his commanding officer was not, in the circumstances, inclined to grant him special favours.

Tony looked astonishingly well, Jan thought: thinner and balder, but not wasted or sunken-eyed. Indeed, the sparkle of schoolboy mischief was still in his eyes, even more so than before, perhaps because he had been stuck in a succession of horrible boarding-school-type establishments for three years. ('Picnic? I'll give you picnic!' As the taxi drove past St James's Park, Jan could hear her nannie Lala's words.) She knew how much he must be treasuring these first moments of family life regained. But was he, like herself, privately agonizing about the question of that night's sleeping arrangements?

Looking out of the taxi window at the thin and war-weary Londoners scurrying about near Victoria Station, Jan tested her conscience. She was deeply moved – she had known she would be – to see these people who must have lived through the bombing, and to see the city of her childhood so changed, with unexpected empty plots and vistas where buildings had been. But she did not feel the violent assault of guilt which other Londoners claimed to have felt on returning from wartime exile. She reflected that in her own way she, too, was war-weary after five nomadic years as Allied propaganda.

The taxi passed Wellington Square, but did not stop. The house Jan glimpsed at the far end on the left looked shut up and neglected. It was uninhabitable, Tony explained, having been vacant for several years, and the basement kitchen had dry rot.

'Just here, please.' They drew up outside King's Court North, a 1930s block of flats next to Chelsea Town Hall where Jan's childhood friend Frankie Whitehead lived; she had arranged to put them up for a short time in a flat belonging to a friend. She greeted the new arrivals from America with delighted hugs, and didn't mention bedrooms. They all went straight out to supper at the Queen's Restaurant in Sloane Square, a favourite of Tony and Joyce's from pre-war days. Some other friends came too, including Anne Talbot. It was an evening of celebratory reunion, with funnier-than-ever stories from Tony (the comedy enhanced by the blackness of the German-prison context) and lots of laughter and catching of eyes across the table. Anne observed 'Tony and Joyce': they seemed to be as good a 'team' as ever, giving one another leads in conversation. What was the truth? Was it not odd that on their first night together for five years they should choose to have dinner in a large group, rather than alone? Anne would no doubt find out.

After supper they walked home, and Jan noticed the length of Tony's stride: he must be revelling in stretching his legs after the years of confinement. She lagged behind to have a private word with Frankie, and suspected that Tony might earlier have done so too. Frankie did not raise an eyebrow, and nor did Tony when Frankie said, in the hallway of the spare flat, 'Now, it's time you all went to bed, and this is the way you'd better arrange it – Janet in the small bedroom, Tony in the large one, Jan in the living-room and Robert in the tiny bedroom in my flat.' The hurdle had been crossed: and, once crossed, Jan supposed it would be easy to arrange things similarly in Wellington Square.

The next day, Saturday 28 May, Tony took his wife and children for a walk. They walked all day, through Kensington Gardens to Campden Hill and beyond, on and on, left and right, through countless streets and squares. They had to run to keep up with him: crotchets, once again, to his minims. Tony told Jan about the Brunswick Boys' Club scheme: £13,000 had been raised in the prisoner-of-war camp, in the form of promissory notes. She was impressed by this active altruism in him. She recounted anecdotes from her lecture tours – she knew he would laugh at 'My dearrr, I feel purrrged', and the 'Mrs Miniver's Fruit Salad Plate'. He told her about his other plan, to stand as the Conservative candidate for Perth and East Perthshire, an ambition which was part of his vision of himself as a rural gentleman. It was such a safe Conservative seat that if he were to be adopted, he would almost certainly win. The election was to take place in a fortnight's time, and he suggested that all four of them should go up to Perthshire to do a spot of what he called 'baby-kissing', in aid of his cause.

Legs aching, Jan, Janet and Robert collapsed onto the sofa in the furnished flat. The next day, and the day after that, Tony again took them for walks, through miles of bomb-damaged streets, pausing only to foregather for drinks every now and then with friends who had been 'in the bag' with him or for lunch at the Lansdowne Club. On Monday evening they were joyfully reunited at last with Nannie, who since the beginning of the war had been running the children's crèche at the Lyons food factory. She agreed to come and live with them again as soon as 16 Wellington Square was fit for habitation.

King's Court North was too small, Tony said on Tuesday. He would sleep at the St James's Club from now on. He hoped nobody would mind. 'No – that's a good idea, darling – do,' said Jan. Janet and Robert were told that it was merely a matter of shortage of space.

It was five days before she put pen to paper to Dolf, who was still in California. 'The children and I', she wrote, 'are founding a Society for the Rehabilitation of Exhausted Wives and Children of Hundred-Per-Cent Fit Returned POWs – starting off with a monumental foot clinic. Tony has walked the 3 of us off our feet since we've been back.' She then wrote this tribute to Tony's resilience:

Really, the British are an indomitable people. He was 42 when he went overseas into action, and had never known any real hardship, hunger or humiliation: and now, after going through the Battle of Egypt – the *defeat* part, not the intoxicating victory march of El Alamein; after 3 years in 6 different prison camps in 3 different Axis or occupied countries; after spending a winter in the Italian mountains dressed in thin desert uniform (khaki shirt and shorts) plus an old tartan plaid wrapped around him; after going literally barefoot for seven months, in order to save his only pair of shoes for a possible escape march; after being shackled in unheated closed cattle trucks on the long journeys between the various camps (during one of which journeys, taking it in turns with the others to peer out of a small crack in the truck, he fell madly in love with what glimpses he could get of the Tyrol); after being under almost continuous heavy bombardment for a year (from our own planes over Brunswick, 2 miles away, which they reduced to flat earth); after going for months without any parcels, mail or news of his family getting through to him; and after spending the final four months in a state of semi-star-vation: after all this, he emerges unscathed physically, improved mentally, passed 100% fit by the doctors, a good deal thinner, very slightly balder, politically conscious for the first time in his life, sweet-tempered and humorous as ever, and hell-bent to plunge into politics and walk up mountains stalking deer . . . I GIVE UP – and so does the enemy.

(Tony's only comment on the shackling business, which he must have hated very much, was 'Silly buggers – they didn't realise we'd all learned to pick locks in our school days. We got them all off long before the end of the journey.')

Dolf had asked her not to write to him until she had had time to judge the situation fairly. This was how she judged it. Dolf should 'cancel all blondes', because there was a good chance that he and she would be able to be together a great deal in the future.

It seems – I gather from Frankie, for of course he would die sooner than make the spiritual effort of saying so to my face – that Tony is immensely proud of my work in the US, and thinks it would be a tragedy if I didn't continue it. I'm sufficiently conscious of my own faults and irritatingness to realise that he is probably damn glad that I've found an outlet for my Winstonian energies at last, and I'm sure he sees – as I do – that the situation provides us with an excellent and face-saving excuse for being apart for several months in the year, without any formal separation and stuff. We still have a great fondness and respect for each other. On the surface, and indeed as far down as the topsoil or even the subsoil, we enjoy each other's company, and we have a deep satisfaction and pride in our co-parenthood of the children.

'Without any formal separation and stuff . . .' Dolf, reading this, saw his life stretching ahead, this forbidden love affair carrying on for years, always unofficial, always interrupted by heartbreaking farewells. By clinging to 'the family pattern', as she called it, Jan was asking him to be a perpetually waiting side-character. He could not, he decided, close his eyes completely to the attractions of blondes.

The meeting to adopt the Conservative candidate for Perth and East Perthshire took place at the Station Hotel, Perth, on 9 June. The candidates were Mr A. J. O. Maxtone Graham and Mr A. Gomme-Duncan. All Tony asked of his wife (knowing her left-wing leanings) was that she should promise not to stand against him as a Labour candidate if he was adopted. Jan and the children were invited by one official to listen to the speeches. A different official then mistook them for members of the Conservative Association, and handed them voting papers. Resisting temptation, they handed them back, unmarked: only members of the Association were supposed to take part. Alan Gomme-Duncan won the adoption by two votes. Had it not been for the scruples of his wife and children, Tony would almost certainly have become an MP in the 1945 General Election. He took his defeat in good humour, and decided to spend the funds earmarked for election expenses on renting a house in the West Highlands for a two-month shooting, stalking and fishing holiday. (Cultoquhey, requisitioned by the Army, was not released until 1947).

It sounded wonderful: the Western Highlands were 'practically Austria', Jan felt; and the chosen place was Appin, the country of her lifelong hero Alan Breck of *Kidnapped*. She would be able to roam in the hills to her heart's content, dreaming of Dolf and David Balfour. Tony's desire was to recreate the paradise of pre-war Scottish family summers: tea on tartan rugs, trout, salmon, grouse, pheasant and venison for dinner, drawing-room games in the evening, constant laughter and physical exercise to drown out any strains in his marriage.

But Jan had a way of turning holidays sour. The pressure to be 'having a lovely time' brought out the worst in her: it was the negative side of the same cussedness which made her the life and soul of the crowd on any derailed train, or ship battered by a Force Seven gale. Previous holiday bad moods, notably in Vienna in 1929 and Los Angeles in 1943, paled by comparison. Even Robert, who had no inkling of the cracks in his parents' marriage, began to sense, in Appin, that something was wrong, though his mother reassured him that Tony's irritableness was just 'prisoner-of-war neurosis'.

Tony told Jan he had arranged the holiday partly 'to give her a good rest' but, indiscriminately generous as ever, proceeded to invite a stream of guests (his golfing friends for the most part), some of whom forgot to bring their ration books, and one of whom (a former POW, Harry Webb) instantly embarked on an affair with Janet. There were sixteen in the house, and the only employed help was one washer-up for four hours a day. Food and petrol were short, and power cuts were frequent because the fast-running burn which powered the private electricity system had dried up in the August heat.

Many months later, Jan described the holiday to Dolf: 'It was one long round of cooking on an enormous old kitchen range, gutting rabbits and birds, cutting up venison, hoisting huge iron saucepans, and walking two miles to the telephone and many more miles in search of something to shoot. Some of our guests were co-operative, some (notably Janet and the S.O.B. she had an affair with) were not.' But the people who were there remember it differently. Jan's helpfulness in the kitchen was, in reality, short-lived – it was Tony's sister Ysenda who did most of the rabbit-gutting and saucepan-heaving; Jan actually purloined the best saucepan in the house to pursue a 'manic ploy' (as Janet called it) which involved boiling up cows' feet to make glue.

Jan saw Tony as the one who was impossible to live with. 'My main mistake in my first letter to you,' she wrote to Dolf months after the event, 'was to use the adjective "sweet-tempered" about Tony. I did not realise then, so well did he conceal it, how much the POW business had affected his temper. He turned out to be irritable & quick-tempered & even, eventually, admitted this, after several blazing rows and much verbal rudeness (which is entirely unlike him). He got into a state of neurotic depression & couldn't persuade himself to get out of bed, etc. – you know the symptoms.'

She did not admit that she, too, was bringing poison to the marriage. How could she do otherwise, when her heart was not in it? Tony irritated her because he fell short of Dolf in all the characteristics which now mattered to her; and she was as irritable as Tony.

One day she vanished, leaving a note on the hall table: 'I have gone to join my friends the gypsies in the heather.' She was gone for a night and a day, no one knew where. It was exasperating for everyone, and upsetting for Tony.

'The nicest part of the whole holiday,' she wrote innocently to Dolf afterwards, 'was the horse, Dick, which the farmer lent me, and on which, at one particular moment when the situation

became intolerable, I ran away for 24 hours, staying in a farm-
house and catching up on sleep.'

This letter to Dolf was not written until November 1945. For
five months, from the end of May onwards, Jan cut herself off
from him: she had decided it was the only way to give her
marriage a decent chance of working. Tony saw, in Appin, that
it was not, but (being a bottler-up and avoider of 'scenes') he
could not bring himself to say so to Jan's face. They communi-
cated through Anne Talbot, who was one of the house-party.
Jan confided to her about Dolf, and she claimed to have known
all along. Tony (not yet aware of the depth of Jan's love for Dolf)
told Anne that as far as he was concerned the marriage was
over, and they should separate. Jan persuaded him, through
Anne, that this would be grossly unfair to the children, and that
they hadn't given themselves a chance in the old, familiar,
roomy surroundings of Wellington Square, which they both
loved and which was the last place in which they had been truly
happy together.

This was a new twist in the plot, one which Jan could not have
foreseen while daydreaming on trains during the war years.
Then, she had vaguely hoped that some opportunity would
come, without her having to instigate it, which would give her
an easy escape route from the marriage. And now, here it was:
Tony was suggesting a separation. But she couldn't agree. Not
only that: she actively (through the medium of Anne) persuaded
him to change his mind. For honour's sake, and her conscience's, she knew she must convince herself that her motive
for leaving him (if she ever did) was not that life would be better
with Dolf, but that life had become irretrievably intolerable
with Tony. She was not yet convinced of this. Her children were
very much in her mind, especially Robert, who was about to
start at Stowe, and to whom (being the youngest) the 'family
pattern' mattered particularly. For her children's sake she was
prepared to argue against herself in this way, and to forgo Dolf
if she could find a joyless but bearable *modus vivendi* with Tony.

So she and Tony threw their energy into making 16 Wellington Square habitable. Everything in its fourteen rooms was
grimy with Blitz dust. Tony, working at Harris & Dixon again,

was finding office life futile and unfulfilling. He came home each evening not to play with trains but to move furniture and put up shelves, with a sense of pointlessness and crushing disappointment in his heart. A dance for Janet: that was it, they would give a débutante dance, he decided. Perhaps that would warm the house up, filling it once again with laughter, champagne and jazz music. The invitations went out: 'Mrs Anthony Maxtone Graham At Home . . .' Needless to say, it was a successful evening on the surface, but dismal beneath. Janet, still pining for Thomi Schmidt, was unimpressed by the young men her parents had invited, most of whom she had not met before. Being 'hostess and mother' made Jan feel acutely old.

'Well,' Jan wrote eventually to Dolf, ' the cage is ready, but the bird doesn't fly back.' You could dust a house, you could install a new kitchen, you could give a dance, but you couldn't breathe warmth into a house without happiness, and this was still lacking. Tony and Jan stopped having rows and an atmosphere of icy politeness descended, which was worse. On 28 October, able to bear the loneliness no longer, Jan wrote to Dolf. She apologized for her long silence.

I HAD to cut myself off from you in order to make a fair trial of this business here and not be torn to pieces with nostalgia all the time. I have tried, honestly, to make a go of it, but I can't live like this. I'm not exactly unhappy, just paralysed, and hungry for expressed affection. Now that Robbie's at school there is nobody to touch, except a cairn puppy the farmer in Argyll gave him, which I look after and which cuddles up to me on the sofa and is very like Rob – small, quick, intelligent and loving.

Promise me, darling Liebes, that even if you have got involved with somebody else, & are living with her, or married to her, by the time I come over in the spring [for the publication of A Pocketful of Pebbles], you will at least put your arms round me & hold me close, & say something zärtlich.* (Damn – I knew that writing to you would plough me up & rouse everything that I have to suppress day and night.)

*Tender.

Jan with Robert's cairn Culi, in 1945

She steeled herself against 'the expected thrust in the vitals', as she called it: the letter from Dolf which would inevitably follow, explaining that he had taken the sensible decision, and had found a charming girl, not blonde, a pianist actually, twenty-seven years old, interested in architecture . . .

But it wasn't a letter, it was a cable. And its message made Jan 'melt with zärtlichkeit'. She wrote straight back to him, her longest letter ever – thirty-six pages. 'My darling darling sweet love . . .'

> It seemed to me almost impossible that you should still be 'uninvolved and unchanged' after all my long silence & our intolerable separation. Oh, Liebstes, Liebstes, how wonderful that you still feel the same.
>
> . . . The long and the short of it is that life in these circumstances is impossible. It is not life at all, but a limbo, a half-animal existence – no, not as warm as that. It cannot last. I am neither truly domestic nor creative, & I can't sleep, & I can't write, & I can't thaw out at all except with very old friends (and ex-'Friends' who are now friends only).

She described the months since sailing from Halifax: the stormy Atlantic crossing, the terrible holiday in Scotland, the exhausting cleaning of Wellington Square, and she brought Dolf up to date, showing him how the war had polarized Tony and her:

> It became increasingly clear [in Scotland] that what he was finding it impossible to control was the fact that he is once more, & even more than before, madly irritated by my whole personality, voice, outlook & presence. In theory he is 'very fond of me', 'couldn't possibly dislike me', & other similar half-compliments which are more wounding than any insults. We have arrived at a sort of *modus vivendi* which consists of my keeping out of his way as much as possible and watching every word & gesture when I *am* alone with him so as not to madden him. He doesn't irritate me, except very occasionally (mostly when he's trying to do something practical in the way of carpentry etc., and being both clumsy and pigheaded about it). He simply stultifies and nullifies and sterilizes me. The worst thing of all is his inability or unwillingness to discuss any of our joint problems, until they're so far gone as to be almost insoluble . . .
>
> Almost everybody I know is in the same state, if that's any consolation. A wise woman writer has suggested that there should be a moratorium on all marriages, owing to the war, & that any 2 people

who want to re-marry should do so. The housing shortage is appalling. The latest Gallup poll says that 1 adult in 3 is trying to find different accommodation. We have turned into a nomadic nation.

Tony and Jan's friends kept saying to them, 'Aren't you two
lucky to have this lovely house to come back to!' ('And the sword
turns in the wound again.') The house was, in fact, 'an ice-
house'. The drawing-room was coldly tidy and unlived-in, the
fire lit only when visitors came. Tony, when he was at home,
spent most of the time in his upstairs bed-sitting-room, the
room in which Robert had been born. Jan spent most of the time
in her bed-sitter studio ('a heavenly room, in which one could
be *so* happy'). Janet found the atmosphere in the house so
unbearable that she bought a Baby Belling and lived indepen-
dently in her bedroom when she was not out at her business
course. Robert was away at Stowe, and Jamie had still not
returned from Yugoslavia. Nannie was the only binding presence: she lived on the top floor and was out at work all day, 'but
thank God she is here most nights for supper & provides a diver-
sion & a link for the 3 of us.'

Longing to touch bits of London which reminded her of Dolf,
Jan visited Mme Luhn, the landlady at 100 Denbigh Street who
had called him down to the telephone that evening in November
1939. There she was, and her *pot au feu* was still simmering on
the stove. Jan walked westwards along the river and knocked on
the door of 113 Cheyne Walk, the place of assignations, where
she and Dolf had heard tugs hooting and the evening-newspaper
seller shouting of Nazi advances as they lay together postponing the moment of parting. Jan's friend Charles Spencer opened
the door. 'You wouldn't possibly have a room to let, would you?'
Jan asked him. 'I have, actually,' he said. 'Not the one you used
in 1940 – the one just across across the hall.'

Jan took it, cheaply. She now had a bolt-hole from the 'ice-
house'. But nothing could stop 'the Jungles' coming back, which
they did, soon after she had finished writing the November letter
to Dolf. Until then, the busyness of getting the house in order
had kept depression away, and had prevented her from facing up
to her creative sterility. But now 'the Jungles' were worse than

ever: she found herself beset by irrational as well as rational glooms, and was caught once again in the vicious circle of illness and unhappiness interacting and making each other worse. Her doctor treated her for anaemia, low blood-pressure, and change-of-life depressions, and every night for two months she took sleeping-pills, which had, as she later described it, 'a devastating effect'.

Just before Christmas, Jamie came home. The fire was lit in the drawing-room. With Robert home for the holidays and the family reunited, it looked on the surface (for a few days) almost as if the Minivers had come back to life. Jamie played Meccano with Robert, and Robert was thrilled to rediscover the older brother he had not seen for five and a half years. But Jan, still in her 'Jungles', felt like an outsider, watching the family party through a window. At the end of the Christmas holidays the boys went away again. Emerging in the New Year from the worst of the 'hell' – enough, at least, to be able to write a letter – Jan wrote to Dolf on 17 January 1946, her fingers stiff and cold because of the fuel shortage:

> I have lost all joy & gaiety, & there is hardly anybody here I really give a damn about. I don't see how I can go on existing like this, in this hell of nothingness. And yet, when I try to face the alternative, of splitting up and busting things up for Rob, I just can't bear the prospect of it. It wouldn't be so bad for Janet, who is practically on her own anyway, but she does need a 'background' of some kind when she's just beginning to go to dances, & I feel that even an only apparently united home is better than none.

Perhaps Jan remembered from her own childhood that, awful though it had been having parents who were icily polite to one another, having separated parents who were openly hostile to one another and nowhere one could truly call 'home' had been even worse.

> I see no immediate prospect of coming to America, and when I shall see you again God only knows – unless some miracle happens & our star lights up again. It is so very, very faint now, Liebes, that I can hardly see it twinkling at all. Was it all a dream, our happiness, &

did we really once exist, and be together, and laugh & have fun? I feel more and more unreal, and more and more entrapped in the cast of some play where I don't belong. The only real thing here is Robert, with his shining intelligent eyes & his loving heart.

It was difficult, in the immediate post-war period, to get an exit permit for America unless you were going on Government business, or to do something which would help the dollar exchange. Clark Getts, the lecture agents who had ruled Jan's working life during the war years, were clamouring for her to come back and embark on another tour. If she accepted, she would almost certainly be able to 'swing it', as she put it, and get a passage. But she couldn't bring herself to take it on. The tiringness and loneliness of the last one still haunted her. She was determined to stay out of Clark Getts's clutches.

Her sense of isolation was compounded by the 'unintimacy' which had developed between her and Janet. But at last, in early 1946, they had a frank talk. Janet told her mother why she was feeling miserable and uncommunicative: she not only hated the atmosphere of the house and the dreariness of post-war England, but she was missing her friends, and pining for Thomi, and saw no way of getting back to America. Jan's heart melted at this, because it was so much the same story as her own. She told Janet about her love for Dolf – though she did not confess that the affair had been going on for six years. Janet was amazed – shocked – worried – delighted – she loved and admired Dolf – but what would be the outcome?

The 'star' was fainter than Jan knew. During those two months of silence, between November 1945 and January 1946, while she was deep in the 'Jungles' and not writing to Dolf, he was stationed in Indiana on his last stint in the Army before being discharged in March 1946. And there, on leave in Indianapolis, he met 'l'Indianapolitaine' or 'the Indiana Compromise', as Jan later called her: a blonde, aged twenty-two, full of physical attraction, and irresistible.

The letter in which he confessed this has not survived, but from Jan's reaction it seems that Dolf played it down: she was bold enough to say (after admitting that the news was 'agony'),

'I know that no relationship that you or I will ever have with anybody else could ever be in the same street with yours or mine.' Her method – just as in the infidelity-imagining letter of 1944 – was to draw on the depth of the relationship between her and Dolf, and to brush aside any others as shallow and not worthy of discussion. All she needed to be sure of, she said, was that the visit to New York she was planning for the publication of *A Pocketful of Pebbles* (which had been postponed till the summer) would not coincide with a 'visit from Indianapolis'.

She was not certain of the journey to America: her application to the Department of Overseas Trade ('My publishers want me to be there to promote sales by means of personal appearances') had not yet been accepted. 'I guess you feel the same about it as I do,' she wrote to Dolf on 8 April, '– a big longing combined with a small dread, because it's only, so to speak, another "furlough", & must lead to another separation.'

But the very prospect of seeing Dolf, now a civilian again, and back working at the Avery Architectural Library at Columbia, and of being once again the centre of attention at book-signings, rekindled her 'Winstonian' energies. She dared to get in touch with the BBC, and was welcomed with rapture. 'I've been on the air quite a lot,' she wrote to Dolf, 'transatlantic quizzes, & reading my own poetry on the North American Service. It's unspeakably relieving to be coming out of that bloody jungle at last: I've never lived through such hell as this winter has been, and I hope I never shall again.'

The Department of Overseas Trade said 'Yes'. She could go. Delighted, she wrote to Frank Morley of Harcourt Brace telling him she would be in New York for publication day. Her letter crossed with one from Dolf telling her that her visit would coincide exactly with the 'visit from Indianapolis'. It was, she wrote back to him, 'the most damnable tangle.'

I could not endure to be in NY while she was there – it would be intolerable for all 3 of us. So I must just postpone my visit. Difficult, because the whole point was to be there on the day of publication, not 3 weeks later. I've written to Frank Morley to say 'owing to further family complications' I now won't be able to arrive until the end of June. God knows what he'll think. Oh, damn, damn, damn . . . what a mess! I can't help seeing, in a detached way, how grimly funny it is in its way.

Once again, she braced herself for the inevitable letter in which Dolf would advise her not to come to New York at all, because he was going to marry *'l'Indianapolitaine'* and had been trying to break it to her gently. His letter arrived. She didn't dare to open the envelope, but sat looking at it and feeling sick.

. . . And then when I finally summoned up enough guts to read it, it was like a sweet balm pouring all over me, & I felt (for the first time in months) warmed right through & not lonely any more.

You're right, Liebes. Involvements are more trouble & anguish than they are worth. Even real love brings enough anguish, God knows, in a world like this, all full of Displaced Persons – but real love *is* worth it, every time.

It was to the poor girl from Indianapolis that Dolf had to break news gently. Her last words to him were, 'My dearest wish is that someone would love me as much as you love that woman.'

'Oh darling honey Liebes Du – I am really & truly, wirklich und warhäftig, coming!' Jan wrote to Dolf on 27 May. She had a seat booked on an aeroplane, the Flying Dutchman. 'I'm arriving on 29 June & can stay till 2 Aug. when I must get back for Robbie's holidays.' She planned to rent an apartment so she wouldn't feel 'alien & visitorish' in a hotel.

The Dutch Airlines publicity dept. has rung me to say that reporters will be waiting for me at La Guardia – so for God's sake don't meet me, because it would be simple hell not to run into your arms. Besides, I'll probably faint dead away with sheer joy when I see you, which would be most awkward if done in public. I'll ring you up as soon as I get to a telephone, & then I'll come right over to your apt. & stand on the exact spot on the floor where I said goodbye to you 14 months ago (or 14 million years, or 14 minutes, whichever way you choose to think of it).

Ask Pauly to get in 6 dozen oranges, please. I shall drink a gallon a day at first, I expect.

The face lit up by the photographers' flashes at La Guardia was thinner and more careworn than the one which had sailed away fourteen months before, and the hair was greyer. But the eyes which greeted Dolf were unchanged. The poem Jan had written to him in 1940 in her schoolgirl German still held true:

> Staatenlos, heimatlos
> Gehen wir immer,
> Staatenlos, schwer zu sein,
> Heimatlos, schlimmer.
>
> Staatenlos? Heimatlos?
> Nein, liebes, nein,
> Weil du mein Heimat bist,
> Und ich bin dein.*

---

* 'Stateless and homeless, we go our way: it is hard to be stateless, worse to be without a home. Stateless? Homeless? No, beloved, no: for you are my homeland, and I am yours.'

Chapter Fifteen

I am a captive in a cobweb's mesh;
Frail is its tracery, yet I cannot stir;
Fast as I tear the strands, they grow afresh
And hold me here with you, a prisoner:
Habit, long musty, set in instinct's place,
Pale duty, and a maze of trivial ties,
And craven kindness – since I am loathe to face
Your wounded and uncomprehending eyes.
Steel chains might yet be snapped, and I be free:
But O! these clinging cobwebs strangle me.

From 'Cobwebs', in *Betsinda Dances*

'THAT WAS A wonderful, heavenly 38 days' leave,' Jan wrote to Dolf on the aeroplane back to Britain on 7 August 1946. 'It got happier and happier, and all the jungles & bitched-upness that we'd both been going through got smoothed out, like a rumpled sheet in the wake of an iron. We're both of us so difficult for other people (it seems) and so unrestful and temperamental – and yet for each other we are perfect – so easy, so restful, and so constant.'

'It got happier and happier' suggests that it was less than happy to begin with. Exhausted after the nomadic years of war, hardened by fourteen unfulfilling months apart, bewildered by one another's recent efforts at infidelity, they now had to embark on yet another existence, this time with Jan as short-term visitor and Dolf as resident, employed citizen. But gradually during these thirty-eight days of readjustment, as the 'bitched-upness' faded, Jan emerged from confusion into a state of clarity about her parallel lives.

The time had come, she decided, when she must free herself from the strangling cobwebs of her marriage. Evenings with Dolf, home from the Avery Library in her rented apartment on East 70th Street, gave her a glimpse of possibilities which made a resumption of life in Wellington Square intolerable, even absurd. It would mean going back to the strain of acting a part for which she was miscast, after tasting the ease of naturalness.

During the war, the thought of breaking up her marriage had been almost unthinkable: Jan had shuddered at the violence of its effect. It would have undermined her whole 'Mrs Miniver' persona, vital as Allied propaganda, and destroyed her reputation. It would have been cruel to Tony in his prisoner-of-war camp, and unsettling for the already unsettled children. But now, the pressure to maintain an outward show of marriedness had eased. She was no longer the professional 'happily married woman', so fearful of scandal that she fled from a hotel in O'Neill, Nebraska just because someone recognized her voice in a washroom. Tony was a civilian, and her youngest child was now aged fifteen. The sheer boredom and spiritual sterility of living with Tony, day after day, month after month, had taken the sting out of any decision to part. No one could say they hadn't tried. It seemed now that the choice was obvious, between what was natural and what was artificial. For years she had clung, privately, to the guilt-inducing state of 'having her cake and eating it' – to the stability of an upper-class marriage and the excitement of an affair – and this, she knew, would be hard to give up. She was keenly aware of the pain she would inflict by breaking up the 'family pattern', but there was now an overwhelming sense of inevitability that this must happen. She would have to take the consequences.

Having put her personal life above her career by postponing her trip to New York until three weeks after the publication of *A Pocketful of Pebbles* in May 1946, she could hardly be surprised that the book began to sink without trace. It was a patched-together and plainly produced collection of her poems, fables and wartime lectures, plus the pre-war *Try Anything Twice* – a compendium of fifteen years of her wit and wisdom, full of good stuff, but out of date and lacking unity. There was no introduction, and no guiding voice to carry the reader from the pre-war to the wartime frame of mind. The *New York Times* gave it a bad review, and it produced only a trickle of royalties. The title, chosen by Jan, did not help. Without the magic word 'Miniver' (Jan forbade the inclusion of the dreaded name) it meant nothing to most people. The book's luke-warm reception dented her writer's confidence, already low. She realized she would have to produce powerful, and fresh, material if she was ever to be a bestselling author again.

A few days after her arrival at Prestwick Airport on 8 August, she and Tony agreed to separate, and to seek a divorce.

'You, bless you,' she wrote to Dolf, 'understand how little the actual divorce matters in all of our lives: it is the mere formal burying of a corpse – or rather of a skeleton which is so bared and whitened by sun and vultures that it doesn't even stink any more, but has acquired a certain stark integrity and bearable-ness. The hellishly miserable time was when it still had flesh on it but needed burying, and when we were still trying, first, arti-ficial respiration and, second, a kind of amateurish embalming.'

Breaking the news to Robert was as dreadful as she had pre-dicted: he was as upset as she had known he would be. Now she had done it. The pattern was broken. But there was one last week of family life before the planned date of separation. In this week, a new friendliness filled the air at Wellington Square. 'The atmosphere in the house is so peaceful and even gay,' Jan wrote to Dolf, 'that it must seem even more incomprehensible to Robbie that we are going to part.'

Packing and sorting out her belongings, Jan managed not to cry. But one thing moved her very much. Walking into Tony's bedroom when she didn't know he was in, she found him fast asleep.

He was curled up on a little sofa which was the first piece of furni-ture we bought, and looking very small and thin and sad. When people are asleep, they should not be looked at unawares by other people. Their defences are down & their masks are off. Poor Tony: he has so much sweetness in him. 'Twenty-three years with the wrong woman' has cramped his style and soured him, but he will be free now and will blossom again into his natural gaiety. I think he is hating this week, and feeling – as anybody well might – that if we can get on as well as this for a short time, why can't we do it always? But he knows really, as I know, that these few days owe their harmony & serenity to the fact that they *are* a finale. The concert is nearly over, and the people who have trains to catch are already groping for their hats.

'Incidentally,' Jan wrote to Dolf in the 'P.S.' at the end of that letter written in the last week with Tony, 'I bought a house yesterday, 17 Alexander Place.' Her jewellery (about which she was unsentimental) had recently been stolen from the car, and with the help of the insurance she had enough money to buy this leasehold house in South Kensington. Of all the impulsive purchases she ever made, this was perhaps the rashest: she was intending to live in New York for eight months of each year. 'But I came to the conclusion that it was more important to have my bigger "residence" this side of the Atlantic, not only because I want to make a nice home for Robbie, but also because when I'm on the other side, with you, I'm so happy that I don't need possessions.'

In her days as a *Times* Fourth Leader writer, producer of 'Miniver' columns and wartime lecturer in America, Jan's distinctive voice had been that of the cheerer-up, the noticer of small pleasures, the anatomizer of happiness. Now, as her mind was growing darker, she began to reveal the other side of that talent, and to use the same powers of observation to anatomize unpleasantness. It was perhaps the mental equivalent of her apparent urge to dissect porcupines. Rather than glossing over the activities of 27 August, the macabre last afternoon of her marriage, she described them in detail to Dolf. At two o'clock she took Culi (the cairn terrier which the farmer in Argyll had given Robert) to a 'large, sinister house' in Kensington to be 'married'.

I was greeted by a tall thin cruel icy-faced Belgian doctor. His wife was away & there was no one in the house except him & me & the two dogs. We left them in the back kitchen to get on with it (it had a slippery tiled floor on which Culi skidded). We watched them through the glass doors for a bit, Dr Borel being very cold & impersonal & technical, & me standing there thinking, 'For Culi, this day is the beginning of family life: for me, the end.' Then we went upstairs to find a drink, & he couldn't find it, so he walked around showing me his pictures by people I didn't know about, & I kept thinking, 'The Jungle is coming back & I need a DRINK.' Finally he had to go to a meeting & I had to get back to cook dinner (the last I'll ever cook for Tony). So we went off in two taxis, & I finished cooking the dinner which Nannie had got under way & it was excellent – roast wild goose and a sort of soufflé thing – and afterwards we all washed up (the last time, I kept thinking quite dispassionately, that he and I shall stand at a sink together). Then we all went upstairs & had coffee & played a few records, & then I excused myself & went to bed with as large a drink as rationing would permit, & the wind howling outside the windows.

The next day was clear and sunny, and 'fresh as the freshness of new life that we were both starting on'. Jan cooked pancakes and coffee for the family, and then Tony's hired car arrived, to take him to catch a train to Scotland. He hugged Janet and Robert, but not Jan: Janet and Nannie thought this unpardonable, but Jan thought it 'perfectly understandable and therefore forgivable'.

Then [Jan continued to Dolf] Tony turned & went into the car & up Wellington Square & out of my life. And I sat down with my back to the window, & finished my breakfast, & lit a cigarette & opened my letters & read *The Times*. There was no need to put on an act: it was no act. It was just like drawing a line under a signature, or throwing away the husk of a walnut from which the kernel has been eaten.

Later in the morning, an immense feeling of relief began to grow in me, which has been ripening ever since like a beautiful swelling purple plum. Darling, I am free. Je suis libre. Ich bin frei. Have you taken it in? I can hardly believe it, even yet.

That same week, Janet left for America to take up a job working as a secretary for *Good Housekeeping*, Robert went to Scotland with Tony for three weeks' stalking, and Jamie arrived in London. He had at last been granted compassionate leave from the Army, on the grounds that he was needed at home to 'patch up his Old Folks' affairs', as he put it. But when he arrived, Jan convinced him that he was too late. So he spent much of his leave sitting with her on the roof-garden, and she felt she was meeting him properly for the first time. 'To paraphrase the old cliché about one's children's marriage,' she wrote to Dolf, 'I have lost a husband and gained a son. I never really knew him before, except during the school holidays before the war. And even then, not properly, because I always had to keep up a pretence of being Parental and Happily Married. Suddenly we have both become *people* – and, darling, he is delightful.' They discovered their joint tastes for wine, Strega, Bach, olives, John Donne, travel, dirty jokes, and getting one's house into 'a gorgeous mess'. These initial impressions of life post-marriage were encouraging. Perhaps this was what it was going to be like: you changed from being a parent to your children to being their friend.

In October Jan sailed to New York, where she stayed for five months. Short of money, having spent it on Alexander Place, she decided to revel in poverty. She pretended to her family that it was through force of necessity that she was obliged to look for accommodation in Hell's Kitchen, the unsalubrious area around the West 50s and 9th Avenue, near where the Lincoln Center now is. But in truth she was actively seeking a slummy existence as an antidote to the final months of icy grandeur in Wellington Square. There was also an element of self-punishment: the charade of being a happily married, secure 'Mrs Miniver' wife was well and truly over, and she wanted to steep herself in the potential consequences. She stayed for two weeks in a seventh-rate hotel with cockroaches on the floor ('not the black English kind which go "squoosh" but the slim American kind which go "squeesh"'). There was, even now, no question of living with Dolf: she was still married, and when they parted in the early morning they still had to look out of the window to make sure no one was watching.

With a single-mindedness which had a whiff of the manic

about it, Jan walked the streets around Hell's Kitchen for four-teen hours a day (as she claimed), asking strangers if they knew of an apartment or room to let. She had twenty-five shopkeep-ers and several taxi-drivers helping with her search. Eventually a shoe-shop-keeper named Casey found her a 'tiny little dirty place' on West 62nd Street, belonging to a dentist named Levine. She gave Mr Levine her references: the head of the BBC, the head of the radio section of the British Information Services, the head of *Information, Please!*, the British Consul, and the British Ambassador.

> Levine read down the list [she wrote to Jamie and Robert], turned to me and said, 'Yeah. But does Casey know you?' Which to my mind is *epic*. Casey's shop is 8 ft by 14 but he is respected in the neigh-bourhood & his recommendation counts for more than the British Ambassador's. This seems to me a superb example of the best kind of democracy.

Jan moved in, with the help of Bennes Mardenn (her eleva-tor-attendant friend, who was now a drama teacher) and his retinue of hard-up students. They made furniture out of orange crates, and sat on them at night singing folk music. A stockpot simmered on the small stove: the butcher supplied Jan with bones and chickens' feet, and she lived on what she called 'Dynastic soup'. Her East Side friends, including Tony's sister Rachel Townsend, were shocked to hear of her living in the slums among criminals. 'Ah, but you see,' Jan told them, 'the burglars live on my side of town but they do their burgling on your side of town.'

Despite her address, she carried on living the life of a radio celebrity, appearing on *Information, Please!* and doing BBC broadcasts. She wrote a fierce letter to the *New York Times* pro-testing against an article which had suggested that sending food parcels to Britain was no use because they hardly ever arrived. Statistics refuted this claim, she wrote: they did arrive, and Britain needed them badly. Writing that letter was as close as she was prepared to go towards lecturing on Anglo-American rela-tions. Another reason for living in Hell's Kitchen was to make herself as uncontactable as possible by the Clark Getts agency. She and Dolf spent their evenings and weekends together, quietly, going to concerts and plays and dining with close friends. Crossing the Atlantic Ocean – which she had to do again in March, for the Easter holidays and the divorce hearing – had lost its novelty. Being on board the *Queen Elizabeth* was 'like staying at the Taft Hotel with a hangover'. Sitting in the draughty Tourist Class lounge being served weak coffee by overworked stewards and unable to penetrate any of the 'family clumps' on armchairs, she yearned for the friendly chaos of the SS *Bayano* in 1945. Here, one didn't touch a rope, or see a sailor, from morning till night. 'Large ships are no fun unless you like bridge or "horse-racing" or other horrors.' Noel Coward, whom she knew slightly, was also on board, in First Class, but she was not feeling strong or successful enough to dress up and consort with the famous.

In flooded and rationed England she went by train straight to Stowe, to visit Robert for the weekend, and again was freezing cold and saddened.

It's lovely to see him – but apart from that the weekend is being intensely boring, dreary and uncomfortable. One hangs about in the hotel or hangs about in the school, trying to keep warm, & outside it rains, and there's nowhere to sit or BE. I always hated school visits, but Stowe is the worst because you have to take taxis back or forth to Buckingham three or four times a day, since there are no 'meals for parents' at the school and nothing whatever to do between meals in the town. (There's nothing to do at the school either, but at least it's faintly warmer & there are books here & there.)

Everybody is browned off. The taxi driver said last night that there doesn't seem to be anything left to live for in England now – only more work & more discomfort & less food & no prospects for a young man. It seems perfectly possible that GB is going to lapse into being just a Balkan state, after all its long grandeur & civilization.

I must now go & get ready for yet another journey to the school, for morning chapel. God . . .

In the chapel she gazed at the boys' faces. 'They all looked so thin,' she wrote to Dolf, 'so thin, so pale, and most of them so chinless. And so terribly alike in type. How the country needs some melting-pot blood. It's getting it, of course, in the Lower Classes, my deah, but the others . . .'

On her way ·back to London she stayed with her brother Douglas and his wife. This was more comfortable, physically, 'but God! they look so old and tired, both of them. And everywhere you go it's the same story – panic about the food situation, both now and in the future. At least it would be panic if they weren't English & tired: as it is, it's a sort of dulled resignation. Our present coldness & wetness is less than half the trouble. It's the utter buggering-up of the harvest that's the serious thing. I can't see any prospect of improved conditions for years now.'

Back at 17 Alexander Place, she sat upstairs in Robert's room, the only one with a gas fire (electricity in London was cut off between nine and noon and two and four), feeling a gnawing hunger all day and rushing downstairs to open a tin of sardines while Nannie was out searching for potatoes.

The divorce hearing was to take place at Parliament House in Edinburgh in May, and the thought of it was beginning to give Jan 'the jitters'. Fate had provided a nice tie-in for the newspapers to pick up on: her divorce from Tony would coincide with Greer Garson's from Richard Ney – a double debunking of the Miniver myth of marriage. ('The Ney marriage', according to Greer Garson's biographer, 'unravelled in a mire of accusations and ugly quarrels' towards the end of 1946.)

Tony, on the nights of 22 and 23 February 1947, had done what was known as 'the gentlemanly thing': to enable Jan to sue him for divorce, he spent two nights at a hotel in Glasgow, The Bristol, with an unnamed 'professional co-respondent'. They signed the register as 'Mr and Mrs A. Maxtone Graham' and for the benefit of 'witnesses' pretended to share the double bed, but in fact took turns on the sofa. Strictly speaking, this kind of collusive pantomime was illegal, but it was regularly winked at by the legal establishment. Jan was spared the ordeal of being exposed in the Press as 'Mrs Miniver the adulteress', as must have happened had Tony sued her for divorce. They agreed to go to the Scottish Court, partly to avoid publicity, and partly to avoid the six-month 'decree nisi' waiting period still obligatory in any English divorce.

As the day of the hearing drew nearer, Jan focused her mind on to the days beyond it. 'I shall feel completely different when the actual case is over,' she wrote to Dolf. 'I have a feeling that this is the last time I'll ever be in the least Jungular, & that this is only the final culmination of a long strain of misery.' A letter from Dolf arrived.

It occurred to me [she wrote back], as I walked towards the front door to pick up the mail off the mat and saw the familiar envelope lying there, that I feel just as quick and warm a rush of excitement and tenderness on seeing a letter from you as I did in 1939/40. It is the *only* compensation from being apart from you. Otherwise separations are increasingly horrible and indeed unbearable. I want desperately that people should KNOW we belong to each other; I want to make some kind of gesture to declare my pride and joy in our unique companionship. The longer I pursue this line of thought, the nearer it brings me to the point where it would not take a very big push to . . . well, I suppose it's no good talking about it yet awhile anyway.

Robert came home for the holidays and pottered helpfully about the house, connecting wires. Jan needed money to do up Alexander Place. She sold her diamond clips for £65 to pay for a carpet. She sold some tray-cloths and doilies and 'other horrors' to Peter Jones for £5, but couldn't bring herself to sell a damask cloth belonging to her mother's family and dated 1800 in cross-stitch, because she knew it would be cut up and the bits resold to hotels. 'But no doubt this inhibition will disappear when I need some other things badly enough. I'm beginning to hate all possessions, except musical or portable ones. I had a grisly job yesterday, turning out the family medicine cupboard, full of reminiscent smells recalling the children's bronchitises and so on. Altogether London is too full of ghosts.'

Jan travelled to Edinburgh by train, with Nannie for company. Cut off from Maxtone Grahams, they booked into a hotel. 'Three damned nights in Edinburgh,' Jan wrote to Dolf, 'and not even the fun of seeing T's mother, whom I still love.'

Her undefended action for divorce was heard at the Law Courts on 7 May. Much of her evidence was perjured, but this was all part of the pantomime. First, she was required to swear (falsely) that the divorce was not collusive. To prove, as was required, that Tony was domiciled in Scotland, she had to say that he now lived at his mother's house in Edinburgh and had 'lived all his life in Scotland apart from absences caused by business or military reasons'. Finally, she had to swear to her belief in the Glasgow adultery story. Regarding her relationship with Tony, her evidence was more truthful: 'The marriage was very happy at first, but after about eight years Tony's attitude towards me underwent a change, and by about 1936 marital relations between us had ceased. On his return from prisoner-of-war camp, I found that his attitude towards me had not changed, and matters between us remained as they had been before the war.' Without demur, the judge granted her a decree of divorce, and costs.

Darling love: It's over, and it went through all right, and I'm back in London, and I found your sweet telegram waiting for me – and, oh honey, it was unspeakably ghastly. The wigs & gowns and the mechanical legal faces and the gloomy old Parliament House, and the utter squalor of the whole thing, so remote from anything that had ever been happy or tender. Nannie's presence – not in the Court, but in the awful hotel where we had to spend 3 nights trying to keep warm, and sitting in the Lounge, and listening to the genteel murmurs of the fellow guests, or tramping the streets & going to bad movies to pass the hours away – Nannie's presence, as I was saying, was the only thing that saved me from going completely nuts. And then the 9-hour journey back, trying to keep one's mind on a book in order to forget the ordeal . . .

Surely the 'Jungles' should have vanished, along with the marriage from which she had at last escaped? They had been caused, she had always believed, by the strain of her double life, which was now a single one. She had envisaged the train journey south from Edinburgh as a blissful ride of freedom; she had imagined that she would return to a state of unattached girlhood, her life simplified, the rotten bit cleanly amputated.

But it was not like that. She had left the marriage behind, but the misery came with her on the train.

The only person who could help was Dolf: she fastened her hopes on him. 'I feel sore and bruised through & through, and I think it will take me a long time to get over it. I am numb about Tony, but not about the "pattern" of happiness and the children's childhood. I want you to take me in your arms and MAKE the Jungles go away, and make me into one whole person again, instead of this divided wretch.'

A few weeks later, sitting at the desk in Dolf's apartment in New York while he was in the same room playing the piano, she wrote to him again:

How the pendulum has swung! For so many years, you were the dependent one, full of fears and panicking dreams, and I was the strong one who pulled you into contact with the outside world and tried to give you back your confidence in yourself. And now it is all reversed and *you* are the one who has to be strong & help me fight my terrors & conflicts & 'the green eyes in the night'. For God's sake, sweetheart, go on being strong for me & make me get back my own strength. Please go on believing in me as much as I have always believed in you, and please go on exercising the gentleness and patience which you have shown throughout this black time.

Dr Lawrence Kubie first appears in Jan's engagement book on 4 September 1947, towards the end of a swelliering summer during which Dolf worked at his job at Avery and Jan achieved little. She tried various doctors, who prescribed nerve tonics and injections, and various psychotherapists, who required her to talk about her childhood on a couch, but with Kubie, an Austrian Jewish psychoanalyst who specialized in 'blocked' artists, she found at last someone whom she warmed to, and who combined the two things she badly needed: expert professionalism and a willingness to allow a professional relationship to develop into a deep (though not sexual) friendship. She needed the element of love in order to blossom in any relationship, and she had an extraordinary capacity for bringing it out, especially in intelligent men, who responded to her wisdom and her frailty. From September to November she had four or five appointments with Kubie each week, and when she ran out of money to pay his fees he allowed her to come free of charge.

She swung, he told her, between the two poles of 'great freedom and release of energy in work and play', and being 'slowed up, with a loss of confidence and a tendency to be emotionally dependent on others.' His listening and his speaking seem to have done her good – or perhaps she merely swung from one pole to the other – because by the time she sailed to England for the Christmas holidays on the RMS *Mauretania* on 30 November, her attitude to large ships, and to the school chapel at Stowe, had undergone a change for the better. On board ship, though the sea was still 'wet, cold, boring and far too big', she found a nice table-mate, a sixty-year-old widow going back to Lowestoft. 'We talk about Yorkshire pudding recipes & so forth & it's all very soothing.' In the school chapel, where last year she had seen mere thin, blue-blooded chinlessness, she now saw 'Corinthian columns rising up behind their Earnest Young Faces & stuff & stuff, and I felt highly numinous & practically believed in God.'

She was on the 'high veldt' rather than in the 'jungle swamps' during her ten weeks in England, and she basked in it. Her house in Alexander Place, where Jamie, Janet and Robert stayed with her for Christmas, became a studenty den of carpentry, half-finished electrical jobs, musical instruments and woodshavings on the floor. Nannie lived permanently in one room, as caretaker. Jan slept each night in her 'darling' sleeping-bag, which enhanced the gypsy or camping-ground atmosphere that she yearned to create. She and Jamie drank red wine at all hours, though never before eleven in the morning. The doorbell rang with visitors of all ages dropping in to drink wine or sing with the guitar, Anne Talbot the most frequent of all; and one afternoon a Herr Tischler dropped in, to deliver Dolf's violin which he had managed to extract for him from Nazi Vienna. Tischler stayed for hours and joined the musical party, playing a duet with violin and guitar to which Jan sang in German. This was the way of living which came naturally to her.

On this 'high veldt' her broadcasting nerve came back, and the BBC snapped her up. She was overflowing with ideas and energy. She wrote a twenty-eight page letter to Dolf on 14 January 1948.

First things first.

1 Congratulations about 'Das Haus' [a poem Dolf had written, which had been praised by fellow Austrians].

2 Yes, of course, do let's get married. Anything else would be absurd, really. I'm enchanted that you've booked a provisional holiday – though of course nothing is settled or inexorable or trap-like, & we won't actually consider ourselves engaged until we meet (which thank God will be in less than a month – oh Liebstes!).

3 Sorry about handwriting. You see, I've been making a tool cabinet because the BBC asked me if I had a hobby & I said yes, carpentry, & they asked me to do a television broadcast about it, which I've just done, and I had to make a thoroughly good single-handed job of the tool cupboard, with brass hinges & handles, so that it would look all right on the screen, & I went up in blue jeans to Alexandra Palace, & it was all tremendous fun & I got 15 guineas for it. I've always contended that the best thing is to go on doing the things you are really interested in, & eventually somebody will come along & pay you for doing them.

4 I have done some other broadcasts, & have made the price of my passage to America. I'm doing one on Monday ('Woman's Hour') about Hill-Billy children, & I did one on Christmas Day on the BBC Christmas Party, playing a game where you had to tell a story about 4 previously unseen objects, without preparation, lasting exactly 4 minutes. Moddestamento detto, I am God's gift to radio & television, & all the departments at the BBC, practically, are after me for one thing or another.

5 I've taken to ART at last. Two weekends ago I went to stay with my brother, & he gave me an old Staffordshire zebra which had belonged to our father (which art, undoubtedly, in Heaven) & it had one foreleg missing. So I made a new one out of a pipe-cleaner & some plastic wood. Then I made a black bishop for Douglas's chess set with a pipe-cleaner, a French franc, a coat-button, 2 metal fly-buttons, a wooden bead, and a blob of sealing-wax. Last weekend, staying with friends in Amberley, I decided to make a zebra foal, but

I couldn't get pipe-cleaners or plastic wood in the village. I was itching to model late at night & couldn't sleep, so I made it instead out of electric light wire & candle ends melted down in a frying-pan. I found pictures of zebras in the Children's Encyclopedia, but I couldn't take in flat pictures, so I went out in the dark & found a live donkey in a field & felt it all over to see where its bones & muscles came (keeping it quiet meanwhile by giving it a cigarette, which it chewed with malicious avidity) . . .

She justified this manic artistic urge by reminding Dolf (who was not approving of her endless diversification) that she needed to develop her visual sense in order to write the scripts for films, so that he could be freed from his 'boring, unworthy and ridiculously underpaid' job at the Avery Library. She and Ernest Shepard had just been to the cinema, she told Dolf, to see Alexander Korda's *Anna Karenina*, and they had come back on a freezing bus warm with excitement about camera angles. She had contacts with Ealing Studios, Rank, and Korda, 'plus a more or less standing order with MGM': all she needed was to be able to *see* scenes in her head, and then her latest idea for a film (with the working title *Monday is Washing Day*), would come to fruition, 'and then, darling, we'll both be FREE at last.'

It was clear to Dolf that going out into the dark to feel donkeys' muscles was getting Jan further away from, rather than nearer to, her true métier of writing. There was a thin line, in these headstrong and tomboyish pursuits, between eccentric charm and battiness. But the relationship had gone beyond the stage where exasperation could do any serious damage. Their love, after eight and a half years of adversity, had grown roots. The taking of vows seemed the most natural next step in the world.

A few months later, Jan was to ask him a dark question, disguised in frivolous language: 'Darling, what *have* you been and gone and married?'

Chapter Sixteen

From this day on, our love shall be
Open, for all the world to see:
And folk will smile who once would frown,
Saying, 'At last you've settled down.'

That's what they think: but we know better.
Theirs is the spirit, ours is the letter.
Our ship, which nine long years has tossed,
Helpless and helmless, nearly lost,
Upon the steep and perilous seas
Of a crazed world's complexities,
Can now, with gathering speed and force,
Pursue a swift and steady course.

Let those whose goal is comfort hanker
For calm, for harborage, for anchor:
We two shall share our double realm –
I at the sheet, you at the helm.
Under bare poles we've ridden out the gale:
Come, love, no settling down – but setting sail.

'The Blue Peter', written on the morning of J.S's wedding to Dolf,
1 March 1948

'IT WAS A very short but dignified (just like me) ceremony,' Jan
wrote to her brother Douglas after the wedding, 'mentioning
God, but leaving out all the other schmaltz.' A civil ceremony
conducted by 'a very nice fat man', Mr Murray H. Stand, it was
over by 11.30. After lunch with Pauly, Janet and a few close
friends, Dolf and Jan moved furniture into their new apartment
at 150 West 82nd Street, their love 'open for all the world to see'.

Dolf agreed with all of Jan's wedding-morning poem, apart from the last line. He would have preferred 'Come, love, no setting sail – but settling down.' It seemed to him that they had done more than enough setting sail already.

'The wedding was on 1 March and the secret is only just out,' wrote the *New York Times* a week later, embarrassed not to have picked up on it sooner. 'The new Mr Miniver, Austrian by birth, is now a naturalized American . . .' Dolf and Jan read this on their sofa, during their stationary honeymoon at home. There was no hint of scandal in the paper, only surprise. No journalist found out that the love affair had been going on since 1939.

Jan's long-repressed urge to show to the world her 'unique companionship' with Dolf found its release in the organizing of the post-wedding party: 'Mr and Mrs Adolf Placzek request the pleasure of your company . . .' It was to be a cocktail party at home on 20 May, and she invited almost everyone she could think of – literary friends, actors, broadcasting colleagues, author-acquaintances – and ordered in wine, pretzels and olives for more than a hundred guests. They came: the room was as cramped as a subway train, and Dolf felt that he – a junior librarian – was of no interest to any of these people. Standing in the doorway and longing to go out for a walk, he said to an unknown guest, 'Well, I'd like to have met Ogden Nash, at least', to which the man (also longing for a walk) replied, 'I *am* Ogden Nash.'

After the party there came a time of easy domesticity. Dolf's editions of Goethe's poetry and Jan's of John Donne's were side by side on the same bookshelf at last. In May Jan entered her favourite state, book-wise: Harcourt Brace commissioned her to write an autobiography of the first twenty years of her life. They wanted it in October, for publication in the spring of 1949, and they talked of pre-publication in serial, which would bring in $15,000 on top of the advance. There were months to go until October, so Jan relished the prospect of glory and income without feeling it mattered if she didn't start writing quite yet. Dolf worked at Avery, and she wrote him an untidy poem, 'Kalbshaxen' ('Veal Shanks'), expressing the culinariness of early married love.

Liebstes:
I cannot imagine anything lovelier, mein Schlumperdinck,
Than hearing your key in the lock, coming home from your work,
And standing over the stove, cooking *Kalbshaxen* . . .
And smelling the smell of garlic (which you pretend to despise)
And of Love (which you worship without pretending),
And saying 'Hello', and watching you lie down on our *Ehebett*,*
Weary with unworthy *Beamtenarbeit*⁺
And close your beautiful tragic-humorous eyes,
And watch your full-lipped tragic-humorous mouth relax in sleep,
And go back to the little stove and tend the *Kalbshaxen*,
And season them with pepper and salt and oregano and garlic
     and love
– Above all the strong, sweet, pungent, aromatic herb of love,
Which is sweet-sour, suitable for feast-days and fast-days,
And utterly, beautifully Kosher,
And wait for you to wake up and share with me
Our dinner of herbs (and *Kalbshaxen*) Where Love Is.

In July they set sail, bound for England on the SS *America*. The typed card on the door of their cabin said 'Mr Dolph Placzek. Mrs Placzek.' They kept it. Now Jan could show him off all over again. She took him to meet her brother Douglas, who was charming, though more eccentric than ever: he had installed a toy train signal by his place at the dining-room table, and when he couldn't stand any more of his wife's chattering he put the signal at 'stop'. They went to Wimbledon to meet 'Fuffs', who had looked after Jan in her teens. They had dinner at the Ritz Grill with Charles and Oscar Spencer, in whose flat in Cheyne Walk they had had their early assignations.

A long weekend in Paris with Robert was part of their plan for these fourteen days together in Europe. Paris! Images filled their heads. Dolf yearned to see the buildings, and the pictures in the Louvre, Jan to sit at café tables on pavements, listening to cars on cobbles and glimpsing lives through upstairs shutters. Robert longed to see 'abroad', never having been taken to

---

* Marriage-bed   †Office-work

On board the SS America: *Dolf, Jan, Pauly, Susan*

the Continent as a child. Jan hoped Robert would relax with Dolf as they strode through the Tuileries discussing mansard roofs. But it didn't work. It was yet another strained holiday. The air was stiflingly hot, the days seemed to drag on for ever, and there was no easy communication between Jan and Robert, or between Dolf and Robert. He had not yet come to terms with his mother's divorce and remarriage, and his way of dealing with the awkwardness and his sense of wrongness was to become very quiet. Notre Dame and Chartres Cathedral were balm for the buttress-starved Dolf, but for Jan and Robert, squinting upwards clutching their Baedekers, they were tiring for the feet and somehow un-nourishing for the mind.

Dolf sailed back to New York, his holiday entitlement used up, but Jan stayed in Britain for another month. She took a train to Scotland to see Jamie, who was working as a student farmer near Kelso before going to the Edinburgh Agricultural College (as the laird's eldest son, he wanted to train to run the farm at Cultoquhey). Sitting in a hay-loft, or by the edge of a field where oats were being cut, detached from her life, her desk, her telephone and her unpaid bills, comforted by the industrious proximity of her son, Jan found – after years of being unable to write prose – that, miraculously, she was writing her autobiography. Onto pads of 'Old Chelsea China' lined paper, words flowed out of her by the thousand: incisive vignettes of her parents' unhappy marriage, rambling digressions about the 'mountain range' which separated childhood from adulthood, whimsical passages about downstairs loos and the smell of potpourri, touching descriptions of a child torn between the 'upstairs' and 'below-stairs' worlds of an Edwardian household. Across the Atlantic, Harcourt Brace were waiting for this, arms outstretched, and she was not failing them. 'I have a kind of race with the reaper-binder, which takes about 18 minutes to make one round of the 27-acre field,' she wrote to Dolf. 'The circuit, naturally, gets slightly quicker each time, but it still takes me as long to write 500 words.' And, the next day: 'I sat in Jamie's loft workshop with a writing-board made of planks, and wrote nearly a chapter of my book – 3,000 words – until my pen ran out of ink & my veins of blood from the damp cold. We had our lunch sandwiches in the car for warmth. I went for a walk up the hill after lunch & communed with rabbits in a pinewood.' She had found another existence which suited her perfectly. She and Jamie dined one evening (at the Queen's Hotel in Kelso, where they were staying) on grouse sent from Cultoquhey by Tony, who had no idea Jan was there. 'It's lovely being in a part of Scotland where one doesn't own any of the land, & isn't related to any of the people who do,' she wrote to Dolf. She and Jamie did drive to Perthshire one Sunday to visit Tony's sister Ysenda Smythe. 'I can assure you,' wrote Jan, 'I felt not the smallest regret that I was no longer The Laird's Lady.'

To get full value out of this new sensation of being anonymous in Scotland, Jan suggested a day's poaching. She and Jamie 'played hookey' from the farm and drove to a flooded burn in the wild hills near the English border. They threw a piece of fence planking across for a bridge. Jamie fished, while Jan collected firewood (which was scarce, so she ripped bark off fenceposts) and built a fireplace, and lit dead bracken as kindling. Jamie came back with five small trout, which he gutted and Jan fried on a flat stone in butter scraped out of their sandwiches, seasoned with wild thyme. 'A band of Indians appeared down the road,' she wrote to Dolf, 'in the person of a band of Local Gentry, but luckily they were too far off to see what we were cooking, & Jamie's rod lying in the heather: & anyway they couldn't have got across the water if we'd withdrawn the plank bridge . . .'

It was yet more rebellious tomboyishness verging on the batty: but what worried Dolf was the taking of a day off from writing her book. He knew that momentum, with Jan, was vital. One day off, and the whole enterprise could start to disintegrate.

His fears were not unfounded. Arriving back on 17 September in New York (where her first intention, as she forewarned Dolf, was to '*plunge* into bed with you and merge my body and soul with yours'), Jan found that she had again lost the knack and the discipline of writing. Dolf had been promoted at Avery: he was now Assistant Librarian, helping to make decisions about important acquisitions for the library, and his hours were slightly longer than before. Jan railed against his responsible diligence. Her destiny, she still believed, was to set him free from the 'mouldy (literally) library' – but she was aware that his small monthly pay-cheque was for the time being their chief source of income, and that they needed it to pay the rent. She felt lost without him during the daytime: her terror of being alone had returned. In a poem she described the thoughts of a dependent wife:

> I love three sounds within the house –
> The ticking of the clock,
> And the singing of the kettle,
> And the sound of his key in the lock.

Partly, she was afflicted by the disinclination to write which almost all writers are familiar with: the feeling that any household job is preferable to facing a blank sheet of paper. Her prowess with odd jobs made temptation all the stronger. 'If I went home,' she wrote later, describing the experience of writer's block, 'the nail-holes in the plaster would stare at me, gaping for speckle as fledglings gape for worms; and the buttons would regard me with round accusing eyes, implying that they couldn't be blamed for not doing their duty if they were not given the proper conditions to work in. Children can be reproachful, animals even more so, but there is nothing to touch the martyred unctuousness of inanimate objects in need of attention.'

But the problem went deeper than this. Bennes Mardenn, who remembers every day with Jan as if it were yesterday, recalls that during the autumn of 1948 Jan showed him the chapter from her manuscript in which the young Joyce saw the parents of her friend Kathleen Gascoigne having a mock-quarrel, before the father picked up the mother and carried her out of the schoolroom, laughing and talking. 'Jan wept when she showed me that. It brought up too much. Her love for her mother and father, and their loathing for each other, tore her apart.' In the hay-loft in Scotland, detached from her own worries, she had mustered the inner strength to tackle the emotive subject of her childhood; but now, back at her own desk amid the paperwork of divorce and exile, she could no longer think clearly. 'The stress on her mind [Jamie wrote later] inhibited her from reliving her childhood accurately enough to commit it to paper.'

'She walked with the palms of her hands *out*,' Bennes remembers, '– the defenceless walk. I have not seen that before or since.' Her frailty touched him deeply. She asked him if he would mind coming to sit quietly in the apartment with her during the daytime, getting on with his work in another room. He did this. When he didn't have anything to do, he brought pretend work. In this way, avoiding solitude, Bennes overlapping with Pauly and Pauly overlapping with Dolf, Jan tried to stave off despair. But it came. She fell headlong into the worst depression she had yet experienced. All the joy of the past year – impromptu music-making at Alexander Place, inspired broadcasting, suddenly-flowing writing, poaching in the Borders – turned out to have been the exaggerated bright side of a condition which inevitably revealed its equally exaggerated dark side. And when you were in the dark side of the cycle, the bright side seemed illusory.

But how could she be depressed, when she was married to Dolf? Wasn't this what she had longed for, and pinned her hopes on? The quotation from Bernard Shaw's *Man and Superman* is apposite – 'There are only two tragedies in life. One is not to get your heart's desire. The other is to get it.' The final hurdle in the journey to happiness had been crossed, but she still felt like a 'divided wretch'. Contentment and inner peace still eluded her, and there was no one left to blame but herself.

Was it the case that marriage to Dolf was an anti-climax after nine years of illicitness? Did their love dwindle slightly, in the daily drudgery of buying and cooking veal shanks and washing up the saucepans afterwards? It did not dwindle, Dolf has claimed, vehemently, and all the evidence in Jan's later diaries and letters bears him out. Their love remained as strong as ever after marriage, and continued to grow deeper by the day.

There was depression in the family, and it may be that Jan would have suffered manic swings whatever had happened in her life – even if the war had never come and she had sat out a long, superficially happy marriage with Tony. It was, partly, a hereditary medical condition. But it is clear that circumstances had exacerbated it. She had got herself into a vicious circle, worrying about money, and about not writing her book: worrying so much that she could not eat without vomiting, which made it even more difficult to work on the book, which made her worry still more. She was heartbroken by the loss of the 'family pattern' and being separated from the children, who didn't write many letters. Even a non-depressive woman might suffer sleep-depriving pangs of anxiety and remorse on finding herself in such a situation. But for someone prone to depression like Jan, such anxieties could be the catalyst of deep despair.

She could not bring herself to write a letter, let alone a book.

When I say physically impossible to write a letter [she wrote to her brother Douglas later, when he, too, was having a nervous breakdown], I mean just that: a literal, even if psychologically-induced,

paralysis of the limbs which makes the effort of taking up a piece of
paper and making marks on it with a pen so monumentally, incon-
ceivably difficult that, sooner than do it, one rushes to the loo and
vomits instead: the only relief that's left to one, after one has got to
the stage of not being able to cry. That was one of my worst horrors
– excelled only by the *sheer* horror of having to answer the telephone. ('What – me answer that screeching devilish contraption?
Actually pick it up and say "Hello?" and perhaps hear some bad
news, or a voice I don't like, or a bank manager saying something
nasty, or even a nice boring person who wants to come to dinner?
Impossible. I won't, I can't, I shan't, I'd sooner die, who the hell do
they think I am, don't they know that I am in hell and mustn't be
bothered? Let it ring – no, don't let it ring – throw something at it,
and stop it, and meanwhile just let me lie down on the floor, preferably under a table, and put a bearskin rug over my head and DIE . . .')
Does that ring a bell, or don't you have that one?

She could not face psychiatric help, and lived on a diet of
sleeping-pills, sherry and cigarettes, unable to keep food down
and sobbing herself to sleep in Dolf's arms. Without telling her,
he called in Dr Lawrence Kubie to see her. She was furious that
he should have done so, and screamed; Dolf moved out of the
apartment for a week. But Kubie took the matter in hand. He
gave her pills to calm her nerves, and insisted that she start
having appointments with him again. She agreed; and he realized, while listening to her sobs, that the 'swings' between the
over-active drive and the retarded-depressive drive were now
out of control.

Just before Christmas Jan received a letter from Curtis
Brown, the literary agents who had taken her on after the war
(after years with A. P. Watt): 'I'm afraid "Displaced Persons" [a
poem she had written] has now been seen and declined by the
New Yorker, the *Post, Ladies' Home Journal, Collier's, Woman's
Home Companion, Atlantic Monthly, Harpers*, and *Tomorrow*.
I'm afraid there are no further likely markets for this one and
so, sadly, I'm returning the manuscript herewith.' These were
all, except for the *New Yorker*, magazines which had published
Jan's poems in earlier years. A few days later another letter followed: 'I'm afraid "Green Warfare" has reached the end of the

road.' 'Pome' was declined by seventeen publications. She had apparently even lost the art of writing publishable poetry.

But Curtis Brown were delighted with the first seven chapters of her autobiography, taking her life up to her early teens, which she had sent them in September. They suggested having illustrations drawn by E. H. Shepard. Glory was so near: all she needed to do was get herself to the age of twenty, and the autobiography would be finished.

But the picking up of a pen remained out of the question. On 4 February 1949, on Dr Kubie's recommendation, she was admitted as a voluntary patient at the Austin Riggs Center at Stockbridge, Massachusetts: a 'psychiatric sanatorium', a 'nursing-home hotel' – or, as Jan and her co-patients liked to call it, a 'loony-bin'.

Here, a four-hour train journey from New York, in white-shuttered seclusion, she sobbed on the couch of Dr Kubie's friend Dr Allen B. Wheelis, the Center's resident psychoanalyst. Appointments with him took place every other day, and seemed to lead to nowhere. The clock ticked. Jan snuffled and blew her nose and wiped her glasses and put them on again, and then started crying again and took them off, and Dr Wheelis receded into a blur, and she blew her nose and put her glasses on again; and so it went on until the appointment was over and he said 'We'll stop there.'

Between these appointments, life became a succession of gaps of time which had somehow to be got through.

Describing her first day at Miss Richardson's Classes in Great College Street, Westminster, aged six, when writing her autobiography a few months earlier, Jan had said that she had discovered she liked being a New Girl, and that this feeling had stayed with her all her life. She could not have known, as she wrote it, that she would soon be a New Girl all over again in an institution uncannily similar to a boarding school, but that this time she would be almost incapable of enjoyment.

It was like a boarding school in that the corridors smelled of polish, the food was institutional (mushy spaghetti, and meatballs hard enough to play billiards with), friends tended to stick together in groups in the common rooms, there was a carpentry workshop in the grounds and a shop to buy snacks, and the tables were laid for breakfast immediately after the supper had been cleared. It was an expensive institution: Jan was there free of charge, 'on a scholarship', and slightly frowned on by the 'full-tariff girls'.

But it was actually a grotesque version of an Angela Brazil school paradise. The evening sight of the laid breakfast tables was a torment for the residents: it signified the changelessness of their mental states. The stage was set for another pointless day, just like the one which had nearly ended. All the residents were suffering from some kind of anxiety neurosis: some, like Jan, were so mentally and physically paralysed that they could hardly bring themselves to walk the fifty yards from the therapy centre back to the main building. Others were the opposite: all too keen to 'act out' their neuroses by running naked round the grounds, shouting. The first thing you did here, on waking up, was to take half a Seconal sleeping-pill, or 'goof-ball', and try to postpone consciousness. Then, when the Beethoven's-Fifth-Symphony 'ta-ta-ta-tum' knock came to wake you up, you lit a cigarette in bed and smoked it, holding it between shaking fingers. Appetiteless, and with knees wobbling, you went to the dining-room and forced down cereal before going straight out to the corridor to smoke. Then, if your appointment on the couch was not till 11.30, there was a two-hour gap to fill.

Jan's two friends here were Hope Patterson and Harriet Harvey. There were male residents as well – Harold Ross, the editor of the *New Yorker*, came here for rest and recuperation in the 1940s – but at this time in her life, Jan was seeking the company of women rather than men. She was quite changed from the 'kittenish' 'child-wife' who had so infuriated Anne Talbot on the Rumanian duck-shooting holiday in 1929 by her insistence on being the constant centre of male attention. Now she longed to talk to women, especially ones who were suffering like her, and to help them. The three sat on rocks talking about husbands, failed marriages, the dread of solitude, 'the Willies' and 'the Tarantulas' (their names for 'the

Jungles'), and the 'Change of Life' (as the menopause, often blamed for mid-life depression, was called). All too familiar with psychiatrist's jargon, they parodied it, sprinkling their chat with 'let me rephrase that', 'we're skirting around the periphery', 'you are free to leave at any time you wish', and 'we'll stop there'. If someone said she didn't feel like playing chess, the rejoinder would be, 'Resisting, huh? Come on, try to be a little co-operative.'

A strict unwritten code developed among these women: if one of them was feeling desperate and asked you to 'shoot a little pool' to bridge the gap before lunch, you went and played pool with her, however black you might feeling, however little you cared whether any ball went into any pocket.

'The Shop' – the carpentry workshop – was open for four hours a day, closed on Sundays. While it was open, Jan was there. In the depths of her depression, though waking each morning with 'the jitters' and 'the Willies', she finished an inlaid chess table which was by far the most carefully-worked piece of furniture she had ever made. 'At one moment,' she wrote proudly to Jamie, in an effortfully cheerful letter, 'it had no less than 23 clamps on it overnight.'

Three months after she had arrived – and still with no improvement in sight – Dr Wheelis suggested that it might help to 'unblock' her if she attempted to get down on paper some of the thoughts which went through her head during the monotonous days. So on the morning of 17 May, returning to her room after her breakfast cigarette, she forced herself to sit down at her typewriter. 'This is an experiment,' she began.

Yesterday was a particularly awful day. Mondays are always bad, especially after a good weekend – and the weekend had been better than usual, full of that sweet flowing interchange of thoughts and feelings between Dolf [who visited her at weekends] and me which is the mainspring of our rare relationship. In spite of all our worries and problems and joint nostalgia, it was a good weekend. By contrast, as well as intrinsically, yesterday was hell . . .

She went on to describe a typical day at the sanitorium:

After lunch comes a very long Gap. You long sometimes to take a nap: but you have learned from experience that you will wake up with an even worse attack of 'tarantulas', and will regret having exposed yourself to the horrors of two awakenings during the twenty-four hours instead of one. Sometimes you have letters to answer, and sometimes you go for a drive or a walk. None of these occupations is boring in itself – it's just that all the time, but absolutely *all* of the time, the agony and worry are going on inside you, and the sense of futility, and the despair at getting nowhere. And outside the spring is going on, and you can't *feel* it, and you think of that line out of Coleridge's 'Dejection: an Ode', when he's talking about sunsets and mountains and so on: 'I see, not feel, how beautiful they are.'

She described the feeling of being 'blocked' as a writer:

It's no good people saying, 'Sit down for an hour or two a day and WRITE!' You can't spin writing out of your own belly like a spider spinning a web: it's something that comes partly from outside, or rather, it's a two-way process, born of your own relationship with the universe . . . I'm like a radio set that's on the blink: I can't tune in any more to any programme worth listening to – only to soap operas and third-rate commentators. And yet I know that all the time the ether is full of Brandenburg Concertos and superb performances of *Antony and Cleopatra*.

She filled fifteen pages: and the act of writing about the tawdriness of the 'hell' did have the effect of helping her to see her way out of it. Two days later, during her appointment with Dr Wheelis, she read aloud to him what she had written. When she had finished, he said, 'I find that very moving.' It seemed a pity, he said, that it couldn't be published somewhere, and he asked her to carry on writing. He went to the bookshelf and produced some pamphlets for her to read, about 'Artistic Experience' and 'Aesthetic States of Mind', and Jan was encouraged and touched. This was what happened to her mood:

I left his office and walked back to the Shop in a state of definite and recognizable euphoria – that state which in my experience you only get into (no, not only, but most often) when you are either in love or have just written something which you feel is good and genuine, especially if it has just 'moved' somebody else whose opinion you value, whether to tears or laughter. I found myself walking spring-ily, and I thought of the rightness of all the old clichés, such as 'walking on air', 'being in high spirits', and 'having a light heart'. I felt walking was far too prosaic a means of progression, and that it would have been more appropriate to my mood to go all the way from Wheelis's office to the Shop turning cartwheels.

When she reached the lawn in front of the main house, she saw 'Polish John', the gardener, in his bare feet, pushing the mowing machine, and she realized that for the first time since her depression she was able to smell the grass – always for her and for Dolf a symbol of joy. Not only could she smell it: she could also feel in her own shod feet the sensation Polish John must have been feeling in his bare ones. The 'two-way' relation-ship with the universe was beginning to return.

On 6 June Dr Wheelis suggested that she try going home to New York for the weekend. She was nervous about this, partly because she was worried about what people there might think. 'I can imagine myself running into Fatso Kubik, our Czech superintendent,' she typed, 'and him looking at me and seeing that I am apparently in perfect health, with a sun-tan, as fat as a pig, and then me having to explain that I'm only back for the weekend and shall be leaving again on Sunday night: and I can imagine him going down to his apartment in the basement and discussing it with his wife and saying, "Well, it don't look to *me* like there's anything wrong with her. Why don't she come back and stay back? Sump'n screwy about the whole set-up."' But she went. Dolf collected her from Grand Central and she felt 'like a farmer's wife on her first visit to the Big City', shocked by the traffic jams and hooting horns. He carried her over the threshold into the apartment. She went round touching every-thing, and embraced her Staffordshire zebra. After dinner at their local Italian restaurant (annoyingly called 'Tony's'), Dolf played the piano while Jan unpacked, and they went to bed early in the sweltering heat. She woke the next morning with 'slight Jungles' but made breakfast for Dolf. 'It was the first time he had had breakfast made for him for over four months, and he was most touchingly thrilled about it.'

In this quiet, homely, unadventurous way her recovery continued, and she left Stockbridge for good in July, five months after her arrival.

August was spent away from the heat of New York, on Island 727 of the 30,000 in Georgian Bay, Ontario, staying with Bev and Marian Robinson. A photograph survives of this vacation: a picnic scene, in which a smiling Jan is holding her pocket-knife threateningly towards Dolf's face. She could still be an unnerving person to be at a picnic with. She peppered her talk with four-letter words (which invariably came as a shock to anyone who expected her to be like Mrs Miniver); but apart from her swearing and her occasional knife-wielding, she was good company.

A manic gesture with the pocket-knife

In New York she was on the radio and television again, appearing on quiz programmes and doing 'Guest Spot' jobs, and she signed a contract with Columbia Broadcasting. 'You can be forgotten in America,' she wrote to her brother, 'because they have been so goddamned loving that they've run you ragged with popularity, and you think you're down & out & flat-broke & will never stage a comeback – and then you do one little 15-minute radio show, as I did last week, & within 24 hours they're all on your neck again.'

But she and Dolf were none the less almost 'flat-broke', and could not legally break the lease on an apartment which they could no longer afford.

Our rent at this apartment sorry flat is so screwing sorry fucking high [she wrote to Douglas], namely $1680 a year for two repeat TWO rooms, that we are perpetually one jump ahead of the sheriff, which doesn't worry me because I was born with a silver bailiff in my mouth, but *does* worry Dolf, who comes of a respectable Viennese family. He had two 'firsts' yesterday: (1) he found his own name in *Debrett* – a thing that his grandfather, the Grand Rabbi of Moravia, would hardly have foreseen happening; and (2) he had his first bounced cheque returned, from the Columbia Men's Faculty Club. So I had to take a *taxi* down to the Guaranty Trust (it's so expensive being broke, don't you find?) and cash a cheque, and Dolf braved the Faculty Club cashier. He was terribly upset and embarrassed about it last night. 'Do relax, darling, and let me go to sleep,' I said to him. 'Everybody in *Debrett* has bouncing cheques . . . Two terms absh-lutely sh'nonymous . . .'

But then something happened which was a little bit eerie, but which brought a sudden prospect of financial rescue. MGM were in the process of making a sequel to *Mrs Miniver*, to be called *The Miniver Story*: and they had taken a liberty with Jan's fictional character. She wrote to Jamie explaining the state of affairs:

We are in the midst of two delicious bits of legal proceedings, one against our landlord, who is the son of a bitch, and one against Metro-Goldwyn-Mayer, who is so to speak the bitch that our landlord is the son of. Briefly, it seems that MGM have nearly finished making the sequel to *Mrs M.*, and that Mrs M. dies of cancer in the last act. I have (genuinely) received no less than three offers recently to do a sequel myself, and the gist of my case is, 'Oy, you carn' do that there 'ere.' We are very much hoping, and it looks pretty promising, judging by the obviously damp state of the MGM attorney's pants, that they will what's delicately called Prefer To Settle It Out Of Court. If not, then they'll bloody well have to settle it *in* court. Bastards. Even if I didn't want to accept the offers, they've still got no right to make it impossible for me to do so by killing the old girl off.

MGM did settle it out of court. On 15 February 1950, after coming home from seeing *The Third Man* at the cinema ('Dolf and Pauly cried in their beards and were *ganz* nostalgic, and it was simply thrilling, and if you haven't seen it you must,' Jan wrote to Jamie), Jan received a cheque from MGM for $13,000 – $5,000 for the sequel, and $8,000 in damages for killing off Mrs Miniver. They celebrated with Kümmel. 'Let's not waste all this lovely money,' Jan said. 'Let's spend it.'

She did not find it difficult. The swing from penury to riches echoed her swings from depression to euphoria. In June she and Dolf sailed to England, where they missed Robert. He was nineteen, doing his two-year National Service in the Scots Guards, and had been commissioned and sent to Malaya with his regiment a few weeks before she arrived. This, for Jan, was 'sickeningly disappointing' as well as worrying. Robert was not communicating with her by letter, and she longed to see him. She and Dolf spent time with Jamie in Scotland, and went to Paris to meet Janet, who was staying there; Jan and Janet got on badly, and Jan returned to New York feeling that two of her three children were out of sympathy with her.

But she also returned with a comforting prospect in view: Jamie was to sail to America in September, and he and she planned to go on a road trip for three weeks. She wanted to show him the country she had grown to know and love during the war years, and he wanted to look at American livestock and farming methods. But she found that, rather than looking forward to his visit, she was merely dreading his leaving, even before he had arrived.

Still reckless with the proceeds of the MGM damages, Jan and Dolf moved into a ground-floor apartment at 68 West 68th

Street which had its own garden ('Moving house is my favourite indoor sport,' Jan wrote to Jamie). While they were settling in and putting plants into pots, *The Miniver Story* opened in London at the Empire, Leicester Square. (It had been filmed in Britain, in a quest for the 'realism' which had been missing the first time.) 'Remember the Minivers!' proclaimed the MGM advertisements. The public, it turned out, preferred to remember the Minivers as they were in the original picture, rather than be re-introduced to them looking tired and ill in post-war Britain. The film lost Metro-Goldwyn-Mayer $2,311,000. The only good thing the *Punch* critic could say about it was that Mrs Miniver's death in the last act at least ensured there would be no further sequels, 'for which on the whole we may be grateful'.

It is a dreadful film. Its direction by H. C. 'Hank' Potter merely emphasizes how good William Wyler's was. In the original film, no scene went on for too long; in the sequel, every scene does, and a pall of gloom hangs over the whole. Greer Garson and Walter Pidgeon still play the leading roles, Garson looking middle-aged and careworn and Pidgeon lacking the wit and wryness which made the first film uplifting in spite of its tragic events. The children are all utterly changed. Vin is absent altogether, his death in the Battle of Britain fleetingly mentioned: Garson had refused to act with her former husband Richard Ney. Judy, now played by Cathy O'Donnell, is a cold, depressed post-war maiden, and Toby, played by James Fox, has grown into a charmlessly precocious and loud-voiced twelve-year-old. The audience knows Mrs Miniver is dying of cancer – the film opens with her visit to the doctor for the diagnosis ('not less than six months, not more than a year') – but Clem doesn't, and the first hour is spent in the dreary tension of waiting for her to collapse and then break the news to him. In one of the dullest scenes of the film, she and Clem dance together, slowly and sadly, in his office overlooking a bomb-site, to the music of a barrel-organ playing outside. After seeing to it that Judy marries a good honest local boy rather than the cad she is in love with, Mrs Miniver dies. Clem is left with the last words, reflecting on her goodness and wisdom.

The film opened in at Radio City in New York in October; but

Jan was not there. She never saw it. Though she always dissociated herself from the character, she knew privately that a bit of her was, or had once been, Mrs Miniver, and nothing would induce her to witness her death at the hands of a Hollywood studio.

Jamie arrived in New York, and off he and Jan went on their agricultural tour of America.

Liebstes [she wrote to Dolf from Cabin 2, Bass Point Camp, Lake Rd 14b, Missouri on 17 October 1950], Remind me never to be away from you for so long ever any more. Silly, ain't it, to get so mixed up with another human being that one feels a 3 weeks' separation is a kind of amputation? (And besides, I am as randy as hell.) At the same time, I'm glad you weren't able to come with us, because you would have been bored to a frazzle and sick at the stomach with fast driving, and with the inspissated foulness of the food we've been forced to eat. *Really* what I think of American cooking . . .

Jamie is a very sweet companion, and we have lots of jokes all the time, and lots of hill-billy music on the car radio. We stop here & there by the wayside when we see interesting breeds of pigs, sorry, hawgs, or cattle, & go and ask the owner about them. The heat at the Kansas City show was terrific, & even Jamie got a mite tired of looking at bulls' behinds . . .

The whole country is too big, & all the middle part ought to be compressed & shrunk like one of those South American Indian human heads.

Was it middle America that had changed, or was it Jan? She was not sure. All she knew was that she was falling out of love with the country which had so enchanted her during her wartime travels. In those distant, gasoline-rationed years, each small town she visited had seemed fascinatingly different from the last: now, she was aware only of their 'ghastly, ghastly sameness'. Was it just that there were no charming, dowdy sponsors waiting to greet her at each town or give her a 'bokay' on railway platforms? Or was it that a new complacency was settling where unspoiltness had been? It was perhaps a bit of both. Showing Jamie America, she wrote afterwards, felt 'like introducing him to somebody one has married but has in the meanwhile fallen out of love with and now sees the faults of.'

She waved goodbye to Jamie as he boarded his ship back to Britain and came home to an angry letter from Janet about a radio-phonograph Jan had sold without asking Janet's permission: and these two things tipped her over into the new depression she had felt coming. All the good that Stockbridge and Dr Wheelis had done a year before seemed to have been undone. She was back where she started. The symptoms were the same: confusion, perpetual tension and sobbing, an inability to keep food down, revulsion against cooking and letter-writing, a disinclination to answer the telephone, a feeling of inadequacy in company, and a dread of being alone.

Desperate to recapture the magic that had worked eighteen months before, she started typing a diary of her days to show to her new psychiatrist in New York, Dr Jackel, recommended by Dr Wheelis. His method during appointments was not to ask her a single question. 'I begged him to ask me questions,' Jan wrote in her first instalment on 12 December 1950, 'but he said the usual stuff about how if he asked questions it would put ideas into my head about what he considered important. I started trying to tell him about my childhood, and my parents not getting on, and how I felt a dread of the repeating pattern: but in the middle of it all I was overcome with discouragement and despair and folded up almost entirely.'

Now she had every reason to panic. If each 'cure' from depression was only temporary, was it worth being cured at all?

Will it go on this way for the rest of my life? If so, I can't see the point of being alive, with this dread of recurrence hanging over me. The happiest thing would be to get killed in an accident at one of the moments when one is normal and on top of the world: but that kind of thing doesn't happen, and anyway, when I'm on top of the world I have such a keen zest for life that I don't want to die, ever. Was it real, that sense of joy, that welling-over of love and sympathy towards one's fellow-beings, that energy, that desire to help make the world better for people, that urge to create things? If it was real, how can it have so utterly gone? What is real, and what is unreal?

She carried on with her television and radio appearances throughout this time, and audiences had no idea that she was a nervous wreck when not in public view. With a supreme effort of will, she could act her former self for long enough to ensure that, as she put it, 'the show could go on'. She appeared on the television programme *Celebrity Time* as a co-guest with the critic John Mason Brown, in which they had to play charades and tell 'riveting little anecdotes' about their literary careers. Jan felt 'jittery' all afternoon, and found the endless waiting beforehand, with camera rehearsals, almost intolerable. 'But it went off all right – as far as anything so idiotic *could* be all right. There were fifty people in the studio, spending nine hours preparing for half an hour of almost complete crap.'

Each week in February and March 1951 she was on the panel of a television programme called *We Take Your Word*, in which the players had to make up the etymology of a given word. Two were false, one was correct: it was an etymological *Call My Bluff*. This was Jan's response to the word 'pumpernickel': 'A young lieutenant in Napoleon's army arrived on horseback at an inn in Prussia one evening, tired and hungry. After arranging for his horse, Nicolai, to be watered and stabled, the officer demanded his own dinner. The innkeeper's wife brought him an unfamiliar dark bread which he took a bite of and then threw on the floor with disgust. "C'est bon pour Nicolai!" he said.'

The audience laughed and clapped: but by the middle of the night, Jan was back in a state of despair. The act of typing long tracts about her days was not helping this time. The magic which had worked so well at Stockbridge, she realized, must have been like an amulet or a magic charm in a fairytale, which only worked once.

In the mornings, when Dolf went out to work, someone always came to sit with her. One day, when neither Bennes nor Pauly could come, Pauly arranged for one of her Viennese friends to come instead: and this visit induced in Jan a final wail of despair.

Well, she arrived – a nice, quiet little woman with a kind face. She asked whether there wasn't some mending or something that she could do for me, and I managed to find her a few stockings and slips that needed washing, which she is at present doing in the bathroom. No doubt she is wondering how the hell I can be in this state and yet still be able to go on doing the radio and television jobs. She must think I'm such a phoney – or maybe she understands more about such things than I imagine she does. Poor thing – she lives quite alone in a little apartment on 98th Street, and she has very little money and – at the moment – no job. She was in concentration camp in Europe and lost everything, like so many of them. And here am I, by comparison so damned lucky and well-off and successful – what must she think of me for being 'depressed'? It's one of those cases which one *feels* ought to make one ashamed of grumbling about any-thing – but it just doesn't *work* that way. If one's in this kind of state, one loses the ability to make comparisons. Hell is absolute, not com-parative. How am I to get out of it? How, how, how?

There was a way out. In August 1951 Jan was diagnosed as having breast cancer, and a mastectomy was carried out at once. Her revulsion against living was replaced by a deep and justified fear of dying.

Chapter Seventeen

Honour the true believer,
  The man whose feet have trod
Life's road of fret and fever
  Sustained by trust in God.
Whatever foes assailed him
  He faced them fair and square:
His strong sword never failed him –
  Faith in the power of prayer.

Crown him with wreaths of laurel,
  Of myrtle and of bay:
With that I have no quarrel –
  Yet spare one slender spray
For him who, unbelieving,
  Unpious, undevout,
Long wandering and weaving
  Among the pits of doubt,
Faced, prayerless and unweeping,
  The flying spears of grief,
Unarmed, yet proudly keeping
  Faith with his unbelief.

'Prayer', written in hospital, August 1951

THERE WAS SOMETHING to blame again, and something official to be brave about. Though Jan was terrified of cancer, with its implications of impending death, the shock gave her the violent jolt she needed to regain a sense of the preciousness of life. In bed, she wrote a poem to her surgeon: '... And though in the glass I look like heck to me, I'm grateful for this neat mastectomy.' She also wrote the poem quoted overleaf, which she paraphrased in a letter to Jamie: 'If one never bothers with the Old Man in one's good moments, it doesn't seem quite cricket to pester him during one's bad ones.' Her ink, once again, was beginning to flow.

Physically, the mastectomy caused in her a *coup de vieux*. She was fifty: but she now felt and looked old. Privately she was horrified with the 'butchery' which had been done to her body. 'She never wanted me to see her naked again,' Dolf remembered. The mastectomy was pronounced successful by the doctors: she was supposedly cleared of cancer, but her face was puffy with the medicine and alcohol of the past years, her hair was thin and grey, her sight was bad, and her back ached. 'I'd better get this letter off quickly,' she wrote to Jamie, 'in case any other bits of me drop off or fail to work.'

But, writing to her brother in September 1951, in response to his depressive cry for help ('Personally the only thing I feel at the moment is that I want to die and never come out of anything again. Any advice on how to break the spell of Nervous B.?'), Jan realized that she, concerned now with physical recovery, was the lucky one. '*My* problem is the comparatively simple one of training one group of muscles to do, in addition to their own work, all the work of the front group which used to run from the breast-bone to the armpit (a fan-shaped job called the pectorals). This is just a matter of strains and stresses, and quite an interesting engineering problem to work out. (See a medical dicker or a book on anatomy.) If only *yours* were as easy, my poor darling, either to cope with personally or to give advice about.'

With the clarity of someone who has known but emerged from depression, she described her own 'hell' vividly to Douglas, and then suggested that a way of dealing with it was to accept the 'conflicting roles' which one was trying to play. These were hers:

1 Jan Struther, the well-known and successful writer, lecturer, radio-performer etc. (with a subdivision called Jan Struther, the much-too-little-known and really pretty terrific serious poet whose depth and brilliance will only really be appreciated by a discerning literary public after she is dead!)

2 ex-Joyce Maxtone Graham, a fugitive from a country-house chain-gang, who, while she is damned glad not to be saddled with the boredom of Showing Visitors the Garden, does occasionally hanker after the comparative physical easiness of the Old Days.

3 Joyce, the mother of Jamie, Janet and Robert, who misses the children and wishes she lived closer to them so that she could at least see them every few weeks, or months, and be in close touch with their everyday lives, love affairs, etc.

4 Jan Placzek, the happily-married wife of a most exceptionally kind, understanding, considerate, witty, charming and creative man with whom she has been in love – and he with her – since the very day they met, twelve-years-ago-come-November 21st.

5 Jan, the expatriate European, who likes many things about America, notably the comparative social informality, the extremes of climate, and the enormous variety of its geographical features; but who dislikes a great many other things about it such as the hysterical silliness of its politics, the monotony of its architecture, and – with a large handful of wonderful exceptions – the bloody futility of its inhabitants' conversations: and who, every now and then, gets an almost physical ache to hear a cowbell in the Alps, or a peal of bells from an English church tower (so long as she wouldn't have to go to the service!), or to see a really old, muddly, quiet village clustered round a manor house, with NO STRAIGHT LINES ANYWHERE.

6 and this is a very important role in the repertory, and one which most grown-ups don't understand or even know about – Joyce Anstruther, aged somewhere between eight and twelve, the little frog-faced girl whose favourite occupation was playing desert islands in the rubbish tip with the gardener's sons, BUT who didn't realize at the time (or, as a matter of fact, till quite recently) that what made that era of one's life so idyllic was that there was always one's Nannie in the background who could pick one up if one fell out of a tree and would unfailingly tuck one up at night and 'pat one to sleep'; the woman of 50 who, even now, when she should be writing an article or story, is apt to spend the whole morning watching an interesting caterpillar in the garden, or constructing a piece of furniture out of packing-cases: who, in fact, ought to be smacked.

For years, she had been trying various approaches: she had tried confining herself to one of these roles – which led to frustrations and discontent – and she had tried combining them all – which led to physical and nervous exhaustion. What she was learning to do now, with Dolf's help, was to recognize that they all existed, that they were all part of her, and that she need not feel ashamed or guilty about any of them, since they were all quite natural. There was no hint in this letter to Douglas that her brush with cancer had helped her finally to snap out of depression: this was Dolf's personal observation.

The family from which she had separated herself by coming to live in America was working itself into new patterns. Janet, at Christmas 1950, had become engaged to Patrick Rance, a delightful ex-Regular-Army Major and High Anglican vicar's son, a lover of butterflies, books, Bach and France. They were married in Perthshire, and Tony gave a grand reception for them at Cultoquhey. Jan did not go: as she wrote to Jamie, 'I'd hate her to have a repetition of the Atmosphere that obtained when Tony and I were married.' She did not meet Patrick until after the wedding, but glowing reports of him came from everyone who met him; and all the crossness seemed to have gone out of Janet, who was turning into a mature, settled, loving daughter and mother-to-be. Jamie became engaged to a charming Scottish girl, Diana Macgregor. And Tony now had a woman friend who was helping him (as Jan had hoped someone would) 'to blossom into his natural gaiety'. Her name was Peggy Barne, and she was a mother of five from Suffolk, who had first met Tony at Pirbright Camp during the war when her husband, Lieutenant-Colonel Michael Barne, was stationed there. 'Tony's Peggy', Rachel Townsend wrote to Jan, 'is beautiful, and calming (and full of jokes) – highly sympathetic.' She also loved golf.

The children, now grown-ups, were finding their paths through life; and Jan began to get on with hers, trying to cast the anguish of the past years aside. Though she no longer had her children nearby, or Europe, or the social status of 'the Laird's Lady', or the ability to finish a book, or the magic touch with Hollywood, she had Dolf, and for the moment she was ready to embrace the tranquillity that this brought. There was a sense of 'All passion spent'. Dolf had stood by her during her depression, when she had been almost intolerable to live with: now she wanted to be for

In the garden at 68 West 68th Street with Anne Talbot and Cleveland Ward, 1951

him the wife that he needed. There was a change of key: whereas before she had been driven through life by burning causes, both public and private, now her ambitions and pleasures were more muted. This slowing-down of the tempo was balm after depression and physical illness.

She sat on a mahogany chair drinking tea out of a Wedgwood cup and discussing poetry with Mr Adjeman, the Armenian junk-shop owner a few blocks away. On Mondays, when her black cleaner Cleveland Ward came, she chatted to him all morning and gave him lunch in the garden. She acquired two kittens, who channelled her energy for love; buying their liver or Puss-e-Ration was an errand she enjoyed. There was the garden to look after. 'What with the kittens and the garden and about twenty-two plants in pots, we have a kind of mixed farm,' she wrote to Jamie. Weekdays were a limbo between the weekends, when Dolf was at home all day and the two of them could go together to East Harlem in search of tropical fruit, or to the Greek quarter to buy vine leaves. Saturdays were 'the dominant seventh' of the week, she wrote, describing this period of her married life: 'but when all's said and done, the most important thing about Saturday is the knowledge that Sunday, the *Schlussakkord*, still lies ahead.' They read the Sunday papers at intervals throughout that 'closing chord' of the week, so that by the evening, they were 'pleasantly drugged with scraps of miscellaneous information, random quotations from the ephemeral oratory of the week, vague mental pictures of the shape Fifth Avenue women are going to assume in the next few weeks, horribly dodgy ways of messing up salad greens: and, above all, a sense of belonging.'

She was becoming unashamedly workshy. On hearing that

Janet had given up a magazine job because it didn't give her enough responsibility, her response, expressed to Jamie, was 'Amazing – fancy *wanting* more responsibility!'

She thought up an idea for a new television game-show, a one-woman show to 'teach housewives not to be such cows and bores' – in other words, to introduce them to some of her own interests, such as carpentry and household repairs. Her idea was to do it once a week for $200, but the producers were so keen that they wanted her to do it twice a week for $400, and to sign her up for a year. 'So I said, *"So lang soll ich leben"* and told them all to go jump in the lake,' she wrote to Jamie. 'What is the use of earning $400 a week if you are too utterly pooped even to spend $200?' But she carried on doing her 'guest spot' radio appearances: she needed the money, having long since spent the remaining MGM damages money on doctors', surgeons', dentists' and osteopaths' bills.

In May 1952, she and Dolf sailed to England for the third time. They met Jan's son-in-law Patrick, her future daughter-in-law Diana, and her first grandchild, Susanna Rance. They visited Robert, who was now at Trinity College, Cambridge. It was lovely to see them all; but each visit was too short – lunch, or tea, or an afternoon's walk along the Backs. She was truly now a visitor to the country which had once been her home. 'That visit to England,' Dolf remembered, 'felt like a farewell.' The last country house they visited, at Dolf's request, was Coleshill in Berkshire, built in 1650. Later in 1952 it burnt down, and Dolf saw this afterwards as a symbol.

It was Jan's last visit to England, and she seemed to know this, because on the journey back to New York she wrote one of her last poems, 'Westbound Voyage', about the seven days of 'de-creation' which were the preparation for saying goodbye:

> When it comes to leaving a world which you have made
> It is necessary to destroy it a little during the journey
> To avoid the death of the heart.

> You are given the statutory seven days:
> Everything must be done in the proper sequence
> But the order must be reversed.

The first day, you look back upon your world
And see that it was good. You rest, gathering
Strength for the de-creation.

The second day, the last-created things
Are the earliest to go: the boy, the spaniel,
And the old woman on the stair.

The third day, the fishes and the birds:
The peacock in his pride, the skylark rising,
The trout in the upland stream.

The fourth day, you quench the mild sun,
The penny moon, and all those constellations
Which belong to a northern sky.

The fifth day, roll up the fretting seas,
The flowered rocks, the hand-tented wheat-stooks
And the grass bright as baize.

The sixth day, the firmament is doomed –
That small sky whose marriage with grey waters
Gave birth to so much green.

The seventh day, darkness and light must go:
The short summer darkness, soft as a moleskin,
And the long, long light.

This is the worst of all. Boy, dog and bird
Will stay in your exiled heart: but how to recapture,
In the other world, that long, long summer light?

But when she got back to New York she found herself being
swept up in a new burning cause: the Presidential Election in
November, in which the Democrat Governor Adlai Stevenson
was running against the Republican General Eisenhower. She
wanted Stevenson to win, as did most enlightened, liberal
Americans, and the strength of her feelings brought forth her
first-ever political poetry. 'Stevenson's Speech' expressed
Stevenson's ability to be understood by people from all walks of
life, while never speaking down to them. On the night before the
election she wrote a poem for publication in anticipation of his
victory, the last line of which was 'They truly liked the General

– but chose the caviar.' But the electorate chose the General, not 'the caviar', and Jan, staying up all night with friends to hear the results, threw herself onto the floor and wept. She felt more than ever out of touch and sympathy with middle America. Ten years before she had had her finger firmly on the pulse of American feeling; now she could no longer find it.

Rachel Townsend, Tony's sister, had become Jan and Dolf's great friend. Whenever they were feeling nostalgic for Europe, they could visit her at 1 Beekman Place and play Canasta or Racing Demon and bask in her un-American accent, and Jan could hear news about the Maxtone Graham former in-laws and cousins, of whom she was very fond. Anne Talbot now lived downstairs: Rachel had taken her on as tenant of the lower floor of the Townsends' 'duplex' apartment. Both Rachel and Anne provided a link with Jan's past, which she craved. As in the past, they were to prove invaluable friends in the coming months.

One morning in December Jan went to her typewriter and started clattering away on it; in three weeks out poured the first 118 pages of another book, 'Cactus and Columbine' – the book about America she had been vaguely planning to write ever since she first arrived in 1940. Harcourt Brace, who had returned the manuscript of Jan's unfinished autobiography to her in February when she sent back their advance, were thrilled once again. If she could finish 'Cactus and Columbine' by March 1953, it would be published in the autumn. 'I've been writing away like mad at my new book,' Jan wrote to Janet just before Christmas. 'I've done about 18,000 words and for the first time in my life I'm enjoying writing prose and finding it quite smooth & easy.' But it seems that breaking off to write that letter to Janet was a rash thing to do, because the book never got beyond those 18,000 words. Justifiably this time, Jan lost confidence in it.

In the fifth chapter there is a ring on Jan's doorbell, at 4.15. Who could it be, she wonders. It is too late for the mail, and too early for the garbage man. It could only be a Fuller Brush man, or someone trying to sell her set another set of the *Encyclopedia Britannica*.

'Hullo?'

'It's me,' said a pleasant feminine voice. 'I hope I'm not too early.'

'Not a bit,' I said, with the forced cordiality born of guilt.

I must have invited somebody to tea – but whom? Tea is a meal which has dropped itself from the rhythm of my gastric juices for twelve years.

The visitor turns out to be Mrs Miniver. This is the book's conceit: Jan meets Mrs Miniver again, and shows her around America. They discuss old times as they potter about New York making astute remarks to one another. Jan, it seemed, still could not quite lay the ghost of Mrs Miniver to rest: she needed to revive her once more, in order to exorcise her completely.

It was a good idea, in theory, but in Jan's hands in late 1952 it did not work. The unfinished typescript remains as stark proof of the decline in her prose writing, a pleasure to read if, but only if, you know and love her already. The book was supposed to be light – and it is full of her usual fertility of metaphor in describing the weather, and the seasons. But by this time in her life Jan had, in her heart, gone beyond lightness. Dialogue with Mrs Miniver in a supermarket queue was no longer her natural genre. If she had been honest, her meeting with Mrs Miniver would have been a bitter clash between two parts of herself, the book a riveting and truthful glimpse into the 'conflicting roles' of her life. But this was supposed to be a travel book about America, and Jan was determined not to venture into the deep waters of her past. The result was relentless jollity.

It demonstrated, too, the extent to which Jan was still enslaved by Mrs Miniver. It was not just that she felt compelled to revive 'the old girl', and to breathe new life into her – perhaps partly in response to the fatal damage done by MGM. She was also enslaved in that never again, after those few months on the Court page of *The Times* in 1938 and 1939, did she find the perfect form for her published prose. She never ceased to be good at writing letters – with them, she knew precisely who her audience was. But when it came to books, the vastness and variedness of the reading public daunted her, and she did not know whom she was addressing.

She had not realized at the time how perfect a vehicle for her writing the 'Miniver' essays had been. They had not been her idea, so she had been free from the paralysing sense of total responsibility which dogged her later books. She had not even set out to write 'a book': the essays had just turned into one, as if by magic. By creating a character who was part-fictional and part-herself, she had been spared the embarrassment of self-revelation while still managing to describe a version of her own life with pin-point accuracy. And her audience, the readers of *The Times*, had been select and ready-made. Having once found the ideal conditions for her prose and invented a natural character on whom to hang her observations, she could never easily move on.

So she gravitated back to talking, which she was good at and was paid for, and which required short bursts of wit and summonings-up of general knowledge in front of a microphone or a television camera. It was in this direction that her career was heading when in March 1953 she went for her regular six-monthly check-up with the surgeon, which always gave her 'the most hellish jitters' beforehand. She was 'perfectly OK', the surgeon told her, and she came out breathing freely with relief. But 'by a macabre coincidence,' she wrote to Janet afterwards, '*The Miniver Story* was running at the neighbourhood theatre that same week . . . I did NOT go & see it. Indeed I never have and never want to. Too, too Pirandello, my deah . . .'

At Cape Cod in June she felt dizzy and sick and became incoherent in her speech; the local doctor suggested that she might be suffering from Ménière's Disease. 'Or Miniver's Disease?' Jan retorted. But in New York, a brain tumour was diagnosed, and Dolf was told that no surgery was possible. Jan was taken to the Columbia Presbyterian Hospital; the radiologist there, Gerhard Schwarz, turned out to have been at school with Dolf, at the Wasa Gymnasium in Vienna. Rachel, Janet (who had flown over from England at the news), Dolf and Bennes took turns at Jan's bedside as loving letters arrived from Robert, and Jamie, and Nannie. For three weeks she drifted in and out of consciousness, and on 20 July, with Dolf on one side of her bed and Janet on the other, she died.

She never reached the autumn of life which most grandmothers achieve, so the supposition of this poem, written when she was pregnant with Janet in 1928, was not realized. But it is a poem her six granddaughters read and think about.

'Advice to my Future Granddaughter'

While I am young, and have not yet forsworn
    Valour for comfort, truth for compromise,
I write these words to you, the unknown, unborn
    Child of my child that in this cradle lies:
'Live, then, as I live; love as I love
    With body and heart and mind, the tangled three;
Sell peace for beauty's sake, and set above
    All other things ecstasy, ecstasy.'

And if, grey-haired by the fireside,
    Filled with the withered wisdom of October,
I frown upon your April; if I chide
    And murmur, 'Child, be good,' or 'Child, be sober,'
      Then, then (I charge you now) no longer stay:
      But laugh, and toss your head, and go your way.

Epilogue

DOLF NEVER SLEPT at 68 West 68th Street again, but took a suitcase to his mother's apartment. He forced himself to hold down his job at Avery Library, though his heart was broken.

Jan's funeral took place at the Fifth Avenue Presbyterian Church, but she was not buried in New York. 'Imagine being buried in *Queen's!*' she had said, with a frown of distaste. Her ashes were taken to the parish church at Whitchurch in Buckinghamshire, where she had lived as a child, and a simple service of interment was held.

In 1957 Dolf married Beverley Kalitinsky, née Robinson, Canadian niece of the Beverley Robinson to whom Jan had told her secret at the Republican dinner party during the war. Dolf and Bev had forty-three years of cloudless happiness together, united in their love of architecture, German, French and English literature, music and conversation with friends young and old, in their book-filled apartment with a Mozart or Beethoven sonata open on the grand piano. Dolf never fathered a child, but Bev had a daughter from her first marriage, and the step-children and step-grandchildren from both his marriages remained Dolf's family.

Between 1960 and 1980 he was Avery Librarian, expanding the collection by purchases abroad and helping to make it internationally known as one of the greatest architectural libraries in the world. If Jan had 'set him free' from his junior job there, this might not have happened. He was made an emeritus professor on his retirement, after which he was Editor-in-Chief of the four-volume *Macmillan Encyclopaedia of Architects* and founding editor of a still larger project, *The Buildings of the United States*, the American 'Pevsner'.

I visited him and Bev at their apartment in West 87th Street in 1998 and 1999, and we talked for days, sitting near the chess table which Jan had made at the Austin Riggs Sanatorium in the depths of her depression. Dolf died in New York on 19 March 2000, a few days after his eighty-seventh birthday, and his obituary – like Jan's – appeared in the London *Times*. His memoirs of growing up in Vienna and of Viennese refugees in New York were published to great acclaim in Germany and Austria, at the very end of his life. His sister Susan still lives in New York.

Tony married Peggy Barne in 1952. After the house of Cultoquhey was sold in 1955 they lived happily at Aberlady Mains House in East Lothian, near Muirfield Golf Course, and travelled a great deal together. Tony died in an aeroplane over India in 1971.

Jamie was twice married and twice divorced, and had three children. After farming at Cultoquhey he became a freelance journalist, and in 1976 he opened the smallest restaurant in Britain, with only one table, in Peebles High Street. Later, much more successfully, he became the world's leading dealer in vintage fishing-tackle.

Janet and Pat Rance had seven children. In 1954 they took over the village shop in Streatley, Berkshire, which Pat transformed into one of the best-known cheese shops in the country. Janet wrote for the *Reader's Digest*, and Pat wrote definitive books on French and English cheese. They died at the end of the 1990s, and 'Lord of all hopefulness' was sung at both their funerals.

Robert, my father, became a Scottish advocate, then an estate agent, and then an entrepreneur and a Planning Inspector. In 1962 he married Claudia Page-Phillips, *née* Tannert, who with her Jewish Austro-Hungarian parents had fled from Austria to England in 1938. They live in Sandwich, Kent, in the house in which I was born.

Acknowledgements

I HAVE BEEN greatly helped, in researching and writing this book, by many people. Dolf Placzek's telephone call to me in June 1998 launched me into the project when I was hovering round the edge. He and Bev were inspiring, and sympathetic to the biographer's need to get to the bottom of Jan's complicated character. Dolf's last telephone message to me before he died expressed (in his thick-as-ever Viennese accent) delight that the story was being told. I am also grateful to Bennes Mardenn, Harriet Harvey, Susan Stern, Ruth Hanbury-Tenison, John Maxtone Graham, Michael Maxtone Graham, David Townsend, Ian Anstruther and Merlin Sudeley, for helping me with research and talking to me so candidly about Jan; to Nicola Beauman, for giving me initial confidence in the project; to Rupert Christiansen, for solidifying that confidence; and to Grant McIntyre, for his well-judged guidance. My father Robert Maxtone Graham, expert archivist, verifier and indexer, was an invaluable eye-witness and a constant but never intrusive support. Janet Rance's notes, and Jamie Maxtone Graham's papers, lent to me by his son Robert, helped me greatly, as did Victoria Rance's, Anthony Gardner's, Geoffrey Barraclough's and my mother Claudia Maxtone Graham's insights and comments. Kathleen Dunpark undertook some research for me at the Court of Session in Edinburgh. Henry Villiers gave me access to his aunt Anne Talbot's diaries. Joy Grant provided me with notes which she had made on Jan. David Drew-Smythe of New South Wales gave me access to documents inherited from his grandfather Douglas Anstruther, and compiled the Jan Struther website. David and Daphne Smith gave me time to write during the school holidays. I am grateful also to the Library of Congress, the London Library, the A.P. Watt archives, the Chatto & Windus archives, the British Film Institute Library and the FDR Library. My husband Michael (who played piano duets with Dolf during our last visit to him in New York in 1999) helped me each day in the quest for the essence of Jan and the *mots justes* to express it. This book is dedicated to him.

Further Reading

Mrs Miniver and *Try Anything Twice* were last published in London in the paperback series Virago Modern Classics, both with introductions by Valerie Grove. An American edition of *Mrs Miniver* was published in 1990.

Editions and translations are described in my father's illustrated *Bibliography of Mrs Miniver and of the other books by Jan Struther*, copies of which are at the British Library, London Library, Cambridge and Oxford University Libraries, National Library of Scotland, Library of Congress, and University of Pennsylvania Library (where Jan was awarded an honorary D. Litt. in 1943).

An Internet edition of *Mrs Miniver*, and of that *Bibliography*, can be freely downloaded from the first of the following list of useful websites:

www.bigfoot.com/~idds/home/janstruther.htm is my cousin David Drew-Smythe's 'Jan' web page, which also has links to:
www.reelclassics.com/Movies/Miniver/miniver.htm which includes many articles about the 1942 film and its cast.

www.google.com if searched under 'Jan Struther' or 'Mrs Miniver' will reveal hundreds of more or less relevant websites, including those listed above.

www.digital.library.upenn.edu/books is the 'On-Line Books Page' of the University of Pennsylvania. Links to Author/Struther will lead to the text of the following works, freely available on the internet: *Mrs Miniver*, *Try Anything Twice*, her hymns, and all poems printed in her five volumes of collected verse.

robert@sandwichkent.freeserve.co.uk is my father's email address. He has available for sale, by post, some copies of the Futura paperback of *Mrs Miniver* (1980).

Index

Page numbers in **bold type** indicate illustrations; the initial 'J' stands both for Joyce and for Jan.

Index

Index

Hahn, Kurt, CBE (1886–1974, founder of Gordonstoun School), 108
Halifax, Earl of (1881–1959, British Ambassador to USA), 164
Halifax, Nova Scotia, and the VE day riots there, 230
Hanbury, Ruth (1901–2000, J's cousin and childhood friend, married Gerald Tenison of Lough Bawn, Co. Monaghan, Eire) 18, 196
Hanbury-Tracy, see Sudeley
Harcourt Brace Inc., publishers, 137, 140, 146, 152, 162, 230, 249, 268, 296
Harvey, Harriet (fellow patient), 277
Harvey School, Westchester County, NY (Robert's school), 164
Haycock, Lizzie (J's grandparents' maid), 12, 14
Hess, Dame Myra, DBE (1890–1965, pianist), 119
Hewitt-Myring, Philip (born 1900 in Paris; journalist, London; Robert's godfather), 81
Hilton, James (1900–54, author, main screen writer of *Mrs Miniver*), 158, 161, 168, 177
Hirsch, Gladys (fellow pupil), 18
Holland, Mrs Martin, teacher, 18
Horton, see Curtis Brown
Hudson, Lucy ('Lala', J's nannie), 7, 14, 28, 236

'Indiana Compromise', 248–50
Information Ministry, 138, 140

Jackel, Dr (NYC psychiatrist), 286
Jamie, see Maxtone Graham
Jan, see Struther
Janet, see Maxtone Graham
Jessel, Vera Pearl (fellow pupil, later Mrs Clive Martyn, 1899–1928), 18
Johnson, Celia, DBE (1908–82, actress, Mrs Peter Fleming), 228
Joshua, Nell (fellow pupil), 18
Joyce, see Struther

Karloff, Boris (1887–1969, horror film actor), 207
Kieran, John (1882–1981, NYC sports journalist), 152–3
Kubie, Lawrence (Austrian-born psychoanalyst in NYC), 263, 275–6

Lala, see Hudson
Launde Abbey, near Oakham (Col. Edward Dawson's house), 45, 47
Lazarus, René (fellow pupil), 18
Lee, Canada (Lionel Canegata, 1907–52, welterweight boxer turned actor), 222–3
Lehmann, Rosamond, CBE (1901–90, novelist), 113, 147
Levant, Oscar (1906–72, pianist and actor), 195
Lewis, Peggy (fellow pupil), 18
London, 1–139 and 232–292, *passim*; Albert Hall, Kensington, 250; Alexander Place, South Kensington, 255, 260–1, 264; Battersea Park, 125; Bloomsbury House, Great Russell Street, 106–7, 114, 117; Caroline Place (now Donne Place), Chelsea, 85; Cheyne Walk, Chelsea, 122, 246; Curzon Street, Mayfair, 22, 31; Denbigh Street, Pimlico, 117, 121, 246; Halsey Street, Chelsea, 85, 120, 196; Imperial War Museum, 19; Kilburn Polytechnic, 25; King's Road, Chelsea, 4, 42, 235–6; Little College Street, Westminster, 20; Lloyds of London, 42, 84; National Gallery wartime concerts, 119, 123, 139, 196; Ormeley Lodge, Ham, 12, 14; Scotland Yard, 31; South Street, Mayfair, 22; Swan Walk, Chelsea, 22; US Embassy and Consulate, 138; Walpole Street, Chelsea, 42; Wellington Square, Chelsea, 38, 53–5, 81, 84, 196, 236, 238, 242–3, 246, 254; the dining-room, **55**
Lord Baldwin's Appeal for Refugees, 104
Lubbock, Cynthia (fellow pupil, later Mrs Alexander Wedderburn, 1899–1986), 19

Mason, Michael Henry (1900–82, yachtsman and travel writer, of Freeland, Oxfordshire; Janet's godfather), 50
Mardenn, Bennes, drama teacher, NYC, 223, 258, 273, 287
Margie, J's secretary, NYC, 221
Marx Brothers, 177, 207

Index

Maxtone Graham family, originally of Cultoquhey, Crieff, Perthshire, 35, **73**, 296;
(Ellen) 'Ann', 1899–1991, née Taylor, of Cape Cod, first wife of Patrick, 149;
Anthony George, 1854–1930, Tony's bachelor uncle, 36, 71;
Anthony James Oliphant, 'Tony', born Edinburgh, 23 July 1900, J's first husband: 30–**37**, 38, **74**, 76, 83, 96, **106**, 137, 139; joined Scots Guards at Pirbright Camp, 145, 162; to North Africa, **176**; prisoner of war, 182, 184; POW life, 238; impresario, 192–4; camp theatre, **193**; 211–13, 216–17, 224; post-war ambitions, 226, 237; liberated, 229; reunited with J, 235; effect of POW life, 238, 241; tries for Parliament, 240; wants separation, 242; unfulfilling work, 243; irritated by J, 243; described when asleep, 254; leaves Wellington Square, 256; 'gentlemanly thing', and divorce, 260–2; wedding reception for Janet at Cultoquhey, 292; remarries, 292, 302; sells Cultoquhey; moves to Edinburgh and then to Aberlady, East Lothian; his death, 8 June 1971, 302;
Claudia, formerly Page-Phillips, née Tannert, Robert's wife, the author's mother, 302;
Diana Evelyn, née Macgegor, Jamie's first wife, J's daughter-in-law, 292, 294;
(Margaret) Ethel, née Blair-Oliphant, 1861–1952, wife of Jim, family historian, mother of Tony, 35, **73**, 261;
James (Jim), 1863–1940, Chartered Accountant in Edinburgh, Tony's father, 35–6, 71, **73**, 84, 226.
James Anstruther (Jamie), J's eldest child, born 10 May 1924 at Walpole Street, 40, **41**, 52, 64, 67–8, **73**, 83, 90, **106**, 107–8, 120–1, 131, 162, 184, 192, 196, 212, 216–17, 235, 246–7, 257, 264, 270, 278, 283, 285, 292, 294, 298; later career, two marriages, and children, 302; died November 2001

Janet Mary, J's only daughter, born 24 March 1928 at Sydney Street, married Patrick Rance, q.v.; 52–3, 65–6, 70, **73**, 100, **106**, 108, 120–1, 131, 137–9, 143, 154, 164–6, 181–2, 186, 205–8, 219, 222, 228, 230, 232, 235, 237–8, 240–1, 243, 246, 248, 256, 267, 283; 292–4, 298; career, marriage, seven children, and her death, 18 December 1996, 302;
Michael and John, born 1929, twin sons of Patrick, 65; **73**;
Mungo, Lt. Col. in the Jacobite army, 1719, died 1763; his 'Litany', 35;
Patrick, 1903–65, of 45 Tregunter Road, later of 17 Alexander Place, South Kensington; stockbroker; married twice; Tony's younger brother, **73**, 149;
'Peggy', Margaret Louise Rosalind Barne, née Percival, died 1994, Tony's second wife, 292;
Peter, born 1927, died in New Guinea, 1963, eldest son of Patrick, 64, **73**
Robert Mungo, J's youngest child, born 6 May 1931 at Wellington Square, 54, 65, **73**, 81, 100, **106**, 108, 120–1, 131, 137–9, 154, 164–6, 181–2, 186, 205–8, 221, 223–4, 230, 232, 235, 237–8, 240, 242–3, 246–8, 250, 254–6, 259–61, 269, 283, 298; career, marriage to Claudia, and their daughter Ysenda, 302;
Ysenda, of Edinburgh, 'Os', J's sister-in-law, 1895–1990, see Smythe;
Ysenda, of London, the author of this book, born 31 December 1962, 302
Mayer, Louis B. (1885–1957, Hollywood film mogul), 168, 177, 204–5, 207
Metro-Goldwyn-Mayer (MGM), 1–2, 98, 158, 160, 168–9, 180, 204, 282
Monson, 9th Baron, died 1940, and his American-born wife, died 1943, described, 46
Moseley, Miss, teacher, 16–17
Munich crisis of 1938, 100–2

'Nannie', see Good.
Nash, Ogden (1902–71, humorous writer), 89, 268

307

Index

Index

Roosevelt, Franklin D. (1882–1945, President), 2, 154, 163–4, 172, 203
Rose, J's maid, 222
Russell, Sheridan (1900–91, musician and hospital almoner, of Cheyne Walk, Chelsea), 107, 114, 139, 140, 183
Rye, Sussex, and the cottage on the golf course, 77, 81–4, 90, 105, 120–3

Sandars, Clare, played Judy Miniver, and her father Eric, 179, 185
Sandberg, Carl (1878–1967, poet), **222**
Sanders, Peter (Arthur Thomas 'Peter'), 2nd Lieut, Grenadier Guards, 1900–20, son and heir of the future Baron Bayford, 31–4
Sandwich, Kent, 105, 302
Schmidt, Thomi, of Binghampton, NY, 224, 228, 243, 248
Schurr, Dr Max, of NYC, 212
Schwarz, Gerhard, radiologist, NYC, 298
Scots Guards, Tony's, Jamie's and Robert's regiment, 176, 184, 196, 235, 283, 292
Scratch Society, of London, for young writers, 20
Severn, Christopher, played Toby Miniver, 179
Shepard, Ernest H., OBE (1879–1976, artist), 62–4, 81, 266, 276; his illustrations, **63–6**
Sherriff, R. C. (1896–1975, a screen writer of *Mrs Miniver*), 168
Smith, Revd Sydney (1771–1845), quoted, 164
Smythe family (pronounced 'Smith') of 38 Heriot Row, Edinburgh:
Patrick Cecil, OBE, Writer to the Signet (1888–1969) 131, 143, 271;
Ysenda Mabel, his wife ('Os', née Maxtone Graham, J's sister-in-law, 1895–1990) 57, **73**, 131–2, 136, 143, 192, 216, 241, 271;
Patrick Mungo, their first son, jazz pianist (1923–1983), **73**
(David) Philip, their second son (1925–1959), 64, **73**
Charles Maxtone, their youngest son (1928–95) 64–5, **73**, 143
Spencer, Charles Nicholas, and his wife 'Oscar' (artists, of Cheyne Walk, Chelsea) 44, 122, 246, 269
Stevenson, Adlai (1900–65, presidential candidate) 295

Stirling-Home-Drummond-Moray family of Abercairny, Perthshire, 48
Stowe School, Buckingham, Robert's school, 242–3, 246, 259, 264
Struther, Jan (Joyce Anstruther, Joyce Maxtone Graham, Jan Struther Placzek):
OUTLINE OF EVENTS:
Born 6 June 1901, London;
Parents, *see* Harry Anstruther and Dame Eva Anstruther; they separated, 15;
Photographed at age 2, **11**; with her mother, **21**; at age 18, **26**;
Education, 16–19;
Writer, journalist and poet with pseudonym Jan Struther from age 18, 21;
Learns shorthand and typing, 25; first job at Scotland Yard, 31;
The modern maiden, **32**;
Her first love, Peter Sanders; his suicide, 31–3;
To Egypt with her father, 33–4;
Meets Tony and they fall in love, 30, 34; they marry, 36, **37**;
Balkan journey, 50–2;
Births of elder son Jamie, 40; of only daughter Janet, 52; and of younger son Robert, 54;
Photographed with the three children **26**; with Jamie, **41**;
Life at Wellington Square, 53;
Wrote hymns, 56–60;
Wrote in association with Ernest Shepard, 62–6;
Holidays in Scotland, 57, 71–6, 107; shooting with Tony, **46**; at Crieff Games, **75**;
They take a cottage on Rye golf course, 77–8;
Begins to be bored by Tony, 76–8; and Tony's changed attitude to her, 97;
Start of mutual infidelity, 81, 83;
Economising, 84; they move to an unsatisfactory smaller house, 84; and soon move again, 85;
First signs of depression, 84, 96;
Peter Fleming suggests writing articles for *The Times* Court page, 88, 90;
First *Mrs Miniver* article in *The Times*, 90;

Index

Index

Index

Modern Critical Interpretations

The Tales of Poe

Edited and with an introduction by

Harold Bloom
Sterling Professor of the Humanities
Yale University

Chelsea House Publishers ◇ *1987*
NEW YORK ◇ NEW HAVEN ◇ PHILADELPHIA

Library of Congress Cataloging-in-Publication Data
The Tales of Poe.
   (Modern critical interpretations)
   Bibliography: p.
   Includes index.
   Summary: A collection of critical essays on Poe's tales of
horror arranged in chronological order of publication.
   1. Poe, Edgar Allan, 1809–1849. Tales. 2. Horror tales,
American—History and criticism. [1. Poe, Edgar Allen,
1809–1849. Tales. 2. Horror stories—History and criticism. 3.
American literature—History and criticism] I. Bloom,
Harold.   II. Series.
PS2618.T32T3   1987   813'.3   86-34307
   ISBN 1-55546-011-9 (alk. paper)

Contents

Editor's Note

This book brings together a representative selection of the most useful criticism available upon the tales of Edgar Allan Poe. The critical essays are reprinted here in the chronological order of their original publication. I am grateful to Wendell Piez for his aid in editing this volume.

My introduction sets the tales, and particularly "Ligeia," in the total context, problematical and influential, of Poe's literary work. The chronological sequence of criticism begins with Robert L. Carringer's study of how Poe's centers of space threaten the protagonists of his stories. Barton Levi St. Armand, centering upon "The Fall of the House of Usher," shows how Poe's use of the Gothic mode replaced the Sublime by "a numinous, nameless dread."

"The Cask of Amontillado" is read by Walter Stepp as an instance of ironic doubling, while Brian M. Barbour relates Poe's tales to their author's ironic rejection of American tradition and society. In a deconstructive analysis, Gregory S. Jay translates several of the tales as parables of "textual intercourse," a fit reading of the relation between Poe and French intellectual tradition.

Examining Poe's images of death, Gerald Kennedy praises the tales as refusing to join in the evasion or denial of mortality. Ken Frieden ends this volume with an advanced exegesis of narrative monologue in Poe, which he finds to be a perpetual transgression of the customary limits of monologue.

Introduction

Valéry, in a letter to Gide, asserted that "Poe is the only impeccable writer. He was never mistaken." If this judgment startles an American reader, it is less remarkable than Baudelaire's habit of making his morning prayers to God and to Edgar Poe. If we add the devotion of Mallarmé to what he called his master Poe's "severe ideas," then we have some sense of the scandal of what might be called "French Poe," perhaps as much a Gallic mystification as "French Freud." French Poe is less bizarre than French Freud, but more puzzling, because its literary authority ought to be overwhelming, and yet vanishes utterly when confronted by what Poe actually wrote. Here is the second stanza of the impeccable writer's celebrated lyric, "For Annie":

> Sadly, I know
>   I am shorn of my strength,
> And no muscle I move
>   As I lie at full length—
> But no matter!—I feel
>   I am better at length.

Though of a badness not to be believed, this is by no means unrepresentative of Poe's verse. Aldous Huxley charitably supposed that Baudelaire, Mallarmé and Valéry simply had no ear for English, and so just could not hear Poe's palpable vulgarity. Nothing even in Poe's verse is so wickedly funny as Huxley's parody in which a grand Miltonic touchstone is transmuted into the mode of Poe's "Ulalume." First Milton, in *Paradise Lost*, 4.268–273:

> Not that fair field
> Of Enna, where Proserpine gathering flowers

1

> Her self a fairer flower by gloomy Dis
> Was gathered, which cost Ceres all that pain
> To seek her through the world;

Next, Huxley's Poe:

> It was noon in the fair field of Enna,
>   When Proserpina gathering flowers—
>   Herself the most fragrant of flowers,
> Was gathered away to Gehenna
>   By the Prince of Plutonian powers;
> Was borne down the windings of Brenner
>   To the gloom of his amorous bowers—
> Down the tortuous highway of Brenner
>   To the God's agapemonous bowers.

What then did Baudelaire hear, what music of thought, when he read the actual Poe of "Ulalume"?

> Here once, through an alley Titanic,
>   Of cypress, I roamed with my Soul—
>   Of cypress, with Psyche, my Soul.
> These were days when my heart was volcanic
>   As the scoriac rivers that roll—
>   As the lavas that restlessly roll
> Their sulphurous currents down Yaanek,
>   In the ultimate climes of the Pole—
> That groan as they roll down Mount Yaanek,
>   In the realms of the Boreal Pole.

If this were Edward Lear, poet of "The Dong with the Luminous Nose" or "The Jumblies," one might not question Baudelaire and the other apostles of French Poe. But the hard-driven Poe did not set out to write nonsense verse. His desire was to be the American Coleridge or Byron or Shelley, and his poetry, at its rare best, echoes those High Romantic forerunners with some grace and a certain plangent urgency. Yet even "The City in the Sea" is a touch too close to Byron's "Darkness," while "Israfel" weakly revises Shelley's "To a Skylark." Nineteenth-century American poetry is considerably better than it is generally acknowledged to be. There are no other figures comparable to Whitman and Dickinson, but at least the following are clearly preferable to Poe, taking them chronologically:

Bryant, Emerson, Longfellow, Whittier, Jones Very, Thoreau, Melville, Timrod and Tuckerman. Poe scrambles for twelfth place with Sidney Lanier; if this judgment seems harsh, or too arithmetical, it is prompted by the continued French overvaluation of Poe as lyricist. No reader who cares deeply for the best poetry written in English can care greatly for Poe's verse. Huxley's accusation of vulgarity and bad taste is just: "To the most sensitive and high-souled man in the world we should find it hard to forgive, shall we say, the wearing of a diamond ring on every finger. Poe does the equivalent of this in his poetry; we notice the solecism and shudder."

II

Whatever his early ambitions, Poe wrote relatively little verse; there are scarcely a hundred pages of it in the remarkable new edition of his complete writings, in two substantial volumes, published by the Library of America. The bulk of his work is in tale-telling and criticism, with the exception of the problematic *Eureka: A Prose Poem,* a hundred-page cosmology that I take to be Poe's answer to Emerson's Transcendental manifesto, *Nature.* Certainly *Eureka* is more of a literary achievement than Poe's verse, while the popularity and influence of the shorter tales has been and remains immense. Whether either *Eureka* or the famous stories can survive authentic criticism is not clear, but nothing could remove the stories from the canon anyway. They are a permanent element in Western literary culture, even though they are best read when we are very young. Poe's criticism has mixed repute, but in fact has never been made fully available until the Library of America edition.

Poe's survival raises perpetually the issue as to whether literary merit and canonical status necessarily go together. I can think of no other American writer, down to this moment, at once so inevitable and so dubious. Mark Twain catalogued Fenimore Cooper's literary offenses, but all that he exuberantly listed are minor compared to Poe's. Allen Tate, proclaiming Poe "our cousin" in 1949, at the centenary of Poe's death, remarked, "He has several styles, and it is not possible to damn them all at once." Uncritical admirers of Poe should be asked to read his stories aloud (but only to themselves!). The association between the acting style of Vincent Price and the styles of Poe is alas not gratuitous, and indeed is an instance of deep crying out unto deep. Lest I be considered unfair by those devoted to Poe, I hasten to quote him at his strongest as a storyteller. Here is the opening paragraph of "William Wilson," a tale admired by Dostoyevski and still central to the great Western topos of the double:

Let me call myself, for the present, William Wilson. The fair page lying before me need not be sullied with my real appellation. This has already been too much an object for the scorn—for the horror—for the detestation of my race. To the uttermost regions of the globe have not indignant winds bruited its unparalleled infamy? Oh, outcast of all outcasts most abandoned!—to the earth art thou not forever dead? to its honors, to its flowers, to its golden aspirations?—and a cloud, dense, dismal, and limitless, does it not hang eternally between thy hopes and heaven?

This rhetoric, including the rhetorical questions, is British Gothic rather than German Gothic, Ossian or Monk Lewis rather than Tieck or E. T. A. Hoffmann. Its palpable squalors require no commentary. The critical question surely must be: how does "William Wilson" survive its bad writing? Poe's awful diction, whether here or in "The Fall of the House of Usher" or "The Purloined Letter," seems to demand the decent masking of a competent French translation. The tale somehow is stronger than its telling, which is to say that Poe's actual text does not matter. What survives, despite Poe's writing, are the psychological dynamics and mythic reverberations of his stories about William Wilson and Roderick Usher. Poe can only gain by a good translation, and scarcely loses if each reader fully retells the stories to another. C. S. Lewis, defending the fantasies of George Macdonald, formulated a curious principle that seems to me more applicable to Poe than to Macdonald:

> The texture of his writing as a whole is undistinguished, at times fumbling. . . . But this does not quite dispose of him even for the literary critic. What he does best is fantasy—fantasy that hovers between the allegorical and the mythopoeic. And this, in my opinion, he does better than any man. The critical problem with which we are confronted is whether this art—the art of mythmaking—is a species of the literary art. The objection to so classifying it is that the Myth does not essentially exist in words at all. We all agree that the story of Balder is a great myth, a thing of inexhaustible value. But of whose version—whose *words*—are we thinking when we say this?
>
> (*George Macdonald, An Anthology*)

Lewis replies that he is not thinking of anyone's words, but of a particular pattern of events. Of course that means Lewis is thinking of his own words. He goes so far as to remember when I first heard the story of Kafka's *Castle* related in conversation and afterwards read the book for myself. The reading added nothing. I had already received the myth, which was all that mattered.

Clearly mistaken about Kafka, Lewis was certainly correct about Macdonald's *Lilith,* and I think the insight is valid for Poe's stories. Myths matter because we prefer them in our own words, and so Poe's diction scarcely distracts us from our retelling, to ourselves, his bizarre myths. There is a dreadful universalism pervading Poe's weird tales. The Freudian reductions of Marie Bonaparte pioneered at converting Poe's universalism into the psychoanalytical universalism, but Poe is himself so reductive that the Freudian translations are in his case merely redundant. Poe authentically frightens children, and the fright can be a kind of trauma. I remember reading Poe's tales and Bram Stoker's *Dracula,* each for the first time, when I was about ten. *Dracula* I shrugged off (at least until I confronted Bela Lugosi murmuring: "I never drink—wine!") but Poe induced nasty and repetitious nightmares that linger even now. Myth may be only what the Polish aphorist Stanislaw Lec once called it, "gossip grown old," but then Poe would have to be called a very vivid gossip, though not often a very eloquent one.

III

Critics, even good ones, admire Poe's stories for some of the oddest of reasons. Poe, a true Southerner, abominated Emerson, plainly perceiving that Emerson (like Whitman, like Lincoln) was not a Christian, not a royalist, not a classicist. Self-reliance, the Emersonian answer to Original Sin, does not exist in the Poe cosmos, where you necessarily start out damned, doomed, and dismal. But I think Poe detested Emerson for some of the same reasons Hawthorne and Melville more subtly resented him, reasons that persist in the most distinguished living American writer, Robert Penn Warren, and in many current academic literary critics in our country. If you dislike Emerson, you probably will like Poe. Emerson fathered pragmatism; Poe fathered precisely nothing, which is the way he would have wanted it. Yvor Winters accused Poe of obscurantism, but that truthful indictment no more damages Poe than does tastelessness and tone deafness. Emerson, for better and for worse, was and is the mind of America, but Poe was and is our hysteria, our uncanny unanimity in our repressions. I certainly do not intend to mean by this that Poe was deeper than Emerson in any way whatsoever. Emerson cheerfully and consciously threw out the past. Critics tend to share Poe's easy historicism; perhaps without knowing it, they are gratified that every Poe story is, in too clear a sense, over even as it begins. We don't have to wait for Madeline Usher and the house to fall in upon poor Roderick; they have fallen in upon him already, before the narrator comes upon the place. Emerson exalted freedom, which he and Thoreau usefully called "wildness." No one in Poe is or can be free or wild, and some academic admirers of Poe truly like everything and everyone to be in bondage to a universal past. To begin is to be free, godlike and Emersonian-Adamic, or Jeffersonian. But for a writer to be free is bewildering and even maddening. What American writers and their exegetes half-unknowingly love in Poe is his more-than-Freudian oppressive and curiously original sense and sensation of overdetermination. Walter Pater once remarked that museums depressed him because they made him doubt that anyone ever had once been young. No one in a Poe story ever was young. As D. H. Lawrence angrily observed, everyone in Poe is a vampire—Poe himself in particular.

IV

Among Poe's tales, the near-exception to what I have been saying is the longest and most ambitious, *The Narrative of Arthur Gordon Pym,* just as the best of Poe's poems is the long prose-poem *Eureka.* Alas, even these works are somewhat overvalued, if only because Poe's critics understandably become excessively eager to see him vindicated. *Pym* is readable, but *Eureka* is extravagantly repetitious. Auden was quite taken with *Eureka,* but could remember very little of it in conversation, and one can doubt that he read it through, at least in English. Poe's most advanced critic is John T. Irwin, in his book *American Hieroglyphics.* Irwin rightly centers upon *Pym,* while defending *Eureka* as an "aesthetic cosmology" addressed to what in each of us Freud called the "bodily ego." Irwin is too shrewd to assert that Poe's performance in *Eureka* fulfills Poe's extraordinary intentions:

> What the poem *Eureka,* at once pre-Socratic and post-Newtonian, asserts is the truth of the feeling, the bodily intuition, that the diverse objects which the mind discovers in contemplating external nature form a unity, that they are all parts of one body which, if not infinite, is so gigantic as to be beyond both the spatial and temporal limits of human perception. In *Eureka,* then,

Poe presents us with the paradox of a "unified" macrocosmic body that is without a totalizing image—an alogical, intuitive belief whose "truth" rests upon Poe's sense that cosmologies and myths of origin are forms of internal geography that, under the guise of mapping the physical universe, map the universe of desire.

Irwin might be writing of Blake, or of other visionaries who have sought to map total forms of desire. What Irwin catches, by implication, is Poe's troubling anticipation of what is most difficult in Freud, the "frontier concepts" between mind and body, such as the bodily ego, the non-repressive defense of introjection, and above all, the drives or instincts. Poe, not just in *Eureka* and in *Pym,* but throughout his tales and even in some of his verse, is peculiarly close to the Freudian speculation upon the bodily ego. Freud, in *The Ego and the Id* (1923), resorted to the uncanny language of E. T. A. Hoffmann (and of Poe) in describing this difficult notion:

> The ego is first and foremost a bodily ego; it is not merely a surface entity, but is itself the projection of a surface. If we wish to find an anatomical analogy for it we can best identify it with the "cortical homunculus" of the anatomists, which stands on its head in the cortex, sticks up its heels, faces backwards and, as we know, has its speech-area on the left-hand side.

A footnote in the English translation of 1927, authorized by Freud but never added to the German editions, elucidates the first sentence of this description in a way analogous to the crucial metaphor in Poe that concludes *The Narrative of Arthur Gordon Pym:*

> I.e. the ego is ultimately derived from bodily sensations, chiefly from those springing from the surface of the body, besides, as we have seen above, representing the superficies of the mental apparatus.

A considerable part of Poe's mythological power emanates from his own difficult sense that the ego is always a bodily ego. The characters of Poe's tales live out nearly every conceivable fantasy of introjection and identification, seeking to assuage their melancholia by psychically devouring the lost objects of their affections. D. H. Lawrence, in his *Studies in Classic American Literature* (1923), moralized powerfully against Poe, condemning him for "the will-to-love and the will-to-consciousness, asserted against death itself. The pride of human conceit in KNOWLEDGE." It is illuminating that Lawrence attacked Poe in much the same spirit as he attacked Freud, who is interpreted in *Psychoanalysis and the Unconscious* as somehow urging us to violate the taboo against incest. The interpretation is as extravagant as Lawrence's thesis that Poe urged vampirism upon us, but there remains something suggestive in Lawrence's violence against both Freud and Poe. Each placed the elitist individual in jeopardy, Lawrence implied, by hinting at the primacy of fantasy not just in the sexual life proper, but in the bodily ego's constitution of itself through acts of incorporation and identification.

The cosmology of *Eureka* and the narrative of *Pym* alike circle around fantasies of incorporation. *Eureka's* subtitle is "An Essay on the Material and Spiritual Universe" and what Poe calls its "general proposition" is heightened by italics: *"In the Original Unity of the First Thing lies the Secondary Cause of all Things, with the Germ of their Inevitable Annihilation."* Freud, in *his* cosmology, *Beyond the Pleasure Principle,* posited that the inorganic had preceded the organic, and also that it was the tendency of all things to return to their original state. Consequently, the aim of all life was death. The death drive, which became crucial for Freud's later dualisms, is nevertheless pure mythology, since Freud's only evidence for it was the repetition compulsion, and it is an extravagant leap from repetition to death. This reliance upon one's own mythology may have prompted Freud's audacity when, in the *New Introductory Lectures,* he admitted that the theory of drives was, so to speak, his own mythology, drives being not only magnificent conceptions but particularly sublime in their indefiniteness. I wish I could assert that *Eureka* has some of the speculative force of *Beyond the Pleasure Principle* or even of Freud's disciple Ferenczi's startling *Thalassa: A Theory of Genitality;* but *Eureka* does badly enough when compared to Emerson's *Nature,* which itself has only a few passages worthy of what Emerson wrote afterwards. And yet Valéry in one sense was justified in his praise for *Eureka.* For certain intellectuals, *Eureka* performs a mythological function akin to what Poe's tales continue to do for hosts of readers. *Eureka* is unevenly written, badly repetitious, and sometimes opaque in its abstractness, but like the tales it seems not to have been composed by a particular individual. The universalism of a common nightmare informs it. If the tales lose little, or even gain, when we retell them to others in our own words, *Eureka* gains by Valéry's observations, or by the summaries of recent critics like John Irwin or Daniel Hoffman. Translation even into his own language always benefits Poe.

I haven't the space, or the desire, to summarize *Eureka,* and no summary is likely to do anything besides deadening both my readers and myself. Certainly Poe was never more passionately sincere than in composing *Eureka,* of which he affirmed: *"What I here propound is true."* But these are the closing sentences of *Eureka:*

> Think that the sense of individual identity will be gradually merged in the general consciousness—that Man, for example, ceasing imperceptibly to feel himself Man, will at length attain that awfully triumphant epoch when he shall recognize his existence as that of Jehovah. In the meantime bear in mind that all is Life—Life—Life within Life—the less within the greater, and all within the *Spirit Divine.*

To this, Poe appends a "Note":

> The pain of the consideration that we shall lose our individual identity, ceases at once when we further reflect that the process, as above described, is, neither more nor less than that of the absorption, by each individual intelligence of all other intelligences (that is, of the Universe) into its own. That God may be all in all, *each* must become God.

Allen Tate, not unsympathetic to his cousin, Mr. Poe, remarked of Poe's extinction in *Eureka* that "there is a lurid sublimity in the spectacle of his taking God along with him into a grave which is not smaller than the universe." If we read closely, Poe's trope is "absorption," and we are where we always are in Poe, amid ultimate fantasies of introjection in which the bodily ego and the cosmos become indistinguishable. Again, I suspect this judgment hardly weakens Poe, since his strength is no more cognitive than it is stylistic. Poe's mythology, like the mythology of psychoanalysis that we cannot yet bear to acknowledge as primarily a mythology, is peculiarly appropriate to any modernism, whether you want to call it early, high or post-modernism. The definitive judgment belongs here to T. W. Adorno, certainly the most authentic theoretician of all modernisms, in his last book, *Aesthetic Theory.* Writing on "reconciliation and mimetic adaptation to death," Adorno blends the insights of Jewish negative theology and psychoanalysis:

> Whether negativity is the barrier or the truth of art is not for art to decide. Art works are negative *per se* because they are subject to the law of objectification; that is, they kill what they objectify, tearing it away from its context of immediacy and real

life. They survive because they bring death. This is particularly true of modern art, where we notice a general mimetic abandonment to reification, which is the principle of death. Illusion in art is the attempt to escape from this principle. Baudelaire marks a watershed, in that art after him seeks to discard illusion without resigning itself to being a thing among things. The harbingers of modernism, Poe and Baudelaire, were the first technocrats of art.

Baudelaire was more than a technocrat of art, as Adorno knew, but Poe would be only that except for his mythmaking gift. C. S. Lewis may have been right when he insisted that such a gift could exist even apart from other literary endowments. Blake and Freud are inescapable mythmakers who were also cognitively and stylistically powerful. Poe is a great fantasist whose thoughts were commonplace and whose metaphors were dead. Fantasy, mythologically considered, combines the stances of Narcissus and Prometheus, which are ideologically antithetical to one another, but figuratively quite compatible. Poe is at once the Narcissus and the Prometheus of his nation. If that is right, then he is inescapable, even though his tales contrast weakly with Hawthorne's, his poems scarcely bear reading, and his speculative discourses fade away in juxtaposition to Emerson's, his despised Northern rival.

V

To define Poe's mythopoeic inevitability more closely, I turn to his story "Ligeia" and to the end of *Pym*. Ligeia, a tall, dark, slender transcendentalist, dies murmuring a protest against the feeble human will, which cannot keep us forever alive. Her distraught and nameless widower, the narrator, endeavors to comfort himself, first with opium, and then with a second bride, "the fair-haired and blue-eyed Lady Rowena Trevanian, of Tremaine." Unfortunately, he has little use for this replacement, and so she sickens rapidly and dies. Recurrently, the corpse revivifies, only to die yet again and again. At last, the cerements are stripped away, and the narrator confronts the undead Ligeia, attired in the death-draperies of her now evaporated successor.

As a parable of the vampiric will, this works well enough. The learned Ligeia presumably has completed her training in the will during her absence, or perhaps merely owes death a substitute, the insufficiently transcendental Rowena. What is mythopoeically more impressive is the ambiguous question of the narrator's will. Poe's own life, like Walt Whitman's, is an American mythology, and what all of us generally remember about it is that Poe married his first cousin, Virginia Clemm, before she turned fourteen. She died a little more than ten years later, having been a semi-invalid for most of that time. Poe himself died less than three years after her, when he was just forty. "Ligeia," regarded by Poe as his best tale, was written a bit more than a year into the marriage. The later Freud implicitly speculates that there are no accidents; we die because we will to die, our character being also our fate. In Poe's myth also, ethos is the daemon, and the daemon is our destiny. The year after Virginia died, Poe proposed marriage to the widowed poet Sarah Helen Whitman. Biographers tell us that the lady's doubts were caused by rumors of Poe's bad character, but perhaps Mrs. Whitman had read "Ligeia"! In any event, this marriage did not take place, nor did Poe survive to marry another widow, his childhood sweetheart Elmira Royster Shelton. Perhaps she too might have read "Ligeia" and forborne.

The narrator of "Ligeia" has a singularly bad memory, or else a very curious relationship to his own will, since he begins by telling us that he married Ligeia without ever having troubled to learn her family name. Her name itself is legend, or romance, and that was enough. As the story's second paragraph hints, the lady was an opium dream with the footfall of a shadow. The implication may be that there never was such a lady, or even that if you wish to incarnate your reveries, then you must immolate your consubstantial Rowena. What is a touch alarming to the narrator is the intensity of Ligeia's passion for him, which was manifested however only by glances and voice so long as the ideal lady lived. Perhaps this baffled intensity is what kills Ligeia, through a kind of narcissistic dialectic, since she is dominated not by the will of her lust but by the lust of her will. She wills her infinite passion towards the necessarily inadequate narrator and when (by implication) he fails her, she turns the passion of her will against dying and at last against death. Her dreadful poem, "The Conqueror Worm," prophesies her cyclic return from death: "Through a circle that ever returneth in / To the self-same spot." But when she does return, the spot is hardly the same. Poor Rowena only becomes even slightly interesting to her narrator-husband when she sickens unto death, and her body is wholly usurped by the revived Ligeia. And yet the wretched narrator is a touch different, if only because his narcissism is finally out of balance with his first wife's grisly Prometheanism. There are no final declarations of Ligeia's passion as the story concludes. The triumph of her will is complete, but we know that the narrator's will has not blent itself into Ligeia's. His

renewed obsession with her eyes testifies to a continued sense of her daemonic power over him, but his final words hint at what the story's opening
confirms: she will not be back for long—and remains "my lost love."

The conclusion of *Pym* has been brilliantly analyzed by John Irwin,
and so I want to glance only briefly at what is certainly Poe's most effective
closure:

> And now we rushed into the embraces of the cataract, where a
> chasm threw itself open to receive us. But there arose in our
> pathway a shrouded human figure, very far larger in its pro-
> portions than any dweller among men. And the hue of the skin
> of the figure was of the perfect whiteness of the snow.

Irwin demonstrates Poe's reliance here upon the Romantic topos of
the Alpine White Shadow, the magnified projection of the observer himself.
The chasm Pym enters is the familiar Romantic Abyss, not a part of the
natural world but belonging to eternity, before the creation. Reflected in
that abyss, Pym beholds his own shrouded form, perfect in the whiteness
of the natural context. Presumably, this is the original bodily ego, the
Gnostic self before the fall into creation. As at the close of *Eureka,* Poe
brings Alpha and Omega together in an apocalyptic circle. I suggest we
read Pym's, which is to say Poe's, white shadow as the American triumph
of the will, as illusory as Ligeia's usurpation of Rowena's corpse.

Poe teaches us, through Pym and Ligeia, that as Americans we are
both subject and object to our own quests. Emerson, in Americanizing the
European sense of the abyss, kept the self and the abyss separate as facts:
"There may be two or three or four steps, according to the genius of each,
but for every seeing soul there are two absorbing facts—I and the Abyss."
Poe, seeking to avoid Emersonianism, ends with only one fact, and it is
more a wish than a fact: "I will to be the Abyss." This metaphysical despair
has appealed to the Southern American literary tradition and to its Northern
followers. The appeal cannot be refuted, because it is myth, and Poe backed
the myth with his life as well as his work. If the Northern or Emersonian
myth of our literary culture culminates in the beautiful image of Walt
Whitman as wound-dresser, moving as a mothering father through the
Civil War Washington, D.C., hospitals, then the Southern or countermyth
achieves its perfect stasis at its start, with Poe's snow-white shadow shrouding the chasm down which the boat of the soul is about to plunge. Poe's
genius was for negativity and opposition, and the affirmative force of Emersonian America gave him the impetus his daemonic will required.

VI

It would be a relief to say that Poe's achievement as a critic is not mythological, but the splendid, new and almost complete edition of his essays, reviews and marginalia testifies otherwise. It shows Poe indeed to have been Adorno's "technocrat of art." Auden defended Poe's criticism by contrasting the subjects Baudelaire was granted—Delacroix, Constantin Guys, Wagner—with the books Poe was given to review, such as *The Christian Florist, The History of Texas,* and *Poetical Remains of the Late Lucretia Maria Davidson.* The answer to Auden is that Poe also wrote about Bryant, Byron, Coleridge, Dickens, Hawthorne, Washington Irving, Longfellow, Shelley, and Tennyson; a ninefold providing scope enough for any authentic critical consciousness. Nothing that Poe had to say about these poets and storytellers is in any way memorable or at all an aid to reading them. There are no critical insights, no original perceptions, no accurate or illuminating juxtapositions or historical placements. Here is Poe on Tennyson, from his *Marginalia,* which generally surpasses his other criticism:

> Why do some persons fatigue themselves in attempts to unravel such phantasy-pieces as the "Lady of Shalott"? . . . If the author did not deliberately propose to himself a suggestive indefinitiveness of meaning, with the view of bringing about a definitiveness of vague and therefore of spiritual *effect*—this, at least, arose from the silent analytical promptings of that poetic genius which, in its supreme development, embodies all orders of intellectual capacity.

I take this as being representative of Poe's criticism, because it is uninterestingly just plain *wrong* about "The Lady of Shalott." No other poem, even by the great word-painter Tennyson, is deliberately so definite in meaning and effect. Everything vague precisely is excluded in this perhaps most Pre-Raphaelite of all poems, where each detail contributes to an impression that might be called hard-edged phantasmagoria. If we take as the three possibilities of nineteenth-century practical criticism the sequence of Arnold, Pater, and Wilde, we find Poe useless in all three modes: Arnold's seeing the object as in itself it really is, Pater's seeing accurately one's own impression of the object, and the divine Oscar's sublime seeing of the object as in itself it really is not. If "The Lady of Shalott" is the object, then Poe does not see anything: the poem as in itself it is, one's impression of the poem as that is, or best of all the Wildean sense of what is missing or excluded from the poem. Poe's descriptive terms are "indefinitiveness" and "vague," but Tennyson's poem is just the reverse:

> She left the web, she left the loom,
> She made three paces through the room,
> She saw the water-lily bloom,
> She saw the helmet and the plume,
>   She looked down to Camelot.
> Out flew the web and floated wide;
> The mirror cracked from side to side;
> "The curse is come upon me," cried
>   The Lady of Shalott.

No, Poe as practical critic is a true match for most of his contemporary subjects, such as S. Anna Lewis, author of *The Child of the Sea and Other Poems* (1848). Of her lyric "The Forsaken," Poe wrote, "We have read this little poem more than twenty times and always with increasing admiration. *It is inexpressibly beautiful*" (Poe's italics). I quote only the first of its six stanzas:

> It hath been said—for all who die
>   there is a tear;
> Some pining, bleeding heart to sigh
>   O'er every bier:
> But in that hour of pain and dread
>   Who will draw near
> Around my humble couch and shed
>   One farewell tear?

Well, but there is Poe as theoretician, Valéry has told us. Acute self-consciousness in Poe was strongly misread by Valéry as the inauguration and development of severe and skeptical ideas. Presumably, this is the Poe of three famous essays: "The Philosophy of Composition," "The Rationale of Verse," and "The Poetic Principle." Having just reread these pieces, I have no possibility of understanding a letter of Valéry to Mallarmé which prizes the theories of Poe as being "so profound and so insidiously learned." Certainly we prize the theories of Valéry for just those qualities, and so I have come full circle to where I began, with the mystery of French Poe. Valéry may be said to have read Poe in the critical modes both of Pater and of Wilde. He saw his impression of Poe clearly, and he saw Poe's essays as in themselves they really were not. Admirable, and so Valéry brought to culmination the critical myth that is French Poe.

VII

Whose head is swinging from the swollen strap?
Whose body smokes along the bitten rails,
Bursts from a smoldering bundle far behind
In back forks of the chasms of the brain—
Puffs from a riven stump far out behind
In interborough fissures of the mind . . .?

Hart Crane's vision of Poe, in the "Tunnel" section of *The Bridge,* tells us again why the mythopoeic Poe is inescapable for American literary mythology. Poe's nightmare projections and introjections suggest the New York City subway as the new underground, where Coleridge's "deep Romantic chasm" has been internalized into "the chasms of the brain." Whatever his actual failures as poet and critic, whatever the gap between style and idea in his tales, Poe is central to the American canon, both for us and for the rest of the world. Hawthorne implicitly and Melville explicitly made far more powerful critiques of the Emersonian national hope, but they were by no means wholly negative in regard to Emerson and his pragmatic vision of American Self-Reliance. Poe was savage in denouncing minor transcendentalists like Bronson Alcott and William Ellery Channing, but his explicit rejection of Emerson confined itself to the untruthful observation that Emerson was indistinguishable from Thomas Carlyle. Poe should have survived to read Carlyle's insane and amazing pamphlet "The Nigger Question," which he would have adored. Mythologically, Poe is necessary because all of his work is a hymn to negativity. Emerson was a great theoretician of literature as of life, a good practical critic (when he wanted to be, which was not often), a very good poet (sometimes) and always a major aphorist and essayist. Poe, on a line-by-line or sentence-by-sentence basis, is hardly a worthy opponent. But looking in the French way, as T. S. Eliot recommended, "we see a mass of unique shape and impressive size to which the eye constantly returns." Eliot was probably right, in mythopoeic terms.

Poe's Tales: The Circumscription of Space

Robert L. Carringer

Poe's stature as a writer of fiction is based principally upon about fifteen items: a small collection of detective stories (written in the first half of the 1840s) and about a dozen of those bizarre and morbid romances he called "arabesques" (all but two, "MS. Found in a Bottle" and "The Cask of Amontillado," written between 1835 and 1843). The peculiar nature of the dilemma *Pym* got Poe into becomes clear when one examines a dominant pattern of experience in these major tales. "The prevailing invitation of Poe's narrators," Terence Martin reminds us, "is for us to witness an act or process of destruction." In every one of the major arabesques an act or process of destruction is central to the plot: plague and bloody red death in "The Masque of the Red Death"; the illness and death of a woman in "Morella," "Ligeia," and "Eleonora," and of twins in "The Fall of the House of Usher"; the prospect of violent death brought about by powerful external forces in "MS. Found in a Bottle," "A Descent into the Maelström," and "The Pit and the Pendulum"; and murderous attacks on others, which entail self-destructive consequences, in "Berenice," "William Wilson," "The Tell-Tale Heart," "The Black Cat," and "The Cask of Amontillado." There are other features that give this material a kind of fundamental sameness despite the variety of motifs and situations. Most of Poe's best writing (all but "The Masque of the Red Death" in the above group) is in the form of first-person narratives. Often there are specific incidents or details that link the narrator with the author. Characteristically,

From *PMLA* 89, no. 3 (May 1974). © 1974 by the Modern Language Association of America.

Poe's protagonists exhibit a morbid preoccupation with various forms of physical disintegration (especially decay and putrefaction), and Poe has an almost clinical regard for the representation of mental excitement, especially those forms of terror that are aroused by the prospect of death or derangement for his narrators. His imaginative commitment, as D. H. Lawrence remarked many years ago, is to "the disintegration processes of his own psyche."

There is abundant evidence, in Quinn's biography and elsewhere, that Poe was almost compulsively masochistic. Awareness of such details, however, has led more often to speculative psychology than to literary criticism, but recently there have been attempts to view Poe's destructiveness in terms other than those of neurotic personality.

Richard Wilbur argues in an extremely influential essay that Poe's destructiveness is, paradoxically, a fundamentally creative impulse whose aim is to obliterate earthly experience in what Poe called "a wild effort to reach the Beauty above." According to Wilbur, this otherworldly impulse signifies the yearning of a divided nature to be whole again, a conflict that is finally objectified into the cosmic scheme of *Eureka,* Poe's late prose poem on the final reunification of matter and spirit in the universe. In his chapter on Poe in *The Design of the Present* John Lynen also argues that a longing for a spiritual ideal of beauty underlies Poe's destructiveness, though Lynen holds that it should be understood literally, not as an allegory on psychological states. Destructiveness in Poe, he believes, is a calculated strategy of indirection, of "expressing things through their opposites"—beauty through the grotesque, rebirth in a higher consciousness through a (necessary) dying in this one.

This line of argumentation rests on several assumptions: that Poe's questing after what he calls ideal beauty should be taken entirely seriously; that this quest, which is the stated intention of his poetry, is the underlying motive of his fiction as well; that this quest anticipates the theme of ultimate reunification of matter and spirit in the universe, which receives mature expression in *Eureka*; and that *Eureka* is the philosophical key to all of Poe's serious work. This entire structure of assumptions can be called into serious question. Despite the important studies of *Eureka* by Davidson and others, it is still respectable to hold that this work can be seen in somewhat the same light as "The Philosophy of Composition," another after-the-fact attempt at pseudoscientific system-building designed to explain certain obsessive peculiarities in their creator's imaginative work. Important studies from *The Histrionic Mr. Poe* to Terence Martin's have testified to Poe's "posing" and his incurable love of playing games. There is as much reason to regard the quest for ideal beauty as a pose as there is to regard it as anything else. Moreover, his use of wan and ghoulish maidens and putrefying corpses as earthly symbols of spiritual beauty has all the makings of a typical Poe joke. There *is* a strong yearning for unattainable feminine figures on the part of some Poe protagonists. It is especially strong in the early poetry and in those early tales such as "Berenice," "Morella," and "Ligeia" in which a male protagonist longs to be reunited with a lost wife or lover. Around 1839, however, the need that this motif represented appears to have been significantly modified or fulfilled (or perhaps he merely tired of it); for after Roderick Usher collapses into death in his dead sister's embrace, the impulse ceases to provide the stimulus for Poe's best work. Thereafter, it appears most characteristically in prosaic, otherworldly dialogues between abstract masculine and feminine figures, and when the earlier motif reappears it is significantly modified, as in "Eleonora," in which the bereaved lover returns to the world and takes another woman with Eleonora's blessing, bestowed from beyond the grave. "William Wilson" (published next after "Usher"), Poe's definitive alter-ego narrative, initiates a new phase in the fiction; and for several years Poe's most interesting narratives (discounting the detective stories) involve a first-person protagonist in some form of self-encounter. As a matter of fact, almost simultaneously with the publication of one of the best of these, "The Pit and the Pendulum," he explicitly renounced the "idea of the Beautiful" as a legitimate province of the tale, and held that verisimilar presentation of ratiocination, terror, passion, or horror is a more suitable interest for a writer of short fiction. One could argue that Poe's supreme achievement in fiction is a series of stories based on this formula written from 1839 to 1843 which depict first-person narrators discovering their capacity for violent, irrational behavior. As Harry Levin and others have pointed out, his chief contribution to fiction is a technique for effectively portraying the impact of those discoveries on consciousness, and I suspect that the chief value of the tales for most readers is as highly realistic, technically sophisticated allegories on the consequences of self-destructive impulses.

Besides physical disintegration and psychological terror, we may note as a third identifying characteristic of a story by Poe a strong impulse to delimit space. Indeed, as we shall see, there is a way in which this third characteristic can be used as a means to explain the other two. Few readers can have failed to notice that most of the time in most of the stories the Poe protagonist is conspicuously *within* something. In six of the thirteen tales previously named, the principal activity takes place within a single room, and within a series of rooms in two others. Tombs figure prominently in four, secret compartments in three others. Even outdoors activity (which is uncommon) is very carefully framed (as in "Eleonora") by natural limits such as hillsides, steep cliffs, or overhanging foliage. Most key moments of action in Poe conspicuously involve severely restrictive enclosures, from stuffy Gothic rooms to deep, dark pits to damp, musty caves to whirlpools, coffins, tombs, and various kinds of secret recesses within a wall or underneath a floor. Poe was very much aware of the persistence of this trait, and in "The Philosophy of Composition" he tried to account for it by explaining that "a close *circumscription of space* is absolutely necessary to the effect of the insulated incident." That is, in terms of his theory of fiction, a tale must have an absolute consistency of tone and atmosphere in order for it to achieve a unified effect; a circumscribed setting is part of this overall economy of form. But Richard Wilbur points to a curious paradox in "William Wilson." During the course of the story Wilson makes his way from Stoke Newington to Eton, from Eton to Oxford, and then to Rome by way of Paris, Vienna, Berlin, Moscow, Naples, and Egypt. "And yet for all his travels," Mr. Wilbur observes, "Wilson never seems to set foot out-of-doors." This paradox occurs even more tellingly in tales involving actual movement in space. In both "MS. Found in a Bottle" and "A Descent into the Maelström," in a reversal of all conventional associations, Poe manages to have his narrator delimited by space *on the ocean.* Poe's comment may be a perfectly valid esthetic observation for those stories to which it applies, but clearly the persistence of the motif into other situations suggests the appropriateness of alternative explanations.

According to Wilbur, Poe's withdrawals are a typical Romantic allegory on the artistic process and circumscription symbolizes "the isolation of the poetic soul in visionary reverie or trance." "When we find one of Poe's characters in a remote valley, or a claustral room," Mr. Wilbur continues, "we know that he is in the process of dreaming his way out of the world." But the worlds into which Poe's protagonists dream their way are fraught with their own special dangers and threats. Prominent among the dangers is one that confronts several protagonists at their moments of truth. One lies at the bottom of a dark pit and is about to be crushed to death by its closing walls. Another moves through the diminishing space of seven rooms to a final confrontation with bloody death in the seventh. Still another is lured through the diminishing space of a cave and bricked up at last in a narrow recess in the wall. We should note, first, that to circumscribe a Poe character is usually to involve him in some form of violent destructiveness. Clearly, then, circumscription is somehow intimately bound up with that penchant for disaster that characterizes the typical

Poe protagonist. As the preceding examples indicate, it is not circumscription alone that is most important but rather what that state signifies, the possibility of being further circumscribed, that is, the threat of being confronted with diminishing space. This is what lies behind that curious paradox in the sea "voyages." In both of them Poe finds a pretext that allows him to reverse all conventional associations that hold the sea to be a place of infinite expanse, and in each one at the climax has his narrator being borne along diminishing concentric circles toward violent death. The major terms of this formula (circumscription involves destruction) appear in other guises. For instance, two 1843 masterpieces, "The Tell-Tale Heart" and "The Black Cat," both involve a secret crime of the narrator's, the evidence of which is buried away in a narrow enclosure. Both narrator-protagonists are irresistibly drawn back to their secret hiding places, and the same irrational impulse compels them to reveal their crimes and thereby open the path to their own destruction. As in the sea and pit narratives, destiny for the narrator-protagonist is a crucial encounter with diminished space. Wilbur reaches his conclusion by dealing primarily with those narratives like "Berenice," "Ligeia," and "The Fall of the House of Usher" which are set principally in the narrator-protagonist's ornate private chamber; but we should recognize how space is unstable even in these. Poe's rooms in these stories, as Mr. Wilbur notes, are usually very prominently enclosures within enclosures. But in all three the narrator's compelling motive is to be further circumscribed. He has suffered a loss of his beloved and will be whole again only after his earthly identity has been destroyed and he has been reunited with what is shut away in the tomb.

If Poe's protagonists exhibited a morbid fear of enclosures, one could label it a sign of claustrophobia and leave it at that. But it is not space itself that threatens. Rather, it is some unknown and irresistible thing that lurks at the point where space ends. One is faced, therefore, with a key question: What is at the center of diminishing space?

Among the characteristic forms that appear at Poe's centers are girls in coffins, murdered victims, and natural images of destruction (such as whirlpools). Again, there is diversity, but there is also a way to see an underlying consistency among these different forms. The clue is provided, I think, by "William Wilson," perhaps the single most important Poe story for an understanding of the sources of his fiction in his life. The central conflict in "William Wilson" is between moral and premoral aspects of being; the second William Wilson is the objectified conscience of the libertine first Wilson. In the story, moral being is threatened and finally destroyed by the unchecked impulses of its dissolute counterpart. Specifically, sexuality proves to be the last straw: the second Wilson appears just after the first has admitted to having sexual designs on the young wife of an aged Duke, and his appearance sends his counterpart into a murderous rage. Sexuality is a frequent threat for Poe protagonists: Poe's most productive period begins with a narrative involving a disguised bloody act of desexualization, the pulling of Berenice's *vaginae dentes*, and in the various sequels earthly women are safely shut away in tombs while a lover yearns for cold, sexless "ideal" women. His last major story, "The Cask of Amontillado"— set, significantly, like the climax of "William Wilson," in carnival (carnal?) times—progresses atypically to entrapment rather than disclosure and ends with the protagonist's libertine alter ego safely buried away (forever?) in a secret recess deep in the bowels of a cave. One might argue convincingly that "threat of sexuality" is really Poe's central theme, and that "the idea of the Beautiful" is merely one form of sublimation. But over-simplification of this sort is a disservice that has been rendered to Poe all too frequently. In "The Man of the Crowd," which followed shortly after "William Wilson," the libertine alter ego is presented as a kind of archetype of criminality. It is better to say more generally that the central conflict facing many of Poe's artist-surrogates is the one dramatized in the two narratives considered together: a conflict between two aspects of their own natures, their rational and moral selves versus the source of their capacity for "criminality" and destructive violence, their premoral natures. Other kinds of plots can be seen as variants on this conflict. For instance, the two sea "voyages" are metaphorically descents from rationality and order down into an inner source of destructive primal energies, symbolized by the boiling eye of a whirlpool. To drop a capital letter to lower case is to reveal an underlying metaphor in the death-of-women narratives: the yearning for "Psyche, my Soul" is a yearning for presexual psychic harmony; the obligatory entombment of earthly women in these narratives is a way of suppressing primal (sexual) energies. The conflict between contending facets of the self is often at the base of narratives involving murdered victims. Two of the best of these, "The Tell-Tale Heart" and "The Black Cat," resolve themselves in terms of an implied play on words. In both stories, the narrator, in a paranoid frenzy, destroys the threatening eye of an innocent antagonist. Later, an irrational impulse drives him to uncover the crime. There in the secret place is the victim but not the offensive organ. The progression of the story is implied by the pun: that which the narrator destroyed, an "Evil Eye," an objective fact, becomes the means of his own undoing, the subjective condition that it symbolizes, an "evil I." As in "William Wilson" a destructive act redounds upon its perpetrator with equally self-destructive force.

Why is it, Howard P. Vincent asks in *The Trying Out of "Moby-Dick,"* that "so many of the world's literary masterpieces have been studies of travel?" "The answer," he replies, "lies in the nature of the basic metaphor, common to all of them, of the voyage as a symbol of spiritual forthfaring: that even as the physical soul seeks new sights in strange places so the human soul in its necessary process of growth goes out into the sea of life. The fundamental metaphor of the voyage applies to Romantic allegories of withdrawal into self as well as to accounts of actual voyages. Just as unlimited expanses of ocean, prairie, or wilderness suggest an "area of total possibility" for the young American Adam, Poe's enclosures suggest his fictional universe of negative possibility and the severely restricted prospects and interests of his protagonists. By the same token, his centers of space are physically threatening to his protagonists because the internal condition that they symbolize is also threatening to the protagonist's rational and moral nature. For there, at the center of space toward which the protagonists of "Berenice," "A Descent into the Maelström," and "The Tell-Tale Heart" are driven, is an image of a thing that is also an image of themselves.

The "Mysteries" of Edgar Poe: The Quest for a Monomyth in Gothic Literature

Barton Levi St. Armand

In exploring the mysteries of Gothic taste, it is easy for the critic to forget that the whole genre was, first and foremost, a fashion, a style, and a mode of interior decoration. That the particular interior being redecorated was human consciousness itself is ancillary to the nature of Gothic as primarily an aesthetic revival which somehow managed to provide Romanticism with its first full set of swaddling clothes. The remarkable thing about this taste is that we can chart its serpentine course almost from work to work in terms of the development of theme, character, and popularity of novel modes and means of decoration. The Wandering Jew, who plays only a minor walk-on part in Lewis's *The Monk,* for example, emerges as the main character type of Maturin's *Melmoth.* Mrs. Radcliffe's Appenines somehow contribute both to Shelley's "Mont Blanc" and to the frozen Arctic land-scapes of his wife's *Frankenstein.* The Venetian segment of *The Mysteries of Udolpho* becomes the whole focus of a tale like Poe's deliberately Byronic "The Assignation"; we cannot fully understand the rationale of its conclu-sion or the presence of "the cracked and blackened goblet" clutched in the marble hand of Poe's dead voluptuary unless we know that Radcliffe's hero-villain Montoni avoided death by using a special type of Venetian glass which splintered and bubbled when poison was poured into it. In such ways, both major and minor, one can chart the growth of Gothic romance from the first appearance of the species in the *Otranto* of 1764 to such late examples as Faulkner's *Absalom, Absalom!*

From *The Gothic Imagination: Essays in Dark Romanticism,* edited by G. R. Thomp-son. © 1974 by the President and Regents of Washington State University. Wash-ington State University Press, 1974.

Yet, even considering Gothicism as a particular formal structure or burgeoning type, the extreme left-wing or avant-garde of Romanticism, with a curious organic vitality seemingly built into it, certain problems arise. These problems are those continuing ones of device and depth, control and connotation, adaptability and meaning. A mode can evolve so fast that, in an attempt to utilize the best of what the recent past has been as well as what the present is still yearning to be, it reaches a point of critical mass which collapses from within and leaves only an empty eclecticism. In the case of the Gothic genre, in all its manifestations—architectural and social as well as literary—this circumstance becomes doubly true. For the Gothic was an alien revival which took root in an age devoted to one supreme mode—that of Classicism, with its fidelity to decorum, uniformity, and the rule of law. To preserve its vitality, the Gothic always needed some new exotic quality, some as-yet-untapped antiquarian element, to grow and to flourish. Hence its frank sensationalism, its fantastic "outreaching comprehensiveness of sweep," to quote the American Gothicist, Herman Melville. The Gothic was nothing if not new and varied; yet at the same time, there was an unexpected mental growth as well, a dimensional growth in acuity of intelligence and refinement of consciousness. The problem was to impose or synthesize a style which would control, deepen, and extend the mode's previous line of development. In specific literary terms, it was the same process which led William Blake to purify the experimental chaos of the *Poetical Sketches* by utilizing the ingenuous hymns of Dr. Watts and so produce at last the *Songs of Innocence* and the *Songs of Experience*. Later, Blake was similarly to transmute the pseudo-Celtic meters of James Macpherson's *Ossian* (1762) into the bardic thunder of the *Prophetic Books,* proving that the mode, the style, the species bred in the unlikeliest places and consorted with the most disreputable models in order to bring forth a superior type.

In our own century, William Butler Yeats, emerging from that same Celtic twilight and its peculiar conjunctions of primal myth and Romantic fustian, of Blake and Macpherson, was to speak of "masterful images" that grew out of pure mind yet began in a "mound of refuse or the sweepings of a street." What remains important, however, is the fact that the Celtic and the Druidical were both manifestations of the taste for barbaric revivals which was to become known generally as "Gothic." The variety and adaptability of the style, from William Beckford's Oriental Gothic in *Vathek* to Herman Melville's remarkable cetological subspecies in *Moby-Dick*, masked an underlying search for a monomyth which could exploit the possibilities of this fanciful interior decoration while it unified Romantic multiplicity and became at the same time a paradigm for expressing fundamental human experience. The nature of this experience was in most cases (surprisingly enough given the Gothic's stiff anticlerical and anti-Catholic bias) profoundly inward, even "religious" in the broadest sense. It may have begun in Walpole's antiquarian fascination with a lost world of medieval superstition as a means of relieving the boredom of eighteenth-century social realities, but the religious impulse in Gothicism soon galloped from a concern with talking pictures and bleeding nuns to a consideration of man's position in a terrifying and inscrutable universe, an obsession with individual destiny and damnation, and a determined exploration of the mysteries of the soul itself.

"Mystery" is a word which we automatically associate with the Gothic genre since it found its way over and over again into so many Gothic titles, the most famous, of course, being *The Mysteries of Udolpho* (1794) by Ann Radcliffe. But the dimensions of the idea of Gothic mystery can lead us into a consideration of just what the control of the genre by an underlying monomyth entails. At the primary level, for example, the "mysteries" of Udolpho are common detective-story mysteries involving the solution of a contrived puzzle: what was the hideous thing behind the black veil which caused the sensitive Emily to swoon so plaintively and so frequently during her incarceration within the dark battlements of Udolpho? It was, we discover at the end of this monumental romance, only a medieval remnant of monkish superstition, a waxen votary object left as a penance by a long-vanished ancestor of the House of Udolpho. Yet Emily's timid lifting of the black veil has much deeper psychic resonances when, in later Romantic fiction, that veil becomes the Veil of Isis which, as Esther Harding explains, is also "the ever-changing form of nature, whose beauty and tragedy veil the spirit from our eyes. Shelley develops this symbol in his *A Defence of Poetry* and deepens the connotations of the metaphor even further when he remarks that "Poetry lifts the veil from the hidden beauty of the world, and makes familiar objects be as if they were not familiar." Similarly, it is not Mrs. Radcliffe's invention of a trick ending to the Gothic tale which insures her a place in the larger chronicles of literary culture and the history of Romanticism in particular. To be sure, the wild voices heard in the night are found to be the wind whipping through eroded battlements and the mysterious nocturnal melodies are always traced to a very real but concealed musician; yet this is not what caused De Quincey to call her a "great enchantress" or Keats to acknowledge her as "Mother Radcliffe." Rather, to paraphrase Poe, Radcliffe's terror is not of Italy but of the soul, and her horror is only a small part of the larger landscape of sensibility—of limitless spiritual and psychological "mystery"—which she was the first to enter and explore. Through her heroine Emily, Mrs. Radcliffe helped to spread suddenly open the gorgeous fan of the Romantic consciousness and accomplish what Wordsworth called "widening the sphere of human sensibility." Emily's voyage through the Alps and Appenines toward Udolpho becomes, then, another metaphor for that quest which the Romantics themselves cultivated and often internalized. This was a journey on which the Neo-Classic sensibility was unwilling to embark, as it kept strictly within the limits of a Reason which feared excesses of the imagination and an overstimulation of the faculties of the soul. Indeed, Emily's unfortunate father, M. St. Aubert, a figure of melancholy common sense who warns Emily about the "evils of susceptibility" at the beginning of the *Mysteries,* actually has to alight from the coach when it pauses on its magic journey in order to renew his contact with the earth. Ostensibly, he crawls so intently over the landscape because, as a typical rationalist, he has a botanical passion for classifying (and so limiting the possibilities of) natural phenomena. Eventually, however, St. Aubert dies of the effects of the journey itself, a journey in which as it continues "the mountains seemed to multiply, as they went, and what was the summit of one eminence proved to be only the base of another," or, "the scene seemed perpetually changing, and its features to assume new forms, as the winding road brought them to the eye in different attitudes while the shifting vapours, now partially concealing their minuter beauties and now illuminating them with splendid tints, assisted in the illusions of the sight. It is of this constantly shifting confusion of the real and the ideal, of noumena and phenomena, of the dazzle of the veil, that M. St. Aubert finally expires, and, in truth, it can be said that he died, like the Age of Reason itself, of an overexposure to Romanticism. What Mrs. Radcliffe has done, with her pages and pages of landscape description which never seem to end (in which more and more sublime vistas continue to unveil themselves through the rolling mists and rainbow fogs), is to make the momentous connection between the life of nature and the life of the mind which made Romanticism itself into a true revolution of the human consciousness. Emily does not merely contemplate these sublime scenes, but she actually helps to create, through the ever-expansive faculties of her Romantic imagination, the mountains beyond mountains and the plains behind plains. Her mediumistic powers of reverie and feminine weaving of the warp of landscape with the woof of dreamscape are halted only by a traumatic confrontation with the dark and limiting male reality of Udolpho itself:

> Emily gazed with melancholy awe upon the castle, which she
> understood to be Montoni's; for, though it was now lighted up

by the setting sun, the gothic greatness of its features, and its mouldering walls of dark grey stone, rendered it a gloomy and sublime object. As she gazed, the light died away on its walls, leaving a melancholy purple tint, which spread deeper and deeper, as the thin vapour crept up the mountain, while the battlements above were still tipped with splendour. From these, too, the rays soon faded, and the whole edifice was invested with the solemn duskiness of evening. Silent, lonely and sublime, it seemed to stand the sovereign of the scene, and to frown defiance upon all, who dared to invade its solitary reign. As the twilight deepened, its features became more awful in obscurity, and Emily continued to gaze, till its clustering towers were alone seen, rising over the tops of the woods, beneath whose thick shade the carriages soon after began to ascend.

(Mysteries of Udolpho)

From a conveniently modern Jungian perspective, we could say that the Anima has here met the Shadow. Yet it was not for Mrs. Radcliffe to follow the profound implications of her method, for those implications were at once too dangerous and disturbing for her own retiring sensibility to sustain. Rather, it was for others, like Edgar Allan Poe (who, in his tale "The Oval Portrait," described the chateau to which the wounded narrator is brought as "one of those piles of commingled gloom and grandeur which have so long frowned among the Appenines, not less in fact than in the fancy of Mrs. Radcliffe) to explore fully those novel elements implicit in *Udolpho,* which were in fact the mysteries of the progress, experience, and destiny of the Romantic soul. In undertaking this quest, Poe also had to solve the problem which had eluded Mrs. Radcliffe in her own attempt to embody such a pilgrimage, for finally *The Mysteries of Udolpho* is subverted by its own freedom and eclecticism. The romance disintegrates from and succumbs to an imitative fallacy, an overindulgence in openness and limitlessness, as Emily becomes supplanted by another heroine the Lady Blanche, and Mrs. Radcliffe's own interests turn from the adventures offered by a picaresque travel narrative to the more genteel enchantments of a sentimental and well-bred fairy tale. This eclecticism and lack of definition, springing from the eternal process of Romantic reverie, was to plague as well such artists as Shelley, whose conflict of Demogorgan and Jupiter in *Prometheus Unbound* is a similar struggle of freedom with tyranny, as is the opposition between the Los and Urizen of Blake's late epics. The common Romantic problem remained the synthesis of an archetypal monomyth which would not destroy the surface mix and float of those novel elements which preserved the beauty and majesty of the free Romantic temperament. In specifically Gothic works of a less epic character, the further dilemma was to preserve the novelty, variety, and dark sensationalism which composed the fabric of the genre while also suggesting a profound spiritual and emotional depth. This is the enigma which challenged Poe when, in describing the effect of the sight of the House of Usher upon the narrator of his most famous tale, he wrote that, "It was a mystery all insoluble; nor could I grapple with the shadowy fancies that crowded upon me as I pondered."

Poe confronted this mystery in a typically "Gothic" way; that is, in spite of the fact that, as an anatomist of the imagination, he had mastered all of the genre's obvious popular elements and even felt some condescension toward it as a set of counters which he could manipulate at will, he decided to utilize in "The Fall of the House of Usher" its most radical manifestation for his own particular purposes. The most avant-garde of the Romantic revivals when he was writing the tale in 1839 was the Egyptian mode, and it is my contention that, in experimenting with a daring mixture of the Gothic and the Egyptian, Poe managed to create a work of art which fulfilled the search of the Romantics for a monomyth which functions at two distinct levels: the surface level of the picturesque, or the decorative, and the subterranean level of the subliminal and the archetypal. For, in resurrecting the Egyptian mode as part of the dramatic stage setting of his tale, Poe also revived the pattern of initiation ritual which underlaid the symbols of the Egyptian Mysteries, the Mysteries of Isis and Osiris, as they were understood by his own age. That ritual had already found its way into the ceremonies of the countless secret societies (such as the Masons and the Odd Fellows) which abounded in the America of the early nineteenth century. In *The Modern Eleusinia; or, The Principles of Odd Fellowship Explained by a Brother of the Order* (published in Nashua, New Hampshire, in 1844) the anonymous author, speaking of the Eleusinian Mysteries, expresses both a Romantic eclecticism and the fascination of his age at all levels with these "secrets of the soul":

> Their object seemed to be to teach the doctrine of one God, the resurrection of the good to eternal life, the dignity of the human soul, and to lead the people to see the Shadow of the Deity, in the beauty, magnificence, and splendour of the universe. The Mysteries of Isis . . . varied in some of their forms, from the Eleusinian, yet they all had one common design; namely, by the most solemn and impressive ceremonies, to lead the minds of the Neophytes, to meditate, seriously, the great problems of

human duty and destiny, to imbue them with a living sense of the vanity and brevity of life, and of the certainty of a future state of retribution, to set forth, in marked contrast, the beauty of Virtue and Truth, and the deep bitterness, and tormenting darkness of Vice and Error;—and, lastly, to enjoin on them, by the most binding obligations, charity, brotherly love, and inflexible honor, as the greatest of all duties, the most beneficial to the world, and the most pleasing to the Gods. By their rites, many of which we should now think rude and childish, rites commencing in gloom and sorrow, and ending in light and glory,—they dimly shadowed forth, the transition of man from the savage to the civilized state, from ignorance to science, and his constant progress, onward and upward through the Ages, to still sublimer revelations. By them, they also signified, that the soul's exaltation, and highest good, were to be approached, only by the way of tears, and sacrifice, and toil.

Here we have, optimistically and floridly, the outline of the same monomyth which is being enacted in the cavernous glooms of "The House of Usher." As Kathleen Raine notes in her *Blake and Tradition*, "The Eleusinian Mysteries were in fashion in and about 1790," and they soon merged with a general interest in things Eastern, Oriental, and especially Egyptian.

Little of the physical evidence of this Egyptian Revival remains with us today, though there were famous architectural examples such as "The Tombs" (a New York prison in Egyptian style in which Melville's Bartleby found his undeserved end) and we still have the towering obelisk of the Washington Monument as a witness to its brief but powerful influence on public taste. A popular interest in Egyptology had been spurred with the finding of the Rosetta Stone in 1799 by Napoleon's armies, and, after its cession to the British in 1801, it became, along with other Egyptian antiquities, almost as curious and sensational an exhibit as the Elgin Marbles were to be in 1807. The deciphering of hieroglyphics became the rage among antiquarians, and researches were carried on by a host of eminent scholars. Besides prison buildings, cemetery gates and entrances were done in a pylonic form copied from Nile temples, for, while the Gothic style of architecture was naturally associated with religious ideas of spiritual aspiration (hence its use for ecclesiastical and college buildings), the Egyptian mode was considered to be more suited for the contemplation of darker, more impenetrable mysteries. As Frances Lichten writes of this revival:

The first decorative inspirations derived from the contemplation of these archeological wonders seem weighted with immense solemnity—the Victorian architect, if not the Victorian designer, was sensitive to the portentousness of Egyptian art and used it for equally serious purposes, calculated to move the beholder to thoughts of death. Nor did he miss the correspondence of cat-acombs with the idea of prisons; therefore prisons styled in the Egyptian manner breathed forth their gloomy implications, even in the United States.

In American literature, as in American art and architecture, the Egyptian Revival produced no really lasting monuments and so always remained something of an underground style. But the Egyptian mode carried with it, as we have seen, a whole host of complex and intricate mythic associations, and it is my contention, to repeat, that many of these associations inform and help to shape the overall design of the Gothic castle or manor house of literature, which, like much of the architecture of its time, mixes Gothic arches with Egyptian obelisks. The haunted castles and mansions of such tales as Poe's "The Fall of the House of Usher" are, I believe, eclectic structures in which a Gothic frame is supported by a basically Egyptian foundation, and the mystery all insoluble of their effect has a direct relation to the larger Mysteries of Initiation into temple secrets concerned with the exaltation of the soul and its torturous rebirth.

I

The exact nature of these Egyptian Mysteries, meant to be imparted in the labyrinths of temple and pyramid, springs from the ancient religion which was practiced in Dynastic Egypt from an almost immemorial time until it was adopted, first by the Greeks, and then by the Romans. Finally, it reached an apex in the cult of Isis, which flourished in the world capitals of the early Christian era. Alexandria (the site of the Great Library whose volumes of sacred lore were later used by Arab invaders to fire the waters of the public bath) became the center for this mystery cult and the perpetuation of its ritual, as the sun god, Osiris, sacred to the pharaohs, was transformed into the more cosmopolitan and eclectic deity, Serapis. As Harold Willoughby summarizes in his study of Mystery initiations in the Greco-Roman world, *Pagan Regeneration,*

> The ancient system had centered in the god, Osiris; but in the reformed cult of Hellenistic times he was replaced to a consid-erable extent by a new divinity, Serapis, and popular interest was transferred to the more appealing personality of Isis. She dominated the Hellenistic cult quite as Demeter held the supreme

place in the Eleusinian mysteries, or the *Magna Mater* in those that emanated from Phrygia. In the ancient Osirian religion, the public ritual with its strong appeal to the masses was important. In the Hellenized worship of Isis, the significant ceremonials were those secret rites that had such deep meaning for the individual. These were only some of the ways in which the new cult showed adaptation to the very personal needs of individual religionists in the Hellenized world.

So in the first and second centuries A.D. the Mysteries of Egypt became the Mysteries of Isis, just as in the Dark Ages they were to become the Mysteries of Hermes, centering on alchemy and the transmutation of lead into gold as a means of symbolizing the tenets of basically the same esoteric ritual and philosophy. The Mysteries always involved a hieratic initiation into an arcane knowledge of immortality, knowledge achieved by a purification of the soul and a rite of passage through various prescribed trials and tests. It is a tribute to the truly sacred and secret character of this ritual that we know of its details only in fragments salvaged from ancient classical historians and a few Doctors of the Church. Even Herodotus, speaking of the performance of the Egyptian Mysteries at Saïs, felt constrained to tell his readers that "I could speak more exactly of these matters, for I know the truth, but I will hold my peace." What we do know, then, comes mainly from a handful of authors who are themselves the fathers of the occult tradition known generally as Hermeticism, which includes later alchemical and mystical commentaries as well as the few original texts which survived the wreck of the ancient world and the apparent extinction of learning during the early Middle Ages.

Poe's works, for example, contain learned references not only to Herodotus, Diodorus, and Plutarch, but also to Lucius Apuleius, who included in his *Metamorphoses* (better known in English as *The Golden Ass*) the most famous description of Isiac ritual which we possess. Apuleius, a Neoplatonic philosopher of the second century A.D., followed Plutarch's model in holding back the most sacred details of the initiation rite as "things too holy for utterance," for "both tongue and ear would be infected with like guilt did I gratify such rash curiosity." Poe also mentions such authors as Tertullian and Iamblichus, both of whom discussed the Mysteries in one form or another, and he makes further reference to Demeter and Isis, who were considered by Diodorus to be interchangeable forms of the same goddess (the reform of the Osiris cult merged many aspects of the native Greek Eleusinian Mysteries with the Mysteries of Egypt). In "A Descent into the

Maelström" there is even a reference by Poe to the seventeenth-century Jesuit occultist Athanasius Kircher. Kircher's most famous work was the massive *Oedipus Aegyptiacus* (1652), a compendium of Egyptian, alchemical, and kabbalistic lore which contained in its final volume a description of the Mensa Isiaca, a hieroglyphic stone tablet once thought to describe in detail the full process of initiation, which Kircher relates to the *De Mysteriis Aegyptiorum* of Iamblichus, among others. There were, too, already in existence literary transmutations of these sources, such as Jean Terrasson's eighteenth-century romance, *Sethos,* and Novalis's *The Novices of Saïs* (1798). Coming closer to the time of Poe, we could say, as H. Bruce Franklin says of Melville's knowledge of Egyptian myth, "For contemporaneous versions and explanations [he] could have opened the pages of innumerable magazines, travel books, encyclopedias, and polemical tracts."

But, for Poe, there is firm evidence of a more specific contemporary source for his acquaitance with a highly romanticized narrative of initiation into the Mysteries of Isis. In 1840, a year after "Usher" was published, Poe reviewed *Alciphron: A Poem* (1839) by the Irish poet Thomas Moore, who had already caught the public fancy for things exotic with his long Oriental fantasy *Lalla Rookh. Alciphron,* however, was only a redoing in verse of what Moore had already done in his short prose romance *The Epicurean* (first published in 1827), with which Poe was undoubtedly familiar, for in his review of *Alciphron* he mentions that the narrator is head of the Epicurean sect at Athens, a fact that is mentioned only in the romance and not in the poem. Burton R. Pollin has already traced the influence of *Alciphron* and *The Epicurean* on Poe's prose fantasy, "Shadow—A Parable," but no one has yet considered its influence on "The Fall of the House of Usher." For Moore's work provided not only that Romantic-Gothic eclecticism which gives the tale a novel and even sensational character, but also the underlying monomyth of initiation ritual which secretly unifies and deepens its metaphysical dimension.

Poe begins his review by praising Moore in no uncertain terms for his imaginative re-creation of a lost and exotic world, writing that "Amid the vague mythology of Egypt, the voluptuous scenery of the Nile, and the gigantic mysteries of her pyramids, Anacreon Moore has found all of that striking *materiel* which he so much delights in working up, and which he has embodied in the poem before us." Like Byron, Poe refers to Moore as "Anacreon," for in 1804 Moore had first made his name with a translation of the *Odes of Anacreon,* by the Classic poet famous for his short lyrics on the subjects of love and wine. Both *The Epicurean* and *Alciphron,* which Moore admits were directly influenced by Terrasson's *Sethos,* attempted to accomplish something much more ambitious, however. Poe's summary of the poem (which can stand for the romance as well) gives some indication of the scope of Moore's philosophical and antiquarian interest:

> The design of the story (for plot it has none) has been less a consideration than its facilities, and is made subservient to its execution. The subject is comprised in five epistles. In the first, Alciphron, head of the Epicurean sect at Athens, writes, from Alexandria, to his friend Cleon, in the former city. He tells him (assigning a reason for quitting Athens and her pleasures) that, having fallen asleep one night after protracted festivity, he beholds, in a dream, a spectre, who tells him that, beside the sacred Nile, he, the Epicurean, shall find that Eternal Life for which he had so long been sighing. In the second, from the same to the same, the traveller speaks, at large and in rapturous terms, of the scenery of Egypt; of the beauty of her maidens; of an approaching Festival of the Moon; and of a wild hope that amid the subterranean chambers of some huge pyramid lies the secret which he covets, the secret of Life Eternal. In the third letter, he relates a love adventure at the Festival. Fascinated by the charms of one of the nymphs of a procession, he is first in despair at losing sight of her, then overjoyed in seeing her in Necropolis, and finally traces her steps until they are lost near one of the smaller pyramids. In epistle the fourth (still from the same to the same) he enters and explores the pyramid, and, passing through a complete series of Eleusinian mysteries, is at length successfully initiated into the secrets of Memphian priestcraft; we learning this latter point from letter the fifth, which concludes the poem, and is addressed by Orcus, high priest of Memphis, to Decius, a praetorian prefect.

For our purposes, the most interesting segment of *The Epicurean* is chapters six to eleven, which, as Poe indicates, contain a full and highly dramatic rendering of an initiation into the Egyptian Mysteries. It is interesting, too, that Poe refers to these Mysteries as "Eleusinian," thus reflecting like the anonymous author of *The Modern Eleusinia,* the eclecticism which merged all these forms of secret cult worship under the general heading of "Egyptian secrets." The Eleusinian Mysteries centered on the myth of Persephone, daughter of the earth goddess Demeter, and her rape and abduction to the Underworld by the dark daemon god Pluto. Eleusinian ritual involved the symbolic interment of Persephone and a search for her by Demeter in a passion drama which was so similar to the death of the sun god Osiris and his enchainment by the evil force, Typhon, that Lucius Apuleius (in discussing the Mysteries of Isis) says of his initiation that "I drew near the confines of death, I trod the threshold of Proserpine, I was borne through all the elements and returned to earth again."

This examination returns us to the beginning of "The Fall of the House of Usher" and the effect of that structure and its surrounding landscape on the spirits of the narrator. For the sight of the House of Usher does not inspire awe and feelings of the sublime, but rather a shrinking dread and those dim apprehensions about impenetrable secrets, solemn catacombs, and morbid depths which Egyptian architecture was supposed to awaken in the Romantic mind. Indeed, the narrator confesses to experiencing only "an iciness, a sinking of the heart—an unredeemed dreariness of thought which no goading of the imagination could torture into aught of the sublime." The Gothic mode of architecture was an objective correlative, one might almost say, for a sublime response on the part of the onlooker. But in the Gothic mode of literature, the literature of horror, as it is sometimes called, the transcendent feeling of the sublime is replaced by a numinous, nameless dread. Poe's narrator cannot even torture his imagination into producing a minimally sublime transport, for in gazing upon the House of Usher, he has the same forebodings as those nineteenth-century Romantics who meditated upon the ruins of the Temple of Karnak or the Great Pyramid at Giza.

II

Let us turn, then, to a detailed consideration of this most famous of Gothic short stories. The opening of Poe's tale, I suggest, is in the general Romantic tradition of a meditation on ruins, made popular by such eighteenth-century works as Volney's *The Ruins; or, A Survey of the Revolutions of Empires* (1791), and popularized by countless nineteenth-century poets and graphic artists. In Poe's contemporary America, we need only to look to a series of paintings like Thomas Cole's *The Past* and *The Present* (1838), Asher B. Durand's *The Morning of Life* and *The Evening of Life* (1940), or John Vanderlyn's *Marius Brooding on the Ruins of Carthage* (1807) to find an appropriate aesthetic parallel. But Poe's meditation, I would again emphasize, is on a very particular kind of ruin, a ruin in which the Mysteries of Egypt and Isis have been, or are about to be, performed. This is the famous Gothic Waste Land which confronts the narrator of "Usher":

During the whole of a dull, dark, and soundless day in the autumn of the year, when the clouds hung oppressively low in the heavens, I had been passing alone, on horseback, through a singularly dreary tract of country, and at length found myself, as the shades of the evening drew on, within view of the melancholy House of Usher. I know not how it was—but, with the first glimpse of the building, a sense of insufferable gloom pervaded my spirit. I say insufferable; for the feeling was unrelieved by any of that half-pleasurable, because poetic, sentiment, with which the mind usually receives even the sternest natural images of the desolate or terrible.

The narrator continues his attempt to define the effect of these stern images on his spiritual faculties by concluding with an elusive but significant reference:

I looked upon the scene before me—upon the mere house, and the simple landscape features of the domain—upon the bleak walls—upon the vacant eye-like windows—upon a few rank sedges—and upon a few white trunks of decayed trees—with an utter depression of soul which I can compare to no earthly sensation more properly than to the after-dream of the reveller upon opium—the bitter lapse into every-day life—the hideous dropping off of the veil.

Like a skull half-sunk in the desert sands, or a sphinx partially uncovered by desert winds, the House of Usher confronts the narrator with the shock of a sepulchral *memento mori,* and, in describing its effect, he thinks automatically of a fragment of the Mysteries associated with Egypt, the land of death, sphinxes, and pyramids, and their reigning goddess, Isis. His phrase, "the hideous dropping off of the veil," refers to a motif better known to the early nineteenth century than to us, though it was revived, appropriately enough, in the 1870s by that grand mistress of the occult and esoteric, Madame H. P. Blavatsky, founder of the Theosophical Society. In her *Isis Unveiled, A Master-key to the Mysteries of Ancient and Modern Science and Theology,* which attempted to merge Eastern mysticism with the Western occult tradition founded on Hermeticism and Neoplatonism, Madame Blavatsky announced,

In our studies, mysteries were shown to be no mysteries. Names and places that to the Western mind have only a significance derived from Eastern fable, were shown to be realities. Rever-

ently we stepped in spirit within the temple of Isis; to lift aside
the veil of "the one that is and was and shall be" at Saïs, to look
through the rent curtain of the Sanctum Sanctorum at Jerusalem;
and even to interrogate within the crypts which once existed
beneath the sacred edifice, the mysterious Bath-Kol.

Madame Blavatsky finished her typically obscure rhetorical flourish
with a mention of the "Bath-Kol," the mysterious oracle of God which
certain rabbis maintained had spoken spontaneously within the precincts of
the Tabernacle at Jerusalem, but her reference to the veil of Isis has the
same source as Poe's reference to "the hideous dropping off of the veil" in
his description of the melancholy effect of the House of Usher. For, in his
treatise on the Egyptian Mysteries *De Iside et Osiride,* Plutarch, the first-
century Roman historian, had written of the Egyptian priesthood that

> their philosophy is involved in fable and allegory, exhibiting
> only dark hints and obscure resemblances of the truth. This is
> insinuated, for example, in the sphinx, a type of their enigmatical
> theology, and in such inscriptions as that engraved on the base
> of Minerva's statue at Saïs, whom they regard as identical with
> Isis: "I am every thing that has been, that is, and that shall be;
> nor has any mortal ever yet been able to discover what is under
> my veil."

Only those fully initiated into the cult of Isis, which conferred upon
her initiates the like status of godhood or immortality, were permitted to
lift the veil of Isis. Hence the equation by Poe's narrator of a sickness unto
death and ultimate despair with an unwarranted and blasphemous "hideous
dropping off of the veil." The reference, as mentioned in connection with
Radcliffe, was a common one in Romantic literature. Novalis writes in his
The Novices of Saïs, for example, that "I, too, then will inscribe my figure,
and if according to the inscription, no mortal can lift the veil, we must seek
to become immortal; he who does not seek to lift it, is no true novice of
Saïs." Thomas Moore, in *The Epicurean,* has his hero Alciphron say of Isis
(after he has arrived in Egypt to study "the mysteries and the lore") that
"At Saïs I was present during her Festival of Lamps, and read, by the blaze
of innumerable lights, those sublime words on the temple of Neitha;—'I
am all that has been, that is, and that will be, and no man hath ever lifted
my veil.' " And, as in Hawthorne's *Blithedale Romance,* where Zenobia
suggests by her legend of "The Silvery Veil" that the Veiled Lady's mysterious drapery might even conceal "the face of a corpse" or "the head
of a skeleton," *The Epicurean* contains an episode in which Alciphron

raises the veil of a strangely silent figure at a feast and finds it to be a hideous mummy.

Like the silver skeleton present at the banquet of Trimalchio in Petronius's *Satyricon,* the mummy is a reminder to remember death in the presence of life; and its effect on Alciphron is once again much like the effect of the House of Usher on Poe's narrator, for the Epicurean confesses, "This silent and ghostly witness of mirth seemed to embody, as it were, the shadow in my own heart." It is a witness, too, in much the same way in which the pyramids, as watchtowers of time, generate shadowy fancies in the mind of Alciphron when he contemplates the ruins of the monuments of Memphis. Usher's House, we might note, is also as mummified as the corpse of any emblamed pharaoh of the Dynasties, for Poe writes of its "extraordinary dilapidation" that

> there appeared to be a wild inconsistency between its still perfect adaptation of parts, and the crumbling condition of the individual stones. In this there was much that reminded me of the specious totality of old woodwork which has rotted for long years in some neglected vault, with no disturbance from the breath of the external air.

The total effect of the House of Usher on Poe's narrator, then, is paralleled by the effect of the Pyramids of Memphis upon Moore's Epicurean:

> There was a solemnity in the sunshine resting upon those monuments—a stillness, as of reverence, in the air that breathed around them, which stole, like the music of past times, into my heart. I thought what myriads of the wise, the beautiful, and the brave, had sunk into the dust since earth first saw those wonders; and, in the sadness of my soul, I exclaimed,—"Must man, alone, then, perish? must minds and hearts be annihilated, while pyramids endure? O Death! even upon these everlasting tablets—the only approach to immortality that kings themselves could purchase—thou hast written of our doom, awfully and intelligibly, saying,—'There is for man no eternal mansion but the grave.' "
>
> (*The Epicurean*)

Alciphron perhaps voices those thoughts too deep for tears which oppress Poe's narrator, who, gazing at the mansion of the Ushers, also thinks unconsciously of the "long lapse of centuries" and "the consequent undeviating transmission from sire to son, of the patrimony with the name, which had, at length, so identified the two as to merge the original title of the estate in the quaint and equivocal appellation of the 'House of Usher.' " The narrator, unable to articulate the feeling of insufferable gloom which causes such "an iciness, a sinking, a sickening of [his] heart," here matches Alciphron, who exclaims, "My heart sunk at the thought; and for the moment, I yielded to that desolate feeling, which overspreads the soul that hath no light from the future." It is precisely to exorcise this feeling that Alciphron undertakes his mission to undergo the trials of mystery initiation, in the hopes of gaining an immortality which will forever banish his fears about the vanity of human wishes and the transience of human accomplishment. The meditation on ruins thus merges naturally and imperceptibly with the immemorial *ubi sunt* tradition, but, whereas Alciphron manages to shake off his feeling of ultimate desolation, the same emotion continues to pervade and to permeate the atmosphere of the House of Usher, as well as to afflict its master, the unhappy Roderick.

If the House of Usher can be considered, in its effect at least, to be a structure of Egyptian dread and magnitude, combining the uses to which such an image was put by the Romantic mind—temple, crypt, and prison—then Roderick Usher is indeed the master of this temple, as well as its entombed Pharaoh and its holy prisoner. He is the priest-king, chief celebrant, and hierophant of its Hall of Labyrinths, the Osiris who must descend into the depths of night in order to be reborn again in mystic marriage with his sister-wife, Isis. As Harold Willoughby writes,

> According to ancient cosmology, the sun each night visited the subterranean regions. In the rite of initiation, therefore, the votary as a new Osiris made both the infernal and the celestial journey like the sun. At midnight he saw the sun brightly shine in the realm of the dead, and likewise he mounted up into the heavens and saw the gods celestial as well as the gods infernal. In doing all this he was but playing the part of the dying and rising god Osiris in the salvation drama of the Isis cult.
>
> (*Pagan Regeneration*)

In visiting the House of Usher, the narrator is also visiting the House of the Dead, being guided (like the neophyte of the Isis rituals) through the subterranean regions, the vaults and crypts within the pyramid or underneath the Temple of Isis itself: "A valet, of stealthy step, thence conducted me, in silence, through many dark and intricate passages in my progress to the *studio* of his master." This master, the true conductor of the mysteries, is, again, Usher himself, for his very name echoes the meaning of the term "hierophant," which, as Carl Kerényi tells us in his study of the Eleusinian rites, means the priestly demonstrator of the holy mysteries.

The narrator of "The Fall of the House of Usher" is an unwilling initiate who has failed to comprehend the significance of the Mysteries he has witnessed and the passion-drama in which he has participated. Thus, he reports his experience in Gothic terms which frame the narrative according to the conventions of the *Schauerroman,* the tale which is more of Germany than of the soul. He can be considered as a partially unreliable reporter, like those early Church Fathers, who talk of the initiation rites as only so much nonsense and pagan mumbo jumbo, more mystification than mystery. This latter supposition accounts for Usher's characterization of the narrator as a madman precisely before the climax of the ritual Usher has been enacting, with his sister Madeline playing the part of the Isis-Persephone figure. The narrator is "mad" precisely because he does not recognize, or realize, the import of the chance for divine wisdom and revelation, with the concomitant gift of immortality, which has been offered to him by the gods themselves.

The first part of "The Fall of the House of Usher" can thus be read as an esoteric or even subterranean performance of an Egyptian Mystery rite, with Usher assuming the part of the hierophant and the narrator as an uncomprehending witness. The story follows, indeed, the five stages of Mystery initiation outlined by Lewis Spence in his study *The Mysteries of Egypt.* The first part can be seen as the necessary steps of contemplation, purgation, and a journey through the higher and lower regions, while the climax can be considered as embodying the culminating aspects of union and rebirth.

III

Long discipline and contemplation were a requisite part of the initiation process itself. As Edouard Schuré writes of the questing neophyte:

> Before rising to Isis Uranus, he had to know terrestrial Isis, had to learn the physical sciences. His time was divided between mediatations in his cell, the study of hieroglyphics in the halls and courts of the temple, as large as a city, and in lessons from his teachers. He learned the science of minerals and plants, the history of man and peoples, medicine, architecture, and sacred music. In this long apprenticeship he had not only to know, but to become.

In this respect, the narrator is the apprentice and Roderick is the master of the peculiar Pythagorean discipline taking place within the Halls of the Temple which is the House of Usher. While in Egypt studying the Mysteries, Pythagoras was said to have learned the fundamentals of geometry and the theory of the celestial orbs as well as all that pertained to computation and numbers. These he used to construct his abstract philosophy of numerical and harmonic progression. Thus Poe's narrator says of his intimacy with the recesses of Usher's spirit, "We painted and read together, or I listened, as if in a dream, to the wild improvisations of his speaking guitar." We do get a more direct hint, however, as to exactly what texts are studied in the discipline. "Our books," he remarks,

> —the books which, for years, had formed no small portion of the mental existence of the invalid—were, as might be supposed, in strict keeping with this character of phantasm. We pored together over such works as the Ververt et Chartreuse of Gresser; the Belphegor of Machiavelli; the Heaven and Hell of Swedenborg; the Subterranean Voyage of Nicholas Klimm by Holberg; the Chiromancy of Robert Flud, of Jean D'Iandaginé, and of De la Chambre; the Journey into the Blue Distance of Tieck; and the City of the Sun of Campanella.

As T. O. Mabbott and others have noted, "All of Usher's library . . . consists of real books, and, although Poe may have seen few of them, they all concern in one way or another the idea that spirit is present even in inanimate things and that the world, or macrocosm, has relations to the the microcosm, man." The books have usually been seen as only an extension of Roderick's belief in the sentience of all things. Yet it is not the books themselves and their content (for some, like Klimm's *Subterranean Voyage*, are merely satirical studies in the vein of Swift's *Gulliver's Travels*) but rather their titles which take on an occult significance. Most of them deal with a journey to the underworld, and we have seen that the journey of the sun god Osiris to the infernal regions was a central part of Egyptian ritual. "I drew near the confines of death," said Apuleius, "I trod the threshold of Proserpine, I was borne through all the elements and returned to earth again." And, he adds to this mystic revelation, "I saw the sun gleaming with bright spendour at dead of night, I approached the gods above, and the gods below, and worshipped them face to face" (*Mysteries of Egypt*).

Swedenborg's *Heaven and Hell,* for example, deals not only with an occult theory of correspondences but also with "the gods above" and "the gods below" as seen face to face by this Swedish mystic. Most of the other titles in Usher's library concern subterranean journeys and what one should expect to find in these infernal regions, thus paralleling the most famous *vade mecum* to the underworld, the sacred Egyptian *Book of the Dead*. For the Mysteries performed in life were considered only as a prelude to the same ritual to be enacted after death. The descent into an artificial darkness in the Temple of Isis was thought to be a symbolic re-creation and anticipation of the descent of the soul into Hades through the Door of Death. As Plutarch wrote, "When a man dies, he is like those who are being initiated into the mysteries. . . . Our whole life is but a succession of wanderings, of painful courses, of long journeys by tortuous ways without outlet" (*Pagan Regeneration*). And Thomas Taylor, the eighteenth-century translator of so many mystic and Neoplatonic texts, added in his *Dissertation on the Eleusinian and Bacchic Mysteries* that "as the rape of Proserpine was exhibited in the shews of the mysteries, as is clear from Apuleius, it indisputably follows, that this represented the descent of the soul, and its union with the dark tenement of body."

What Lewis Spence has to say about the antiquity of the sacred Egyptian texts, however, may explain why Poe includes among the library titles in the dark tenement of the House of Usher such an item as Campanella's *City of the Sun*. "The Book of the Dead," he writes, "was preceded by the Pyramid Texts, which recount the manner in which Egyptian royalty succeeded to union with the God [Osiris]. His soul bathed in the sacred lake, he underwent lustration with Nile water, and he then crossed the Lake of Lilies in the ferryboat. He ascended the staircase of the sun and reached the city of the sun, after magically opening its gates by a spell, being announced by heavenly heralds" (*Mysteries of Egypt*).

The titles in Usher's library, then, comprise an esoteric guide to the underworld of Usher, itself a journey into the blue distance of Mystery initiation. This journey ends with a transcendent vision—the City of the Sun, the golden state of Isis unveiled, in holy union with her brother-husband Osiris, who himself has been resurrected after death and dismemberment by the ecliptic powers of darkness. These latter powers the Egyptians personified by the god Set, whom Greeks designated as the wind monster Typhon. In the Eleusinian Mysteries, which Poe obviously thought were identical with the original Egyptian rites, the liturgy charted the course of Persephone through the precincts of Hades, to which she had been abducted by the god of the underworld Pluto. In the passion drama performed in the labyrinths of the House of Usher, this shadowy part is taken by the physician who has in his keeping Roderick's sister. Madeline is temporarily interred in one of the numerous vaults within the main walls of the building, for, like Persephone, she will be resurrected in the return to life and union which is the hierogamic marriage of Isis and her hierophant, Roderick, acting the part of the reborn sun god.

The proper guide for the descent into these infernal regions is thus *The Book of the Dead*. As Spence tells us, this book "is a magical book, inasmuch as the sorcery of everyday life is placed at the disposal of the dead in order that they may escape destruction in the journey toward the Otherworld by means of spells and magical invocations" (*Mysteries of Egypt*). The chapters of this most antique of volumes describe the monsters and enemies that the dead soul will encounter in its wanderings, revealing their secret names which, when uttered, allow the soul to control a host of destructive demons. Thus "Belphegor," in Poe's eclectic catalogue of demonology, is the name of the Ammonitic devil who lurked in the shadows of rocks and crevices, seducing the daughters of Israel until he was openly denounced by the angry prophet Hosea.

Another important section of *The Book of the Dead* is devoted to the judgment of Osiris, in which the soul is interrogated by forty-two judges to determine whether it is fit to take equal station with the sun god or be devoured by the howling monster who waits without. The last three books mentioned as part of Usher's library function precisely as this kind of symbolic scripture, familiarizing the soul with the demons to be met in the coming infernal journey; and following, as *The Book of the Dead* should follow, the Pyramid Texts. The list even culminates in a work that can be translated quite literally as the book of "The Watches of the Dead." Poe's narrator continues:

> One favourite volume was a small octavo edition of the *Directorium Inquisitorium,* by the Dominican Eymeric de Gironne; and there were passages in Pomponius Mela, about the old African Satyrs and AEgipans, over which Usher would sit dreaming for hours. His chief delight, however, was found in the perusal of an exceedingly rare and curious book in quarto Gothic—the manual of a forgotten church—the *Vigilae Mortuorum secundum Chorum Ecclesiae Maguntinae.*

We have thus come to the trials, inquisitions, and tortures that the questing soul, the aspirant of the Mysteries, must face if he is to obtain the right to confront Isis unveiled, for the *Directorium Inquisitorium* cherished by Roderick is actually a work by Nicholas Eymeric de Gerone, inquisitor-general for Castile in 1356, which gives an account of the tortures of the

Inquisition. It is for this that the instruction, purgation, and discipline have been instituted and the reason that the arcana, the *Hiera* (the sacred objects), have been revealed to the narrator, who is to accompany Usher on the infernal journey in the same way in which the neophyte is conducted, or ushered, by the hierophant.

One of the most important of these arcana, prophetic of the entombment of the sun god, is the series of strange paintings which Roderick executes as part of the discipline which occupies his waking hours before the descent into the Underworld. As the narrator writes of the uncanny effect of these paintings,

> From the paintings over which his elaborate fancy brooded, and which grew, touch by touch, into vagueness at which I shuddered the more thrillingly, because I shuddered knowing not why;—from these paintings (vivid as their images now are before me) I would in vain endeavor to educe more than a small portion which should lie within the compass of merely written words. By the utter simplicity, by the nakedness of his designs, he arrested and over-awed attention. If ever mortal painted an idea that mortal was Roderick Usher. For me at least—in the circumstances then surrounding me—there arose out of the pure abstractions which the hypochondriac contrived to throw upon his canvas, an intensity of intolerable awe, no shadow of which I felt ever yet in the contemplation of the certainly glowing yet too concrete reveries of Fuseli.

The narrator refers here to the Swiss artist of the weird and the grotesque, friend of Blake and a fellow-illustrator of visions and nightmares. But Usher's paintings are abstract in the same way that his musical studies are intense, formal, and intricate, for they form part of the larger pattern of exact instruction in the larger monomyth of the Mysteries. They are also like the "scenic representations," the "chambers of imagery," which Thomas Moore's Alciphron has to pass through in order gain admittance to the sanctuary of Isis. Edouard Schuré, in his imaginative re-creation of an initiation ceremony, based on the same Romantic sources with which Poe was familiar, writes of one segment of the ritual that

> A Magus called a *pastophor,* a guardian of sacred symbols, opened the grating for the novice and welcomed him with a kind smile. He congratulated him upon having successfully passed the first test. Then, leading him across the hall, he explained the sacred

paintings. Under each of these paintings was a letter and a number. The twenty-two symbols represented the twenty-two first Mysteries and constituted the alphabet of secret science, that is, the absolute principles, the universal keys which, employed by the will, become the source of all wisdom and power.

(*The Great Initiates*)

Schuré relates these arcana to the Tarot deck and suggests that the Tarot cards themselves represent symbolic fragments of initiation into the Mysteries of Egypt and Isis. Although only one of Roderick Usher's awe-inspiring paintings is described (and it seems to have no relation to Tarot symbolism), Usher does act as a *pastophor* in exhibiting it to the narrator. The work fits into the chain of occult symbolism that is developed through the titles of the books in Usher's library. As the narrator relates,

One of the phantasmagoric conceptions of my friend, partaking not so rigidly of the spirit of abstraction, may be shadowed forth, although feebly, in words. A small picture presented the interior of an immensely long and rectangular vault or tunnel, with low walls, smooth, white, and without interruption or device. Certain accessory points of the design served well to convey the idea that this excavation lay at an exceeding depth below the surface of the earth. No outlet was observed in any portion of its vast extent, and no torch or other artificial source of light was discernible; yet a flood of intense rays rolled throughout, and bathed the whole in a ghastly and inappropriate splendour.

Usher's painting might be entitled "The Burial of the Sun," for (as Willoughby has already noted, referring to the statement of Apuleius that "I saw the sun gleaming with bright splendour at the dead of night") the novice made the same journey as the sun god Osiris. *The Book of the Dead* tells us that this journey involved a descent into the nether regions of night and darkness and then an ascent up the golden staircase of the sky to final enthronement in Heliopolis, the holy City of the Sun. Thus at the end of his initiation into the Mysteries of Isis, Apuleius writes, "I was adorned like the sun and made in the fashion of an image." Willoughby comments of Lucius's symbolic resurrection that "This was essentially a rite of deification, and Lucius with his Olympian stole, his lighted torch, and his rayed crown was viewed as a personification of the sun-god" (*Pagan Regeneration*). The ancient Egyptians called part of the original ritual which centered around the resurrection of pharaoh as a representative Osiris figure "the Rite of the Golden Chamber," and it is just such a golden chamber which Usher limns—the inner vault, the *sanctum sanctorum,* the burial chamber of a pyramid and the tomb of a god.

The ghastly and inappropriate splendor of Usher's vault is paralleled, too, by the unearthly phosphorescence of a cavern that Moore's Alciphron stumbles upon as part of his Mystery initiation in the depths of a pyramid at the necropolis north of Memphis. Moore writes,

> While occupied in these ineffectual struggles, I perceived, to the left of the archway, a dark, cavernous opening, which seemed to lead in a direction parallel to the lighted arcades. Notwithstanding however, my impatience, the aspect of this passage, as I looked shudderingly into it, chilled my very blood. It was not so much darkness, as a sort of livid and ghastly twilight, from which a damp, like that of death-vaults, exhaled, and through which, if my eyes did not deceive me, pale, phantom-like shapes were, at that very moment, hovering.
>
> (*The Epicurean*)

Usher's painting, I think, does not so much look forward to the development of modern abstract art and nonobjective expressionism as it looks backward to Pythagorean geometry and the mysterious labyrinths of the pyramids. It is not Usher, however, but his sister Madeline who is interred in such a vault, for, being the exact twin of her brother ("sympathies of a scarcely intelligible nature had always existed between them"), she undergoes the passion of Persephone, prematurely buried in the sinks of Hades, while he underrgoes the passion of Osiris, slowly being torn apart and dismembered while she struggles for resurrection in the tomb. Her malady, as Poe specifically tells us, is cataleptic in nature; and the first trial of the Mystery initiation was a literal simulacrum of the death of the neophyte and his wandering, as a lost and questing soul, through the infernal regions. Schuré even speaks of "the seeming cataleptic death of the adept and his resurrection," but that resurrection is accomplished only by the trials and tortures foreshadowed in a book like the *Directorium Inquisitorium*—trials which are ultimately "elemental" in nature.

Lucius Apuleius had said of his initiation into the cult of Isis that "I was borne through all the elements." The elemental trials which are common both to *The Epicurean* and "The Fall of the House of Usher," then, are the ordeals of earth, fire, water, and air. In Usher's case, the trial by earth is obviously the entombment of his sister Madeline in the crypt, as well as his own entrapment in the labyrinthine dungeon of the house of his fathers. Similarly, the trials by air, fire, and water all culminate in the whirlwind which gathers in the vicinity of the mansion at the end of the tale, and in the vaporish activity of the tarn, which is supercharged with a weird phosphorescence. The tarn thus becomes the molten barrier which must be passed or endured if the initiation is to be successful. The narrator describes the scene in the following terms:

> The impetuous fury of the entering gust nearly lifted us from our feet. It was, indeed, a tempestuous yet sternly beautiful night, and one wildly singular in its terror and its beauty. A whirlwind had apparently collected its force in our vicinity; for there were frequent and violent alterations in the direction of the wind; and the exceeding density of the clouds (which hung so low as to press upon the turrets of the house) did not prevent our perceiving the life-like velocity with which they flew careening from all points against each other, without passing away into the distance. I say that even their exceeding density did not prevent our perceiving this—yet we had no glimpse of the moon or stars—nor was there any flashing forth of the lightning. But the under surfaces of the huge masses of agitated vapor, as well as all terrestrial objects immediately around us, were glowing in the unnatural light of a faintly luminous and distinctly gaseous exhalation which hung about and enshrouded the mansion.

In this context, it is interesting to note that Set or Typhon, the legendary force of darkness that temporarily overcame Osiris, was often conceived of as a storm or whirlwind. In fact, in Jacob Bryant's *A New System; or, An Analysis of Ancient Mythology* (first published in 1774) the author says of the Greek Typhon (from which the modern term "typhoon" is partially derived), "By this was signified a mighty whirlwind, and inundation: and it oftentimes denoted the ocean; and particularly the ocean in ferment." Certainly the tarn of Usher is a ferment, an unholy ferment which combines all the elements of earth, water, fire, and air, though the narrator attempts to explain away such unnatural appearances by reassuring Roderick with the Radcliffean explanation that they "are merely electrical phenomena not uncommon—or it may be that they have their ghastly origin in the rank miasma of the tarn." In *The Epicurean* Alciphron's trial by the elements of air and wind can be profitably compared with the sound and fury of Poe's tempest and its effect on the beholders of this midnight cyclone. The glare of an unnatural light during the hours which should be consecrated to darkness may also again remind us of Apuleius and his testimony that "I saw the sun gleaming with bright splendour at dead of night." Moore writes of the trials of air and fire:

> Just then, a momentary flash, as if of lightning, broke around me, and I perceived, hanging out of the clouds, and barely within my reach, a huge brazen ring. Instinctively I stretched forth my arm to seize it, and, at the same instant, both balustrade and steps gave way beneath me, and I was left swinging by my hands in the dark void. As if, too, this massy ring, which I grasped, was by some magic power linked with all the winds in heaven, no sooner had I seized it than, like the touching of a spring, it seemed to give loose to every variety of gusts and tempests, that ever strewed the sea-shore with wrecks or dead; and, as I swung about, the sport of this elemental strife, every new burst of its fury threatened to shiver me, like a storm-sail, to atoms!
>
> (*The Epicurean*)

Thus is Typhon, the Lord of Winds, unleashed with the same power that, with its "impetuous fury," almost lifts the narrator and Usher off their feet in Poe's tale. The "brazen ring" is missing from Poe's version of the trials, but there is a "shield of brass" and a whole pattern of hierarchical symbolism (which centers on the progression of the planetary metals) embodied in the fanciful history which Poe calls the "Mad Trist" of Sir Launcelot Canning. This is the work which the narrator reads to Roderick at precisely the same time that Madeline frees herself from the tomb. Yet, beneath the Gothic exterior of this pseudo-Grail romance once again lurks another Egyptian Mystery—the art and science of transmuting these metals, known popularly as alchemy, which also helps to structure the monomyth of "The Fall of the House of Usher." I have already explored this connection elsewhere, but what is important about the "Mad Trist" in the context of the original Egyptian Mysteries is the fact that it functions as a pageant or dumb show of the trials and torments that the questing aspirant has to endure. The ordeals of entering the City of the Sun, the "palace of gold, with a floor of silver," include the struggle with the monster of doubt and will, the Dragon "of pesty breath," Typhon, and the successful confrontation with the obstinate hermit, the Master of the Mysteries, who holds the key to the gates of full initiation. At the same time, Madeline is enduring the trial of earth, the ordeals of the labyrinth, and the premature burial which shadows forth the death of the old self and the rebirth of a new, untrammeled soul. This struggle issues in the final Mystery which the narrator is permitted to witness, the full *hieros gamos* of priest and priestess, Osiris and Isis, Roderick and Madeline, which fulfills the paradox that absolute purity of soul can only be attained by a physical ravishment. Since both Madeline and Roderick have attained the status of gods, however, their union is a sublime, awe-inspiring one which the narrator chooses to report under the guise of a typical Gothic catastrophe, echoing that "utter astonishment and dread" which he first evinced upon his entry into the catacombs of Usher:

> As if in the superhuman energy of his utterance there had been found the potency of a spell—the huge antique panels to which the speaker pointed threw slowly back, upon the instant, their ponderous and ebony jaws. It was the work of the rushing gust—but then without those doors there *did* stand the lofty and enshrouded figure of the lady Madeline of Usher. There was blood upon her white robes, and the evidence of some struggle upon every portion of her emaciated frame. For a moment she remained trembling and reeling to and fro upon the threshold, then, with a low moaning cry, fell heavily inward upon the person of her brother, and in her violent and now final death-agonies, bore him to the floor a corpse, and a victim to the terrors he had anticipated.

The veil of Isis has been lifted, then, with sublime consequences for Madeline and Roderick, whose earthly tenement is superseded by the radiant glories of Heliopolis. But this revelation has only "hideous" repercussions for the narrator, who has failed to comprehend the full significance of the Mysteries he has witnessed. The closing scene of "The Fall of the House of Usher" is described in the terms of an apocalypse, a catastrophe like the archetypal Gothic climax of Horace Walpole's *The Castle of Otranto,* where a clap of thunder shakes the castle to its foundations, the walls are thrown down with a mighty force, and the poor witnesses think the last day is at hand. "There came a fierce breath of the whirlwind," the narrator of "Usher" exclaims, "—the entire orb of the satellite burst at once upon my sight—my brain reeled as I saw the mighty walls rushing asunder—there was a long tumultuous shouting sound like the voice of a thousand waters—and the deep and dark tarn at my feet closed sullenly and silently over the fragments of the 'House of Usher.' " This is not a description of an apocalypse, however, but of a new genesis, and it constitutes a conjunction rather than a catastrophe. Earth, water, air, and fire are now transcendently united, as Sun and Moon are sublimely conjoined. The initiation is complete, and, as the anonymous author of *The Modern Eleusinia* puts it, after the "deep bitterness, and tormenting darkness of Vice and Error," and "by the way of tears, and sacrifice, and toil," we have reached and actually witnessed "the soul's-exaltation."

IV

Beneath the Gothic tracery of the walls of "Usher" one can glimpse the massive Egyptian pylons which structure and support the House itself. But at the same time, we have traveled far from the hothouse Romanticism of Thomas Moore's *The Epicurean,* which points to the later Romantic decadence of works like *Salammbô, The Temptation of St. Anthony,* and *Salomé.* Beginning in the nostalgia and yearning for the past which was perhaps the strongest of the early Romantic senses, the Egyptian style soon degenerated into the felicities of historial romance, as the search for a unifying monomyth was similarly transferred from the realm of literature to the realm of science. Moore's *The Epicurean* is what we would have to term, without any pejorative meaning intended, mere romance; it illustrates the early fascination with the exotic and the eclectic which was to return in an even more overwhelming degree toward the last days of the Romantic Age.

What was lost in this shift was the traumatic connection between landscape and consciousness, the widening of the sphere of sensibility which conjoined the sense of place with the sense of self and which made the Romantic imagination into a new medium and a new universe, a metaphysical temple full of enchanting clerestoreys as well as demonic tunnels and howling labyrinths. Mrs. Radcliffe, in associating the landscape of the Alps and the Appenines with the high consciousness and snowy sensibility of her heroine, Emily, had begun all unwittingly a process which was to culminate in the daring use of metaphor which made the landscape of the House of Usher into a simulacrum of the desert places of the human soul. The "hideous dropping off of the veil" witnessed by the narrator was at one and the same time a privilege and a curse; a privilege for those, like Usher, prepared to go beyond the "trembling of the veil" (as Yeats titled his own autobiography) and a curse for those, like the narrator himself, who delved into the Mysteries of the soul without putting aside their rationalism, failing to realize that the precinct which they had entered was, in fact, holy ground. Thus is the narrator of "Usher" afflicted by shadowy fancies and an unfathomable melancholia at the beginning of Poe's tale and thus is he cursed with an unmediated Faustian knowledge at its end.

The quest for a monomyth involving the trials and progress of the soul was to become, as we have mentioned, more and more of a secular rather than a literary endeavor, as the eclecticism in which Romanticism began at last exhausted and subverted the Romantic consciousness itself. Beginning with the attempt of Athanasius Kircher to produce a compendium of occult knowledge in his *Oedipus Aegyptiacus* (1652–55), the scholarly synthesis of ancient religious history and the Mysteries of myth continued in a work we have already quoted, the enormously influential *A New System; or, An Analysis of Ancient Mythology* (published by Jacob Bryant in three volumes from 1774 to 1776). Poe was undoubtedly familiar with this work, for he refers to Bryant's "very learned 'Mythology' " in "The Purloined Letter," and in *Eureka* he quotes with approval Bryant's declaration that "Although the Pagan fables are not believed, yet we forget ourselves continually and make inferences from them as from existing realities." Bryant proceeded to reduce all antique mythologies to one grand monomyth, which could be traced to the primal event of the Flood, so that "All the mysteries of the Gentile world seem to have been memorials of the Deluge." Bryant's syncretism was continued by disciples such as George Stanley Faber, whose *Dissertation on the Mysteries of the Cabiri* (1803) bore the typical fulsome and self-explanatory subtitle: *Being an Attempt to Deduce the Several Orgies of Isis, Ceres, Mïthras, Bacchus, Rhea, Adonis, and Hecate, from an Union of the Rites Commemorative of the Deluge with the Adoration of the Host of Heaven.* The historical quest, then, subsumed particular concerns with the nature and destiny of the individual soul in a general interest in mythology. The goal became the elusive monomyth that tied all myths together as a fossilized "epic of humanity" which portrayed the evolution from sympathetic magic to sophisticated religion. Sir James George Frazer climaxed this search in 1890 with the publication of the first two volumes of *The Golden Bough,* which was the virtuoso attempt of a trained classicist to solve the seemingly insoluble Mysteries of the Grove of Nemi.

Frazer, however, only resurrected and codified the occult and esoteric lore which had already provided such a treasure trove of eclectic symbolism for Romantics such as Moore and Poe. Moreover, Frazer also pointed to the connection between consciousness and landscape, between the individual and the magical environment which he inhabits, by emphasizing the legend of the Fisher King, whose psychic health and well-being ensured the fertility of his kingdom. The wounding of the King, who is also chief priest and hierophant—what Edouard Shuré calls "The Great Initiate"—causes his kingdom to lapse into decay and decline, producing the Gothic Waste Land which, as Stephen Mooney has pointed out, is common both to Eliot's famous poem and to Poe's "The Fall of the House of Usher." In the notes to *The Waste Land,* Eliot listed among the sources for his poem the "Adonis, Attis, Osiris" chapter of Frazer's *The Golden Bough,* which dealt in massive detail with the folklore of the Mystery religions, and especially with the role of the sacred marriage, which we have already discussed in relation to Poe. He also cited Jessie Weston's book on the Grail legend, *From Ritual to Romance,* as a direct inspiration for "the title, . . . the plan, and a good deal of the incidental symbolism of the poem."

From Ritual to Romance is a scholarly classic which attempts to prove that the Grail romances are derived from the vegetation rites of those same Mystery religions and that the main features of the Grail story—the Waste Land, the Fisher King, the Hidden Castle with its solemn Feast, and the Mysterious Feeding Vessel, the Bleeding Lance and Cup—are elements transmuted from the original monomyth of initiation ceremonies. Under this rubric, Usher, with his obscure illness and impotence, is also of course another kind of Fisher King, while the House itself becomes the Hidden Castle or sinister Chapel Perilous and its surrounding landscape of decayed and noxious vegetation is the Perilous Cemetery or Waste Land noted by Mooney. The "Mad Trist" of Sir Launcelot Canning (the title of which is reminiscent of *The Geste of Syr Gawaine,* another Grail romance mentioned by Miss Weston) continues the chivalric imagery, for the trencher or ringing brass shield that Poe's hero Ethelred must win is very like the sacred vessel of the Attis rite, which, as she points out, was both tympanum and cymbal. Weston concludes that the Grail romances are veiled accounts of Mystery initiations and she deduces that

> The earliest version of the Grail story, represented by our Bler-heris form, relates the visit of a wandering knight to one of these hidden temples; his successful passing of the test into the lower grade of Life initiation, his failure to attain to the highest degree. It matters little whether it were the record of an actual, or of a possible, experience; the casting into romantic form of an event which the story-teller knew to have happened, had, perchance, actually witnessed; or the objective recital of what he knew *might* have occurred; the essential fact is that the *mise-en-scène* of the story, the nomenclature, the march of incident, the character of the tests, correspond to what we know from independent sources of the details of this Nature Ritual. The Grail Quest was actually possible then, it is actually possible to-day, for the indication of two of our romances as to the final location of the Grail is not imagination, but the record of actual fact.

Poe's narrator, too, passes, or at least beholds, the first trials of initiation like the wandering knight at the threshold of the hidden temple, but his failure to recognize the full significance of the esoteric symbolism and ritual displayed by the hierophant loses him his chance for the highest degree. Indeed, the whole ambiguous narrative technique of "The Fall of the House of Usher" is implicit in Weston's description of this earliest of the Grail romances. When we turn to Eliot's *Waste Land* (which is an attempt to write another variety of *Modern Eleusinia* by imposing an occult monomyth on the chaos of contemporary life), we find the same kind of allusions to the presence of profounder Mysteries. The Egyptian mode surfaces in the name and practice of Eliot's sleazy fortune-teller, Madame Sosostris, and in her wicked pack of cards, the Tarot deck; to Weston, as to Schuré, there was no doubt that "parallel designs and combinations" of Tarot symbolism "were to be found in the surviving decorations of Egyptian temples" (*From Ritual to Romance*). Adding to the Egyptian symbolism, Eliot also utilized Far Eastern and Oriental sources, constructing a modern eclecticism which actually dramatized the search for meaningful archetypes in much the same way that Weston and Frazer used comparative techniques in their anthropological studies, or, though Eliot would have been horrified at the suggestion, much as Madame Blavatsky had sought for the monomyth amid all the esoterica of her *Isis Unveiled*.

What remains important is the fact that, while the unifying legend of the Grail romance and its occult meaning, uncovered by Frazer and Weston, made the quest for a monomyth possible again for Eliot in 1922, it was also possible for Poe in 1839. Ultimately, Poe and Eliot have the same sources and the same concerns, for, like all modern seekers for that myth (whether literary or anthropological), they try to reverse the direction of the quest away from romance and back toward ritual, that task which Jacob Bryant defined in his subtitle of *A New System; or, An Analysis of Ancient Mythology* as the attempt "to divest Tradition of Fable; and to reduce the Truth to its Original Purity." An awareness of this tradition, in turn, may force us to realize that, given its antecedents, *The Waste Land* is more truly "Gothic" in character than its first readers ever imagined. But the tradition also demonstrates that Poe, in successfully using the monomyth of initiation ritual to structure and to deepen the vital eclecticism of "The Fall of the House of Usher," was not only an adept of Gothic prestidigitation, but that he had mastered as well the most complex thaumaturgies of Romantic art.

The Ironic Double in Poe's "The Cask of Amontillado"

Walter Stepp

In Poe's "The Cask of Amontillado," a heraldic emblem offers a suggestive entrance into the story. Descending into the catacombs of Montresor's failed family, Fortunato says, "I forget your arms." It is one of his numerous blind, unintentional insults. The proud Montresor, biding his time, blinks not and replies: "A huge human foot d'or, in a field of azure; the foot crushes a serpent rampant whose fangs are embedded in the heel."

> "And the motto?"
> "Nemo me impune lacessit."
> "Good!" he said.

The brief scene highlights the major plot dynamics of Poe's great story: the clumsy insult, Montresor's menacing irony, and Fortunato's further blindness to this irony. ("Good!") Montresor flashes countless "clues" like the one above before Fortunato's rheumy eyes—signals of his impending doom, but Fortunato does not perceive. The clues are part of the larger "system" or "demonstration" motif of the story: Montresor, the diabolical rationalist, systematically demonstrates again and again that the arriviste, Fortunato, does not *know*, cannot distinguish. Montresor, at the end of his life, has addressed his narrative to "You, who so well know the nature of my soul," and it is as if he were performing before some ultimate audience, saying, "You see? I show him the picture of his own death, and he says 'Good!' " An unspoken corollary of this speech I have imagined for him might read, "And yet, this buffoon, this Fortunato . . . 'is rich, respected,

From *Studies in Short Fiction* 13, no. 4 (Fall 1976). © 1977 by Newberry College.

admired; he is happy, as once I was.' *He* is the heir of Fortune!" And so Montresor proceeds to demonstrate the illegitimacy of this heir.

The heraldic emblem represents all the irony of life that Fortunato cannot comprehend. But it is the more interesting, I think, for what it says of Poe's knowledge of his evil protagonist (the two being so often equated in Poe's case). For the emblem suggests a deeper motivation that Montresor does not understand, either, but which Poe seems to have built upon. The Latin verb in the motto makes clear what is clear anyway—that Montresor identifies himself with the golden foot, ponderously triumphing over the lashing serpent. When he holds up the dire image before Fortunato's unseeing eyes, he has in mind no doubt the golden legitimacy of his vengeance, a just and unquestionable retribution for the thousand lacerations he has borne in silence. He will tread him into the ground, and indeed he does seal poor Fortunato in stone.

Such is Montresor's reading of the emblem, it seems reasonably clear; but another reading—Poe's, I think—does not so easily identify Montresor with the foot. The snake is the more obvious choice. Secrecy, cunning, serpentine subtlety—these are the themes Montresor demonstrates best of all. And the huge, golden boot fits very snugly the Fortunato that Montresor presents to us—large, powerful, and very clumsy. The larger story shows very well how to read the emblem: a giant has blindly stepped on a snake.

Moreover, to arrive at my main point, the emblem represents a scene of mutual destruction. Allegorically speaking, the foot and the serpent are locked together in a death embrace: neither can escape the ironic bond that is between them. Through this allegory, then, I want to point to the deeper relationship between the two men, a deeper motive for murder, and, finally, a deep, ineffably horrible sense of retribution for the crime. This last may be especially difficult to see, in view of the fact that much of the slow horror of the tale derives from just that sense that Montresor has indeed escaped retribution for his deed, that he has acted out his readers' most terrible fantasy: to murder "without conscience." This is the chief burden of his demonstration, told with appropriately dry matter-of-factness. He ends by letting us know he has lived fifty triumphant years since the murder of "the noble Fortunato." My allegory, then, is certainly not Montresor's.

Is it Poe's? I shall say that Fortunato rather ironically represents the familiar Poe *doppelgänger,* and that, as in Poe's earlier, more explicit allegory, "William Wilson," the double corresponds with conscience. (That "with" is a nice hedge for the moment.) The correspondence is unmistakably pat in the earlier story; "Cask" suggests that Poe's command of his theme has considerably deepened in that the double now is a reversed image—a "negative" double, if you will, an ironic double. (Well, all doubles are; I mean something further in that the double is not recognized "as such" by Montresor.) I think most readers have noticed the rather perfect symmetry of opposition between Montresor and Fortunato; most readers should, for that is the chief burden of Montresor's systematic demonstration. Montresor frames a "facade-system" to deny his double, the irony being that he denies him so systematically that he ends by creating a perfect double-in-reverse. The analogy with a photographic positive and its negative is rather exact here—not because life operates so, but because of Montresor's compulsive program, his obsessional wish to demonstrate that "He is not I." Or: "I am not he." The right emphasis ought to emerge from the demonstration to follow.

I think I need mention only a few instances of the systematic oppositions that Montresor's procrustean method presents to us, enough to recall its obsessive symmetry. Most importantly, Fortunato is broadly drawn as a character entirely befitting his carnival motley and clownish bells. He appears as the open, gullible extrovert, an innocent possessed of that same ignorant vanity that caused the original fall from grace; he thinks he knows enough to sample the apple the serpent tempts him with. He believes the sacred Amontillado is meant for *him,* but he is a drunkard, Montresor lets us know, certainly not a man of his companion's fine taste. Every delicacy, every pearl of ironic distinction, is utterly lost on this man: "He is not I; I am not he."

But it should be said that Montresor more than once obliquely acknowledges that there is more to Fortunato than his portrait is designed to show. Montresor does acknowledge certain sympathies with Fortunato, which point to what is being denied by the rationalist's demonstration. He begins, "He had a weak point—this Fortunato—although in other regards he was a man to be respected and even feared." Here at least, in the beginning, Montresor is quite conscious of his portraiture's limitation, and perhaps that is enough to convince us that he is not himself caught up in his own "sincerity"—Montresor's word for his rival's weakness: "In painting and gemmary, Fortunato, like his contrymen, was a quack, but in the matter of old wines he was sincere." Montresor plays on this sincerity even as Fortunato practices on gullible millionaires. Fortunato is hoist by his own petard, and Poe intimates that Montresor is too, I think; but of course the mine of irony lies deeper with him. If Fortunato's "sincerity" is his connoisseurship, Montresor's is his system. But that is the larger point; here let me emphasize their clearer level of affinity: they are both successful "quacks."

"The rumor of a relationship"—the phrase is from "William Wilson"—sifts out in a few of Montresor's oft-noted "slips." One most touching occurs when Fortunato is near death. Montresor speaks of "a sad voice, which I had difficulty in recognizing as that of the noble Fortunato." The epithet may be taken as an obvious piece of sarcasm in keeping with the general ironic tenor, but I do not find that Montresor allows himself the double-edge when addressing "you who so well know the nature of my soul." Then he keeps to hard, dry understatement of fact. (An exception might be Montresor's final utterance: "*In pace requiescat.*" And even then, if there is indeed a bond between them . . .)

And most readers have noted this piece of apparent rationalization: "There came forth [from out the niche] only a jingling of bells. My heart grew sick—on account of the catacombs." There is also Montresor's failure to satisfy the "definitive" conditions he has set down for himself, the code of honorable vengeance. "A wrong is unredressed when retribution overtakes its redresser," Montresor says, and whether he satisfies that clause is being debated here. "It is equally unredressed when the avenger fails to make himself felt as such to him who has done the wrong." Satisfaction is not debatable here; Montresor fails, for of course Fortunato never knows why he dies. He does not know the avenger "as such." Indeed, his nemesis has gone to great lengths to show that Fortunato is not *capable* of knowing such a man. He merely knows that Montresor has deceived him and that his fortune has run out. To connect with our larger theme, then, Montresor has failed "definitively" to achieve his vengeance in a way that suggests he does not understand its motive much more than does Fortunato. Why *did* he fail? It would have been simple enough to state the formal motive: You have wronged me thus and so; therefore you die. Whether we explain it as a prideful blindness (system always assumed its rationale is self-evident) or as an unwillingness to raise the ambiguous question, the irony of Montresor's "oversight" derives deep from the common substance of the two apparently opposed characters. As the emblem foretold, Montresor is bound with Fortunato and "dies" with him.

But it is the "mocking echo" motif that is most suggestive of the two men's relationship. (I take the phrase from Hawthorne's "Young Goodman Brown," another kind of double story.) Montresor's chosen method of demonstration and torment is to resound Fortunato's innocent words, striking a sinister edge in them known only to himself and his sole confidant, his reader. I am suggesting something further, a strange case of what one might call "murderous identification." I am thinking of the obvious case of "William Wilson," in which the protagonist learns too late the retribution for slaying one's conscience. Two examples: When Fortunato at last realizes his murderer's intentions, he vainly tries to humor him.

> "But is it not getting late? Will they not be awaiting us at the palazzo, the Lady Fortunato and the rest? Let us be gone."
> "Yes," I said, "Let us be gone."
> *"For the love of God, Montresor!"*
> "Yes," I said, "for the love of God!"

And Fortunato is heard no more, silenced at last by his own words thrust back at him. Certainly the most horrific—because so understated—example of this diabolical doubling occurs immediately preceding this last. While Montresor has been laying the tiers of his masonry, Fortunato has been sobering up and presumably comprehending the imminence of his death; "a low moaning cry from the depth of the recess. It was *not* the cry of a drunken man." This is followed by a long and "obstinate" silence. When the wall is nearly completed, "A succession of loud and shrill screams, bursting suddenly from the throat of the chained form, seemed to thrust me violently back." Montresor quickly puts down his momentary fright and reassures himself of the "solid fabric of the catacombs." Then, "I reapproached the wall, I replied to the yells of him who clamored. I re-echoed—I aided—I surpassed them in volume and in strength. I did this, and the clamorer grew still." I have always wanted to see a skilled actor play that scene; rather, two skilled actors. Fine points matter especially here, to see in Montresor's performance just the fine, ironic blend of "quackery" and "sincerity." Fortunato's dazed agony would be a study, too, as he witnesses the weird spectacle of this devil out-clamoring his victim's agonies—eerie harmonics there. And perhaps in this terrible way, Montresor demonstrates how one defeats the double—by beating him at his own game, doubling *him* up. Just as the subtler quack dupes the lesser, so perhaps Montresor "re-echoes" an "echoer."

Again, the parallel with "William Wilson" helps here. There it was the uncanny voice of the double-as-conscience that was most devastating. *"And his singular whisper, it grew the very echo of my own."* But William Wilson was not so well defended as Montresor; he tried the direct frontal assault and lost. Montresor, it would seem, achieves his triumph by reversing roles with his double, in effect *usurping* the double's occupation. Now *he* becomes the menacing echo and sends his double to the doom meant for himself, as it happened to Wilson.

By systematically denying every impulse represented by "the noble Fortunato," Montresor perhaps restores the perfect, lucid order that prevailed when the Montresors "were a great and numerous family." That is to say, a mental equilibrium, false though it may be, has been restored. I am speculating now that the decline of the Montresor family represented a devastation of disorder to the compulsive Montresor, signifying to him the price of his impulsivity. I suggest this term, of course, because it is the direct antithesis of the cool, controlled character Montresor represents himself to be. I have tried to show Montresor's ambivalence toward the impulsive parvenue, the childlike Fortunato, indeed innocent to the end since he never "knows." As in "William Wilson," Montresor is "galled . . . by the rumor of a relationship," but in spite of the double's "continual spirit of contradiction, I could not bring myself to hate him altogether." Who is "the noble Fortunato"?

In "William Wilson," Poe makes it absolutely clear that the double represents conscience; such a parallel is not clear in "Cask," but it is the case, I think. Fortunato is not the interdictory conscience of "William Wilson," but he is conscience-related: he is guileless, trusting innocence. It may be misleading to call him conscience, but *his* death is required to slay conscience. If it is not so clear that Fortunato corresponds to conscience, perhaps the blame (or credit) may be laid to Montresor's elaborate plan of denial. If Fortunato is a double-as-conscience, such an idea is not likely to be directly verified by a man whose one great wish is to portray himself as a man—nay, *the* man—without conscience. Indeed, the murder of Fortunato might be thought of as a "test case" to confirm just that notion: a man kills his conscience and rests in peace for fifty years. Surely the horror of Poe's little gem rests on the fantasy of the crime without consequences. If a man might do that, as every boy has dreamed of doing, where is "the public moral perspective"? The disposal of a rival becomes as simple as a child's "omnipotent" wish that he should "go away."

"William Wilson" tells the story of a man who murdered his conscience and thus himself; the same story is at work in "Cask," I submit, but with the great difference that Wilson recognizes his folly, while Montresor steadfastly refuses to. This significant difference is at least one reason why I find "Cask" much the more interesting story. Wilson's recognition satisfies, perhaps too easily, our own conscientious understanding of the way things ought to be; Montresor is more difficult, he challenges that understanding. He makes claims on us, if we take him seriously, that Wilson does not. Wilson, for all his prodigality, is, after all, "one of us," the difference being of degree. But Montresor, like Iago, stands in the line of Machiavellians who assert that the public moral perspective is but a façade by which knaves are stung and puppies drowned. We may say that Montresor is at heart a tormented sinner like Wilson, but it requires rather than subtlety to show it, and the villain is not likely to own it when we do.

The question of "comeuppance" in the two stories is a measure of their relative subtlety. In "William Wilson," poetic justice is clear if not profound: He slew his conscience and thus himself. Poe clearly emphasizes an allegorical understanding, and his story serves that purpose admirably well. In "The Cask of Amontillado," the same idea is intimated, but much more ambiguously and with formidable qualifications that make its meaning less easily satisfying. That is, though a reader may discern significant chinks in Montresor's armor, the armor remains—for a lifetime, he tells us. The armor represents a powerful lie, and it is important not to underestimate its power. Its felt presence stands in defiance of any mere allegorical, or purely intellectual, understanding. It is disturbing, it sustains the muted horror of this story, and is not as easily dismissed, I think, as in James Gargano's formulation: "With a specious intellectuality, common to Poe's violent men, Montresor seeks to escape from his own limitations by imagining them as imposed upon him from beyond the personality by outside force. But the force is a surrogate of the self, cozening [the] man toward damnation with all the brilliant intrigue Montresor uses in destroying Fortunato." All which I most potently believe, but I hold it not honesty to have it thus set down, as Hamlet replies to *his* own speech. In the "damnation" of the criminal Montresor, I believe, in theory. Theological grounds being what they are not these days, I might make the case in the good humanistic tradition Gargano espouses. To gain precision and authority, I might go further to document, on psychoanalytic grounds, the suffering that must lie at the heart of "the compulsion neurotic." (I think that is the correct classification.) But, alas, these are general and even problematic premises; they do inform my understanding of Poe's story, but they tend to pale before the immediacy of Montresor's defiant evil. The truth of the story, its meaning, must acknowledge that dilemma of the reader—unless, of course, as is common, we want merely to use the story as "case" to illustrate doctrine. The slow horror of the story rests ultimately on the reader's ambivalent wish-belief that Montresor did indeed triumph, that he did indeed sin with impunity: that he *did* slay his conscience. When Poe had Montresor address his story to "you, who so well know the nature of soul,"—alluding perhaps to the *reader's* role as ironic double—I do not think he intended an easy irony.

Poe and Tradition

Brian M. Barbour

When Poe began as a creative artist in the late 1820s, there was no living American literary tradition for him to inherit. This is why scholars as diverse as Campbell and Davidson, seeking to reverse Baudelaire's ahistorical impetus, have turned inevitably to Coleridge in an effort to link Poe to the ideas of his time. There is nothing factitious about this as there was, perhaps, about Marshall McLuhan's effort thirty years ago to relate Poe to a Ciceronian ideal in the South: Coleridge had the most seminal mind of his century and Poe, particularly (but not exclusively) in his criticism, consciously adapted himself to the greater figure. But writers inherit more than just other writers, and Malraux's well-known dictum to the effect that it is the beautiful painting not the beautiful smile that inspires the artist is no more than a half-truth, good for the beginner without question but inapposite to the mature artist whose work grows out of, even as it seeks to correct, the life around him. L. C. Knights put it this way: "Now the possibilities of living at any moment are not merely an individual matter; they depend on physical circumstances and (what is less of a commonplace) on current habits of thought and feeling, on all that is implied by 'tradition'—or the lack of it." As applied to Poe, this sense of tradition—current habits of thought and feeling and their related values and ideals—is both wider and more exclusive than the conventional sense: wider because literature is only part of social experience, more exclusive because its focus will be primarily American.

From *The Southern Literary Journal* 10, no. 2 (Spring 1978). © 1978 by the Department of English of the University of North Carolina at Chapel Hill.

Poe's creative years coincided with the Age of Jackson, and it was within and against that tradition that his own sensibility developed. As a gifted artist he was alive to its weaknesses and limitations and saw more clearly than most where it fostered and where it thwarted human possibility, including normal sympathetic existence. Values and ideals lie at the center of tradition. "The central value of American culture in the early nineteenth century," John William Ward has argued, was "the assertion of the worth of the totally liberated, atomistic, autonomous individual." The strongest tradition shaping society, in other words, denied both the efficacy of tradition and the reality of society. If this was sometimes a paradox, the times had given it proof. The resulting tendency was to locate the experience of being in the exercise of the will; making straight the way was a certain utilitarian sense of mind, a kind of didactic rationalism that emphasized the immediate solving of practical problems and derided speculation. The drive was towards domination by the self rather than towards integration with other selves and the consequent modifications of ego-assertion. Means usurped ends and rather easily, for the moral consequences of the will-to-dominate of the autonomous self were kept conveniently obscure by the utilitarian theory of mind. It is against these features of the prevailing tradition that Poe needs to be seen. Lewis P. Simpson has shown that the search for an ideal literary *order,* growing out of his ever-projected magazine and exfoliating as an effective influence on American civilization, is the substratum underlying and unifying Poe's whole career. This vision, like his personal psychological experience, set him against any uncritical acceptance of the emerging ethos.

His most valuable stories *embody* a critique of this tradition. "The Purloined Letter," as we shall see, has a dialectical structure in which an outlook is criticized by means of a positive value actually present, but this is not Poe's customary method. His task was to show his society that its central values were not humanly adequate (or, at least, that they contained unsuspected dangerous consequences) and that its ordinary way of thinking kept this out of view. The consensus ran all the other way. In the practical and material realm what Ward calls the central value was well established, having received its classic expression in Franklin's *Autobiography.* Now in the spiritual and intellectual realm Emerson was striving to redefine the *opportunity* offered by the American experience, but with the same emphasis on the atomistic, autonomous self. As Professor Ward has noted, "No less than Jackson, . . . Emerson held a vision of the good society which had at its center the atomic individual, moving freely and without constraint through space and society, dependent upon nothing beyond his own personality and unaided self." The strongest moral voice within the culture was divided in its effect. Emerson was attacking American materialism, but he possessed no coherent social theory; by exalting atomism and individual will he unwittingly strengthened the development of society along lines in which materialism and will-to-dominate were increasingly normative and morally reputable. There was, in short, no effectively established critical position even identifying the fundamental problems. None, that is, outside the great fiction of the period, for the creators of Hurry Harry, Aylmer, Ahab, and Montresor were not deceived about the nature of the self-willing, means-obsessed, atomistic individual. But this fiction had not yet established itself as part of a tradition, for Americans were not yet sophisticated enough to see that profound moral insight was available in "stories."

What habits of thought and feeling would the emerging tradition engender? What were its consequences, beyond the immediate, for human life? Poe's basic technique arose as a way of exploring this tradition without having a recognized countertradition to invoke. It has to be said that the strangeness of his tales often mitigated their intended moral effect, although this was intended to provide a certain stark clarity. His most characteristic tales embody the central value of the self-willing, atomistic, autonomous individual, but they wrench us out of the lenitive atmosphere of American optimism to focus our attention on narrators whose willfulness expresses deep disorder within. We are obliged to see the moral consequences, the dark, hidden possibilities in what we believe. They force us to live through a world empty of nourishing relationships where characters exist in an atomistic void, condemned to the resources of their autonomous selves, a world in which no one is recognized as a person. Two steady, interdependent criticisms are brought to bear: the tradition frustrates the person's growth to wholeness, even leaving, in the emphasis on domination as opposed to integration, a basic and dangerous confusion over what it means to be human; and the utilitarian habits of mind keep this growth obscured, unfelt, and unprepared for. . . .

We are faced with an embarrassment of riches. To fully analyze Poe's finest stories along the lines I have been indicating would extend this paper to Gibbonian lengths. For convenience, therefore, I would like to concentrate on four tales, examining them in some detail; two—"The Purloined Letter" and "The Fall of the House of Usher"—convey Poe's analysis of the American mind, and two—"The Cask of Amontillado" and "Ligeia"—

display his insight into the will-to-dominate of the autonomous individual and its destructive consequences. Before proceeding, however, a word about the narrators. "The Purloined Letter" is unusual not only for its dialectic but also because the narrator is not the real subject. The most liberating moment in the history of Poe studies came when James Gargano demonstrated conclusively that Poe "often so designs his tales so as to show his narrators' limited comprehension of their own problems and states of mind; the structure of many of Poe's stories clearly reveals an ironical and comprehensive intelligence critically and artistically ordering events so as to establish a vision of life and character which the narrator's very inadequacies help to 'prove.' " The popular view of Poe as the exotic creator of *frisson* identified him with his narrators, but in fact the tales are, so to speak, told against them. This accounts for the wide diversity of styles, for he invented ways to convincingly communicate the feel of a variety of psychic disorders. And the function of the ironic structure is to open a moral perspective upon the experience.

"The Purloined Letter" is the last of those three tales—"The Murders in the Rue Morgue" and "The Mystery of Marie Roget" are the others—in which Poe is commonly recognized to have invented detective fiction. Holmes liked to point it out to Dr. Watson as a salutary lesson, and the argument that they two descend from Dupin and Poe's narrator—that the basic elements and configuration of the genre sprang Minerva-like from his head—is a familiar one. These tales are ordinarily called "ratiocinative," but the term is misleading inasmuch as it suggests that what is of greatest importance is a method of Holmes-like deduction whereby Dupin outwits the Minister D——. That piece of detection largely serves as a framework within which Poe can explore the question, What constitutes real intelligence?

Like many of the Romantics, Poe brought into literature a new interest in the workings of the human mind. So strong was this that it made him proof against one of the weaker Romantic tendencies, that towards Primitivism. "The theorizers on Government," he said, with the Contractarian philosophers apparently in view, "who pretend always to 'begin with the beginning,' commence with Man in what they call his *natural* state—the savage. What right have they to suppose this his natural state? Man's chief idiosyncrasy being reason, it follows that his savage condition—his condition of action *without* reason—is his *un*natural state." Like Blake, Poe assimilated Rousseau to Locke as retrograde powers. Locke of course was "America's philosopher" and his view of the mind, filtered through Reid, Stewart, and the Scottish Common Sense school, was dominant in Poe's day. Though Locke is, properly speaking, an empiricist, his immensely influential theory of knowledge . . . had become increasingly identified during the course of the eighteenth century with purely natural and rationalistic ways of thinking. Locke conceived of the mind as a blank page on which ideas of the external world were inscribed through the senses, or as a kind of mechanical organizer of sensations which were fed to it by "experience." *This view appeared very well suited to explain the processes of scientific classification* and experiment or the formation of common-sense judgements on practical matters, *but it tended to create the assumptions that only the physical, the tangible, the measurable were real,* and that consciousness was a prisoner of the senses [italics mine].

To anyone concerned with introspection and the primacy of the mind's own powers, Locke was the enemy.

In America, this diagnosis and the consequent revolt are identified with the Transcendentalists. Using James Marsh's edition (1829) of Coleridge's *Aids to Reflection,* the American Transcendentalists took over the distinction between Reason and Understanding, but they gave it a quite un-Coleridgean emphasis, an emphasis which "The Purloined Letter" shows Poe rejected. For Coleridge, with his lifelong search for unity, Reason and Understanding were complementary powers of the mind, each valuable in its own sphere which corresponded roughly to the moral and the practical. Pure Reason, for example, had no place in politics where it could only result in Jacobinism. But the moral life depended on the promptings of an intuition lying deeper than the Understanding. With the American Transcendentalists this distinction tended to harden into a frozen posture. Reason became an honorific power whose twofold purpose was to communicate with the Over-Soul and to dishonor the "sensual" Understanding. Coleridge valued the Understanding on its own terms. He rejected Godwin because he saw that "philanthropy" can't be achieved if the "homeborn" elements that insure life's continuity and allow virtue to develop—the family, for instance—are done away with. The Transcendentalists, however, were not looking for a means to *explore* reality in its various dimensions; they wanted a means to *discredit* the "sensual" Understanding. As an independent realm, to be valued for what it was, they had no interest in it. Intelligence here comes dangerously close to being freed (ambiguous word) from common experience.

In "Sonnet—To Science" we see the young Poe similarly solve the problem of the prevailing rationalistic outlook by simply rejecting it. In "The Purloined Letter," however, he tries to discern the limits of this outlook and show why it is inadequate as an account of intelligence. The interplay between the mind, the body, and experience suggests a viewpoint similar to Coleridge's and implicitly criticizes Transcendentalism. It will be recalled that the story falls into three parts. In the first G—— comes to Dupin's rooms, relates the problem, and details the steps he has already taken. Dupin listens and gives his ironic advice: "Make a thorough research of the premises." The story turns on the different ways *thorough* is understood. The second is quite short. A month has passed when G—— returns still baffled. He says he is willing to pay a reward of fifty thousand francs for the letter, whereupon Dupin tells him to draw up his cheque and produces the letter. G—— leaves and Dupin enters into a somewhat long-winded "explanation," most of which is concerned with G——'s failure as a "reasoner"; only the last couple of paragraphs treat the action by which Dupin foils D—— and recovers the letter. The interest centers in the explanation.

Why does G—— fail as a reasoner? Calling him "a functionary," Dupin says, "the remote source of his defeat lies in the supposition that the Minister is a fool, because he has acquired renown as a poet." And speaking of D——, he adds, "As poet *and* mathematician, he would reason well; as mere mathematician he could not have reasoned at all."

Clearly, the prevailing rationalistic outlook dominant in America is being criticized. Poe uses narration and dialogue to point up the restless energy of the superficial "functionary," and he contrasts this busyness with the calmer, more attractive rhythm of the reflective Dupin. Out of this comes their contrasting attitudes towards poetry. Dupin has been "guilty of certain doggerel" himself, while for G—— anyone whose interests lie that way is a "fool." Poetry, as the story reveals, though not to G——, is a form of knowledge, the necessary complement, intuitive and tending to the concrete, to mathematics, rational and tending to the abstract. As Dupin argues, both are necessary in a mutually fertilizing relationship before there is full intelligence. The rational principle cannot be divorced from intuitive perception without running the risk of reducing itself to mere cleverness. Or, we might say, a people that has no way of valuing poetry is committed to very limited ways of knowing.

G—— is committed to his "microscope"; and with this goes a certain hubris: " 'The thing is *so* plain. There is a certain amount of bulk—a space—to be accounted for in every cabinet. Then we have accurate rules. The fiftieth part of a line could not escape us.' " But somehow the letter does, ironically defining the limits of this way of thinking about the world. " 'Then we examined the house itself. We divided the entire surface into compartments, which we numbered, so that none might be missed; then we scrutinized each individual square inch throughout the premises, including the two houses immediately adjoining, with the microscope, as before.' " That "two adjoining houses" is a nice comic touch, redoubled energy serving for the lack of insight. " 'But,' " asks Dupin later, with delighted scorn, " 'what is all this boring, and probing, and sounding, and scrutinizing with the microscope, and dividing the surface of the building into registered square inches?' " Our question might well be, Why does Poe call it a microscope? He doesn't mean the familiar compound microscope, he means a magnifying glass; the thing was known and the term was present in the language for him to use (the *OED* gives 1665 for its first citation). Dupin points out that all G—— can do in an unprecedented situation is extrapolate his method, which brings more and more of the tangible (like the two adjoining houses) under review. Poe calls the glass a microscope because he wants, through this linguistic extension, to identify G——'s method with that of scientific rationalism. This outlook, as Hochfield says, "tended to create the assumptions that only the physical, the tangible, the measurable were real." The story undermines these assumptions. The immaterial or spiritual, it argues, is not only real but primary.

Dupin is a poet and the story contrasts his mode of intelligence, the imagination, with G——'s. The use of the "microscope" entails a loss of perspective, a loss, that is, of wholeness of vision. G—— is committed to a reality that is measurable only, the surface of things. The tales's central irony is that even there he cannot locate the letter, for *seeing* in this sense depends on a prior act of mind. He is cut off, in Coleridge's well-known words, from "that deep Thinking . . . attainable only by a man of deep Feeling" and locked into a Newtonian system where mind "is always passive—a lazy Looker-on on an external world." Poetry or the imagination is contrasted with the microscope; the latter divides while the former unifies. And the corresponding unity of the self in the act of knowing is its strength (just as its absence is Dupin's warrant for calling G—— "a functionary"). Poe points out the limits of the dominant American mode of thought, but he also criticizes the orthodox alternative. For Dupin is no Transcendentalist, using Reason to discredit the "sensual" Understanding, finding satisfaction in inverting the dominant view. Intelligence, properly understood, is not detached intellect; it is rooted in the life of the body and is a function of the whole person. When the tale opens Dupin and the narrator are sitting in the darkness "enjoying the twofold luxury of meditation and a meerschaum," and it is through this perspective that everything subsequent is to be seen and judged. "The high perception," as Melville was afterwards to put it, is here wedded to "the low enjoying power." Thought (or meditation: the stress falls on that ingathering that must precede activity) is from the outset of this exploration into the makeup of real intelligence intimately linked with feeling (evoked by the meerschaum), and where there is this copresence even the darkness is not prohibitive.

Poe's criticism of the impoverished sense of mind dominant in utilitarian America is not merely negative; it proceeds from a human center. American thought has customarily oscillated between unleavened materialism and unrooted idealism; but Poe's groundwork is the wholeness of the person operating through the unifying activity of the imagination. It will be useful to keep this in mind when we come to stories more wholly negative in their critique.

Poe feels disdain for the aggressive didactic rationalism of G—— but reaches a different evaluation of the narrator of "The Fall of the House of Usher" who also embodies an essential American attitude towards the mind. The distinction is a moral one, and it reminds us that Poe's social thought, *as realized in his fiction,* is more *ondoyant et divers* than the aristocratic haughtiness and contempt for the mob usually ascribed to him. Within the American tradition, from the White House down, there was widespread belief in the sufficiency of the common sense of the common man. Professor Ward has noted this paradox: "The rejection of training and experience . . . was an important aspect of nineteenth century American thought." The age was convinced that mental discipline was otiose, that real intelligence didn't need formal training, that the mind's inherent powers were adequate to any situation. Underlying this was the assumption, given spurious legitimacy by the Declaration of Independence, that the most important truths were self-evident; and the phrase "common-sense" had received a sort of sanctity from its Revolutionary association. This outlook was of course necessary for belief in the autonomous self. What Poe saw were its limitations, that in most important matters there are qualifications that can only be gained by discipline and experience, developing natural aptitude. What Lionel Trilling once called "the general import" of "The Rime of the Ancient Mariner" applies *mutatis mutandis* to "Usher"; "The world is a complex and unexpected and terrible place which is not always to be understood by the mind as we use it in our everyday tasks."

"What ails Roderick Usher?" Roy Male has asked. "That is the central question of the story." And Darrel Abel in his well-known essay adheres to this emphasis: "Five persons figure in the tale, but the interest centers exclusively in one—Roderick Usher. The narrator is uncharacterized, undescribed, even unnamed." But as usual in Poe the interest lies with the narrator. In this case he embodies the American belief in common sense, but he is taken out of the plain and simple world where this view holds easy sway and he is tested by more severe events. To focus on Roderick, fascinating as he is, is to finesse Poe's intention and meaning. And Professor Abel seems misleading when he says the narrator is uncharacterized. The opposite is true, and this characterization is a basic element in the tale.

Poe uses tone and statement to establish the narrator as the ordinary man of common sense. He is not unattractive. We see evidence of charity in his response to Usher's letter, and he has none of the hubris of Poe's swollen rationalists. But he accepts as axiomatic the adequacy of the untutored intelligence. The tale presents us with a mind incapable of the development necessary even for its own preservation. Consider the opening paragraph from the point where he first sees "the melancholy House of Usher":

> I know not how it was—but, with the first glimpse of the building, a sense of insufferable gloom pervaded my spirit. I say insufferable; for the feeling was unrelieved by any of that half-pleasurable, because poetic, sentiment with which the mind usually receives even the sternest natural images of the desolate or terrible. I looked upon the scene before me—upon the mere house, and the simple landscape features of the domain—upon the bleak walls—upon the vacant eye-like windows—upon a few rank sedges—and upon a few white trunks of decayed trees—with an utter depression of soul which I can compare to no earthy sensation more properly than to the after-dream of the reveller upon opium—the bitter lapse into every-day life— the hideous dropping off of the veil. There was an iciness, a sinking, a sickening of the heart—an unredeemed dreariness of thought which no goading of the imagination could torture into aught of the sublime.

Roderick is not around—he doesn't enter until the eighth paragraph—so this is usually allowed to provide atmosphere. But that account is exiguous, for Poe's theme, method, and the basic configuration of the tale are all outlined here. The theme emerges from the dialectical interplay between his untutored common sense and the instreaming impressions which evade it. The method emphasizes his sturdy refusal to be affected by, or quite admit the reality of, phenomena that seem to lie outside the Newtonian framework until, at the end, he directly experiences what no common sense can ever explain, no science account for.

"I know not how it was," he begins and sets out to undo that initial bafflement. The third sentence ("I looked upon the scene before me") renders the movement of his mind and conveys the reasonable tone. His eye slowly scans the scene and particular images register one-by-one on his consciousness. The adjectives provide an interesting mix of the objective—mere, simple, few, white, decayed—and the subjective—bleak, vacant eye-like, rank—and this indicates the dialectical interplay. The sentence movement is extraordinarily slow and clogged; words are used in combinations the tongue and lips find awkward to make in passing over from one word to the next, giving the effect of great intellectual effort, of a mind puzzled by what lies before it and pondering each successive image in hopes of making a breakthrough. This sense of a search for order (the probable sense of *poetic*) is enriched by the anaphora, which in another context might have seemed frenetic. And this is furthered by the succeeding sentence with its series of false starts ("there was an iciness, a sinking, a sickening"), implying the mind's reaching for and discarding in turn analogies which might generate understanding.

The effort fails. But he is not particularly disturbed, and the paragraph pivots, so to speak: "What was it—I paused to think—what was it that so unnerved me in the contemplation of the House of Usher?" *Think* here means something like "set up a chain of reasoning"—since the preceding perceptions have not arranged themselves into any sort of order—and it is in tension with *unnerved,* which the voice naturally stresses. "It was a mystery all insoluble; nor could I grapple with the shadowy fancies that crowded upon me as I pondered." The flat monotone smothers any concitation; whatever he might say, it is clear that he does not feel the experience as a mystery. And how much of the story is focused by that playing off of *grapple* (with its physical associations) and *fancies* (the word itself slightly dismissive)! Poe shows how the mind further smothers those "crowding fancies" by means of language which is highly abstract and undefining: "I was forced to fall back upon the unsatisfactory conclusion, that while, beyond doubt, there are combinations of very simple natural objects which have the power of thus affecting us, still the analysis of this power lies among considerations beyond our depth." How easily that is said! The undisturbed tone, his chief characteristic, continues to the end of the paragraph. But as the proleptic *mere* gives way to the experienced *shudder* after he looks into the tarn, we have the basic configuration outlined (and the ending adumbrated):

It was possible, I reflected, that a mere different arrangement of
the particulars of the scene, of the details of the picture, would
be sufficient to modify, or perhaps to annihilate its capacity for
sorrowful impressions; and, acting upon this idea, I reined my
horse to the precipitous brink of a black and lurid tarn that lay
in unruffled lustre by the dwelling, and gazed down—but with
a shudder even more thrilling than before—upon the remodelled
and inverted images of the gray sedge, and the ghastly tree-
stems, and the vacant and eye-like windows.

The next paragraph begins with a casually thrown off "Nevertheless."
Nothing is going to ruffle him, but it is clear that his apparent calm is not
the expression of a firm inner poise. The rest of the tale develops this theme.
The narrator's tone never changes no matter how hard he has to strain to
account for phenomena, and this is the key to the tale as a whole. It indicates
the strength of his need to domesticate the experience and keep up the
illusion that everything is explicable within the general Newtonian framework. His untutored common sense, lacking internal discipline, is unable
to develop with the developing experience, and he has no other defense.

As the tale progresses, the narrator crosses the causeway, enters the
house, goes deep within it to Usher's chamber, and finally—in the widely
recognized analogy between House and head or brain—finds himself drawn
into the recesses of Usher's mind: "It was no wonder that his condition
terrified—that it infected me. I felt creeping upon me, by slow yet certain
degrees, the wild influence of his own fantastic yet impressive supersti-
tions." The *OED* gives "doorkeeper" for its first definition of *usher,* and
Poe calls attention to the word in this sense: "The valet now threw open
a door and ushered me into the presence of his master." This is a threshold
world: having crossed the causeway the narrator leaves behind him the
straightforward world of common sense; Usher opens the door on things
undreamt of in the philosophies of, say, Benjamin Franklin and Ralph Waldo
Emerson. The narrator's way of handling this unlooked for experience
varies no more than his tone; the tone in fact is a function of a broader
technique. From first to last he steadies himself by disclaimers, rational
"explanations" of discordant phenomena, the cumulative effect of which
is simply to undermine common sense and authenticate the experienced
actuality of the final, inexplicable event. They cluster around three moments: the opening when he is trying to stave off his uneasiness, the middle
when Usher recites "The Haunted Palace," and the end when he desperately
casts about for ways to deny that what is happening can be. It would not

be convenient to quote them all and in full context, but perhaps a sampling from the first cluster will suggest their quality. Tone as always is important; sometimes it's only a matter of a strategic "but":

> There can be no doubt that the consciousness of the rapid increase of my superstition—for why should I not so term it?

> And it might have been for this reason only.

> There grew in my mind a strange fancy—a fancy so ridiculous, indeed, that I but mention it to show the vivid force of sensations that oppressed me.

> Shaking off from my spirit what *must* have been a dream.

And so on, right down to his assigning "the work of the rushing gust" for the final opening of the door by Madeline before she crosses the ultimate threshold. We notice, however, a progressive straining in these disclaimers, seen in the emphasis given to that last *must,* with its perceptible opening of doubt.

The tension he is under is nicely realized in the long paragraph that follows Usher's recitation of his poem:

> I well remember that suggestions arising from this ballad led us into a train of thought wherein there became manifest an opinion of Usher's *which I mention not so much on account of its novelty* (for other men have thought thus), *as an account of the pertinacity with which he maintained it.* This opinion, in its general form, was that of the sentience of all vegetable things. But in his disordered fancy, the idea had assumed a more daring character, and trespassed, under certain conditions, upon the kingdom of inorganization. I lack words to express the full extent, or the earnest abandon of his persuasion. The belief, however, was connected (as I have previously hinted) with the gray stones of the home of his forefathers. The conditions of the sentience had been here, he imagined, fulfilled, in the method of collocation of these stones—in the order of their arrangement, as well as in the many fungi which overspread them, and of the decayed trees which stood around—above all, in the long undisturbed endurance of this arrangement, and in its reduplication in the still waters of the tarn. Its evidence—the evidence of the sentience—was to be seen, he said (and here I started as he spoke), in the gradual yet certain condensation of an atmosphere of their own about the

waters and the walls. The result was discoverable, he added, in that silent yet importunate and terrible influence which for centuries had moulded the destinies of his family, and which made him what I now saw him—what he was. *Such opinions need no comment, and I will make none* [italics mine].

In the paragraph a marked shift occurs. The first disclaimer is routinely made. By the end he has reached, for the only time in the tale, scorn. Why? Notice the way the third sentence from the end begins: "Its evidence—the evidence of the sentience—was to be seen, he said (and here I started as he spoke)." The key here is the phrase inside the dashes, for it gives the effect of a mind suddenly growing alert to itself and realizing what is implied by that pronoun, the intimacy with Usher's beliefs that it insinuates. The effect is a delicate one, but it seems to indicate a sudden anxious rejection of a half-acceptance of what has been said in the previous sentence. The mind, braced now and solicitous to vindicate itself, impels him to "start" as Usher continues. The closing scorn is the self-conscious expression of the alerted and braced mind. But in the whole movement across the paragraph we have an indication of the strain under which he is operating. What we are seeing, in other words, is a variety of forms of resistance, but no growth.

As the story continues his grasp weakens. He loses any precise sense of calendar time and his disclaimers grow increasingly forced. Finally the last door is opened and common sense is utterly routed. Madeline stands "without the door"; when she crosses the threshold it is to bring death. Two possibilities lie open, death or flight, and, by instinct deeper than common sense, he flies. Life is not defeated, but a certain way of regarding it most certainly is.

Poe presents two aspects of the view of mind dominant in the American tradition, neither of them adequate. Real intelligence, we see, is a matter of sensibility and it has to be able to develop from within the new and unprecedented, not restrict itself to the already known and charted. The moral dimension of Poe's art is not always recognized, but it is there. He holds no animus against the common man clinging to his common sense; he feels a certain sympathy for one whose tradition is so limited and, in the end, dangerous. But he does hold an animus against the theoretician of didactic rationalism whose arguments have determined what the common man has available to him, and who has wrongfully denied life in its depths. This moves in another direction, for such denial has important moral consequences. The American experience had given unprecedented scope to individual will: this could become unrestricted will-to-dominate when it disregarded life's moral complexity and was not controlled from below by a reverence for the mystery of the person.

The American tradition forced on Poe (as on Hawthorne and Melville) his great theme, the will-to-dominate, which is to say the will without this control operating from below and the ideal of the atomistic society forbidding rigorous control from outside. In Buber's familiar terms, the world of *It* displaced the world of *Thou,* manipulation prevailing over meeting and relationship. Poe emphasizes the cost. Other persons become looked upon not as beings to whom we are spiritually bound, but as mere objects in the external world, in short, as part of nature. The centrifugal impulse of society helped keep this obscure, but Poe seized on the hidden implications of this outlook and revealed them with prophetic insight. The will-to-dominate is, for Poe, always pathological and destructive no matter in what temperament it is expressed, and he is as quick to explore the consequences of Romantic will as of the rational didactic. The ironic structure and moral focus are turned on the narrators, romantic or rationalist, and the destructive possibilities of ideals too easily believed in are revealed.

"The Cask of Amontillado" presents a rationalist. It is a late work (1846), but it is for its clarity of development that one is tempted to call it the tale towards which all the others tended. Every word goes to characterize the narrator and at the same time to place him by moral standards of which he is insensible. The shaping irony lies in the fact that his rationalistic outlook is turned on events of a religious, indeed eschatalogical, nature. The time scheme and setting quietly enforce this. The affair with Fortunato lies fifty years in the past. Montresor was then on the bitter side of some disappointment, so he must be well into his eighties and near death as he relates his story to his Confessor ("You who so well know the nature of my soul"). Against this situation Poe rubs both Montresor's story and the attitude he takes in telling it. Like the biblical fool, in his heart he does not fear God.

He is a man obsessed with his own cleverness. In his narrative he takes particular delight in this cleverness, but, unawares, reveals its terrifying human emptiness. The carnival "madness," for example, and Fortunato tricked out in motley initially emphasize, by contrast, his cool reason. And from the first we see him plume himself on his discipline. He is a connoisseur, and his study is himself: "It must be understood, that neither by word nor deed had I given Fortunato cause to doubt my good-will. I continued, as was my wont, to smile in his face, and he did not perceive that my smile *now* was at the thought of his immolation." His view of human nature is of that type of reductive cynicism that usually goes by the name realist: "There were no attendants at home; they had absconded to make merry in honor of the time. I had told them that I should not return until the morning, and had given them explicit orders not to stir from the house. These orders were sufficient, I well knew, to insure their immediate disappearance, one and all, as soon as my back was turned." He finds something exquisite in permitting Fortunato to insist that they go on to the vaults: "Putting on a mask of black silk, and drawing a *roquelaire* closely about me, I suffered him to hurry me to my palazzo." He takes vulpine pleasure in his knowledge of what lies in wait:

> "Enough," he said, "the cough is a mere nothing; it will not
> kill me. I shall not die of a cough."
> "True—true," I replied.

And his wit enables him to triumph even over the unexpected as when Fortunato gives him a sign from freemasonry and he pulls a trowel out from within his cloak. This sense of self is obdurate and proof against *any* appeal:

> "*For the love of God, Montresor!*"
> "Yes," I said, "for the love of God!"

Against this, however, are two moments of inciting or prompting, their strength suggested by their being involuntary and physiological, life from out the depths protesting what the conscious mind is leading on to. These must be quelled and explained away, the grip of the rational mind reinstated. The first comes after the laying of the seventh tier. A period of silence has gone by and Montresor is curious about Fortunato's condition. He holds the torch above the opening and tries to see in: "A succession of loud and shrill screams, bursting suddenly from the throat of the chained form, seemed to thrust me violently back." Though he has consciously desired this, something in him profoundly recoils: "For a brief moment I hesitated—I trembled. Unsheathing my rapier, I began to grope with it about the recess." This, I think, is a fine psychological detail. He is using the rapier to probe the dark, fearful interior; "grope" conveys just the right sense of loss of control: "but the thought of an instant reassured me. I placed my hand upon the solid fabric of the catacombs, and felt satisfied." Here is the essence of his case. There is only the material world, the solid fabric, after all, safely there to the touch. He is restored.

The second comes in the final paragraph. No sound has succeeded his blasphemy about the love of God. Again he tries to get the torch to where he can still see in; he drops it through the tiny remaining hole and it hits the ground: "There came forth in return only a jingling of the bells." A human being has been reduced beyond language to the uncoordinated twitchings of a nervous system: "My heart grew sick—." The inciting is clear, direct—and explained away: "on account of the dampness of the catacombs." There is only the material world. Nothing else is real.

Montresor is characterized by his rationalistic outlook and haughty pride in himself. "Insult," we learn in the opening paragraph, he is far less able to bear than "injury." And it is a further point of this sense of honor that "the avenger" should "make himself felt as such to him who has done the wrong." What he wants is a certain type of feeling, a feeling of domination. This is conveyed in the paragraph that precedes the fearful moment when he is forced to draw his rapier. Soon after beginning the wall he senses, with pleasure, that Fortunato's intoxication—a barrier keeping back full recognition of his plight—has worn off: "The earliest indication I had of this was a low moaning cry from the depth of the recess. It was *not* the cry of a drunken man. There was then a long and obstinate silence. I laid the second tier, and the third, and the fourth; and then I heard the furious vibrations of the chain. The noise lasted for several minutes, during which, that I might harken to it with more satisfaction, I ceased my labors and sat down upon the bones." *Obstinate* is the key word. It indicates how badly Montresor wants to directly experience Fortunato's despair and take from that his *satisfaction*.

He is telling this as a last confession, and the irony is generated by the contrast between his rationalism pridefully centered on himself and the eschatalogical threshold he stands on. He does not feel contrition (without which there is no remission of sin) nor grasp the moral dimension of his story. For him its meaning is clear: he has had his vengeance, wreaked his will upon his enemy. The final sentence evokes his pride in his wit: "*In pace requiescat!*" "May he rest in peace!" The phrase inverts an ancient liturgical formula (just as the opening sentence inverts a proverb); in doing so it completes Poe's meaning. The Latin Mass said in Poe's time ordinarily ended with the priest turning to the congregation and giving it his parting blessing, followed by the words, "*Ite missa est*"— "Go, the mass is ended." The only exception was the Mass for the Dead. In this there was no blessing; the priest simply turned and expressed the hope of the faithful: "*Requiescat in pace.*" Montresor's words are reflexive in their meaning, a point Poe underscores by inverting them. The ending cooperates in the placing of his moral obtuseness; it is he who has been dead in his humanity these fifty years.

Though there are still those who cherish the belief that "Ligeia" is about a woman who comes back from the dead through the agency of her will and another woman's body, the interpretation first developed by Roy P. Basler makes a response relevant to what Poe is offering. "Ligeia" shows "the power of frustrate love to create an erotic symbolism and mythology in compensation for sensual disappointment." There is of course no Ligeia; she is wholly the creation of the narrator's fantasy, the product of an erotomania rooted, I would guess, in a habit of masturbation. The account given by Joel Porte is more or less accurate, but his judgment—"The vitality of the world of dreams is the true underlying theme"—is quite wrong, if only by one word. It is the power, not the vitality, of the world of dreams that is demonstrated, for the theme has to do with the way a diseased fantasy is the enemy of life. Like Monstresor, the narrator here works his will upon another human being without any feeling for what he is doing; he is incapable of any living response to the individual and unique.

W. H. Auden has said somewhere that the tendency of the Romantic hero was to want to be God, and this story provides a case where the generalization actually applies. The story is quite simple and has a simple structure; there is a Ligeia-half and a Rowena-half. The first part is a fantasy; in the second part fantasy impinges on the real world with terrifying results. Poe uses the dark-heroine / light-heroine contrast and a marked shift in style to help establish the differences. The narrator, through Ligeia, experiences himself as worshipped ("idolatry" is a conspicuous word whenever his attention is directed towards her) in and through sexual passion. His response, in his throes, is to believe himself coming close to some ultimate knowledge, only to lose it. This knowledge is occasioned by Ligeia's eyes in moments of intense passion (Poe's pun could hardly be more pointed), and it called a "sentiment" which he "feels." The key to the tale is the quote from Glanvill used as its epigraph. This is introduced by the narrator, not Ligeia, and he avers that it "never failed to inspire me with the sentiment": " 'And the will therein lieth, which dieth not. Who knoweth the mysteries of the will with its vigor? For God is but a great will pervading all things by nature of its intentness. Man doth not yield himself to the angels, nor unto death utterly, save only through the weakness of his feeble will.' " The will which operates is his, though he wants us to believe it is hers. If Ligeia, being all that she is, worships him, what must he be? And she will come back from the dead to go on worshipping him!

In the second half the narrator marries the real person, Lady Rowena Travanion of Tremaine, probably thinking his sexual fantasies can be realized in the world of actual experience. The marriage chamber, at any rate, is arranged to that end:

> But in the draping of the apartment lay, alas! the chief phantasy
> of all. . . . The material was the richest cloth of gold. It was
> spotted all over, at irregular intervals, with arabesque figures,
> about a foot in diameter, and wrought upon the cloth in patterns
> of the most jetty black. But these figures partook of the true
> character of the arabesque only when regarded from a single
> point of view. By a contrivance now common, and indeed trace-
> able to a very remote period of antiquity, they were made
> changeable in aspect. To one entering the room, they bore the
> appearance of simple monstrosities; but upon a farther advance,
> this appearance gradually departed; and step by step, as the vis-
> itor moved his station in the chamber, he saw himself surrounded
> by an endless succession of the ghastly forms which belong to
> the superstition of the Norman, or arise in the guilty slumbers
> of the monk. The phantasmagoric effect was vastly heightened
> by the artificial introduction of a strong continual current of
> wind behind the draperies—giving a hideous and uneasy ani-
> mation to the whole.

What this seems to mean is that the draperies were decorated with figures
that were lewd and which, by the air-current device, could be animated so
as to become pornographic. Rowena recoils from her fate, but he finds a
temporary pleasure in sexual cruelty: "That my wife dreaded the fierce
moodiness of my temper—that she shunned me and loved me but little—
I could not help perceiving; but it gave me rather pleasure than otherwise.
I loathed her with a hatred belonging more to demon than to man." She
experiences deep psychological anguish, while he finds himself reverting
more and more to the fantast's world where the will meets no resistances.
After a period she begins to decline physically—everything in this world
is destructive of vitality—and he poisons her to hasten her along. His desire
is to experience the climactic triumph of his fantasy. And so in the famous
final paragraph he believes Ligeia is coming back through Rowena's corpse
to continue her idolatry to him.

Poe's theme is a moral one: the triumph of fantasy is destructive of
actual living with its demands. Rowena is not met with in the world of
relationship; she is used by the narrator for his enjoyment in the world
of *It*. Like Montresor, he is an imperious, autonomous self for whom others
are atomistic objects to be manipulated. For them the will is neither disciplined by a sense of complexity nor controlled from below by a feeling
for the mystery of the person. In each case this has consequences for the

body. Speaking of "the Romantic retreat from the physical," John Fraser has noted that "the body has been suspect much of the time in American literature, perhaps because it is the body that most ineluctably sets limits to individual human ambitions." These narrators, caught in the grip of a will-to-dominate, recognize no such limits while yet insisting on their own virtue. That situation mirrors in its way what has sometimes been called the irony of American history.

Poe's tales explore, as fiction can, the moral consequences of those ideals and values, and consequent habits of thought and feeling, that formed the American tradition. His limited but real achievement was to reveal, however obliquely, the human consequences of the tradition, to cut through the fogbank of optimism and insist on its destructive potential. Unlike Cooper, Hawthorne, and Melville, he saw little to celebrate in the American experience and his work is almost wholly negative in expression and impact. That is why, perhaps, he spent so much of himself, at the last, constructing the aesthetico-cosmology that arches back to the poetry of withdrawal of the Romantic anchorite. In the end he could not, alone, sustain the necessary tension. There is a sense in which American society defeated him. But not before he had taken its measure.

Poe: Writing and the Unconscious

Gregory S. Jay

> *Can the dispossession of consciousness to the profit of another home of meaning be understood as an act of reflection, as the first gesture of reappropriation?*
>
> RICOEUR, *Freud and Philosophy*

> *But human megalomania will have suffered its third and most wounding blow from the psychological research of the present time which seeks to prove to the ego that it is not even master of its own house, but must content itself with scanty information of what is going on unconsciously in its mind. We psychoanalysts were not the first and not the only ones to utter this call to introspection.*
>
> FREUD, *Introductory Lectures on Psychoanalysis*

> *But evil things, in robes of sorrow,*
> *Assailed the monarch's high estate . . .*
> *And, round about his home, the glory*
> *That blushed and bloomed*
> *Is but a dim-remembered story*
> *Of the old time entombed.*
>
> "The Haunted Palace"

Contemporary critical theory has most insistently haunted two related structures: Romantic literature since Blake, and philosophy after Locke. Some have argued that all "modern" writing should be defined by its response to the Romantics; in philosophy, most particularly on the Continent, it is Kant and Hegel who serve as the commanding centers from

From *The American Renaissance: New Dimensions* 28, no. 1 (1983). © 1983 by Associated University Presses, Inc.

which others try to depart. Thus we should not be surprised that post-structuralist criticism finds Edgar Allan Poe so amiable a subject, for Poe's chief struggle was his attempt to emerge, as a writer and a thinker, from the influential shadow cast by Romantic poetry and Idealist philosophy (German and American). With the aid of recent theorists, we may better understand what Edward H. Davidson asserted in his pioneering study: "that Poe was a 'crisis' in the Romantic and the symbolic imagination. He came near the end (if such directions have 'beginning' and 'end') of the idealist or Romantic expression and mind." But Davidson's formula sounds too passive, however fated Poe's inherited dilemmas may be. Though from "Tamerlane" to *Eureka* Poe's tests show a desire to recover the Ideal, the True, and the Beautiful, his stories and poems and essays constantly repeat a pattern of aggression against the Transcendental. The increasing number of confessional tales, in fact, suggests a compulsive need to confess a kind of "guilt" for the "murder" of what is elsewhere lamented as lost.

The mental flights, reflections, and ratiocinations of Poe's protagonists yield not only this guilt but a related dissolution of self and identity. The horrible results of Poe's ecstatic states upset the Romantic commonplace that proposes an access to the divine through abnormal states of consciousness. Often his narrators seem condemned by genealogy to extraordinary speculations. "I am," writes William Wilson (but which one?), "the descendent of a race whose imaginative and easily excitable temperament has at all times rendered them remarkable." In Wilson's case, introspection produces a doppelgänger who becomes a mortal antagonist. Murder or revenge is regularly carried out against doubles of the self in Poe ("Loss of Breath," "Metzengerstein," "The Tell-Tale Heart," "The Purloined Letter," "The Imp of the Perverse," "The Cask of Amontillado"), as well as against the bodies of those women conventionally symbolizing Sublime Knowledge. "The essential Poe fable," observes Michael Davitt Bell, "however elaborately the impulse may be displaced onto a double or a lover, is a tale of compulsive self-murder." Bell's interpretation of this "murder" as primarily a symbolic destruction of the sexual or sensual self, however, misses the important conjunction of sexuality, philosophy, and textuality in Poe's works.

The dethronement of the self's monarchy by the irruptions of buried passions does signify at the sexual level, to be sure; yet this upheaval represents at another level only one example of the general crisis of self and identity as philosophical concepts, or as viable notions for the writer. The Romantic/Hegelian/Transcendental placement of the self at the center of philosophy's union with Beauty, Spirit, or the Over-Soul makes of coherent personal identity a prerequisite to Truth itself. As the writer's character or identity, be he philosopher or poet, proceeds from that of the text, the Truth of writing becomes susceptible to a double assault. First, there are elements in the text that repeat those of other texts, thus threatening the dream of original identity (Poe's purloinings from other writers are notorious). This fear we find in Poe's obsessions with the burdens of family inheritance and the problems of discerning plagiarism, both of which raise questions about the relationships between creativity and repetition. Second, there are parts of the self that seem not its own, residing in an unconscious which, like Poe's many ancestral mansions, houses the decaying but persistent recollections of an influential past. To bemoan inheritance, rail against plagiarism, or entomb one's double is to seek an exclusion of the other who shadows identity. In so often exposing Truth as a deceptive effect of violence or revisionary experience, Poe finds (often in horror) that fissure which ultimately destroys the Romantic and Idealist structures of reflection he so perversely inhabits and haunts.

Whether "seriously" or "parodically," in "Ligeia" or "How to Write a Blackwood Article," Poe repeatedly employs the language, plots, symbols, and ideas that are his legacy from Gothic fiction, British poetry, and German metaphysics. To read Poe is to interpret the significance of his rearrangements of these family estates. They are undone from within, either by the return of the repressed other or by a hyperbolic mockery of the visionary's pretensions. In both his "arabesques" and "grotesques," Poe's method may aptly be compared to Jacques Derrida's definition of "deconstruction" as "inhabiting" structures "*in a certain way* . . . borrowing all the strategic and economic resources of subversion from the old structure." The subsequent reappropriation results, not in a new mastery of Truth (which is what Dupin would like us to believe), but in an edifying collapse of both terms in the dualism (true/false, construction/deconstruction, self/other, etc.). Like the "House of Usher" and its narrator, deconstructive reflection "always in a certain way falls prey to its own work."

This is to say that a deconstruction of Truth cannot itself be "true" in the old sense. It becomes rather, as in Poe's deployment of his literary borrowings, a rhetoric of signifying effects. Here we recall Poe's aesthetic principle that poetry "has no concern with Duty or with Truth." Without that concern, however, and the desires it engenders, Poe's work is inexplicable. He ceaselessly explores the imagination's power to know the "Supernal Loveliness." Poe's critique of Truth's place in the imagination's work displaces the center of Romantic and philosophical discourse, but strategically that displacement (or "murder") serves as prelude to the appearance of an idea of Beauty that functions in much the same structuring way as Truth once had. Yet Truth is not Beautiful in Poe, or vice versa. The insistent conclusion, contradicting the lingering transcendentalism of Poe's optative moods, is that the "death" of Truth which is the prerequisite of ideal beauty cannot be dialectically resolved. As Joseph N. Riddel has argued, the presence of Beauty remains contaminated by the confession of its fatal means of production. The same holds true for the identity of a self produced by the "murder" of the Other. In either case, we end up in a world where both truth and self are rhetorical effects, and, as such, vulnerable to the unsettlings of identity that language and interpretation always fall prey to.

I

Poe's journeys into the disestablishment of inherited constructs are subversive versions of standard Romantic themes. For his own purposes he took up the Romantic reaction against empiricism and "common sense" philosophy. In "How to Write a Blackwood Article," Blackwood advises the Signora Psyche Zenobia: "Be sure and abuse a man called Locke." Northrop Frye made "The Case against Locke" his opening explanation of Blake's romanticism, and Robert Langbaum begins with Wordsworth's reaction to Locke in his own fine account of literature and identity. The Romantic critique of rational reflection included a general, but variously imagined, substitution of perception for reasoning. Higher, even divine, truths might be approached by a visionary experience whose significant prerequisite is the initial dissolution or making-absent of mundane sensory realities. The list of such enabling experiences is lengthy, and most appear in Poe (e.g., childhood, drugs, dreams, liquor, art work, books, moonlight, remembrance, sleeplessness, mesmerism, sea voyages, madness). The exemplary passages are in Wordsworth, for there the distinct necessity of overthrowing the "absolute dominion" of the "bodily eye," and of replacing it with the creative "recollection," is most clearly articulated. When "the light of sense / Goes out," the "invisible world" stands revealed, though in an aspect more heartening than the terror-inspiring apparitions of the recalled Ligeia or Madeline Usher. Emerson gives the American version in *Nature*'s chapter on "Idealism," a text Poe could hardly not have read:

> If the Reason be stimulated to more earnest vision, outlines and surfaces become transparent, and are no longer seen; causes and spirits are seen through them. The best moments of life are these delicious awakenings of the higher powers, and the reverential withdrawing of nature before its God.

"As a matter of fact," wrote Hegel, "thinking is always the negation of what we have immediately before us."

The recurrent narrative pattern in Poe takes us along with a protagonist on just such an extraordinary voyage of visionary negation, borrowing this structure in a way usually both sympathetic to its aspirations and critical of its results. Example after example could be adduced to demonstrate how such arabesque *rites de passage* work in Poe, not simply as "excuses" for the "supernatural," but as critical variations wrought consciously on the tradition. Even Dupin's ratiocination, which in the trajectory of Poe's career is entertained as a possible substitute for and improvement on the visionary, becomes a double of hypnosis: "I cannot better explain my meaning," says Vankirk in "Mesmeric Revelation," speaking of his insights into God and immortality, "than by the hypothesis that the mesmeric exaltation enables me to perceive a train of ratiocination." In "The Imp of the Perverse," Poe drops such devices of artificial exaltation, positing our impulse to throw ourselves into the "abyss" as a fatal law of character admitting of "no intelligible principle." But such a defensive abstraction of motive comes late in the career, after countless passages like the following from "Berenice":

> My baptismal name is Egaeus; that of my family I will not mention. Yet there are no towers in the land more time-honored than my gloomy, gray, hereditary halls. Our line has been called a race of visionaries; and in many striking particulars—in the character of the family mansion—in the frescoes of the chief saloon—in the tapestries of the dormitories—in the chiselling of some buttresses in the armory—but more especially in the gallery of antique paintings—in the fashion of the library chamber— and, lastly, in the very peculiar nature of the library's contents, there is more than sufficient evidence to warrant the belief.
>
> The recollections of my earliest years are connected with that chamber, and with its volumes—of which latter I will say no more. Here died my mother. Herein was I born. . . . Thus awakening from the long night of what seemed, but was not, nonentity, at once into the very regions of fairy-land—into a palace of imagination—into the wild dominions of monastic thought and erudition—it is not singular that I gazed around me with a startled and ardent eye—that I loitered away my boyhood in books, and dissipated my youth in reverie; but it *is* singular that as years rolled away, and the noon of manhood found me

still in the mansion of my fathers—it *is* wonderful what stag-
nation there fell upon the springs of my life—wonderful how
total an inversion took place in the character of my commonest
thought. The realities of the world affected me as visions, and
as visions only, while the wild ideas of the land of dreams became, in turn,—not the material of my everyday existence—but
in very deed that existence utterly and solely in itself.

Like Usher and Dupin, Egaeus's home is the library. He is a place
where other writings meet, less a soul than an intertextual confluence. His
identity, and that of Poe's work, appears to be that of a shadow cast by
others. Egaeus's "anxiety of influence" (Harold Bloom's term) so holds
him that the "noon of manhood" finds him still in the mansion of his
forefathers, an edifice of historicism as well as textuality. The predicament
afflicts many of Poe's narrators, for the intertextuality of his creations necessarily involves the danger of unoriginality. The significant twist here is
in the result of Egaeus's "inversion" of "everyday existence." This making-
absent of the mundane world and its replacement with the "wild ideas of
the land of dreams" takes him backward into repeating the characteristics
of the past, and of his fathers. Poe draws a structural parallel between a
personal and a literary or cultural unconscious. Egaeus's "wild dreams"
will represent, in good Freudian fashion, the conflicts and desires of his
individual unconscious, thus disrupting his coherent identity with impulses
from elsewhere that he (the idea of the unified self) does not author. At
the level of writing or culture, we are likewise born into a context of
influences; when we come to consciousness of ourselves as individuals, we
do so always already through the categories and axioms we have inherited.
The poetic "anxiety of influence," so evident in Poe's Romantic protagonists
and in his own responses to Coleridge, Byron, Wordsworth, and Shelley,
is only a local manifestation of that general tension between traditions and
individual talents that shapes cultural history as a whole. Thus the "ancestral
mansions" and genealogical systems in Poe's work represent the machinery
of inheritance in the largest sense, and inform, as we shall later see, Poe's
dark criticism of the contemporary American rage for the idealism of literary
and national "self-reliance." Genealogy becomes the aptest structural metaphor because of its theoretical and historical strengths as a system for
denominating and regulating the passage of identity, authority, and property through the mutability of time. It is no accident that so many of Poe's
transcendental seekers of Truth are aristocrats. Poe's attraction to the hier-
archies of aristocracy is one with his temptation toward the Transcendental,

but both fall victim to the discovery of the work of the unconscious and the other, those bastards and outcasts whose exclusion enables the system, and who cannot forever be denied the recognition of their kinship.

Egaeus begins as a version of the "belated" Romantic mind. Berenice's disease (which like those afflicting his other heroines appears to result from no intelligible principle) coincides with a drastic change in his imagination, with ghoulish results. The distinction Egaeus uses to explain how he comes to rip the teeth from the prematurely buried Berenice concerns the difference between the "attentive" and the "speculative" imaginations. The latter he inherits; the former is the "disease" he falls into when Berenice grows ill. The "attentive" fixes on "frivolous" objects of contemplation, such as the "device on the margin, or in the typography of a book." His reveries sometimes involved the "frequent repetition" of a word until it ceased to convey any idea whatever ("Quoth the Raven, 'Nevermore' "?) He hopes to banish the words of the fathers and to transcend their influence. Berenice's fatal illness seems to cause Egaeus's mental derangement, or to enable his effort to dissolve everyday reality. In fact, his disease comes immediately after her spells of epilepsy, trancelike states resembling "positive dissolution" and ending in an abrupt return to life. The same pattern holds for the workings of the "attentive" faculty. Unlike the "speculative," it could not transcend objects, but "pertinaciously returning in upon the original objects as a centre," remained fixated to the world, the body of the other.

His previous attitude toward Berenice—"not as a being of the earth, earthy, but as the abstraction of such a being"—was a "speculation" now diseased by an interior malady, an irruption of the other within the self. For Egaeus, her illness is the insistent return of what had been repressed, her "earthy" self, and his own mortality. What drives him mad as he watches her die is "the singular and most appalling distortion of her personal identity." Thus the "death" of his betrothed occasions his ghastly attempt to assert her immortality by wresting her symbolically pure white teeth from the grave. The horrible paradox governing him is this: the desire for immortal identity runs into a fatal conflict with the immortal identities of others; to "murder" or "repress" those others in the service of one's own identity involves an intense attention to them as objects, and a repetition of them in reflection that subsequently leaves a resistent trace of the other in the dream of originality. Berenice's premature burial makes Egaeus's perverse attempt to transcend mutability possible, but her teeth remain signs both of the body and of Egaeus's own repressed fears. Her mouth signifies (as others have noted) a displaced *vagina dentata*. It resembles other "abysses" in Poe, a negative version of transcendental aspiration. The self leaps into an unconscious beyond that it cannot control, but which beckons with its secret script.

Poe's inquiry into the instability of personal identity shapes much of his work. A variety of topics serve as its vehicle, including metempsychosis, reincarnation, doppelgängers, and spiritual immortality. The interest is especially obvious and keen in the earlier tales and poems written most immediately under the influence of Poe's reading in Gothic fiction, British poetry, and Idealist philosophy. In "Morella," a tale of the transmigration of soul from mother to daughter, the narrator-husband-father tells us of Morella's "profound" "erudition" in the "mystical writings" of the "early German literature." Meeting her "by accident," his soul "burned with fires it had never before known; but the fires were not of Eros." He finds "tormenting" the "unusual meaning" and "vague intensity" of his passions. Since Poe's epigraph comes from Plato's *Symposium,* we can assume that "Eros" here means a sublimating Platonic love that leads to the Divine, and that the narrator begins by repressing the explicitly physical aspect of his attraction to Morella's person. But in his daughter's figure she returns, and he "shuddered at its too perfect *identity*" with Morella's.

Morella's "disquisitions" in "theological morality" cited "above all, the doctrines of *Identity* as urged by Schelling." The narrator summarizes:

> That identity which is termed personal, Mr. Locke, I think, truly defines to consist in the sameness of a rational being. And since by person we understand an intelligent essence having reason, and since there is a consciousness which always accompanies thinking, it is this which makes us all to be that which we call *ourselves*—thereby distinguishing us from other beings that think, and giving us our personal identity. But the *principium individuationis*—the notion of that identity *which at death is or is not lost forever,* was to me—at times, a consideration of intense interest; not more from the perplexing and exciting nature of its consequences, than from the marked and agitated manner in which Morella mentioned them.

Morella's "marked and agitated manner" captivates the narrator. The troubled sublimity of her appearance inspires the arabesque or elevating experience that precipitates him into disaster. Her "manner" is her style, and thus she embodies that "mesmerism" of language Poe finds typical of Romantic literature and German philosophy.

The prospect of immortality, of the repetition of characters, oppresses rather than exalts the narrator's soul: "Shall I then say that I longed with

an earnest and consuming desire for the moment of Morella's decease?"
The syntax indicates her "decease" as a substitute for coitus. The more she
talked of spiritual immortality, the more his repressed desires were
thwarted, as she divorces body from soul in quest of eternal identity. Her
death would put an end to his desire and prepare them for a spiritual union
in death (that embrace in the tomb found from "The Visionary" to "Annabel
Lee"). So her eyes become especially repugnant: "my soul sickened and
became giddy with the giddiness of one who gazes downward into some
dreary and unfathomable abyss." His lust for her death is perverse, a fascination with what the abyss will reveal, even at the cost of that bodily
organ that stands for the self. Those eyes, as Daniel Hoffmann has argued,
are displaced vaginas again, "her meaning eyes" inviting a glimpse into his
own carnal nature, his place in a temporal order of determined creations.
Like the lakes and tarns throughout Poe's writings, those eyes are revisions
into the Romantic topos of the reflective pool, whose spring waters flow
from the pond of Narcissus. The association of abyss, eye, and lake in Poe
suggests the abysmal quality of self-reflection, as the view into the beyond
gives back not a heightened vision of one's true self but a bottomless
speculation on the otherness we find there.

Morella's gradual reappearance in her daughter is, like the death of
Rowena in "Ligeia," a barely disguised wish fulfillment of the narrator's.
He perversely christens his daughter with the dead woman's name: "What
prompted me then, to disturb the memory of the dead? What demon urged
me to breathe that sound? What fiend spoke from the recesses of my soul?"
Morella's transmigration turns into an allegory of the voice of the narrator's
repetition compulsion. The repetition compulsion is Freud's coinage for
the unconscious reenactment in the present of ideas, relationships, or trau-
mas from the past. The present self is literally made an actor in a drama
authored by another, in this case the unconscious. Freud once hoped that
such repetition might be worked over into remembrance, a revision that
masters repetition and establishes the power of present narratives over past
plots. In practice, the issue became "metapsychological" when Freud attempted to explain the repetition of unpleasurable experiences. He argued
that Erotic desire went beyond the pleasure principle in that its reproductive
functions lead to change, rather than to the restoration of a past state. The
repression enabling Freud's Eros, however, is his exclusion of a human
situation by the use of a biological tropology of "germ cells." This allowed
him to make absent the most prominent and forbidding repetition compulsion in Freudian sexuality: the imagining of the sexual act as a return to
the mother. The narrator in "Morella" likewise hopes to cure and master

repetition by recalling Morella's name, but what occurs instead is the involuntary dramatization of his own entrapment in a past fixation. For him, horror is redoubled when his original trauma before Morella's person and style is repeated with his daughter's transformation. The eternal identity of Morella turns into the terror of the past's tyranny over the present. The return of the repressed is immortality's dark double. The narrator's own identity comes undone as the repetition compulsion commands him to enact the script of the unconscious. The narrative text repeats the process, characteristically shrouding its content in a host of protestations of incomprehension and vagueness. The use of a first-person narrative, or of a nameless observer-double, allows Poe's texts to perform the discourse of a self beside itself, a layering of "secret writings." It challenges our notions of authorship and reading. We are prompted to interpret this discourse of the other that haunts the mystified accounts of these men driven to commit and confess acts for which their disturbed consciousness can ostensibly find no intelligible principle. We are tempted to become like Dupin, trying to restore the letter to its proper home.

The problem of identity in "Morella" comes out of Poe's reading in Locke's "Of Identity and Diversity," from *An Essay concerning Human Understanding*. Locke initially defines the "principium Individuationis" as spatio-temporal noncontradiction, "It being impossible for two things of the same kind, to be or exist in the same instant, in the very same place; or one and the same thing in different places." This is obviously not the case with such identities as Ligeia or William Wilson. Locke argues that if we define "identity of Man" as "one Organization of Life in several successively fleeting Particles of Matter," then we shall "find it hard, to make an *Embryo*, one of *Years*, mad, and sober, the same Man, by any Supposition that will not make it possible for *Seth, Ismael, Socrates, Pilate, St. Austin,* and *Caesar Borgia* to be the same man." If we allow "the identity of Soul alone" to make "the same Man," then we fall into "the Notions of those Philosophers, who allow of Transmigration." As the latter would considerably confuse the Last Judgment, Locke sets out to redefine the relation between "*Personal Identity*" and the "*Idea of a Man.*"

In the passage Poe paraphrases in "Morella," Locke reduces the identity of man to a "self" that is noncontradictory, ever-present consciousness, without the play of unconscious forces: "When we see, hear, smell, taste, feel, meditate, or will any thing, we know that we do so." So much for the "imp of the perverse," and for all those Poe protagonists driven by "no intelligible principle":

> For since consciousness always accompanies thinking, and 'tis
> that, that makes every one to be, what he calls *self*; and thereby
> distinguishes himself from all other thinking things, in this alone
> consists *Personal Identity,* i.e. the sameness of a rational Being;
> And as far as this consciousness can be extended backwards to
> any past Action or Thought, so far reaches the Identity of that
> *Person*; it is the same *self* now it was then; and 'tis by the same
> *self* with this present one that now reflects on it, that the Action
> was done.

It is this equation of self with a reflective consciousness both immediate
and recollective that Poe's texts turn into an oddity. Even Locke recognizes
the times of heterogeneity in consciousness: forgetfulness, intoxication, the
instances "when we say such an one *is not himself,* or is *besides himself.*" This
unhappy anomaly he solves by simply excluding these fits of otherness
from personal identity:

> If there be any part of its [the self's] Existence, which I cannot
> upon recollection join with that present consciousness, whereby
> I am now my *self,* it is in that part of its Existence no more my
> *self,* than any other immaterial Being. For whatsoever any Sub-
> stance has thought or done, which I cannot recollect, and by my
> consciousness make my own Thought and Action, it will no
> more belong to me, whether a part of me thought or did it, than
> if it had been thought or done by any other immaterial Being
> any where existing.

This self is a self-discourse, an uninterrupted narrative that excludes
anything violating the control of its self-representations. Locke's "self"
defends against the influence of others, against thoughts or acts it cannot
"own" and which do not "belong" to it. We are not surprised that Locke
was the founding philosopher of "private property." Locke's self only feels
at home in a discourse or consciousness that owns and disposes of its
properties, and which is *essentially* not identifiable with anything or anyone
outside the boundaries of its authorized entitlements. The ordeals of Poe's
narrators tell us much about the fallacy of equating "self" and "self-consciousness." Morella's "immortality" can be read as the action of the narrator's unconscious, and thus as a critique of the "principium Individuationis" supposedly demonstrated by Morella's transmigration. His
horror at her return is a fearful response to the "immortality" of an alien
part of himself.

The plot of "Morella" is typical of Poe in that the death of a beautiful woman is the enabling device that occasions the narrator's excursion into visionary consciousness. The unmaking of his identity that follows proceeds in part from his implicit wish fulfillment, his "guilt" for her death. This guilt is often obscured by a displacement into lament and adolescent melancholy, or occluded by a rhetoric of arabesque frenzy. An example of the latter is in "Ligeia," when the narrator's evident poisoning of Rowena (to enable the "return" of the transcendentalist Ligeia) is presented as an opium dream of terror, in which the "angelic aspect" of Ligeia commits the fatal act. He has already cast Rowena into her "sudden illness" by surrounding her with the arabesque furnishings whose effect is the negation of mundane reality (Rowena's body). The guilt of these men grows more explicit in Poe's career, into "The Fall of the House of Usher" and "The Black Cat." The lament for the lost lady increasingly becomes the hysterical confession of her willful entombment, or, in the poems, the delightful expression of necrophilia, as in "For Annie": "And I lie so composedly, / Now, in my bed, / (Knowing her love) / that you fancy me dead—." The composing of Poe's writings into confessional narratives includes his stories of revenge, of doubles murdered in an allegory of adultery and self-destruction. To understand these developments, we need to turn to the source of Poe's dead ladies, and to the strange adaptation of this plot to Poe's theory of poetry.

II

Poe's war on plagiarism and his lifting of materials from other writers turned to his own purposes an early anxiety of influence experienced under the spell of Coleridge and Byron. A wealth of criticism has disinterred many of Poe's sources, but none have followed Floyd Stovall's passing insight that Poe's "effort to be original" stirred a fanatic attempt "to eradicate all traces of influence" in his poetry. For my purposes, the key poet here is Byron, and the central text his *Manfred*. It provides Poe with many of his stock Romantic devices, including of course the Byronic hero and the dead lady, as well as a simoon, ominous red lights, and a confession narrative. More importantly, Manfred's tale, as Poe reads it, becomes the story of the end of Romantic and philosophical idealism.

Manfred's achievement of Transcendental knowledge is haunted by his mournful remembrance of the dead Astarte. In an "all-nameless hour" he knew her, and in that climax of his quest his "embrace was fatal." Manfred's double ("She was like me in lineaments"), Astarte dies ostensibly as a result of his Satanic, Faustian ambition: "The Tree of Knowledge is not that of

Life." Doubtless Poe fixed on *Manfred* partly because his unconscious felt guilty for his own mother's death. His descriptions of Ligeia, Usher, and others mingle his own features with hers, as in mourning he introjectively identifies with her to "immortalize" her. His ambivalent violence toward such composite figures expresses the tension between self-punishing guilt and a desire for revenge against her for abandoning him as she dies into a spiritual world.

"I loved her, and destroy'd her," wails Manfred. The implicit narcissism of his love, coupled with his otherworldly loneliness, suggests that the search for self-mastery may end in self-murder and an exclusion of the other. Unable to demolish consciousness in forgetfulness or oblivion, he has Astarte conjured up, to ask her forgiveness. She instead pronounces his doom, which works a curious effect on Manfred:

> If that I did not know philosophy
> To be of all our vanities the motliest,
> The merest word that ever fooled the ear
> From out the schoolman's jargon, I should deem
> The golden secret, the sought "Kalon," found,
> And seated in my soul.
>
> (3.1.9–14)

The apparition of the dead, accusing Astarte brings a calm and truth the living lady never inspired. And yet that "If" casts doubt upon this ascension-through-death. His secure sense of guilt empowers at the end his resistance to the demons and his declaration that "The mind which is immortal makes itself / Requital for its good or evil thoughts,— / Is its own origin of ill and end." This psychologizing of his fate turns guilt into the vehicle of truth and the self's identity. In his "crime," in the destruction of the apparently desirable presence, Manfred makes his vision of the "sought 'Kalon,' found." In Manfred's guilt the Romantic dousing of the light of sense becomes the murder of the beautiful lady. The absence of the world, and of its transcendental center, is the precondition of Manfred's self and heroic text. The poem unfolds as the structure of his compulsive remembrance, until Manfred returns to the tower where they loved and she died, much as Poe and his Psyche will unconsciously find themselves suddenly at the tomb of the lost Ulalume. Writing withdraws from immediate presence, displaces what is before it, eclipses (if it can) the old gods, and leaves the trace of a "guilt" for the necessary "murder" of former truths and texts.

In "Byron and Miss Chaworth," Poe explicitly describes the advantages for the poetic imagination in the lady's absence. Although he acknowledges Miss Chaworth's charms, Poe concludes that it was "better" that "their intercourse was broken up in early life and never uninterruptedly resumed in after years":

> If she responded at all, it was merely because the necromancy of *his* words of fire could not do otherwise than exhort a response. In absence, the bard bore easily with him all the fancies which were the basis of his flame—a flame which absence itself but served to keep in vigor. . . . She to him was the Egeria of his dreams—the Venus Aphrodite that sprang, in full and supernal loveliness, from the bright foam upon the storm-tormented ocean of his thoughts.

This affirmation of the Romantic visionary formula hardly seems applicable to the horrific figures of Poe's uncharneled ladies. An axiom like "I could not love except where Death / Was mingling his with Beauty's breath" suggests the poet felt threatened by the lady's presence. An "overdetermined" signifier, Poe's lady stands variously and often simultaneously for: (1) the body, which the lady's presence excites, thus awakening the unconscious work of the instinctive other within the rational man; (2) the cultural inheritance (familial, national, European), which forms an influential other in the mind that dictates to the self; (3) truth as a metaphysical absolute; (4) the truths and beauties of past authors. If "supernal loveliness" requires the "death" of the other, then the ideals of truth, self, or originality depend on a repeated attention to what they seem to exclude. The same applies to the poet's revisions (or "murders") of his precursors. In fact, "supernal Loveliness" is also the term Poe uses in "The Poetic Principle" for that transcendent Beauty poetry vainly aspires to. The "most entrancing" of "poetic moods" doesn't follow the "brief and indeterminate glimpses" of Beauty, but rather from the "petulant, impatient sorrow at our inability to grasp *now,* wholly, here on earth, at once and for ever," a "portion of that Loveliness." In other words, no past poet could have precluded this poet's vision; and besides, failure to transcend now inspires the best poetry.

In the preface to his first volume of poetry, the "Letter to B———," Poe attacks Wordsworth and Coleridge (though he ends by stealing, almost verbatim, the latter's definition of poetry). "He belittles their poetry," writes Stovall, "in order to persuade the reader that it has not influenced his own." Poe joins the debate over the American writer's originality in reference to the "established wit of the world . . . for it is with literature as with law or empire—an established name is an estate in tenure, or a throne in possession." Disparaging Wordsworth's supposed didacticism,

Poe states, "He seems to think that the end of poetry is, or should be, instruction—yet it is a truism that the end of our existence is happiness." The removal of truth from the center of writing, and its replacement by "effect" (the correlative of arabesque elevations like opium or mesmerism) makes for a poetics that disorders logocentric structures such as genealogy or poetic tradition. Writing without such truth is the rhetoric of effects, and it throws us into a speculative abyss wherein we witness the disestablishment of "proper" forms and meanings. The maelstrom, the arabesquely furnished apartment, Dupin's library—these and other such derangements of "reality" are analogous to the space of writing itself, which likewise affects us in substituting its representations for our "normal" presences. The hysterical confession is also such a state, a literary form exemplifying how the telling of truth and the discourse of the other double one another. These spaces of representation provide the same perverse opportunities as those dark reflective waters that often occupy the center in Poe's poems and tales. They form a shadowy critical mirror of that idealism Poe sometimes indulged. In the review of Drake and Halleck, Poe extolls "that evergreen and radiant Paradise, which the true poet knows, and knows alone, as the limited realm of his authority—as the circumscribed Eden of his dreams." Yet we find far different scenes in his work from the pastoralism he lauds, of "the fair flowers, the fairer forests, the bright valleys and rivers and mountains of the Earth":

> My infant spirit would wake
> To the terror of the lone lake.
> Yet that terror was not fright—
> But a tremulous delight,
> And a feeling undefin'd,
> Springing from a darken'd mind.
> Death was in that poison'd wave
> And in its gulf a fitting grave
> For him who thence could solace bring
> To his dark imagining;
> Whose wild'ring thought could even make
> An Eden of that dim lake.

The strangest argument that the Ideal's absence is poetry's law appears as "The Philosophy of Composition," Poe's supposed account of how he wrote "The Raven." The increasing prominence of the confession in Poe affects his criticism, too, so that this piece reads much like "The Black Cat" or "The Imp of the Perverse." Contradicting the latter, however, Poe here seems to have an "intelligible principle" for casting his lady into the abyss. The opening references to Godwin and Dickens alert us that this is a murder mystery: the narrator of it turns out to be both culprit and detective. The critical voice ratiocinates with increasingly insane lucidity the modus operandi of a poetics whose "most poetical topic" is the death of a beautiful woman. The function of the lady's loss is to evoke "mournful and Never-ending Remembrance," the ultimate in Poe's elevating arabesque states of dissolution. The tension between the essay and the poem lies in the distinction between the lover/student's remembrance and the poet's recollection. Poe explains how willfully the student propounds his questions to the monologocentric bird, ending as intoxicated on "nevermore" as others are by drink, antique volumes, or the contemplation of arabesque tapestries. The raven perches on the bust of Pallas, reminding the student that the attainment of past wisdom, or the return of Lenore, is nevermore. He has a terrible case of Bloom's anxiety, reminded constantly of his belatedness, his loss of the muse, and the probability that he shall never attain (or regain) a philosophical, sexual, or literary Eden. (Not for nothing did Poe contrast his doctrine of mesmeric brevity to the "essential prose" lapses of *Paradise Lost,* as if his own "brief poetical effects" could hypnotize us into forgetting Milton's greatness.) Another parody of the transcendentalist, the student/lover is fanatic in his desire for the immortality of truth and beauty (Lenore).

The poet, however, claims a subtler idea of repetition. "The pleasure" of the poem's refrain, Poe writes, "is deduced solely from the sense of identity—of repetition." Originality is the essay's constant topic, and here Poe sees his way to a literary "originality" that is not that of a single immortal identity: "I determined to produce continuously novel effects, by the variation *of the application* of the *refrain—the refrain* itself remaining, for the most part, unvaried." This principle holds for the combinatorial rhetoric of Poe's borrowings from literary tradition, high and low. The student's arabesque trance brings, not the lady, but a death sentence for transcendentalism; Poe's critical account proceeds to confess the requisite erasure of the center, so that absolute repetition may be eluded. (Poe says he chose "pallas" for its "sonorousness," and we note its homophonic resemblance to "palace" and "phallus," and thus to the haunting of the aristocratic, genealogical transmission of identities.) The eclipse of the light of sense in this case reveals a re-vision of the past, not a vision of the eternally present. Or, more powerfully, we come to see that the eternal and immortal are repetitions, and that the poet, if he is to lay claim to his own identity, must control them. Yet the sorrowful spectacle in Poe's works is usually of protagonists controlled by repetitions, as in the case of the student who is possessed by a compulsion to repeat dead wisdom and dead loves.

Poe's appearance as master of repetition in this narrative reminds us of the other detectives and interpreters in his later work who seem to achieve sublimity in the decoding of mysteries. The skepticism of readers toward the "rational" explanation Poe gives of the composition of "The Raven" is well founded when the dubious achievements of Dupin or Legrand are kept in mind. And reciprocally, we cannot question the ratiocination here without wondering if such genuises are not also perpetrating a hoax. "The Philosophy of Composition," which begins by excluding the role of "accident" or of the unconscious from poetic creation, constitutes the identity of its own originality by the same repression that so evidently divides Poe's protagonists. The mastery of speakers in Poe collapses into the whisperings of their doubles, those discourses of the other which irresistibly come to the "surface" when the text leaps into the abyss of self-reflection. If, as I have argued, all these arabesque states of mind in Poe are structurally coincident with the act of writing, then the terror and fascination is that of the writer who knows (whatever that means) that writing dissolves his own identity, purloins his own character. What does the writer do but put his character(s) in circulation? Don't his inevitable displacements and borrowings, and the unconscious figurations of himself in the work, undo his control, make him yet another letter to be purloined in the reading game?

Dupin, as double of the Minister D——, is both poet and mathematician. He continues the traits of earlier Poe heroes, though the cool intuition of transcendent rationality now replaces the ecstatic state of revelation. The fundamental rule of mathematical calculation in this context is noncontradiction: integers must be identical to themselves. One must not be two or ten, else their systematic combination would prove nonsense. Nor must we inquire too closely into the hypothetical necessity of a zero for the system, lest we be drawn into interminable reflections on the interdependence of being and nothingness. The discrimination of identities, the routing of letters back to their homes or of aberrant crimes to their ordered place, is Dupin's primary activity. In "The Murders in the Rue Morgue," the linguistic puzzle allows Dupin to become an accomplice to the exclusion of forbidden sexual passions from human life and language, as he deduces the nonidentity of the orangutang's voice with any human speech. Though this may be a "correct" solution to the story's surface mystery, it is a very deluded explanation of the other within us that has unspeakable desires. The strength of Dupin's (I can't help hearing "dupe") repression is measurable by the hyperbolic care taken in the solemn incrimination of the orangutang. That this animal could be identified with us is a possibility Dupin never entertains, and is thus the one we are made to fasten on. So obviously *outré* is this poor orangutang that readers who accept it merely replay Dupin's own interpretive blindness. This hint of possible interpretive mastery on *our* part, however, for outsmarting Dupin, won't survive the more complicated exchange of identities in "The Purloined Letter."

Dupin's discourse on method in that tale concerns a schoolboy's victorious strategy in the guessing game of even and odd. The boy guesses his opponent's moves through "an identification of the reasoner's intellect with that of his opponent." The analytical reasoner turns himself into the object of scrutiny by becoming the other: "I fashion the expression of my face . . . in accordance with the expression of his, and then wait to see what thoughts or sentiments arise in my mind or heart, as if to match or correspond with the expression." This purloining of character replays the Romantic idea of sympathetic knowledge. In this game, the analytical player erases himself, takes the place of the other, and hopes to profit by the reflection (as indeed the Minister D—— hands over a check for 50,000 francs). Yet we cannot be so simple as to assume a strict correspondence between surface expression and subjectivity, or to think that a binary calculus of reversals ("If he thinks that I think that he thinks . . ." etc.) will suffice. Poe puns mercilessly on "correspond," having Emerson at least in mind and cautioning against a too easy belief in the transmission of identities. Identification with another may be perilous if human subjectivity is heterogeneous or multiple. Which of the other's selves do we identify with, and with which one of our selves do we do it? Through identification we might take into ourselves the others within the other, and deposit them unknowingly in our own unconscious (as we do all the time when we read). Dupin's method depends upon faith in a mastery of what comes about during the arabesque state of being besides oneself under the influence of some other, and upon a concomitant belief in the proper meaning of characters. The story's complications show up the method's fallacies.

The "origin" of the story, however, as Derrida emphasizes, is in the usurpation of the King's authority and mastery by the Queen's evident adultery. The "phallogocentric" letter demonstrates the wandering of meaning from its "proper" home. In restoring the letter to the Queen, Dupin does not return the letter to its proper place, for it can have none, not even where it is addressed. The power of the letter is in the absence of a univocal meaning, in a vulnerability to interpretation that enables its circulation among purloiners who thus "correspond" with each other. The unrevealed "content" of the letter never concerns Dupin, for he has substituted a semiotic game of placement for the hermeneutic game of meaning. His semiotics of the letter restores the idea of the letter's having a proper place, but it does so only through a systematic structuralist blindness that prevents him from reading its other addresses, or his own displacement within the correspondence. Again, he doubles the Minister D——, who is "blinded" and loses the letter when Dupin's hired agents distract him with a staged disturbance in the street below, firing off a musket into a crowd of women and children. Dupin authors a violent primal scene to recapture the letter, and thus hopelessly entangles himself in representations of transgression, castration, ejaculation, and dissemination. Dupin's dream of control is exquisitely expressed in his victorious pronouncement that "the pretended lunatic was a man in my own pay." This triumphant scene, as Dupin narrates it, will within a page become an ironic commentary on Dupin's own blindness to the implications of the inscription he has left in the purloined letter's double.

Dupin is a superficial reader. His deriding of the Prefect for seeking the letter in depths or secret places expresses his wish to avoid private parts. Dupin keeps himself at a distance, theoretically, from depths and abysses. He falls into one, however, through the reading of letters, because the acts of identification in interpretation require the displacement of our own identities and open up the possibility that the other within may engage in correspondences of an illicit, rather than divine, kind with others elsewhere. The maelstrom here is textual, in that reading is read as an arabesque excitement of the mind that may not result in apocalyptic characters, but in the purloining of ourselves. Poe's own writings offer abundant evidence that the act of writing may precipitate disturbing and unwanted revelations, both within the text and within the mind of the reader.

Dupin himself suffers such a fate. At story's end, some perverse impulse prompts him to leave an incriminating signature within the "fac-simile" that he puts in the place of the re-purloined letter. His desire for recognition stems from an old grudge with the Minister D——, and in this inscription he would seem to have achieved a triumphant announcement of his identity as the master. Simple, but odd. The quote, which takes the place of his proper name, is lifted by Poe from Crébillion's rewrite of the tragedy of the House of Atreus. As Riddel has keenly shown, that ancient revenge plot of adultery, theft, revenge, and cursed genealogy seems one that these Parisians are compelled to repeat. Dupin thus sends a letter to D——, but the "letters" belong to another writer. Dupin changes into a character from an old story, and it is unclear in reflection just who is writing who. Revenge is the parable of repetition par excellence, for its machinery dictates a binary choice of roles (victim or avenger) that reverse with each act, thus reducing the identities of the players to the script's tyranny. Dupin sacrifices his own identity and originality to produce an effect on the Minister

D——, and thereby too becomes an odd letter needing interpretation, and the probable victim of D——'s next move. Dupin wants to strike back for an "evil turn" done him by D—— in Vienna, but we may surmise from Poe's purloining of the Atreus legend that Dupin has been acting all along in unconscious correspondence with a primal, ancient, internalized plot. "Nil sapientiae odiosius acumine nimio."

The primal scene here is represented as that "evil turn" in Vienna, a troping which other critics rightly guess to have a romantic content. If the Minister D—— first purloined a lady from Dupin there, then Dupin's rescue of the Queen would put him back into the position of power or possession regarding the woman that he lost to D—— (the summary easily falls into psychomachia). But unless Dupin (and here's a wish fulfillment) is the author of the "original" purloined letter, then the story ends with Dupin in a position of holding only the "truth" of the letter's endless circulation, or with the sublimated ecstasy of his own apparent victory. If we read that "evil turn" as a symbolic castration of Dupin, then we may understand how giving the phallogocentric letter back to the Queen revenges him. Now the Minister D—— is impotent. The phantom King, however, this story's deepest absence, still remains dispossessed of his power and his property. The Queen meanwhile holds an instrument of power that works only in the absence, blindness, or impotence of the reigning Logos. The truth of letters may not be centered in a transcendental home of meaning, for the power of letters depends on their impropriety and indirection. And of course Poe's own text is itself "The Purloined Letter," subject to all these reflections, and a correspondence course in writing's adultery of identity.

III

In sum, the Romantic or Idealist visionary moment of the soul's knowing union with the world becomes in Poe the nightmare of the self's inhabitation by conflicting scripts. This is not to question the strength of Poe's imaginative lamps, but rather to question the identity or location of authorship. When the text negotiates a rhetorical conflict of repression and expression, who writes? Who authors our nightmares? Poe's work shows a morbid sensitivity to this issue, in its narrators (who scarcely know what they say), in its plots (whose characters seem condemned to repeat old stories), and most literally in his "modernist" deployment of quotes, phrases, ideas, characters, names, and fabulated citations taken (consciously or not) from other writers. These traces form the archive of Poe's rhetoric of borrowing, his cryptic writing or his *écriture*. Commenting on the latter term, Richard Poirier has recently said,

> The performing self is never free of its environment, never a so called "imperial" or unconditioned self. No such thing exists in the history of literature, no self ever has been successfully imperial, because nature (and not just the repressiveness of our selves) dictates that the only materials a "free" self can be constructed from are those by which it is imprisoned.

Poirier goes on to defend Emerson against the charge that he was happily oblivious to the traces of the *écriture* against which self-reliance struggles. Poe often used that reading of Emerson as naive idealist for his straw imperial man. In Emerson, Poe could see the combination of Romantic and German themes united in this pronouncement of Hegel's: "The tendency of all man's endeavors is to understand the world, to appropriate and subdue it to himself; and to this end the positive reality of the world must be as it were crushed and pounded, in other words, idealized." Emerson's self-reliance hoped to put the self back into mastery of its own house. Freud's "call to introspection" was Concord's historical dilemma, as Emerson himself described it: "The young men were born with knives in their brain, a tendency to introversion, self-dissection, anatomizing of motives." The apparent intent of "The American Scholar," "Self-Reliance," and "The Over-Soul" is to purge introversion of historicity, to free self-consciousness from personal or cultural determinations of *écriture*.

Ever since the Pilgrims, the American experiment had been to write a revised script on the new land, to constitute and declare an independent identity to resist and redirect the legacy of the Old World. The central text for interpretation was first the Bible, then the political documents of the Revolution, and then what Emerson called "Nature," a "not-me" including culture as a component. Mingling Kant, Coleridge, and Cotton Mather, Emerson formulates philosophy, poetry, and self as grounded in the reading of this Nature: "A life in harmony with Nature, the love of truth and of virtue, will purge the eyes to understand her text." Emerson tries to imagine the purgation of our consciousness of other in his audacious introduction to *Nature,* which cries out for a liberation from the "dry bones of the past." In the place of the repressed influences of the past, Emerson posits the inspiration of Nature's Over-Soul as the center of the introspective self: "Our being is descending into us from we know not whence. . . . I desire, and look up, and put myself in the attitude of reception, but from some alien energy the visions come." This "Revelation" is "always attended by the emotion of the sublime. For this communication is an influx of the Divine mind into our mind." An "ecstasy," "trance," and "certain tendency to insanity" afflict such visionaries, but the light is the Word, and "Revelation is the disclosure of the soul."

Emerson's "influx of the Divine" appears in Poe as the corpse of the sublime. Where Emerson's self-reliant introspection discovers Eternal Identity, Poe's horrified introverts disclose the anomaly of the Living Dead, the mortality of Beauty and Truth, the puzzle of inscriptions and the collapse of identities into their speculative doubles. Harold Bloom, anxious to make Emerson his precursor prophet of earliness, claims "that a poetic repression brings about the Sublime wildness of freedom." Once more Bloom tries to make repetition a master's game, but he can only do so by ruling out his antagonist from the start. Bloom must "deny the usefulness of the Unconscious, as opposed to repression, as a literary term." With the discourses of the other excluded, the "wildness of freedom" follows as an ineluctable wish fulfillment. Poe's texts insistently put the unconscious in the same structural position (culturally, psychologically, even cosmically) as the Over-Soul, or, more accurately, his writing suggests that the Over-Soul is a strategically adopted persona of the unconscious.

Hegel's method was to make the negations and divisions of the self dialectical. The spirit

> sunders itself to self-realization. But this position of severed life has in its turn to be suppressed, and the spirit has by its own act to win its way to concord again. The final concord then is spiritual; that is, the principal restoration is found in thought, and thought only. The hand that inflicts the wound is also the hand which heals it.

(Emerson would have delighted in the felicity of a translation that made the "final concord" spiritual.) Poe, however, fears the metempsychosis or immortal spirit of written thoughts, their ghostly persistence. In "The Power of Words," two spirits talk of the infinity of influence, taking as their mode the original immortality of the Word:

> It is indeed demonstrable that every such impulse *given the air,* must, *in the end,* impress every individual thing that exists *within the universe;*—and the being of infinite understanding—the being whom we have imagined—might trace the remote undulations of the impulse—trace them upward and onward in their influences upon all particles of all matter—upward and onward for

ever in their modifications of old forms—or, in other words, *in their creation of new*—until he found them reflected—unimpressive *at last*—back from the throne of the Godhead. . . . And while I thus spoke, did there not cross your mind some thought of the *physical power of words?* Is not every word an impulse on the air?

The hopeful turn of influence into the creation of new forms again expresses the quandary of tradition and the individual talent. That is also the theoretical theme of "The Fall of the House of Usher," in which the "final concord" does not restore the mansion of the self, but instead replays the power of other impulses.

The narrator, at the start of his quest to restore the foundations of sanity, experiences a "depression of soul" in his inability to translate the sight of the Usher building into "aught of the sublime." This may be explained by his separation from Usher: "Although, as boys, we have been even intimate associates, yet I really knew little of my friend." (Compare "William Wilson.") The narrator's rationality has heretofore come from the distancing of something with which he was once intimately associated, and whose return will undo him. The House of Usher is itself Poe's most hyperbolic image for the transmission of influences within the structures we inhabit. And if its "excessive antiquity" and arabesque furnishings were not enough, Poe dwells on the repetition compulsion of this "ancient family." Its "direct line of descent," with "very trifling and very temporary variation," prompts the narrator's thoughts to "the perfect keeping of the character of the premises with the accredited character of the people" (note the pun on "premises"), prompting him to "speculating upon the possible influence which the one, in the long lapse of centuries, might have exercised upon the other." Finally, it is the "undeviating transmission, from sire to son, of the patrimony with the name, which had, at length, so identified the two as to merge the original title of the estate in the quaint and equivocal appellation of 'The House of Usher.' " Like the power of words, this heritage forms a strange "sentience" in the "home of his forefathers," "above all in the long undisturbed endurance of this arrangement, and in its reduplication in the still waters of the tarn." This "arrangement" is a perverse celestial music, an "atmosphere" of the "importunate and terrible influence which for centuries had moulded the destinies" of the Usher family.

Hoping to "annihilate" the "sorrowful impression" the building makes upon him (correlative to the unhappy irruption of the other back into his consciousness, also taking the form of Usher's letter to him), the narrator seeks relief in representations: "I reflected, that a mere different arrangement of the particulars of the scene, of the details of the picture" would suffice. Thus he stops at "the precipitous brink of a black and lurid tarn," where glimmer "the remodelled and inverted images" of the house. Here the abyss is again identified with reflection, our impish perversity in sinking into representations, and the remainder of the tale unfolds in the space of this re-cognition.

The narrator begins with the delusion that such reflection can restore him to himself. He too is remodelled and inverted as he enters this abysmal mansion, where he replaces the doctor and the lady Madeline as Usher's physician and twin. Within this frame Poe once more gives us the story (Usher's) of a belated imagination, his soul a ruin, his Ideality the product of a sensual repression culminating in his sister's premature entombment. Yet the involvement of the narrator changes the familiar pattern. Usher and Madeline live in the narrator's rhetorical house of therapeutic writing. His project is to revise the Poe script so as to save the imagination from the return of the repressed. The final, ghastly comic, staging of this effort comes when the narrator tries to soothe Roderick by reading to him! The "antique volume" is the "Mad Trist" by "Sir Launcelot Canning" (a quaint appellation Poe later used as his own pseudonym). The joke is on everyone, for this text is a copy of a nonexistent original, the only "truly" fictitious work in Usher's library. Poe's invented volume parodies our desire to be canny readers, to pierce the mystery of uncanny stories. The narrator hopes to treat Usher with writing: "I indulged a vague hope that the excitement which now agitated the hypochondriac, might find relief (for the history of mental disorder is full of similar anomalies) even in the extremeness of the folly which I should read." A good pre-Freudian doctor, the narrator wants to take Usher's diseased libidinal energy ("excitement") and sublimate it, cathect or attach it to a safe object. What he doesn't see is that reading may be precisely the cause of such "excitement," and that the redirection of libidinal energy will only repeat, albeit in distortion or displacement, the original structure of impulses the narrator hopes to quiet.

The ensuing spectacle of the interdoubling of reality and literature is indeed a "Mad Trist" and illustrates Freud's hypothesis that "the uncanny is nothing else than a hidden, familiar thing that has undergone repression and then emerged from it." The narrator reads on blindly, ignoring how the text awakens the unconscious, while Roderick hears mesmerically the echoing of surface and depth. The narrator agrees evidently with those critics who find literature a means of entertainment, or (and it amounts to the same thing) a salvation from being beside themselves by means of a safe transportation to already privileged truths. This literary episode deconstructs the narrator's rationale of reading, exposes with lunatic hilarity his dominant concern with holding the house of his own sanity together.

The story of the "Mad Trist" invites multiple interpretations. Marie Bonaparte finds it an allegory of the Oedipal struggle, with Ethelred slaying the father to gain the mother; this, for her, would be the content of the repressed. Yet Ethelred's entrance by force into the dwelling of the hermit also repeats the motion of Usher's letter to the narrator, as well as that of the narrator's arrival at Usher's mansion. Ethelred is "drunken," in an arabesque state that empowers him to shatter the door, slay the dragon of fire who has replaced the hermit, and gain the protective shield of authority, "breaking up . . . the enchantment which was upon it." Usher (and others) turn the "Trist" into an allegory of Madeline's return, and thus of the return of Usher's own unconscious desires. Usher, however, also seems to accusingly scream "MADMAN" at the *narrator*. The madness of the narrator would be his rationality in reading, his refusal to recognize the other inhabiting the text. Ethelred could be read as the figure of the narrator's quest to break the enchantment of the unconscious that keeps us from truth. Reading would then be an arabesque liberation of formal powers enabling the slaying of the monstrous other. Ethelred's shield would be his phallogocentric emblem, or so antique romance would have it. Madeline's reappearance for her final mad tryst with Roderick is equally unreadable. She is a representation whose "original" identity (as truth, or as the narrator's unconscious, or as Roderick's sensual self) is multiple, a hall of mirrors, and always enchanting. Her return will destroy both Roderick and the narrator, her other double. The failure of the narrator's talking cure reflects upon himself as the identity of the text he reads is haunted by spectral visitations. The stories-within-stories and interpretations-within-interpretations build to an intensity of overdetermination that exceeds the capacity of any single deciphering consciousness or reading strategy.

The narrator "fled aghast" from the scene of all this attraction and repulsion of correspondences. His own writing effort, and the containment of speculation it desired, shatters along with its chief representative. It had seemed to the narrator as if "the superhuman agency" of Roderick's "utterance" had "found the potency of a spell" to open the door for Madeline's enshrouded body. The "potency" of the narrator's own rationalized ejaculations has, in like manner, inadvertently brought forward the figures of the Ushers from within himself. Their collapse into each other's arms is that "fatal embrace" that is Poe's typical negative union. This would seem to purge the narrator cathartically of the conflicts embodied, and so cure himself, but the treatment is not entirely successful. His last reflection occurs looking back at the house. He sees "the full, setting, and blood-red moon" shining through the widening fissure cutting the house in two. This version of the Romantic trope of moonlight for imagination is tinged by the color of blood, and thus pictures a mind colored by thoughts of sex and death. It is these thoughts, archaic and impulsive, nonidentical with the narrative of self-consciousness, that split open the house of himself. The climactic fall of the mansion into its own images serves as the best final commentary on the workings of self-reflection in Poe, and on the effect this can have on the identity of a literary text:

> While I gazed, this fissure rapidly widened—there came a fierce breath of the whirlwind—the entire orb of the satellite burst at once upon my sight—my brain reeled as I saw the mighty walls rushing asunder—there was a long tumultuous shouting sound like the voice of a thousand waters—and the deep and dank tarn at my feet closed sullenly and silently over the fragments of the *"House of Usher."*

Poe sets the *"House of Usher"* apart with quotation marks, in italicized script, as if it were the title of a tale. Riddel has correctly read this scene as a textual deconstruction, the story falling into itself, the proper name in fragments. I would, however, end by recalling that textuality should not be a privileged analytical metaphor. These closing lines, like so much of Poe, won't allow us to extract textuality from sexuality. Inspiration has become daemonized and passionate, "a fierce breath of the whirlwind." The anatomy of the red fissure and "mighty walls rushing asunder" combines a vision of abysmal vaginal horrors with echoes of apocalypse, as if this were a creation catastrophe. The "long tumultuous shouting sound like the voice of a thousand waters" reminds us that the house of generation is both echoic and spermatic: Bloom is right to insist that writing is a family romance, a history of relations. This climax consummates the affair of sex and writing, makes that coupling the final terror, and images its reburial in reflection. The "silence" of the text's "fragments" is not complete, as writing cannot silence the traces left by those shouting voices of the past, for they are also voices of desire.

Desire inspires both lover and writer. The dialectic of Eros and Thanatos some critics find in Poe ought to be replaced by an analytics of eros and *écriture*. One may prematurely bury the corpus of this dilemma, this peculiar intimacy, "sullenly" put it in its place, but the very act of interment leaves its epitaph in script and capital letters. "US" and "HER," tomb of the lovers, house of the poet's relation to the Muse, of Everyman to his Unconscious. The house of writing both participates in and violates the economy of sex. These fragments and fissures picture another castration, a textual/sexual *sparagmos* of the proper that follows from the primal scene of Roderick and Madeline's "Mad Trist." Yet the dissemination of these "thousand waters" generates the recapitation of the *"House of Usher."* Tomb, phallus, text, the *"House of Usher"* rises up at the end in writing, a typographic inverse double of the house and story now disappearing into the tarn. It is, I will suggest, the undecidable significance of this union of sex and writing that makes Poe's work finally "unreadable." The structures of these two discourses embrace without a unifying authority, become rivals for the letter, and draw us as readers into an interminable analysis of textual intercourse.

Phantasms of Death in Poe's Fiction

J. Gerald Kennedy

The tales of Edgar Allan Poe display an elaborate repertoire of supernatural motifs, so well adapted to the evocation of horror that one might suppose the *frisson* to be their exclusive object. Otherwise discerning readers have thus fixed upon such phantasmagoria as evidence of Poe's "pre-adolescent mentality"—to recall the judgment of T. S. Eliot—and concluded that his otherworldly tales amount to little more than gimcrackery. Even those with a scholarly regard for Poe's achievement sometimes assume (as the author invited us to) that mystical elements in the fiction serve mainly to secure the necessary "single effect." Collectively examined, however, his tales reveal the complex function of the supernatural, which typically introduces the predicament that his protagonists must overcome, escape, explain away, or surrender to. The intrusion of the uncanny generates "cosmic panic" (in Lovecraft's phrase) and poses the troubling paradox at the center of Poe's dark vision. Although the preternatural arrives in various shapes—as a demon-horse, a phantom ship, or a reanimated corpse—it commonly dramatizes the interpenetration of life and death, the mingling of metaphysical opposites. A passing glance at the recurrent themes of vampirism, metempsychosis, spiritualism, and spectral manifestation indicates Poe's fixation with the fate of the body and the destiny of the soul. In effect, such motifs carry a significance independent of the narrative scheme in which they emerge; they constitute an esoteric ideography and inscribe a parallel

From *The Haunted Dusk: American Supernatural Fiction, 1820–1920*, edited by Howard Kerr, John W. Crowley, and Charles L. Crow. © 1983 by the University of Georgia Press.

text concerned exclusively with final questions. Through a decoding of this imagery, I want to clarify the four conceptual models which dominated Poe's representation of our mortal condition.

II

Under the ostensible influence of Walpole, Radcliffe, Brockden Brown, Coleridge, Irving, and the German Romantics Tieck and Hoffmann, Poe assimilated the conventions of Gothic Horror. His gravitation toward that mode was probably inevitable, for its narrative configuration seems to have embodied his fundamental perception of the human condition. In his preface to *Tales of the Grotesque and Arabesque* (1840), he described the "terror . . . of the soul" as his essential "thesis." The supernatural paraphernalia of the Gothic, particularly phantasms of death and destruction, afforded a means of articulating this primal fear. In a broad sense, Poe's "terror of the soul" bears traces of the historical and intellectual crisis that produced the Gothic novel; indeed, we cannot make sense of his preoccupation with madness, violence, perverseness, disease, death, and decomposition without recognizing the cultural drama inherent in what David Punter has called the "literature of terror." It is a commonplace notion that the Gothic emerged from the rupture in Western thought between rationalism and Romanticism that occurred in the latter half of the eighteenth century. This formulation, however crude, contains an important truth: Gothic fiction enacts the radical uncertainty of an epoch of revolution in which nearly all forms of authority—neoclassicism, Right Reason, religious orthodoxy, and aristocracy—came to be seen as constricting systems. Ghosts and crumbling castles, wicked lords and diabolical monks served as fictive emblems of a collapsing order. Alone in a landscape of nightmare, the Gothic hero experienced the dark side of Romantic freedom: existential disorientation, wrought by the loss of defining structures. The Gothic paradigm dramatized for the first time the quintessential modern predicament—the plight of an alienated being whose rational skepticism had vitiated his capacity for belief, while paralyzing dread had betrayed the insufficiency of science and logic. It was the peculiar achievement of the Gothic (and, one imagines, the basis of its appeal) to express in playful, imaginative terms the latent fears of Western culture in an urban, industrial, post-rational, and post-Christian era. If this species of fiction presented a search for answers, an elucidation of mysteries, its real force lay, as Punter observes, in the evocation of doubt, in its capacity for "removing the illusory halo of certainty from the so-called 'natural' world."

Through its own illogic, Gothic supernaturalism exposed the limits of reason as an explanatory model. The proliferation of occult themes in eighteenth-century literature amounted, in the view of Patricia Meyer Spacks, to a recognition that "the mind of man is naturally subject to secret terrors and apprehensions" and that supernatural motifs possess a "real and universal" validity. Writers of Gothic Fiction, even those like Ann Radcliffe who were committed to an ultimately rational vision, felt the need to widen the range of narrative possibility and draw upon the imagery of dreams. But the insurgence of literary supernaturalism expressed more than a resistance to Augustan aesthetic constraints; it also manifested a curious response to the rationalizing of religious thought in the eighteenth century. In effect, writers of Gothic novels salvaged elements of popular belief—devils, curses, and spiritual visitations—that had been jettisoned by Christian humanist thought. And their use of supernatural imagery appears to have one other major implication: as a response to death in the face of religious skepticism. Glen St. John Barclay has argued that "any story which in any sense refers to the intervention of the supernatural in human affairs necessarily affirms that the supernatural exists. It holds out the reality of alternative modes or realms of existence beyond the physical limitations of our material life. In doing so, it responds directly to what is certainly man's most abiding concern, the prospect of his own personal annihilation and oblivion in death." One must question the inference that any literary representation of the supernatural affirms its existence in the experiential world—a blatant confusion of art and life—but Barclay's perception of the uncanny in fiction as a response to the fear of "personal annihilation" seems astute. When we consider that the Gothic movement derived much of its impetus from the graveyard school of poetry, we perceive that in the midst of other revolutions in taste, belief, and thought in the eighteenth century, a wholly new and powerful consciousness of death had begun to emerge. In place of the calm acceptance of mortality we might expect in the verse of a clergyman-poet, we find in Young's *Night Thoughts on Death* and Blair's *The Grave* a deepening anxiety about extinction. Such poetry excited curiosity about death and decomposition; it introduced dreams and fantasies about dying; and it conferred upon the tomb and the cemetery a peculiar new importance. The abode of death became associated with preternatural phenomena, as instanced by Blair's depiction of a weird procession:

> Roused from their slumbers,
> In grim array the grisly spectres rise,
> Grin horrible, and obstinately sullen
> Pass and repass, hushed as the foot of night.
>
> (ll. 39–42)

Such images proliferated in the mid-eighteenth century as a funereal sensibility infused popular literature; death was no longer simply an event or moment in writing but its very object.

The association of supernaturalism and mortality acquires broader significance in light of the monumental study of Philippe Ariès, *The Hour of Our Death.* Through research into the burial practices, wills, and memorial sculpture of France (and Western culture generally) since the Middle Ages, Ariès demonstrates that, far from being a universal and static phenomenon, our conception of mortality has undergone vast changes, from the serene, public leave-taking of the medieval "tame death" to the lonely despair of our contemporary "invisible death"—the institutional concealment of the final hour. Perhaps the most striking of Ariès's general conclusions is the observation that before the end of the seventeenth century, "human beings as we are able to perceive them in the pages of history [had] never really known the fear of death." Initially this seems a baseless proposition, for the phrase "fear of death" involves an apparent conflation of several distinct responses—to the idea of death, its imminence, its bodily effects, and its psychic consequences. As a historical judgment, this also seems doubtful; we know, for example, that the deadly plagues of the late Middle Ages inspired terror throughout Europe. But we must bear in mind that the medieval fear of an immediate threat and its spiritual corollary fear of eternal judgment are both quite different from the modern dread of mortality, the crux of the general claim. Ariès associates the onset of contemporary death-anxiety with three broad developments: the secularization of death and the erosion of belief in an afterlife; the growth of self-consciousness and individualism, which diminished the communal aspect of death and made it a private, personal experience; and the advent of science and modern medicine, which converted the corpse into an object of study and death into a physiological process. As indices of these changes, we see in the eighteenth century the appearance of public cemeteries and the abandonment of services once provided by the church; the practice of erecting funerary monuments to commemorate the existence of the common folk; the exhuming of bodies for experimental purposes; and, as noted earlier, the appearance of literary and artistic productions concerned with mortality and grief.

One result of scientific attention to the physiology of death was a mounting curiosity about the connection between the body and the soul. The medieval idea of the *homo toto,* the whole and indissoluble man, was supplanted during the Enlightenment by the concept of a self that divided at death. But what part did the soul play in the agony of dying, and where did it go at the moment of extinction? Ariès notes that "this question, which is at the heart of the medical interest in death, is also one of the central preoccupations of the age." Investigations of cadavers exerted a "profound impact on the imagination of the time," feeding speculation about residual sentience in the corpse and about the prospect of galvanic reanimation. Such research demanded fresh anatomical specimens and thus gave rise to the atrocity of grave-robbing. This clandestine industry swiftly generated a folklore of violated tombs and reviving corpses; it must have contributed to the appearance, about 1740, of a terror hitherto unexpressed in Western culture—the fear of premature burial.

III

This upheaval in attitudes touches almost every facet of cultural experience. With respect to Gothic fiction, the ubiquity of corpses (often bleeding preternaturally) reminds us, as Freud would much later, that the ultimate source of all terror is death itself. In effect, the haunted castle, the subterranean passageway, the secret vault, and the sealed room—all the conventional scenes of Gothic mystery—evoke anxiety because they pose the implicit threat of fatal enclosure. In an age that witnessed what Ariès calls "the first manifestation of the great modern fear of death," we discover a literary form given over to the recurrent staging of ultimate vulnerability. But the Gothic did not remain a static form; when we come upon its recognizable contours in the fiction of Poe, we also encounter new resonances and motifs indicative of changes in the cultural consciousness of death.

Perhaps in reaction to the eighteenth century's prolonged contemplation of the unshrouded corpse and the gaping grave, the dark imaginings once poetically associated with death had shaded into a bland sentimentality about time and transience, about loss and separation. By the early nineteenth century, as Ariès points out, the sense of mortality as "pure negativity" accompanied a fascination with the idea of a spiritual reunion beyond the grave. The ghastly image of death created by the procurement and dissection of cadavers yielded to an extravagant, romanticized vision of "the beautiful death"—a tender, well-planned departure, in which the prospect of an otherworldly rendezvous loomed large. Religious sentiment enjoyed a superficial resurgence in consolation literature, as the hour of death became a fetishized event. Ann Douglas has called attention to the necrolatry inherent in these works: "Such writings inflated the importance of dying and the dead by every possible means; they sponsored elaborate methods of burial and commemoration, communication with the next world, and microscopic viewings of a sentimentalized afterlife." The poetry of Felicia Hemans and her American admirer, Lydia Huntley Sigourney, epitomized the movement in popular culture toward an ethereal image of mortality, purged of gross physical detail. Ariès summarizes the prevailing attitude: "Since death is not the end of the loved one, however bitter the grief of the survivor, death is neither ugly nor fearful. On the contrary, death is beautiful, as the dead body is beautiful. Presence at the deathbed in the nineteenth century is more than a customary participation in a social ritual; it is an opportunity to witness a spectacle that is both comforting and exalting." But this new perception involves aesthetic contrivance: "This death [was] no longer death, it [was] an illusion of art." Indeed, the preoccupation with mortality so evident in magazines, annuals, and contemporary engravings betrays massive cultural self-deception: "In life as well as in art and literature, death [was] concealing itself under the mask of beauty."

What these shifts in sensibility reveal most clearly is the essential instability of Western ideas about mortality since roughly 1700. The reassuring model of "familiar and tame" death, prevalent until the late seventeenth century, vanished with the rise of the modern, industrialized, secular city. In its place emerged a multiplicity of conflicting attitudes and assumptions, producing radical confusion about the nature and meaning of death. The Christian message of resurrection continued to be heard, but clergymen as frequently extolled the beauty of dying, outlined the spiritual benefits of grief, or described the amenities of a domesticated heaven. Proponents of spiritualism grew numerous and by the mid-nineteenth century had established an organized movement. Those still influenced by a deistic or pantheistic saw death as Bryant had painted it in "Thanatopis": a beatific return to the bosom of nature, that "mighty sepulchre" of humanity. Attitudes originating in eighteenth-century graveyard verse continued to obtrude upon the popular consciousness; as I have shown in another essay, the fear of premature burial sustained a flourishing fictional subgenre in contemporary periodicals. Medical experiments upon corpses still excited a horrified fascination, as the popularity of Mary Shelley's *Frankenstein* (1819) suggests. The rise of scientific positivism prompted widespread doubts about the existence of an immaterial soul, to the chagrin of ministers and spiritualists alike.

But amid the welter of contending viewpoints, David Stannard has discerned the "overriding national treatment of death" between the Revolution and the Civil War: "In large measure, if not entirely in response to the growing individual anonymity brought on by changes in their social world, Americans sought a return to their lost sense of community in the graveyard and the heavenly world of the dead; in the process, paradoxically, they effectively banished the reality of death from their lives by a spiritualistic and sentimentalized embracing of it." That is, the death fetish of the early nineteenth century grew from a need to reestablish bonds of commitment in an increasingly impersonal, urban society. But in order for death to become the great Meeting Place, it had to be disinfected and prettified. The effort to invest death with sentimentalized beauty drew the support of many leading writers; Washington Irving's tales "The Pride of the Village" and "The Broken Heart" (in *The Sketch-Book*) epitomize the tearful fare that flooded the publishing scene, promoting the Beautiful Death. This was the very society that, in Mark Twain's *Huckleberry Finn,* produced the lachrymose Emmeline Grangerford: "She warn't particular, she could write about anything you choose to give her to write about, just so it was sadful. Every time a man died, or a woman died, or a child died, she would be on hand with her 'tribute' before he was cold." With respect to popular gift book poetry, there is less exaggeration in Twain's caricature than one would suppose.

IV

Such was the literary and cultural environment in which Poe endeavored to sustain himself as a writer in the early 1830s. That he found the funereal sentimentality of the day a valid rhetorical mode may be surmised from his appreciative regard for Mrs. Sigourney, Letitia E. Landon, Mrs. E. Clementine Stedman, and other purveyors of maudlin stuff. In 1842 he did score the "namby-pamby character" of *Graham's Magazine* in a moment of pique, but there is no evidence that he found the cultural preoccupation with mortality unhealthy, inappropriate, or laughable. By temperament and mournful personal experience, Poe was drawn into the contemporary cult of death. But if he respected the muse of sentiment, he avoided in his tales the conventional sad-but-joyful departure, and he clearly saw through the "mask of beauty" that concealed the grim features of human dissolution. In his "Marginalia" series Poe observed trenchantly, "Who ever *really* saw anything but horror in the smile of the dead? We so earnestly *desire* to fancy it 'sweet'—that is the source of the mistake; if, indeed, there ever was a mistake in the question." Unlike his contemporaries, he refused to soften or idealize mortality and kept the essential "horror" in view; but he also moved beyond the Gothic formula to explore divergent conceptions of death. Through the symbolic notation provided by supernatural motifs, we can identify the features of four principal paradigms: annihilation, compulsion, separation, and transformation.

Annihilation. In his illuminating study *The Denial of Death,* Ernest Becker builds his argument upon a fundamental insight: "This is the meaning of the Garden of Eden myth and the rediscovery of modern psychology: that death is man's peculiar and greatest anxiety." This comment goes far in explaining the stunning contemporaneity of Poe's fiction and poetry. Becker's analysis demonstrates that we experience death as a "complex symbol" that changes as human beings pass through successive stages of consciousness. But the primal, embedded meaning of death, which all of our "immortality projects" seek to overcome, is that of terrifying annihilation. Initially encountered in childhood through the permanent disappearance of loved ones, this terror develops finally into a concept of personal extinction, a recognition of one's creaturely condition—that one is trapped within a body that "aches and bleeds and will decay and die." This elemental anxiety informs much of Poe's fiction; it manifests itself in the wild, deathbed protest of Ligeia: "O God! O Divine Father!—shall these things be undeviatingly so?—shall this Conqueror be not once conquered?" The Conqueror Worm, its "vermin fangs / In human gore imbued," provides a graphic reminder of our bodily fate. An acute interest in the physiology and physical imagery of death in fact typifies Poe's annihilation model. Visible signs of disease, impending death, or dissolution assume as reminders of the ultimate naturalistic process. Poe also draws attention to traditional emblems of death—the skull, the skeleton, the "grim reaper," the moldering corpse—to intensify the anxiety of his protagonists (cf. "The Pit and the Pendulum"). As a metaphorical reminder that one is, to borrow the later phrase of Yeats, "fastened to a dying animal," the annihilation paradigm in Poe frequently involves physical entrapment aboard a ship, inside a house, within a vortex, behind a wall, or (most revealingly) in the tomb itself.

Elements of this model can be found in most of Poe's tales, but its purest expression occurs in "Shadow—A Parable" and in the more impressive sequel, "The Masque of the Red Death." These works have in common an atmosphere of brooding anticipation. Both represent the deliberate immurement of a group fearful of pestilence, and both depict the physical intrusion of death. Each tale implicitly suggests that our most ingenious strategies cannot protect us from this fate, nor can we entirely repress the dread to which that awareness gives rise. Significantly, I think, neither story raises the prospect of a happy reunion in another world. "Shadow" closes with the perception by the "company of seven" of a multitude of spirit voices, "the well remembered and familiar accents of many thousand departed friends," but far from providing reassurance, these voices cause the assemblage to start from their seats "in horror, and stand trembling, and shuddering, and aghast." The annihilation model presents a stark encounter with the death-anxiety from which our "neurotic shield" of repression ordinarily protects us.

As the headnote to "Shadow" makes clear, the title figure is the shadow of death, whose presence imposes a palpable depression: "There were things around us and about which I can render no distinct account—things material and spiritual—heaviness in the atmosphere—a sense of suffocation—anxiety—and, above all, that terrible sense of existence which the nervous experience when the senses are keenly living and awake, and meanwhile the powers of thought lie dormant. A dead weight hung upon us . . . ; and all things were depressed, and borne down thereby." Death weighs upon the group because it is thrice present: first in the pallid countenances of the men themselves as reflected on the ebony table; then in the corpse of "young Zoilus," whose unclosed eyes reveal a "bitterness" (even though the body is "enshrouded"); finally in the "dark and undefined shadow" that issues from the sable draperies and fixes itself upon the door. Here, the supernatural impinges upon the natural world to signify an important concept. The "vague, and formless, and indefinite" shadow, a manifestation "neither of man, nor of God, nor of any familiar thing," projects a view of death as terrifying absence and absolute difference. Its horror derives from its complete unintelligibility. Poe's conception of the shadow also relates mortality to the idea of evil, for the inscription sets up an inherent contrast between the Psalmist, who will "fear no evil" in the valley of the shadow of death, and the narrator Oinos, who suffers "the boding and the memory of evil" within the sealed room. According to Ariès, death lost much of its sacral quality in the eighteenth century when men ceased to believe in hell and "the connection between death and sin or spiritual punishment." No longer a moment of religious significance, the hour of reckoning, death itself became evil, a thing to be avoided. (We begin to see the importance of this association for Poe when we note the elements of the human tragedy specified in the "The Conqueror Worm": Madness, Sin, and Horror.)

A slightly different emphasis develops in "The Masque of the Red Death," where the situation adumbrated in "Shadow" acquires complexity and dramatic effect. There is no need here to review extant interpretations of the tale's color symbolism, nor should we be detained by the "ebony clock," with its too-obvious linking of time and death. What demands closer scrutiny is Poe's characterization of the dreadful intruder and the implications of that portrayal. Cutting through a tangle of critical conjecture, Joseph Patrick Roppolo has called the work "a parable of the inevitability and universality of death." Death cannot be barred from the palace, he argues, because it is in the blood, part and parcel of our humanity, not an external invader. Hence, according to Roppolo, the spectral figure is not a representation of mortality (which is already present) but a figment of the imagination: man's "self-aroused and self-developed fear of his own mistaken concept of death."

This approach has a certain validity—death is indeed in our blood, coded in our genes—and it leads to the interesting hypothesis that Prospero succumbs to his own terror, to the "mistaken" idea that death is a tangible enemy. But it also collapses the supernaturalism of the story and reduces the intriguing figure to a simple misconception, thus distorting the allegorical signification. The notion of the specter as self-delusion loses credibility when we realize that all of the revelers observe "the presence of a masked figure." Either everyone deludes himself in precisely the same way, or else there *is* a figure. Poe's careful description of the "spectral image," as he is seen by "the whole crowd," supports the latter view.

> The figure was tall and gaunt, and shrouded from head to foot in the habiliments of the grave. The mask which concealed the visage was made so nearly to resemble the countenance of a stiffened corpse that the closest scrutiny must have had difficulty in detecting the cheat. And yet all this might have been endured, if not approved, by the mad revelers around. But the mummer had gone so far as to assume the type of the Red Death. His vesture was dabbled in *blood*—and his broad brow, with all the features of the face, was besprinkled with the scarlet horror.

In choosing to symbolize the unmentionable, the "mummer" has violated a taboo and brought death into the open. But why does Poe insist upon the particularity of the Red Death imagery? In the opening paragraph he describes the plague as extraordinarily fatal and hideous: "there were sharp pains, and sudden dizziness, and then profuse bleeding at the pores, with dissolution." Even more terrible, "the whole seizure, progress and termination of the disease, were the incidents of half an hour." That is, the Red Death produces grotesque disfiguration and almost instantaneous decomposition (the horror of M. Valdemar). The putrefaction of the grave becomes a public spectacle as the plague transforms a vibrant individual into a loathsome object. Belief in the uniqueness of personality and the immortality of the soul crumbles at the sight of human carrion. The Red

Death evokes dread because it exposes our creatureliness and raises the question at the core of naturalistic thought: are we finally nothing more than the biological organization of our own perishable flesh?

Such appears to be Poe's conclusion, at least in this parable of annihilation, for when the masqueraders fall upon the stranger, they discover an emptiness behind the corpselike mask.

> Then, summoning the wild courage of despair, a throng of revellers at once threw themselves into the black apartment, and, seizing the mummer, whose tall figure stood erect and motionless within the shadow of the ebony clock, gasped in unutterable horror at finding the grave cerements and corpselike mask which they handled with so violent a rudeness, untenanted by any tangible form.

This discovery reenacts the nineteenth-century perception of death as "pure negativity," a nullity resulting from the "separation of the body and the soul" (Ariès). Poe's portrayal of pure absence signifies "the presence of the Red Death"; the revellers fall, the clock stops, and "the flames of the tripods" expire. Pestilence holds dominion with "Darkness and Decay" over the realm of human experience. The silence of the mummer reigns, and for Poe, silence nearly always implies both the death of the body and the extinction of the soul. In "Sonnet—Silence," written three years before "The Masque of the Red Death," Poe distinguished between "the corporate Silence," which has "no power of evil . . . in himself," and "his shadow," the nameless and (by implication) evil silence that is the death of the spirit. The wordless figure who comes "like a thief in the night," bringing silence to Prospero's domain, presents but a semblance of physical death; he is actually the more dreadful incorporeal silence that affirms the annihilation of the soul.

Compulsion. In "The Imp of the Perverse," Poe accounts for the irrational urge to cast one's self from a precipice, to plunge into an abyss: "And this fall—this rushing annihilation—for the very reason that it involves that one most ghastly and loathsome of all the most ghastly and loathsome images of death and suffering which have ever presented themselves to our imagination—for this very cause do we now the most vividly desire it." This passage at once epitomizes the compulsion paradigm and suggests its relationship to the model already discussed. Death-as-compulsion draws upon the terror of annihilation but finds within it an irrational pleasure, "the delight of its horror." The disgusting character of death, which generates anxiety and aversion in the previous form, now becomes an object of fascination and longing. In *The Narrative of Arthur Gordon Pym* and "A Descent into the Maelström," Poe associated the "perverse" with the image of the abyss, a self-evident symbol of engulfing mortality, and thus indicated its patently suicidal nature. In other works dramatizing the perverse—"The Tell-Tale Heart," "The Black Cat," and "The Cask of Amontillado"—the literal abyss becomes an implied figure disclosed by temptation: the "unfathomable longing of the soul *to vex itself*—to offer violence to its own nature" through displaced self-destructiveness. In each of these tales, an act of murder leads to obsessive revelation; "The Imp of the Perverse" makes explicit the suicidal impulse of the confession: "They say that I spoke with a distinct enunciation, but with marked emphasis and passionate hurry, as if in dread of interruption before concluding the brief but pregnant sentences that consigned me to the hangman and to hell."

Although the death-wish theory of Freud has been largely discredited, the longing for an end to life has (as Eliot's headnote to *The Waste Land* suggests) a persistent tradition of its own. Since the rise of Romanticism, the will to die has become increasingly conspicuous in Western culture. Roughly concurrent with the rise of the Gothic novel and the valorization of "sensibility," Goethe's *Sorrows of Young Werther* (1774) "swept over eighteenth-century Europe like a contagious disease," initiating a vogue for suicide—or, more precisely, unleashing an impulse that had long been held in check by reason, faith, and social convention. Four years before *Werther,* the self-induced death of Thomas Chatterton had had only a limited impact, but in the wake of Goethe's novel and its literary progeny, Chatterton's death became an important symbol: he was, for the Romantics, "the first example of death by alienation." The outbreak of suicide in life and literature in the late eighteenth century expresses far more than a passing fashion; it seems to manifest an intriguing response to the modern dread of death. At first glance, this seems an illogical supposition: how does the wish for death follow from the fear of mortality? We know know that in some cases thanatophobia paradoxically drives the individual toward death as a means of release from the burden of death-anxiety. We understand too that the act on some basic level involves a rejection of the fated biological creature; the mind or self directs violence against the body to eradicate the pain and despair inevitably experienced in the viscera. Hence the Romantic vogue for suicide, which finds expression in Poe, reflects yet another aspect of the quintessential modern affliction that Kierkegaard called the "sickness unto death."

Two of Poe's early tales, "Metzengerstein" and "MS. Found in a Bottle," use supernatural motifs to illuminate the inner world of suicidal compulsion. In "Metzengerstein" a "mysterious steed" seems to embody the soul of the hated Count Berlifitzing, and by carrying the Baron Metzengerstein to his death, it enforces a curse and completes the revenge pattern. But attention to detail indicates that the horse actually embodies the fiendish malignancy of the baron himself, whose "perverse attachment" to the animal stems from an intrinsic likeness: "the young Metzengerstein seemed riveted to the saddle of that colossal horse, whose intractable audacities so well accorded with his own spirit." The beast inspires an instinctive dread: Metzengerstein "never vaulted into the saddle, without an unaccountable and almost imperceptible shudder"; he never names the horse and never places his hand "upon the body of the beast." His fear originates from his first perception of the horse as a tapestried image. Significantly, Poe writes that the baron feels an "overwhelming anxiety" that falls "like a pall upon his senses." The nature of his terror becomes explicit when a preternatural change in the horse's features discloses its symbolic function: "The eyes, before invisible, now wore an energetic and human expression, while they gleamed with a fiery and unusual red; and the distended lips of the apparently enraged horse left in full view his sepulchral and disgusting teeth." Once again, Poe associates evil (the fiery, hellish eyes) with death (the sepulchral teeth) in contriving an image of Metzengerstein's inescapable doom. But here is the essence of the compulsion model: far from banishing the symbol of his future destruction, Metzengerstein compulsively surrenders himself to the creature (and the horror he inspires), finally allowing the horse to carry him into the all-consuming flames.

"MS. Found in a Bottle" adds a significant dimension to this conception of death by suggesting that the narrator seeks more than his own perverse annihilation: he longs to enter the abyss, the vortex, to glimpse the *mysterium tremendum* it contains. In the tale's most frequently cited passage, Poe juxtaposes the terror of extinction and the yearning to pierce the veil of mortality: "To conceive the horror of my sensations is, I presume, utterly impossible; yet a curiosity to penetrate the mysteries of these awful regions, predominates even over my despair, and will reconcile me to the most hideous aspect of death. It is evident that we are hurrying onwards to some exciting knowledge—some never-to-be-imparted secret, whose attainment is destruction." The story's dense supernaturalism virtually obliges one to understand "these awful regions" as a reference to death, for the voyage itself is a parable of the passage toward it. Shortly after its departure from Java, the freighter on which the narrator sails is becalmed in a manner reminiscent of the ship in Coleridge's *Ancient Mariner*. The stillness, a foretoken of death's fixity, expresses itself in two signs: "The flame of a candle burned on the poop without the least perceptible motion, and a long hair, held between the finger and thumb, hung without the possibility of detecting a vibration." Readers of Poe's day would have recognized in these details two familiar methods of verifying death in cases of suspended animation. The analogy becomes more apparent when the sun is suddenly "extinguished by some unaccountable power," plunging the ship into the "pitchy darkness" of "eternal night" and the narrator into a condition of anxiety and "utter hopelessness." Poe's introduction of the phantom ship— appropriately colored a "deep dingy black"—contributes images of aging to the increasingly complex death symbolism; the spectral sailors personify decay, the ineluctable failure of the flesh: "Their knees trembled with infirmity; their shoulders were bent double with decrepitude; their shrivelled skins rattled in the wind; their voices were low, tremulous, and broken; their eyes glistened with the rheum of years; and their gray hairs streamed terribly in the tempest." Yet these wasted figures, phantasms of the narrator's own never-to-be-reached senescence, inspire a "sentiment ineffable," for they approach the fatal vortex with "more of the eagerness of hope than of the apathy of despair." Their immense age and acceptance of death fill the narrator with a sense of novelty and expectation, and so despite irrepressible sensations of horror, he awaits a potential revelation. In this sense the tale of compulsion looks forward to two other models—separation and transformation—in which death is both an end and a beginning.

Separation. In an age that cultivated the idea of the "the Beautiful Death," the last hour became a matter of extravagant preparation. Those stricken with a lingering illness (tuberculosis was the fashionable malady) made the most of their invalidism by composing letters, poems, diaries, and meditational works, filled with reflections upon earthly life and hopes for the hereafter. Belief in a spiritual rendezvous introduced an element of joyous expectancy to the deathbed scene, Ariès notes, but it also caused death itself to be regarded as "an intolerable separation." The parting became a ritualistic event; the offering of flowers—to beautify the image of death—entered into common usage, as did the creation of commemorative jewelry, needlework, and painting. Ariès characterizes this pattern of funereal idolatry as "the death of the Other" because in an important sense, death became an object of scrutiny and the dying person a kind of aesthetic component, an element in the tableau of "the Beautiful Death." This transformation could only have occurred through a suppression of the physiology of decay and the dissociation of mortality from a concept of hell. Ariès remarks, "No sense of guilt, no fear of the beyond remained to counteract the fascination of death, transformed into the highest beauty."

Without the threat of damnation, the notion of heaven also changed, becoming "the scene of the reunion of those whom death has separated but who have never accepted this separation."

Poe's valorization of "the death of a beautiful woman" as "the most poetical topic in the world" thus exploited a common theme in nineteenth-century culture. In poem after poem, his persona experiences the death of a woman as a radical separation from the beloved Other, an estrangement inducing guilt, grief, madness, and lonely visits to the tomb of the deceased. The sequence of stories from "Berenice" through "The Oval Portrait" uses the same poetic premise but with some intriguing modifications: in fiction, the woman's death excites horror, even perverse impatience in the narrator, who observes disgusting physical changes, in place of the beatific reunion of spirits envisioned in consolation literature. Poe dramatized an implicit antagonism, sometimes culminating in a frenzied, mad encounter with the buried woman. The notable exception to this scheme is "Eleonora," a tale that embodies fairly conventional ideas of death and spiritual communion. More representative of Poe's separation paradigm, however, are "Morella" and "Ligeia," works that depict death not as absolute annihilation but as an ambiguous, temporary parting. In a monstrous parody of the death of the Other, Poe represents the return of the beloved not in spiritual terms but as a ghastly reincarnation tinged with vampirism. Through such supernaturalism, he implies that death is neither an extinction of the self nor admission to a heavenly social club. Rather, it is a condition of spiritual confinement and unrest, a dream world where one acts out the desires and hostilities of an earlier existence.

"Morella" dramatizes a metaphysical question that troubled Poe's generaton: his narrator ponder the fate of individual essence—the "*principium individuationis,* the notion of that identity *which at death is or is not lost forever.*" The tale seems to confirm the survival of personal entity when the dying wife ostensibly returns in the person of the daughter whom she has delivered upon her deathbed; the empty tomb, discovered at the story's end, implies the transmigration of the mother's soul. But the story also raises a doubt about the idea of an enduring, transferable identity, for death of the "second Morella" apparently brings to a close the cycle of resurrection. Less ambiguously, the narrative demonstrates Poe's characteristic attraction-repulsion pattern: the narrator's "singular affection" for Morella and the abandon with which he enters into a mystical apprenticeship give way at length to "horror" and "alienation." As in "Berenice," the onset of physical decline obsesses the narrator: "In time, the crimson spot settled steadily upon the cheek, and the blue veins upon the pale forehead became prominent; and one instant, my nature melted into pity, but, in the next, I met the glance of her meaning eyes, and then my soul sickened and became giddy with the giddiness of one who gazes downward into some dreary and unfathomable abyss." This is a fascinating passage: the narrator observes the signs of his wife's impending death and feels himself caught helplessly in a mechanism of self-destruction (the compulsion model). Her extinction somehow entails his own.

Here Poe touches upon the human tendency to feel jeopardized by the vulnerability or aging of one's partner. Ernest Becker notes that "if a woman loses her beauty, or shows that she doesn't have the strength and dependability that we once thought she did," men may experience the ultimate threat: "The shadow of imperfection falls over our lives, and with it—death and the defeat of cosmic heroism. 'She lessens' = 'I die.' " The narrator's revulsion should be understood not as a response to Morella herself but to her mortality; we can trace his disgust back to her "cold hand," to the voice whose melody is "tainted with terror," to the "melancholy eyes"—all signs of the fate she anticipates and symbolizes. His abhorrence of the process of dissolution and his eagerness for the moment of release foreshadow the twentieth-century concept of unspeakable, invisible death—the hidden shame we encounter, unforgettably, in Tolstoy's "The Death of Ivan Ilych."

In effect, "Morella" presents a grotesque inversion of the sweet parting idealized as "the Beautiful Death." The dread evoked by the death of the Other seems central to this model: in "Berenice" the narrator's "insufferable anxiety" leads to the unconscious defilement of his cousin's body; in "The Fall of the House of Usher" Roderick's terror prevents him from voicing his suspicion that Madeline has been interred prematurely; in "The Oval Portrait" the painter grows "tremulous and very pallid, and aghast" as he perceives the fate of his wife. Fear and loathing enter the scheme of "Ligeia" in a different way. After witnessing his wife's fierce struggle to overcome death through a sheer act of will, the narrator remarries and projects his repressed disgust upon Rowena. The image of his second wife's "pallid and rigid figure upon the bed" brings to mind Ligeia's death and "the whole of that unutterable woe with which [he] had regarded *her* thus enshrouded." During the "hideous drama of revivification," Rowena's morbid relapses produce two associated effects: the narrator's shudder of horror at "the ghastly expression of death" and his "waking vision of Ligeia." The mingling of past and present pushes the narrator to the brink of madness: the woman before him is both living and dead, Lady Rowena and Ligeia, an impossible fusion of irreconcilable opposites. Privately, Poe dismissed the idea that the story affirmed the soul's immortality, and he underscored the finality of death: "One point I have not fully carried out—I should have intimated that the *will* did not perfect its intention—there should have been a relapse—a final one—and Ligeia (who had only succeeded in so much as to convey an idea of the truth to the narrator) should be at length entombed as Rowena—the body alterations have gradually faded away." Notwithstanding Poe's omission, the tale as published hardly implies a joyous or lasting reunion; apart from "Eleonora," he rigorously resisted any idealizing of the death of the Other.

What then is the meaning of the apparently supernatural return staged in the separation paradigm? In "Morella" Poe intimates that the reincarnation completes a curse; Morella warns the narrator, "thy days shall be days of sorrow . . . thou shalt bear about with thee thy shroud on earth," perhaps as retribution for the contempt she has received from him. The return of Madeline Usher also savors of revenge; after a bloody and "bitter struggle" to escape her tomb, she destroys the brother who had buried her prematurely, bearing him to the floor "a corpse, and a victim to the terrors he had anticipated." The return of Ligeia seems to victimize Rowena rather than the narrator, but we must remember that, unlike Eleonora, Ligeia never sanctions or encourages her husband's remarriage. Note the avoidance in the gesture by which she signals her reappearance to the narrator: "*Shrinking from my touch,* she let fall from her head the ghastly cerements which had confined it" (italics mine). The point is subtle but important, for we see that the parting marks an irreversible alienation, to which the horrific reunion bears witness. The ultimate implication of the separation model becomes clear: death makes us strangers to each other. In Poe's fiction, the dramatized return of the Other also suggests, paradoxically, that human ties continue to exert a claim and that loss haunts us in the midst of life. If the death of a beautiful woman grants a certain immunity to Poe's protagonist (dissolution is what happens to someone else), the very task of watching and waiting intensifies the consciousness of his own mortality and destroys his hold upon life and reason. Only in "Eleonora" does the narrator accept the death of the Other and commune happily with her spirit. But that situation more nearly resembles a fourth figuration of human destiny.

Transformation. In his 1844 tour de force, "The Premature Burial," Poe wrote, "the boundaries which divide Life from Death, are at best shadowy and vague." Describing one of those "cessations . . . of vitality" known to result in accidental burial, he mused, "where, meantime, was the soul?" The question of the soul's whereabouts during sleep and after death has a long tradition in Western philosophy, stretching back to Plato and Aristotle. But this enigma aroused profound uncertainty for Poe's generation, as gathering religious doubt inevitably came to center on the problem of mortality. The traditional notion of an immortal, individual essence had come under attack from two fronts. Developing medical knowledge had by the early nineteenth century charted the human anatomy so precisely that the venerable belief in a physical seat of the soul (held by Descartes, for example, who exalted the pineal gland) could no longer be sustained. Indeed, skepticism about the soul's very existence increased in direct ratio to physiological understanding. Meanwhile, the Romantic movement, influenced by German idealism, had popularized a transcendental view of man and nature: a world suffused by an Over-Soul that animated human beings (as it did all living things) but that returned unto itself at death, bearing no trace of personal essence. In the face of these popular ideologies, belief in an individuated soul persisted, mainly because that concept was bound up with the individualism that had undergirded Western culture since the early Renaissance. But the apparent failure of religious dogma channeled belief in the soul into secular occultism, both organized and informal.

Matters of death and the soul were never very far from Poe's thoughts. As we have seen, his writing emphasizes the physiological and psychological aspects of dying, suggesting his greater responsiveness to the threat of oblivion than to the prospect of an afterlife. Yet in early poems like *Al Aaraaf* and "Israfel" (as well as tales like "Eleonora"), he could occasionally entertain fancies of transcendence. In a series of four works, which began with "The Conversation of Eiros and Charmion" and ended with "The Power of Words," Poe depicted death as metamorphosis and through supernatural dialogues projected scenes of spiritual reunion and cosmic discovery. In "The Colloquy of Monos and Una," the transformation of the title entities makes possible a retrospective view of death and burial, in which the "evil hour" of separation now appears as a "passage through the dark Valley and Shadow" toward "Life Eternal": a rebirth. After delivering a harangue on earthly problems, Monos relates the "weird narrative" of his own decease, noting the sensory impressions of his last moments, the lamentations of his survivors, preparations for his burial, and the interment itself. He insists that the "breathless and motionless torpor" which was "termed Death by those who stood around [him]" did not deprive him of "sentience." But gradually his senses dim, and Monos becomes aware of a new mode of consciousness, the "sentiment of *duration*," which he terms "the first obvious and certain step of the intemporal soul upon the threshold of the temporal Eternity." Finally the "consciousness of being" yields to a simple sense of place: "The narrow space immediately surrounding what had been the body, was now growing to be the body itself." In reporting this transformation, Poe propounds the idea that the soul and body do not separate at death, that the spirit remains within the mortal frame, still in effect a prisoner of sensation, until the process of decay reduces the body to dust. Yet Poe's final, troubling sentence implies that not even the soul survives this disintegration; what remains is pure absence, "nothingness." But we have the dialogue itself as evidence of an "immortality." Poe appears to suggest that the total annihilation of body and soul must take place before the rebirth or transformation alluded to at the beginning of the work. The self must endure "many lustra" of decomposition ("corrosive hours") before reaching the condition of nullity preliminary to "Life Eternal."

This vision of infinity becomes somewhat clearer in "Mesmeric Revelation." Here the dialogue occurs between Vankirk, a patient dying of tuberculosis, and P., the narrator-mesmerist. On the point of death, Vankirk summons P. to place him in a sleep-waking state, so that he may explore his own "psychal impressions" about the soul. Articulating what may have been Poe's own uncertainties, the dying man admits, "I need not tell you how sceptical I have hitherto been on the topic of the soul's immortality. I cannot deny that there has always existed, as if in that very soul which I have been denying, a vague half-sentiment of its own existence." Under mesmeric influence, and speaking (in the latter portion of the tale) from the beyond, Vankirk elaborates a transcendental theory of God as an all-pervasive spirit, of which the human being is an individualized expression. He affirms of man, "Divested of his corporate investiture, he were God. . . . But he can never be thus divested—at least never *will* be— else we must imagine an action of God returning upon itself—a purposeless and futile action." According to this hypothesis, each of us is trapped within a body that is coextensive with and inseparable from the soul. How then do we escape the tomb? Here is the key to Poe's theory of immortality (and the concept of death as transformation): "There are two bodies—the rudimental and the complete; corresponding with the two conditions of the worm and the butterfly. What we call 'death,' is but the painful metamorphosis. Our present incarnation is progressive, preparatory, temporary. Our future is perfected, ultimate, immortal. The ultimate life is the full design." If we understand "present incarnation" to encompass both flesh and spirit, the metaphysics of "The Colloquy of Monos and Una" becomes intelligible. The temporal body falls away like a chrysalis, revealing the intemporal, "complete" body, the astral body. But Poe is no systematic thinker; in "Mesmeric Revelation" he drops the idea of a season in limbo (called "the alloted days of stupor" in "The Conversation of Eiros and Charmion") and says that "at death or metamorphosis, these creatures, enjoying the ultimate life—immortality" inhabit "SPACE itself" as "non-entities" invisible to the angels. Unfortunately, the final tale in the sequence, "The Power of Words," sheds no light on these mysteries, defining the soul merely as a "thirst" for ultimate knowledge.

These philosophical inconsistencies are perhaps beside the point. What seems significant about the cycle of spiritualized dialogues is Poe's inclination to see body and soul as inextricably bonded. Despite the conception of an unearthly, astral form, an odd materialism informs Poe's notion of the spirit world; "Aidenn" is simply a place where things, substances, are less densely constituted. God is "unparticled matter," souls have bodies, and words have a physical power." It is as if, for all of his mystical inclinations, Poe cannot escape an empirical vision of a bounded world. His depiction of an afterlife seems to express a yearning for a realm "out of space, out of time," beyond the contingencies of mortal existence. Yet in fact his spirit figures carry with them a good deal of earthly baggage—memories, affections, beliefs, political opinions—and spend much of their time (if one can thus speak of the eternal) reflecting upon personal experiences or explaining celestial phenomena according to mundane scientific principles. In short, Poe's visionary texts (and here I include the monumentally confused *Eureka*) project a false transcendence, a phantasmic existence after death, conceptually embedded in a cosmos of matter and energy, a system that culminates in irreversible dissolution: entropy.

V

Among Poe's manifold representations of death and dying, we discern no single formulation that might confidently be described as the essential design. His object as a writer was not, of course, to construct a programmatic analysis of human fate; his thematic diversity and penchant for irony complicate even further an identification of his "real" conceptual matrix. Nevertheless, the imagery of death recurs with such insistence that its imaginative priority seems self-evident. Edward Davidson once described Poe as a "verbal landscapist of death," and in an early poem, "The City in the Sea," we encounter the characteristic scene of silence and desolation, upon which "Death looks gigantically down." For Poe, death was indeed gigantic, not in crude physical terms but as a ubiquitous and oppressive presence. Personal experience, popular culture, and intellectual history conspired to make it so. The pathetic facts of his own life—the successive deaths of his parents, his surrogate mother (Mrs. Jane Stith Standard), his foster mother (Mrs. Allan), and his child bride, Virginia—describe a pattern of loss that must have haunted him like a specter. His inveterate melancholy also fed upon the funereal spirit of the age, as manifested in the sentimental offerings of the gift books and ladies' magazines. And his fear and trembling (to use the phrase of his contemporary, Kierkegaard) further derived from the crisis of authority and understanding that shook Western culture in the eighteenth century. Among other consequences, this crisis seriously challenged or destroyed traditional ways of accepting death and introduced a welter of new, secular conceptions that necessarily contributed further uncertainty. To use the phrase of Becker, it was at this moment that the "eclipse of secure communal ideologies of redemption" produced the anxiety characteristic of the modern age. Since 1700 rapidly changing conceptions of death, symptomatic of a decentered culture, have failed to mitigate or resolve the underlying dread. It it a mark of Poe's genius that he perceived the central problem of death and sensed in his own dubiety the confusion of our existential plight. As Sarah Helen Whitman shrewdly perceived in 1859, the "unrest and faithlessness of the age culminated in him"; Poe was the saddest and loneliest writer of his generation because he "came to sound the very depths of the abyss," to plumb the nature of modern despair.

No story in the Poe canon sounds the depths more effectively than "The Facts in the Case of M. Valdemar," a tale that incorporates elements of all four models previously discussed. A sequel to "Mesmeric Revelation," "Valdemar" further illuminates the disjunction between body and soul as disclosed by mesmeric experiment; it postulates the threshold experience of a man *in articulo mortis*. Like the tales of separation, it portrays mortality as an object of scrutiny; the narrator furnishes expert observations on the physiological decline of his friend. Like characters in the tales of compulsion, M. Valdemar expresses the desire for death ("Do not wake me—let me die so") and longs for release from the mesmeric trance so that his dissolution may be completed. The ensuing spectacle of immediate putrefaction ties the story to the annihilation model and exemplifies the naturalistic horror inherent in death. This is not to suggest that "Valdemar" involves a conscious manipulation of these patterns; rather, the synthetic, composite effect seems the result of an intense concentration of anxiety, a focusing, as it were, of Poe's ambivalent perceptions of mortality.

Despite the fact that Poe in correspondence acknowledged the tale to be a "hoax," "Valdemar" demands serious attention as a conceptualization of death. With excruciating precision, it records the grotesque "facts" of the protagonist's apparent demise:

> The eyes rolled themselves slowly open, the pupils disappearing upwardly; the skin generally assumed a cadaverous hue, resembling not so much parchment as white paper; and the circular

> hectic spots which, hitherto, had been strongly defined in the center of each cheek, *went out* at once. . . . The upper lip, at the same time, writhed itself away from the teeth, which it had previously covered completely; while the lower jaw fell upon with an audible jerk, leaving the mouth widely extended, and disclosing in full view the swollen and blackened tongue.

The disappearance of the "hectic spots" brings to mind, appropriately, the sudden extinction of the sun in "MS. Found in a Bottle," while the revelation of the writhing lip recalls "Metzengerstein," "Berenice," and other Poe tales in which teeth function as a sign of death. This moment of apparent decease has its counterpart in the tale's unforgettable final image, the instantaneous decomposition of Valdemar: "Upon the bed, before that whole company, there lay a nearly liquid mass of loathsome—of detestable putridity." Apart from effecting our revulsion, these details serve a figurative purpose, for "Valdemar" dramatizes the scientific effort—undertaken in the eighteenth century and continuing in our era of medical technology—to understand, control, and perhaps finally conquer the major causes of death. From an empirical viewpoint, cessation of life results from physiological processes that can theoretically be halted or reversed. Even aging has proved susceptible to retardation, and recent developments in genetic engineering and organ replacement bring ever closer the possibility of a technologically guaranteed immortality. However improbable or undesirable this idea seems, one can scarcely deny that the great dream of our scientific utopia lies in the direction of extending life beyond its traditional limits and converting death into a manageable, discretionary experience. Like Hawthorne's Dr. Rappaccini, the narrator of "Valdemar" uses scientific (or pseudoscientific) methods to control the processes of life artificially. His ultimate object is to determine "to what extent, or for how long a period, the encroachments of Death might be arrested" by mesmerism. The stratagem succeeds in postponing Valdemar's dissolution, but when the man is awakened from his vegetative stupor, the grotesque final scene betrays the limitation of human efficacy and reaffirms the sovereignty of death. In effect, the illusion of a scientifically insured immortality disintegrates with Valdemar.

Another key to the symbolic ramifications of the tale lies in the supernatural voice, the "harsh, and broken and hollow" sound that seems to emanate from some deep or distant source, producing a "gelatinous" impression. When the voice declares, "I *have been* sleeping—and now—now—*I am dead,*" it perpetrates what Roland Barthes has called a "scandal of language, . . . the coupling of the first person (*I*) and of the attribute '*dead*' "; it "asserts two contraries at the same time (Life, Death)"; and it effects a "scandalous return to the literal" when "Death, as primordial repressed, erupts directly into language." The last point seems especially pertinent: the tale violates language, logic, and cultural taboo, allowing the unspeakable to speak, the unbearable sight to be seen. It compels us to confront death in all of its visceral repulsiveness, unsoftened by the effusion of sentiment or the prospect of a spiritual afterlife.

As noted earlier, Poe rejected the illusion of "the Beautiful Death" which beguiled his generation, and through the preternatural voice in "Valdemar" he expresses the hard physical and psychological truth at the core of modern consciousness. In this work as in so many others, supernaturalism intrudes upon the world of reason and experience to deliver the message of mortality. The uncanny produces a disruption, shatters the illusion of one's control over the flow of existence; it rivets the consciousness of Poe's protagonists like the first undeniable sign of a mortal illness. It arrives as a threat to the quest for knowledge, beauty, and godlike dominance, driving home a perception of the existential paradox summarized by Becker: "Man is literally split in two: he has an awareness of his own splendid uniqueness in that he sticks out of nature with a towering majesty, and yet he goes back into the ground a few feet in order blindly and dumbly to rot and disappear forever. It is a terrifying dilemma to be in and to have to live with." While Poe could entertain visions of transcendence, he was finally too much the victim of our own crisis of death to exorcise its dread. Yet he faced the "terrifying dilemma" with remarkable tenacity and acuity, producing a literature that seems, in our age of "invisible death," more than ever disturbing and menacing. Little wonder that for many, Poe cannot be taken seriously: to do so is to confront the fearful yet vitalizing truth that our century has done its best to deny.

Poe's Narrative Monologues

Ken Frieden

Edgar Allan Poe's narrative monologues border on madness and disrupt the normally associated conventions of voice. Monologue is solitary speech, whether physically isolated, morally deviant, or semantically opaque; Poe's strongest narrators are not only solitary human beings, for as a fictive consequence of the criminal acts they narrate, they often speak from solitary confinement. But while his narrators appear isolated and deviant, Poe's narratives themselves swerve away from norms. An initial problem is to distinguish between the narrative conventions Poe borrows, transforms, and creates, because the superficially popular genre of his fiction conceals the relationship to English literary tradition. By emphasizing the intensity of reader experience above all else, Poe himself neglects literary history, yet even the most emotionally charged reception of a text is made possible by literary context. Although Poe does respond to conventions of the Gothic novel, his revision of epistolary narrative and conversational poetry is more decisive.

Poe's most compelling fictions succeed as representations of diverse and often pathological characters. Yet if we suspect that consciousness, in literature, is "a fictive appearance generated by language, rather than something language describes or reflects," then we must attend to the devices by which fiction creates the illusion of representing a consciousness. Such devices depend on intertextual relations in literary history. The "I" emerges at various stages and in all genres of English literature, including dramatic

From *Genius and Monologue*. © 1985 by Cornell University. Cornell University Press, 1985.

soliloquy, conversational poetry, and first-person narrative. Whereas the dramatic frame clarifies what it means for a character to say "I," the poetic and narrative "I" raises problems that derive from the disparity between the actual form of writing and the imaginary scene of speaking. Poe revises the conversational mode to present dreams, fantasies, passions, obsessions.

The meaning of first-person narrative in stories by Poe becomes clearer in the context of his eighteenth-century precursors. The earliest epistolary fiction of Samuel Richardson brings the narrator into a peculiar condition of identity with the narrated world. If the surest truth of experience is "I think," the most irrefutable literary assertion is "I write." Yet who is the "I" of such a statement? The fictional "I" creates itself and, simultaneously, its frame. Especially where the letters of only one character constitute a fictional world, there is no clear separation between the narrating persona and the world narrated. After Richardson, then, the scene of writing is an accepted component of the English novel. This scene influences the later development of self-conscious prose and particularly modern internal monologue that pretends to reproduce a scene of unwritten thoughts.

Prior narrative traditions are tame, however, when compared with those introduced by Poe's first-person tales. In a sense, Poe transfers the intensely present "I" of Romantic verse to an analogous "I" of narrative. But his first-person accounts do not merely transpose the conversation poem into a narrative form: Poe's narrated monologues unsettle the representational conventions on which they initially depend. At the same time that a first-person voice reveals exalted states of consciousness, Poe subverts the realistic pretense by focusing attention on the act of writing. The scene of Poe's greatest originality is the point at which he disrupts the conversational tradition by tampering with the unexamined illusion of narrative voice.

"I Write in the Present Tense"

Apart from the obvious, yet superficial, influence of Gothic novels, Poe is most significantly influenced by the first-person form of epistolary fiction. A first-person "voice" is clearly essential to the genre based on personal letters and diary entries.

Samuel Richardson innovates in a monological vein by producing the epistolary novel *Pamela* (1740). Twentieth-century literary norms make the novelty of Richardson's narrative devices difficult to appreciate: Richardson introduces a genre of self-reflective writing while planting the seeds of its undoing. Early in *Pamela,* for example, the heroine represents her past thoughts in a letter to her parents: "O Pamela, said I to myself, why art thou so foolish and fearful? Thou hast done no harm! What, if thou fearest an unjust judge, when thou art innocent, would'st thou do before a just one, if thou wert guilty? Have courage, Pamela, thou knowest the worst! . . . So I cheered myself; but yet my poor heart sunk, and my spirits were quite broken." Recalling her thoughts in the form of a pseudodialogue at a specific moment, Pamela apparently practices what Shaftesbury calls the "Home-*Dialect* of *Soliloquy*." As Shaftesbury's analysis predicts, the soliloquist becomes "two distinct *Persons*" when Pamela reasons with herself. At the height of perplexity she contemplates suicide and thinks: "Pause here a little, Pamela, on what thou art about, before thou takest the dreadful leap; and consider whether there be no way yet left, no hope, if not to escape from this wicked house, yet from the mischiefs threatened thee in it." On one level, this passage works as psychological realism that represents a process of thought. At the same time, the pause in Pamela's thoughts is a pause in her narrative of events, like the dramatic monologue Diderot describes as "a moment of repose for the action, and of turmoil for the character." While these passages represent past thoughts, the narrative form appears to correspond to the represented moment.

Richardson's Pamela also shows a self-conscious awareness of the process of writing. She accounts for her possession of writing materials and at several points notes her time of composition to the hour. Pamela's activity of writing is, in addition, occasionally interrupted by the world she describes. Amid contemplations, Pamela writes, "But I must break off; here's somebody coming." Even more vividly, she writes of her feeling of dread and its influence on writing: "Though I dread to see him, yet do I wonder I have not . . . I can hardly write; yet, as I can do nothing else, I know not how to forbear!—Yet I cannot hold my pen—How crooked and trembling the lines!—I must leave off, till I can get quieter fingers!—" After Pamela describes her inability to write, the narrative breaks. As the fictional Pamela exists only by virtue of her writing, she literally "can do nothing else." Her peculiar self-awareness only slightly disturbs the representational illusion with the recognition that "Pamela" exists only as a fictive writer. We experience Pamela primarily as a writer, but she remains a realistic character within the fiction.

Richardson's novel explicitly narrates Mr. B's approach to Pamela, and it tells a parallel tale of the reader's approach to her texts. Mr. B must fight to obtain Pamela's writings, a struggle which identifies him with the reader, who now holds the texts that are also objects within the fictional world. Like a sympathetic reader, Mr. B understands and loves Pamela all the more for the words she pens; in fact, he only begins to acknowledge the depth of her character through her writing, just as the reader discovers her.

"I write, therefore I am" is the principle of first-person narration. Even for Mr. B, Pamela is most truly herself in her writings. Yet as Mr. B kidnaps and isolates her, she is pushed toward a mode of writing that is not intended to be read. Pamela cherishes the notion that she can be identical with what she writes and defends herself against charges of insincerity: "I know I write my heart; and that is not deceitful." The purity of her manuscripts at first depends on their remaining untouched by Mr. B; when he demands to see all she writes, he undermines the very possibility of writing. Pamela imagines that she will no longer be able to write "with any face"— or heart?—if she must write without monological isolation, in the expectation of Mr. B's readership. In a sense, then, the novel ought to end as soon as she and Mr. B are united; Pamela writes, of necessity, for only as long as they are separated and she contemplates matters that she must hide from him. The scene of writing is linked to the developments that overcome Pamela's solitude by bringing her closer to the reader and to Mr. B.

Henry Fielding proves to be a genuine critic when he subsequently lambastes the new epistolary fiction in his *Shamela* (1741), revealing the essence of Richardson's narrative monologues by means of comic distortions. *Shamela* does not merely parody *Pamela*'s more obvious quirks, such as the ambiguous character of the heroine. Fielding's caricature pokes fun at the improbable narrative device by which Pamela continues to write during the most heated moments of action, and in so doing, Fielding reveals the nature of Richardson's epistolary form.

One of Shamela's most humorous diary entries, purportedly written "Thursday Night, Twelve o'Clock," may serve as an introduction to Poe's revision of narrative conventions. In a style that obliquely prepares the way for Molly Bloom's internal monologue, Shamela describes events as they occur:

> Mrs. Jervis and I are just in bed, and the door unlocked; if my master should come—Odsbobs! I hear him just coming in at the door. You see I write in the present tense, as Parson Williams says. Well, he is in bed between us, we both shamming a sleep; he steals his hand into my bosom, which I, as if in my sleep, press close to me with mine, and then pretend to awake.—I no sooner see him, but I scream out to Mrs. Jervis, she feigns likewise but just to come to herself; we both begin, she to becall, and I to bescratch very liberally. After having made a pretty free use of my fingers, without any great regard to the parts I attacked, I counterfeit a swoon.

Shamela is a counterfeiter both in bed and in her narrative pretense that suggests simultaneity with narrated action. She can as easily feign an impossible narrative stance as she can "counterfeit a swoon." Thus the parody of Pamela's character combines with a comic exaggeration of her manner of writing: Fielding exposes the possibly bizarre consequences of Richardson's innovation. First-person, present-tense writing results in a variety of difficulties, such as the paradoxical illusion that Shamela can simultaneously write her diary and engage in a battle with Mr. B. Nothing in *Pamela* reaches such self-contradictory extremes, of course, yet Fielding aptly captures the potential turns of perversity made possible by Richardson's representations of thought and of moments of writing. One hundred years later, E. A. Poe develops a kindred genre in which diabolical monologists appear menacingly present.

"Why Will You Say That I Am Mad?"

In one sense, then, Poe's first-person narrators stand firmly in the tradition of epistolary fiction as initiated by Richardson and parodied by Fielding. But when Poe situates his work in relation to tradition, he refers most exclusively to poetic models. In "The Poetic Principle," Poe establishes both an aesthetic theory and a canon of "English and American poems which best suit my taste." While Poe argues strongly that he has discerned *the* poetic principle, he describes something that he himself invents, in connection with his own poetic preferences. Poe favors short poems of high intensity, on the basis of a "peculiar principle" of psychology:

> a poem deserves its title only inasmuch as it excites, by elevating the soul. The value of the poem is in the ration of this elevating excitement. But all excitements are, through a psychal necessity, transient. That degree of excitement which would entitle a poem to be so called at all, cannot be sustained throughout a composition of any great length. After the lapse of half an hour, at the very utmost, it flags—fails—a revulsion ensues—and then the poem is, in effect, and in fact, no longer such.

On the surface, Poe's principle of literary taste is a "psychal necessity," the human inability to sustain a state of excitement for longer than half an hour. Imposing a half-hour limit is not literally necessary, Poe imagines a faintly sexual scene, derived from figurative demands of a literary scene in which the excitement "flags—fails—a revulsion ensues," and the poem loses its status as poem. An emotional coupling between poem and reader takes place. But does the poetic principle really derive from "psychal necessity," or does poetry control psychology? Only superficially do Poe's poetics depend on exclusively psychological principles. If Poe admires verses that produce an exalted state in the mind of the reader, he seeks poetic personae that create illusions of similarly exalted conditions.

The poetic principle of elevating excitement produces a present scene analogous to that of Coleridge's convesational poetry. A moment in the speaker's experience corresponds to the reader's exalted experience. One mode of Poe's writing is, then, a radicalization of the poetic genre Coleridge begins with "The Eolian Harp." In his "Letter to B——," he admires Coleridge's "towering intellect" and "gigantic power" yet adds that "in reading that man's poetry, I tremble like one who stands upon a volcano, conscious from the very darkness bursting from the crater, of the fire and the light that are weltering below." Whereas Coleridge "imprisoned his own conceptions," Poe—for the sake of an exalted half hour—strives to free the bound forces, as in "Tamerlane," the dream poems, "The Raven," "The Sleeper," and "Annabel Lee." Poe's tales present even more powerful first-person presences. Often enough, Poe's narrators are themselves imprisoned, yet in some way liberated by the scene of narration. The liberation of bound forces and representation of an exalted consciousness are initial premises for Poe's fiction. Poe gives free expression to *thanatos,* an impulse toward death or destruction; beyond their scenes of murder, Poe's narrators perform their own self-destruction in dramas linked to "the imp of the preverse."

The deviant narrators of "The Tell-Tale Heart," "The Black Cat," and "The Imp of the Perverse" in some ways extend into short fiction the epistolary and conversational modes developed by Richardson, Coleridge, and their followers. Yet Poe's narrators often confront the representational illusion at the same time that they dispute the superficial claim that they are insane. In Poe's texts, the scene of madness combines with a controlled scene of writing; at exactly this point, Poe destabilizes the genre he assumes: rhetorical forms both constitute and question a conversational pretense.

On one level, Poe's mad monologues may be read as expressions of psychological realism. "The Tell-Tale Heart," for example, presents itself as the spontaneous narrative of a murderer: "True!—nervous—very, very dreadful nervous I had been and am! but why *will* you say that I am mad? The disease had sharpened my senses—not destroyed—not dulled them. Above all was the sense of hearing acute. I heard all things in the heaven and in the earth. I heard many things in hell. How, then, am I mad? Hearken! and observe how healthily—how calmly I can tell you the whole story."

As the scene of discourse, we may imagine ourselves in conversation with a confined lunatic. His denial of madness only intensifies the effect of his bizarre claim to have "heard all things in the heaven and in the earth." The opening words imply that we have provoked the speaker by asserting what he denies: far from being insane, he says, "the disease had sharpened my senses," and if we choose to listen, we will share his exalted mood for a few minutes. As soon as we begin to read, then, we find ourselves written into a drama in which we have accused the speaker of being nervous or mad. The narrative opens with a paradox, however, which unsettles the representational illusion. The speaker combines mad assertions with narrative lucidity and presents a disconcerting contradiction between his representing and represented personae. The discrepancy between sane narrator and madman perhaps shows the error of assuming that linguistic normalcy implies psychological normalcy. The narrator is mad, or at least abnormal, according to his own account, because he kills an old man for no reason. He is doubly mad when he imagines he hears the pounding of the dead man's heart and gives away the crime he had concealed. Yet the narrator tells a coherent tale, as if to demonstrate out of spite that he is sane, refuting the ordinary belief that he must be mad. This contradiction overturns mimetic conventions: a literal reading of the mad narrator shows itself to be naive, because only Poe's textual pretense creates the illusion of disparity between madman and sane narrator.

"The Black Cat" follows similar patterns, without the exclamatory wildness of the tell-tale narration. The contradiction is even sharper in "the most wild yet most homely narrative which I am about to pen," for the scene of writing is explicit. Condemned to death, the narrator explains: "To-morrow I die, and to-day I would unburthen my soul. My immediate purpose is to place before the world, plainly, succinctly, and without comment, a series of mere household events. In their consequences, these events have terrified—have tortured—have destroyed me. Yet I will not attempt to expound them." Again Poe invents a situation of radical conflict, in which lurid and lucid details compete. Renouncing all value judgments, the narrator resolves to tell his tale in the most indifferent tones. He explains his peculiar behavior only by reference to a philosophical principle. The speaker has been prone to mysterious states, as when "the fury of a demon instantly possessed me"; the narrator attributes his ultimate downfall to perversity:

> Of this spirit philosophy takes no account. Yet I am not more sure that my soul lives, than I am that perverseness is one of the

primitive impulses of the human heart—one of the indivisible primary faculties, or sentiments, which give direction to the character of Man. Who has not, a hundred times, found himself committing a vile or a silly action, for no other reason than because he knows he should *not*? Have we not a perpetual inclination, in the teeth of our best judgment, to violate that which is *Law,* merely because we understand it to be such?

Similar to an evil genius, the "spirit of perverseness" appears as a reversal of the *daimonion* that turns Socrates away from evil. The spirit of perverseness inverts, turns upside down, subverts: "It was this unfathomable longing of the soul to *vex itself*—to offer violence to its own nature—to do wrong for the wrong's sake only—that urged me to continue and finally to consummate the injury I had inflicted upon the unoffending brute." Rather than speak of some psychological drive that leads men to evil, the narrator points to an abstract, counterrational impulse to violate whatever is—nature or law. The impulse to perverseness, governed by the rhetorical figure of chiasmus, is a kind of hidden nature in man. The mad narrator undoes himself both through his perverse actions and in his submerged story of textual subversion, a tribute to "the power of words." The spirit of perverseness is an anti-*daimonion* that turns the speaker against himself; the overt instigator, a black cat, bears the name of Pluto, god of the underworld.

"The Imp of the Perverse" reveals more explicitly the perverse power of words. Half treatise and half tale, the text opens in the tone of philosophical inquiry: "In the consideration of the faculties and impulses—of the *prima mobilia* of the human soul, the phrenologists have failed to make room for a propensity which, although obviously existing as a radical, primitive, irreducible sentiment, has been equally overlooked by all the moralists who have preceded them. In the pure arrogance of the reason, we have all overlooked it." The neglected primum mobile resists the efforts of reason, of perception, of human purpose. Speaking in the tones of rationality, Poe's narrator points to the limits of reason, beyond which our sesnses must be guided by belief. Experiencing vertigo on the edge of an abyss, we encounter "a shape, far more terrible than any genius or any demon of a tale." A thought takes form: "Because our reason violently deters us from the brink, *therefore* do we the most impetuously approach it." Rather than call us away from evil, the perverted "genius" presses us toward the abyss. The perverse further opposes reason and systems of good and evil because it can at least appear to "operate in furtherance of good."

The narrator condenses the paradoxical perverseness into a definition: "It is, in fact, a *mobile* without motive, a motive not *motivirt* (sic)." Displacing comfortable theological beliefs according to which God is the primum mobile, this alternative, an introjected "mobile without motive," upsets all order. The perverse suggests that there can be motion without any rational ground, and even the apparent motive can be without motivation.

By a perverse logic, the entire analytical discourse is transformed when the speaker describes his present situation. Not only does the apparently unmotivated take on motive; perversely, we become visitors to a prison rather than readers of a philosophical discourse:

> I have said thus much, that in some measure I may answer your question, that I may explain to you why I am here, that I may assign to you something that shall have at last the faint aspect of a cause for my wearing these fetters, and for my tenanting this cell of the condemned. Had I not been thus prolix, you might either have misunderstood me altogether; or, with the rabble, have fancied me mad. As it is, you will easily perceive that I am one of the many uncounted victims of the Imp of the Perverse.

The speaker denies his madness by calling himself a victim of the principle he has outlined. Yet his language hovers between calculation and illogic. The narrator explains "why I am here . . . wearing these fetters" by reference to a cause that is only a perverse absence of cause. From the standpoint of realistic representation, the perverse narrator betrays his deviance through linguistic peculiarities. He begins his tale: "It is impossible that any deed could have been wrought with a more thorough deliberation. For weeks, for months, I pondered upon the means of the murder." Like the narrator of "The Tell-Tale Heart" who comments that "it is impossible to say how first the idea entered my brain," he assumes an understanding of what he has not yet explained. Both fictional speakers break accepted conventions by employing the definite article, where "*the* idea" and "*the* murder" have not been previously explicated. If we read these narrators as mimetic characters, their linguistic deviations may be signs of defective mental processes. From another prospective, however, ill-formed syntax is a contradiction embedded in the narrative by Poe, to enhance the contradictions in the narrator's account.

The narrator undoes himself in a scene of internalized self-address, after the words "I am safe" have become his standard refrain: "One day, whilst sauntering along the streets, I arrested myself in the act of murmuring, half aloud, these customary syllables. In a fit of petulance, I remodelled them thus; 'I am safe—I am safe—yes—if I be not fool enough to make open confession!' " Language overthrows him, for as soon as he asserts one thing, the perverse drives him to subvert this rational thesis:

> No sooner had I spoken those words, than I felt an icy chill creep to my heart. I had had some experience in these fits of perversity, (whose nature I have been at some trouble to explain), and I remembered well, that in no instance, I had successfully resisted their attacks. And now my own casual self-suggestion that I might possibly be fool enough to confess the murder of which I had been guilty, confronted me, as if the very ghost of him whom I had murdered—and beckoned me on to death.

A rhetorical moment takes the place of all ghosts, when "the imp of the perverse" drives the speaker to confess. "The rabble" would understand his behavior as a symptom of madness, but his perversity turns out to be a reflex inherent in words.

"MS. FOUND IN A BOTTLE"

Poe's radical revision of the conversational pretense derives, then, not from the poetic principle of psychological exaltation, but from a rhetorical application of the spirit of perverseness. The mad monologues achieve powerful effects of psychological realism and can be read as the conversations of deranged speakers. Beyond the operation of perverseness in self-destructive behavior, however, Poe's narrators show that language may undermine its own theses. As soon as a murderer tells himself, "I am safe—yes—if I be not fool enough to make open confession," he already assures that he will pronounce his doom. In the tradition of the epistolary and confessional novel, several of Poe's short fictions more radically disrupt the conversational mode by recognizing themselves as writing, and the realistic pretense fades.

"MS. Found in a Bottle" initially confronts the reader with an uncertainty: Is *this* the manuscript found, or will it describe a recovery of some other document in a bottle? The manuscript we read is not, in any obvious sense, found in a bottle. Apparently, the story may be *about* a "MS. Found in a Bottle," or it may actually *be* this manuscript. The story generates the odd illusion that it exists within itself. A perplexing ambiguity makes impossible any clear distinction between the text that represents and the text that is represented. Midway through the narrative, we are informed: "It was no long while ago that I ventured into the captain's own private cabin, and took thence the materials with which I write, and have written. I shall from time to time continue this journal. It is true that I may not find an opportunity of transmitting it to the world, but I will not fail to make the endeavor. At the last moment I will enclose the MS. in a bottle, and cast it within the sea." The bottle is a familiar figure of textuality, of the metonymic relation between form and content, literary container and the thing contained. But the expected configuration is inverted: whereas the container is a bottle within the textual world, what is contained is the text itself. This illusion is also destroyed, however, because the bottle only exists by virtue of the text "inside" that describes its existence. Perversely, the text of "MS. Found in a Bottle" usurps the world it describes by showing that it is identical with that world. The mimetic convention slips away when the text discloses itself merely as a text; the bottle and the wine merge, the container and the contained become inseparable.

Yet the representational level remains: "At the last moment I will enclose the MS. in a bottle, and cast it within the sea." The text masquerades as an object in the world it represents; Poe, by titling the story, pretends to verify this pretense. Poe also "adds" an epigraph that accords a special status to the words of the desperate writer: "Qui n'a plus qu'un moment à vivre / N'a plus rien à dissimuler" ("One who has only a moment to live / Has nothing more to conceal"). According to this proverb, then, no dissimulation can occur if the writer is on the verge of death. In the final lines of the story, "amid a roaring, and bellowing, and thundering of ocean and tempest," the narrator writes that "the ship is quivering—oh God! and—going down!" At this moment, presumably, the text is enclosed in the bottle, just as the ship is swallowed up by the sea. But the representational illusion is also engulfed as the moment of writing becomes the moment of death: we can never remove the text from its alleged bottle, for text and bottle are identical. According to the rhetorical figure, the inside of the bottle should represent its contained meanings, but the fullest meaning of Poe's story is that this text is identical with its inside, the entire text is its meaning, so that in some sense the bottle can never be uncorked.

The writer or speaker in "The Cask of Amontillado" never reveals his present place, yet he embeds figurative clues within the tale he narrates. In connection with the story of ruthless murder, a first level of allegory makes the unfortunate Fortunato a stand-in for the reader. As readers, our mistake is to think we can confidently, safely uncork a text and savor its wine. Within the representational illusion, Fortunato shows the same *faiblesse:*

"He had a weak point—this Fortunato—although in other regards he was a man to be respected and even feared. He prided himself on his connoisseurship in wine." The narrator rightly claims that "I did not differ from him materially"—because, of course, both are textual fictions— "and bought largely whenever I could." Yet they do differ: Fortunato prides himself on an ability at wine tasting; the narrator represents himself primarily as a buyer of wines. Fortunato is like a presumptuous literary critic, while Montressor is a writer who stores his textual bottles in endless vaults. While staging Fortunato's death, the narrator figures himself as a writer within the story. Fortunato makes the mistake of wishing to outdo Luchresi, who is reputed to have a fine "critical turn."

As he walks unknowingly toward his tomb, Fortunato laughs and "threw the bottle upward with a gesticulation I did not understand." This is a potentially troubling moment for the narrator, whose reader has taken the text, or the act of signifying, into his own hands:

> I looked at him in surprise. He repeated the movement—a grotesque one.
> "You do not comprehend?" he said.
> "Not I," I replied.
> "Then you are not of the brotherhood."
> "How?"
> "You are not of the masons."

The speaker is troubled by his victim's continued independence. How can the author of a text or scheme respond to such a rebellion? At this provocation, which is like that of an elusive reader, the narrator turns the situation around:

> "You are not of the masons."
> "Yes, yes," I said; "yes, yes."
> "You? Impossible! A mason?"
> "A mason," I replied.
> "A sign," he said.
> "It is this," I answered, producing a trowel from beneath the folds of my *roquelaire*.
> "You jest," he exclaimed, recoiling a few paces.

At first, "mason" refers to the secret order of Masons, an order that separates itself by means of arcane signs. Yet the narrator quells his reader's rebellion by demonstrating that his signs escape him; we now understand the opening line of the story: "The thousand injuries of Fortunato I had borne as I best could, but when he ventured upon insult, I vowed revenge." Poe's persona takes revenge on his critics, showing their inability to understand what they say by literalizing their figures of speech and demonstrating that their error entombs them. Fortunato believes that the Masonic order controls its secret language, but he learns that its language can control him. The pun on "mason" turns a trowel into an ominously literal sign of the Mason's demise, and Fortunato can only lean heavily on the narrator's arm as he walks toward his death.

"The Cask of Amontillado" suppresses the rebellious reader by writing him into the text and by entombing him in a subterranean vault. The trowel, a figure for the stylus, walls up unfortunate Fortunato, who tries to dismiss Montresor's action as a joke. But the act of writing is utterly serious: as "I forced the last stone into its position; I plastered it up," and the story ends. The Mason, unable to control his trope, finds himself victimized by the perverse action of masonry. The narrator becomes confused with what is narrated, the container with the contained, as if urging us to disbelieve the mimetic conventions that pretend to present the voice of a speaking subject. The reader, too, should be unable to savor his wine, confronted by a double who has become like wine decomposing within a bottle, the corpse within a textual tomb.

Poe takes up the first-person form only to transgress its usual limitations. The "I" no longer rests with a stable representational function, for behind the mask are only contours of the mask. Where the fictionally speaking voice becomes inextricably bound up with the events it speaks, the more solid ground of mimetic fiction crumbles. There remains an enhanced sensitivity to the dynamics of textual illusion.

First-person narratives, from Richardson to Poe, enact the unification of narrator and narrated, narration and event, creator and created. When the mimetic framework is questioned by internal contradictions, self-narrative unsettles the barrier between signifying and referential functions of language. To represent a self, narration reflects itself.

The literary life of self perhaps corresponds to an equally fictional worldly self that depends on performance for its existence. The monos of monologue can no longer stand as a subject or monad and is rather a textual swerve. For monologue is not the *logos* of subjectivity but only the linguistic embodiment of isolation and deviance that reveals perverse origins of the fictive subject.

Chronology

1809   Born in Boston, January 19, the second of three children of David Poe and his wife, Elizabeth Arnold, both actors. Poe's father subsequently abandons the family.

1811   Death of Poe's mother in Richmond, Virginia. The children are taken into different households, Edgar into that of John Allan, a Richmond merchant. Not legally adopted, he is nevertheless renamed Edgar Allan.

1815–20   Resides with the Allans in Scotland and London.

1820–25   Educated in private schools, after the Allans return to Virginia.

1826   Enters University of Virginia (founded by Jefferson the year before), where he studies languages. Gambling debts compel him to leave, after Allan refuses to pay them.

1827   Enlists in army in Boston, where his first book, *Tamerlane and Other Poems,* appears and is ignored.

1828–29   Honorably discharged as sergeant major, Poe lives in Baltimore, where *Al Aaraaf, Tamerlane, and Minor Poems* is published.

1830–31   Enters West Point in May 1830; does well in studies but is expelled in January 1831 after deliberately breaking rules. Breach with John Allan. *Poems, Second Edition* published. Poe lives in Baltimore with his father's sister, Maria Clemm, and her daughter Virginia, then eight years old. His brother, also living with the Clemms, dies in August. Poe begins to write tales.

1832–35   Tutors cousin Virginia Clemm. A number of the tales appear in various journals. Death of John Allan. Poe writes book reviews and becomes editorial assistant for *Southern Literary Messenger.* Moves to Richmond with Virginia and Mrs.

Clemm; becomes editor of the journal, to which he contributes reviews, poems, and stories.

1836 Marries Virginia Clemm, not yet fourteen; her mother stays on as housekeeper.

1837–38 Resigns from the *Messenger* and moves with his household to New York City, where he is unable to secure editorial work. Publishes "Ligeia" and *The Narrative of Arthur Gordon Pym*. Moves to Philadelphia.

1839–40 Works for *Gentleman's Magazine,* where "William Wilson" and "The Fall of the House of Usher" appear. Publishes the two-volume *Tales of the Grotesque and Arabesque* in Philadelphia, late in 1839. After losing his job, he attempts unsuccessfully to found his own magazine.

1841–42 As an editor of *Graham's Magazine,* he prints "The Murders in the Rue Morgue." In January 1842, Virginia Poe suffers severe hemorrhage, never fully recovers.

1843–45 Poe's reputation rises with the prizewinning "The Gold-Bug." Moves to New York City. Despite his lecturing, editing, and extensive publication, Poe is never financially secure. His drinking is increasingly a problem. "The Raven," published in January 1845, is immensely popular. *Tales* published in July 1845, *The Raven and Other Poems* that November. He becomes owner and editor of the *Broadway Journal*.

1846 Abandons *Broadway Journal* because of his depression and financial problems. Moves household to Fordham, New York, where Virginia is cared for by her mother and Marie Louise Shew.

1847 Virginia dies January 30. Poe, himself very ill, is nursed by Mrs. Clemm and Mrs. Shew.

1848 Proposes marriage to the poet Sarah Helen Whitman, who later breaks off the engagement. Publishes *Eureka: A Prose Poem* in June.

1849 A year of rapid decline, marked by heavy drinking and paranoid delusions. Poe travels to Richmond, where he is engaged to Elmira Royster Shelton. Sails to Baltimore, and vanishes. Discovered delirious outside polling booth on October 3, thus suggesting subsequent legend that he was dragged from poll to poll as an alcoholic "repeater." Dies October 7, ostensibly of "congestion of the brain." "The Bells" and "Annabel Lee" appear posthumously.

Contributors

HAROLD BLOOM, Sterling Professor of the Humanities at Yale University, is the author of *The Anxiety of Influence, Poetry and Repression,* and many other volumes of literary criticism. His forthcoming study, *Freud: Transference and Authority,* attempts a full-scale reading of all of Freud's major writings. A MacArthur Prize Fellow, he is general editor of five series of literary criticism published by Chelsea House. During 1987–88, he was appointed Charles Eliot Norton Professor of Poetry at Harvard University.

ROBERT L. CARRINGER is Associate Professor of English and Film Studies at the University of Illinois.

BARTON LEVI ST. ARMAND, known for his writing on Gothicism and Romanticism, including Poe and Wilde, teaches at Brown University.

WALTER STEPP is Assistant Professor of English at Nassau Community College, Garden City, New York. He has written on Henry James.

BRIAN M. BARBOUR has edited anthologies of criticism on Benjamin Franklin and on American Transcendentalism.

GREGORY S. JAY is Associate Professor of English at the University of South Carolina. He is the author of *Past and Present Voices: T. S. Eliot and the Poetry of Criticism.*

J. GERALD KENNEDY teaches at Louisiana State University. He is the author of *The Astonished Traveler: William Darby, Frontier Geographer and Man of Letters.*

KEN FRIEDEN is Assistant Professor in the Department of Modern Languages and Classics at Emory University. He is the author of *Genius and Monologue* and *The Dream of Interpretation.*

Bibliography

Auden, W. H. Introduction. In *Selected Prose and Poetry,* by Edgar Allan Poe. New York: Rinehart, 1950.

Auerbach, Jonathan. "Poe's Other Double: The Reader in the Fiction." *Criticism* 24 (1982): 341–61.

Barthes, Roland. "Textual Analysis of Poe's 'Valdemar.' " Translated by Geoff Bennington. In *Untying the Text: A Post-Structuralist Reader,* edited by Robert Young, 133–61. Boston: Routledge & Kegan Paul, 1981.

Bell, Michael Davitt. *The Development of American Romance: The Sacrifice of Relation.* Chicago: University of Chicago Press, 1980.

Benton, Richard P., ed. *New Approaches to Poe: A Symposium.* Hartford: Transcendental Books, 1970.

Bonaparte, Marie. *The Life and Works of Edgar Allan Poe.* Translated by John Rodker. London: Imago, 1949.

Brooks, Cleanth. "Edgar Allan Poe as Interior Decorator." *Ventures* 8, no. 2 (Fall 1960): 41–46.

Buranelli, Vincent. *Edgar Allan Poe.* 2d ed. Boston: Twayne, 1977.

Butler, David W. "Usher's Hypchondriasis: Mental Alienation and Romantic Idealism in Poe's Gothic Tales." *American Literature* (1976): 1–12.

Carlson, Eric W., ed. *Edgar Allan Poe: The Fall of the House of Usher.* Merrill Literary Casebook Series. Columbus: Merrill, 1971.

————, ed. *The Recognition of Edgar Allan Poe.* Ann Arbor: University of Michigan Press, 1966.

Davidson, Edward Hutchins. *Poe: A Critical Study.* Cambridge: Harvard University Press, Belknap, 1957.

Derrida, Jacques. "The Purveyor of Truth." *Yale French Studies* 52 (1976): 31–113.

Eliot, T. S. *From Poe to Valéry.* New York: Harcourt, Brace & World, 1948.

ESQ 16, suppl. (1970). Special Poe issue.

Felman, Shoshana. "On Reading Poetry: Reflections on the Limits and Possibilities of Psychoanalytical Approaches." In *The Literary Freud: Mechanisms of Defense and the Poetic Will.* New Haven: Yale University Press, 1980.

Fiedler, Leslie. *Love and Death in the American Novel.* Rev. ed. New York: Stein & Day, 1966.

Gargano, James. "The Question of Poe's Narrators." *College English* 25 (1963): 177–81.

153

Godden, Richard. "Edgar Poe and the Detection of Riot." *Literature and History* 8, no. 2 (1982): 206–31.

Halliburton, David. *Edgar Allan Poe: A Phenomenological Study*. Princeton: Princeton University Press, 1973.

Hirsch, David H. "The Pit and the Apocalypse." *Sewanee Review* 76 (1968): 632–52.

Hoffman, Daniel. *Poe Poe Poe Poe Poe Poe Poe*. Garden City, N.Y.: Doubleday, 1972.

Hoffman, Michael J. *The Subversive Vision: American Romanticism in Literature*. National University Publications. Port Washington, N.Y.: Kennikat, 1972.

Howarth, William, ed. *Twentieth Century Interpretations of Poe's Tales*. Englewood Cliffs, N.J.: Prentice-Hall, 1971.

Huxley, Aldous. *Music at Night and Other Essays*. London: Fountain Press, 1931.

Hyslop, Lois, and Francis E. Hyslop, Jr., eds. and trans. *Baudelaire on Poe*. State College, Pa.: Bald Eagle Press, 1952.

Irwin, John T. *American Hieroglyphics*. New Haven: Yale University Press, 1980.

Johnson, Barbara. "The Frame of Reference: Poe, Lacan, Derrida." *Yale French Studies* 55–56 (1977): 457–505.

Ketterer, David. *The Rationale of Deception in Poe*. Baton Rouge: Louisiana State University Press, 1979.

Kiely, Robert. "The Comic Masks of Edgar Allan Poe." *Umanesimo* 1, no. 5 (1967): 31–41.

Kozikowski, Stanely J. "A Reconsideration of Poe's 'The Cask of Amontillado.' " *American Transcendental Quarterly* 39 (1978): 269–80.

Lacan, Jacques. "The Seminar on 'The Purloined Letter.' " Translated by J. Mehlman. *Yale French Studies* 48 (1972).

Levin, Harry. *The Power of Blackness: Hawthorne, Poe, Melville*. New York: Knopf, 1958.

Levine, Stuart. *Edgar Poe: Seer and Craftsman*. Deland, Fl.: Everett/Edwards, 1972.

Levy, Maurice. "Poe and the Gothic Tradition." Translated by Richard Henry Harwell. *ESQ* 18, no. 1 (1972): 19–25.

Lynen, John. "The Death of the Present: Edgar Allan Poe." In *The Design of the Present: Essays on Time and Form in American Literature*. New Haven: Yale University Press, 1969.

Mankowitz, Wolf. *The Extraordinary Mr. Poe*. New York: Summit, 1978.

Moldenhauer, Joseph J. "Murder as a Fine Art: Basic Connections between Poe's Aesthetics, Psychology, and Moral Vision." *PMLA* 83 (1968): 284–97.

Pollin, Burton R. *Discoveries in Poe*. Notre Dame, Ind.: University of Notre Dame Press, 1970.

Quinn, Arthur Hobson. *Edgar Allan Poe: A Critical Biography*. New York: Appleton-Century-Crofts, 1963.

Quinn, Patrick Francis. *The French Face of Edgar Poe*. Carbondale: Southern Illinois University Press, 1957.

Regan, Robert, ed. *Poe: A Collection of Critical Essays*. Englewood Cliffs, N.J.: Prentice-Hall, 1967.

Roth, Martin. "The Poet's Purloined Letter." In *Mystery and Detection Annual 1*. Beverly Hills, Calif.: Donald Adams, 1973.

Seelye, John. "Edgar Allan Poe: *Tales of the Grotesque and Arabesque.*" In *Landmarks of American Writing,* edited by Henning Cohen, 101–10. New York: Basic Books, 1969.

Shulman, Robert. "Poe and the Powers of the Mind." *ELH* 37, no. 2 (1970): 245–62.

Smith, Alan Gardner. "Edgar Allan Poe, the Will, and Horror Fiction." In *American Fiction: New Readings,* edited by Richard Grey. Totowa, N.J.: Barnes & Noble, 1983.

———. "The Psychological Context of Three Tales by Poe." *Journal of American Studies* 7, no. 3 (1973): 279–88.

Tate, Allan. *The Forlorn Demon.* Chicago: Ayer, 1953.

Thompson, G. R. *Poe's Fiction: Romantic Irony in the Gothic Tales.* Madison: University of Wisconsin Press, 1973.

———. " 'Proper Evidence of Madness': American Gothic and the Interpretation of 'Ligeia.' " *ESQ* 18, no. 1 (1972): 30–47.

University of Mississippi Studies in English, n.s. 3 (1982). Special Poe issue.

Vanderbilt, Kermit. "Art and Nature in 'The Masque of the Red Death.' " *Nineteenth-Century Fiction* 22 (1967): 379–89.

Veler, Richard P., ed. *Papers on Poe: Essays in Honor of John Ward Ostrom.* Springfield, Ohio: Chantry Music Press, 1972.

Vitanza, Victor J. "The Question of Poe's Narrators: Perverseness Considered Once Again." *American Transcendental Quarterly* 38 (1978): 137–49.

Wilson, Edmund. *The Shores of Light.* New York: Farrar, Straus & Giroux, 1952.

Woodson, Thomas, ed. *Twentieth-Century Interpretations of "The Fall of the House of Usher."* Englewood Cliffs, N.J.: Prentice-Hall, 1969.

Zanger, Jules. "Poe and the Theme of Forbidden Knowledge." *American Literature* 49 (1978): 533–43.

———. "Poe's American Garden: 'The Domain of Arnheim.' " *American Transcendental Quarterly* 50 (1981): 93–104.

Acknowledgments

"Poe's Tales: The Circumscription of Space" (originally entitled "Circumscription of Space and the Form of Poe's *Arthur Gordon Pym*") by Robert L. Carringer from *PMLA* 89, no. 3 (May 1974), © 1974 by the Modern Language Association of America. Reprinted by permission of the Modern Language Association of America.

"The 'Mysteries' of Edgar Poe: The Quest for a Monomyth in Gothic Literature" by Barton Levi St. Armand from *The Gothic Imagination: Essays in Dark Romanticism,* edited by G. R. Thompson, © 1974 by the President and Regents of Washington State University. Reprinted by permission of Washington State University Press.

"The Ironic Double in Poe's 'The Cask of Amontillado' " by Walter Stepp from *Studies in Short Fiction* 13, no. 4 (Fall 1976), © 1977 by Newberry College. Reprinted by permission.

"Poe and Tradition" by Brian M. Barbour from *The Southern Literary Journal* 10, no. 2 (Spring 1978), © 1978 by the Department of English of the University of North Carolina at Chapel Hill. Reprinted by permission.

"Poe: Writing and the Unconscious" by Gregory S. Jay from *The American Renaissance: New Dimensions* 28, no. 1 (1983), © 1983 by Associated University Presses, Inc. Reprinted by permission.

"Phantasms of Death in Poe's Fiction" by J. Gerald Kennedy from *The Haunted Dusk: American Supernatural Fiction, 1820–1920,* edited by Howard Kerr, John W. Crowley, and Charles L. Crow, © 1983 by the University of Georgia Press. Reprinted by permission.

"Poe's Narrative Monologues" by Ken Frieden from *Genius and Monologue* by Ken Frieden, © 1985 by Cornell University. Reprinted by permission of Cornell University Press.

Index